Enterprising China

Enterprising China

Business, Economic, and Legal
Developments since 1979

Linda Yueh

OXFORD
UNIVERSITY PRESS

OXFORD
UNIVERSITY PRESS

Great Clarendon Street, Oxford OX2 6DP

Oxford University Press is a department of the University of Oxford.
It furthers the University's objective of excellence in research, scholarship,
and education by publishing worldwide in

Oxford New York

Auckland Cape Town Dar es Salaam Hong Kong Karachi
Kuala Lumpur Madrid Melbourne Mexico City Nairobi
New Delhi Shanghai Taipei Toronto

With offices in

Argentina Austria Brazil Chile Czech Republic France Greece
Guatemala Hungary Italy Japan Poland Portugal Singapore
South Korea Switzerland Thailand Turkey Ukraine Vietnam

Oxford is a registered trade mark of Oxford University Press
in the UK and in certain other countries

Published in the United States
by Oxford University Press Inc., New York

British Library Cataloguing in Publication Data

Data available

Library of Congress Cataloging in Publication Data

Data available

Typeset by SPI Publisher Services, Pondicherry, India
Printed in Great Britain
on acid-free paper by
MPG Books Group, Bodmin and King's Lynn

ISBN 978–0–19–920583–7(Hbk)

ISBN 978–0–19–920582–0(Pbk)

1 3 5 7 9 10 8 6 4 2

■ PREFACE

China's transition from a centrally planned economy to a more market-oriented one has been remarkable. Business in China has accordingly been transformed. This book covers the evolution of business developments in contemporary China. Using both economic and legal reforms as the overall framework, it analyses the marketization of industry in China during the thirty-year reform period.

This interdisciplinary approach will contribute to the analysis of business development in China, which can best be understood within a complex framework of laws, politics, and economic reform aims. The distinctive feature of the book is that it views both domestic enterprise reform in China and the evolving treatment of foreign firms in the context of both corporate laws and economic policies.

The book leads the reader through the complex interaction between economics, law, and politics in shaping the business environment in China. It also looks ahead to how business is likely to evolve as economic and legal reforms speed up in the twenty-first century, notably with China's increasing global integration.

And, this volume also incorporates case studies to provide industry-specific analysis as illustrations of the overall macroeconomic and legal developments in China's economy during its first thirty years of reform. The book includes twelve original business case studies integrated into one volume which are great teaching tools and add facts and colour to an issue.

A number of case studies are also kindly contributed by Kun-Chin Lin of King's College, London, Jonathan Story of INSEAD in Paris, and Sanzhu Zhu of the School of Oriental and African Studies (SOAS) in the University of London. Their expertise adds greatly to this volume. Finally, valuable research assistance has been provided by Yan (Bonnie) Cheng, Xiao Mei Li, Ryan Manuel, and Jing Xing, which is appreciated.

■ CONTENTS

▨ FIGURES

■ TABLES

■ ABBREVIATIONS

2SLS	two-stage least squares
3G	third generation
3SLS	three-stage least squares
ABC	Agricultural Bank of China
ADB	Asian Development Bank
ADR	alternative dispute resolution
AMC	asset management company
ASEAN	Association of Southeast Asian Nations
ATC	Agreement on Textiles and Clothing
AVIC	Aviation Industries of China
BAIC	Beijing Automotive Industry Corporation
BAIHC	Beijing Automotive Industry Holding Corporation
BCS	Budgetary Contract System
BIS	Bank for International Settlements
BOC	Bank of China
CAAC	Civil Aviation Administration of China
CAS	Chinese Academy of Sciences
CBRC	China Banking Regulatory Commission
CCB	China Construction Bank
CDB	China Development Bank
CEO	chief executive officer
CEPA	Closer Economic Partnership Arrangement
CIC	China Investment Corporation
CICC	China International Capital Corporation
CIETAC	China International Economic and Trade Arbitration Commission
CIRC	China Insurance Regulatory Commission
CJV	cooperative joint venture
CNOOC	China National Offshore Oil Corporation
CNPC	China National Petroleum Corporation
CNTIC	China National Textile Industry Council
COE	collectively-owned enterprise
CPC	Communist Party of China

CPI	consumer prices index
CRS	Contract Responsibility System
CSRC	China Securities Regulatory Commission
DRC	Development Research Centre
DSB	dispute settlement body
DSU	dispute settlement understanding
EPZ	Export Processing Zone
ETDZ	Economic and Trade Development Zone
EJV	equity joint venture
FAA	US Federal Aviation Administration
FAW	First Auto Works
FDI	foreign direct investment
FIE	foreign-invested enterprise
FSB	Financial Stability Board
FSF	Financial Stability Forum (later re-named Financial Stability Board)
FTA	free trade agreement
FTC	foreign trade corporation
FTZ	Free Trade Zone
G20	Group of 20 major economies
GDP	gross domestic product
GLS	generalized least squares
GM	General Motors
GSM	Global System for Mobile Communications
HMT	Hong Kong, Macao, Taiwan
HRS	household responsibility system
HTDZ	High-Technology Development Zone
ICBC	Industrial and Commercial Bank of China
ICFAI	Institute of Chartered Financial Analysts of India
ICT	Information and Communication Technology
IFI	international financial institution
IHT	*International Herald Tribune*
IMF	International Monetary Fund
IOC	International Olympic Committee
IPR	intellectual property rights
IPO	initial public offering
IRR	internal rate of return
IV	instrumental variable

JV	joint venture
LDC	least developed country
LLC	limited liability company
LLP	limited liability partnership
LSE	London Stock Exchange
M2	monetary aggregate
M&A	mergers and acquisitions
MFA	Multi Fibre Agreement
MII	Ministry of Information Industry
MOF	Ministry of Finance
NBECZ	National Border and Economic Cooperation Zone
NBS	National Bureau of Statistics
NIE	Newly Industrializing Economy
NOC	national oil company
NPC	National People's Congress
NPL	non-performing loan
NYSE	New York Stock Exchange
OCC	Open Coastal City
OECD	Organization for Economic Co-operation and Development
OLS	ordinary least squares
OPC	Open Port City
OTC	over the counter
PBOC	People's Bank of China
P/E ratio	price-to-earnings ratio
PPP	purchasing power parity
PRC	People's Republic of China
QC	quality control
QDII	Qualified Domestic Institutional Investors
QFII	Qualified Foreign Institutional Investors
R&D	research and development
RBS	Royal Bank of Scotland
RMB	renminbi or Yuan
SAIC	Shanghai Automotive Industry Corporation
SAR	Special Administrative Region
SASAC	State-owned Assets Supervision and Administration Commission
SC	State Council
SCB	state-owned commercial bank

SEC	US Securities and Exchange Commission
SETC	State Economic and Trade Commission
SEZ	Special Economic Zone
SIP	share issue privatization
SME	small and medium-sized enterprise
SOAS	School of Oriental and African Studies
SOE	state-owned enterprise
SURE	seemingly unrelated regression estimation
SWF	Sovereign Wealth Fund
T&C	textile and clothing
TAIC	Tianjin Automobile Industry Corporation
TFP	total factor productivity
TRIPs	trade-related aspects of intellectual property rights
TRM	transitional review mechanism
TVE	township and village enterprise
VAR	vector autoregressive model
VAT	value-added tax
VW	Volkswagen
WFOE	wholly foreign-owned enterprise
WTO	World Trade Organization

1 Introduction

One of the most notable features of China's growth in the three decades since market-oriented reforms were introduced in 1979 is the development of a corporate sector that has produced companies which are among the largest and fastest growing ones in the world—with firms such as the computer company, Lenovo, and ICBC (Industrial and Commercial Bank of China) becoming part of the global business landscape. Against a backdrop of transition from an economic system that was almost entirely state-owned as recently as the early 1980s, it is all the more remarkable, and underpins much of China's successful economic development.

The transformation of China's industrial sector from one run by the state to a marketized or nearly marketized one is driven not only by economic policies but also by legal reforms that have occurred alongside. These economic policies and institutional reforms have contributed to the development of a market economy out of a previously centrally planned economic system where the state dictated output and prices as well as nearly all other aspects of supply and demand. China's successful development is often referred to as a 'paradox', as the market has seemingly developed without a sound legal foundation. Instead, economic policies and permissive attitudes towards decentralized regions experimenting with market forces have seemingly managed to instil incentives that have propelled growth.

Although it is certainly true that the legal system is incomplete in that much of it has been developed only since the 1990s and claims of imperfect enforcement of the extant laws mar the usual praise associated with China's development, China has also undertaken a large number of legal reforms that have evolved with the market. For instance, anticipation of an increase in mergers and acquisitions (M&A) activities with greater market opening after the 2001 accession to the World Trade Organization (WTO) prompted the passage of a M&A law in 2003. In other areas, laws were passed to facilitate investment, such as the Law on Chinese–Foreign Equity Joint Ventures, which was the first corporate law of the reform period promulgated in July 1979. It heralded the start of the influx of foreign direct investment (FDI) that has been a notable part of China's success in becoming a global exporting power in the span of only a couple of decades. Without such a law, foreign investors, not accustomed to investing without legal principles governing their rights, would not have chosen China as the destination for their funds to the same extent.

The interplay between legal and economic reforms, therefore, is crucial to understand as part of the assessment as to how the market has developed in China. This is not to attribute the success of market development simply to laws, but rather, this book takes the perspective that laws and regulations which solidify market foundations and property rights have been enacted alongside economic policies that together enable the development of a market system in China. Neither perfect nor complete, the laws promulgated in China nevertheless create property rights (real estate, intellectual property rights such as patents), establish contracting relationships (Chinese–Foreign joint ventures), and govern markets (regulators such as the China Securities Regulatory Commission). Therefore, this volume posits that legal and economic reforms interacted to create, support, and govern the market in China. In some areas, legal reforms have been more important than in others, notably in attracting FDI, while arguably less so in others, for example in developing privately-owned firms, which have arisen as the state has withdrawn from large segments of the economy, thus opening up opportunities for entrepreneurs to enter.

The theme of the book is that the development of the corporate industrial and services sector has followed the approach of China's broader economic and legal transformation: gradual, policy-led, market-oriented reforms are undertaken, resulting in (and on rare occasions, sequenced with) complex economic system changes and legal reform. This book will cover the evolution of the corporate sector in China from the late 1970s to the present under this framework. Importantly, the book will bring together an analysis of contemporary Chinese business developments with the more broadly known story of China's economic and, to a lesser extent, its relationship to legal reforms.

The main theme of the book is that developments in the business sector are very closely intertwined with China's economic and legal reforms—all of which have been undertaken gradually, and premised on the overriding policy command which seeks social and political stability. The book will argue that the evolution of enterprises in China, and Chinese enterprises globally, will depend on both the continuing domestic economic *and* legal reform process and China's ever-deepening engagement with the global economy and with international capital markets. An understanding of contemporary business developments in China will also allow observers to anticipate further evolution in this sector, particularly as China moves towards an increasingly marketized internal economy with a greater degree of global integration as it grows ever closer in economic might to the major economies of the world.

1.1 **Structure of the book**

After this introductory chapter, the second chapter analyses Chinese legal and economic reforms since 1979 to identify the key contributors and policies which have led to the transformation of the enterprise sector from one dominated by state-owned enterprises (SOEs) and collective enterprises (such as township and village enterprises or TVEs) into a diverse corporate sector comprising not only SOEs and TVEs but also privately-owned and foreign-invested enterprises (FIEs). The role of legal as well as economic reforms will be highlighted to provide a fuller picture of the development of the corporate sector. The third chapter assesses the interplay between law and markets to explain the China 'paradox' of having achieved significant growth whilst having a notably weak legal system when institutional development is thought to be a prerequisite to economic development. A complex interaction between formal laws and informal institutions was intertwined with markets in a way that is not dissimilar to what most countries contend with at China's stage of economic development, but with the added complication that a communal property state existed for most of the period.

Following from these overviews, the next chapters will analyse the four major enterprise sectors in China: SOEs, TVEs, private firms, and foreign firms. These chapters will investigate the ways in which legal and economic policies were enacted to further the state's goals in each of these sectors. For instance, the move to reform SOEs involved adopting a form of privatization known as 'share issue privatization' with the aim of corporatizing state-owned firms and making them into shareholding companies that can eventually become privately owned with stock sold to the public. To achieve this, the Company Law of 1993, along with the creation of the stock markets in the early 1990s, was enacted to lay a market-recognized foundation for the policy intent of the corporatization of SOEs.

The motivations behind the policies may differ among these ownership types, but the state used both law and institutional reform to mould and shape the development of the sector. For SOEs, it appears that the state used laws to legitimize the policy enactments to restructure but not privatize all of the state firms. For the collective sector, laws were often enacted post hoc in response to economic necessity but without fundamental ownership reform, as rural TVEs in particular served to maintain industry in the lagging segment of the Chinese economy. In other words, TVEs—a lingering hybrid form of enterprise—appear to serve multiple purposes that suit the overall partial economic transition approach of China. For private firms, it is an entirely different matter. Hampered for the most part by laws that favoured SOEs and collectives as well as foreign firms, private firms arose despite the legal obstacles. Laws pertaining to the private sector tended to be enacted ex post, usually where a market need became unavoidable, such as the securities scandals of the 1990s that prompted improved regulation by the end of the decade. Interestingly for foreign firms, the first laws were enacted to attract multinational investment. Until the 2000s, they had in effect almost a separate legal regime. Although not wholly the case, laws led market development for FIEs, granting them more formal but circumscribed rules that determined their activities. The final chapter concludes with an assessment of business developments in the context of China's particular, incomplete legal and institutional framework, with some thoughts about the future contour of business in China in the twenty-first century.

1.2 Case studies

A total of twelve case studies are featured in the book, some of which were commissioned from experts such as Kun-Chin Lin from King's College, London; Jonathan Story from INSEAD; and Sanzhu Zhu from the School of Oriental and African Studies (SOAS), University of London. Each of the four chapters focused on a specific sector (SOEs, TVEs, private, and foreign firms) will include these original and illustrative case studies. The cases provide a narrative to accompany the text that can shed light on how the legal and policy initiatives have affected a company or industry. In the chapter on state-owned enterprises, there are three cases which epitomize the main reform efforts. The case of Haier shows how gradually privatization has been undertaken in China. Starting off as a SOE, Haier gradually became more commercially driven until it began operating largely as a privately run firm whose white goods are sold around the world, including in the United States and other rich economies.

The second case uses the experience of the state-owned commercial banks (SCBs) to typify the corporatization policy whose aim is to eventually transform state-owned enterprises into joint stock companies, but not to necessarily divest them of state control. The largest of the SCBs, ICBC, typifies this approach. It has had minority equity shareholders which included foreign firms such as Allianz and American Express, as well as having undergone an initial public offering (IPO) on domestic and international stock markets which gave it access to global capital markets. However, it remains predominantly state-owned and only trades a fraction of its shares on bourses. ICBC, therefore, illustrates the corporatization process for Chinese state-owned firms, which have gone some way towards, but not all the way, to becoming privatized shareholding companies. The third case in the chapter examines China's national oil companies (NOCs) and represents a strategic sector that the government wishes to retain. Through consolidation and partial listings, the NOCs have become a triumvirate of firms that dominate the Chinese energy sector. Their evolution illustrates China's on-going industrial policy which includes controlling key inputs to fuel its continuing industrialization and financing overseas investments to secure such commodities. The final case in the chapter is one of three studies of the spectrum of low- to high-technology goods. Such a range represents different facets of industrial capabilities. For instance, the first of these pertaining to high-tech goods will be in the SOE chapter as the research and development (R&D) necessary to achieve innovative capacity is still largely driven by the state and government policy. The illustrative case is that of the civil aviation industry in which China's efforts to develop commercially viable and competitive passenger aircrafts are examined as an indicator of China's capabilities. China still lags behind those advanced economies, but is not atypical of a country at its level of economic develop-ment. Nevertheless, China's intense fostering of the aviation industry signifies its intent to possess an innovative, high-tech sector.

The chapter on TVEs includes a case study of the toy industry. These rural enterprises have been strong engines of growth, particularly in labour-intensive sectors such as toys. The achievement of China in becoming the largest toy maker in the world is linked to the changes in its TVEs and how such enterprises have developed in the face of greater competition from home and abroad. A not dissimilar, though more commercially high-spec, case is found in the chapter on private firms. Lenovo is a good example of a privately started but state-supported firm in China. Its development reflects the changing attitudes and policies of the Chinese authorities towards private enterprises during the reform period. Lenovo also represents the launch of China's 'going out' policy, whose aim is to create internationally competitive firms. When it acquired IBM's personal computer business along with the use of the IBM brand name for five years, Lenovo essentially marked the start of an era of 'going global' for Chinese firms.

The chapter on foreign firms includes four case studies. The active use of FDI policies to attract technology and develop the export sector can be divided into two distinct areas. The first is the policies influencing the FDI vehicle, while the second relates to the moulding of the technological spectrum of the export sector. Two cases illustrate the main types of FDI into China: Chinese–Foreign joint ventures (JVs) and Wholly Foreign-owned Enterprises (WFOEs). Nokia and the telecommunications sector is a case study of China's long-standing FDI policy which was geared at encouraging JVs so that Chinese manufacturers can learn from more advanced foreign firms and eventually become competitors. This was the experience of Nokia, which entered China early on during the initial liberalization of its wholesale and retail sector and enjoyed a dominant market position alongside other foreign companies such as Motorola. Over time, however, they faced increasing competition from Chinese domestic firms in certain segments of the market, such as handsets. The second major form of FDI was WFOEs. Carrefour represents this type of horizontal FDI (as opposed to vertical FDI that refers to cross-border production chains) which does not involve a Chinese partner and is mainly geared at replicating the operation of a foreign firm in a new market, for example retail services. WFOEs, though, faced a set of notable challenges in navigating the only partially open and still largely restrictive Chinese domestic market. Market access, a perennial complaint of China's trading partners such as the European Union and the United States, and other strategic considerations of doing business are captured in this case.

The chapter on foreign firms further includes two cases that represent the low- and medium-tech segments of exports, both highlighting the use of Special Economic Zones (SEZs), not only to develop its employment-generating, labour-intensive industries, but also to facilitate industrial upgrading. China's comparative advantage lies in low-tech goods such as textiles and clothing which utilize its abundant and cheap, but reasonably skilled labour force, including millions of rural–urban migrants. The case of garments illustrates the development of a sector that is potentially the largest global market segment for Chinese exports. Irrespective of the barriers which still exist, China's dominance in low-tech goods has earned it the moniker of being the 'manufacturer of the world'. This case shows how China's export sector in low-technology products evolved. The second case considers the predominance of foreign investment in higher technology areas of Chinese exports. Although China had become the world's largest trader by 2010, around half of its exports have been produced by foreign-invested enterprises since the late 1990s. The case study of the automobile sector, which falls within medium-tech goods, highlights China's continuing need for FDI in the upgrading of its industrial capacity. Because automobiles, in particular, require certain technological capabilities in both upstream and downstream suppliers, it is a sector that often relies on global production and supply chains, and involves importing and exporting intermediate inputs. Despite its efforts, China's indigenous car industry has not produced globally competitive cars, even though its exports appear to be characterized by significant industrial value-added. Harkening back to the case on high-tech goods, the dominance of FIEs in that segment is even more significant where some 80 to 90 per cent of such exports are produced by foreign-invested firms. The car industry recently has turned to China's own domestic market, which has nearly 40 million vehicles, still some 200 million short of the US market, but a faster growing one. The case study, therefore, encapsulates a number of aspects of economic policies: developing the medium-tech export sector, FDI strategy, and building the role of global supply chains in international trade.

The final two cases are found in the last chapter of the book, which provides some concluding thoughts about the effect of laws on market development in the past 30 years and future evolvement. The first case uses as illustration a key component of Chinese laws (and those of many other countries) aimed at promoting innovation, that is, intellectual property rights (IPRs). Patent laws are assessed at the national and regional levels to ascertain the determinants of innovation, a crucial component of long-run economic growth. Despite much lingering weakness in the legal enforcement of IPRs, patents have been growing exponentially, but are determined not just by laws. Instead, patenting is affected by a number of contextual factors, including R&D spending, and exhibits strong regional variation. The growth of innovation in spite of an incomplete legal system bodes well for the future of Chinese growth.

The second case study uses the post-WTO regime of services liberalization to indicate how laws and regulations have, and are likely to, shape the nascent financial markets. China agreed to open its services sector upon accession to the WTO, which meant that a fairly underdeveloped area of the economy had to evolve quickly, including in line with a growing number of global financial norms such as those issued by the international body, the Financial Stability Board (FSB). Banking and capital markets are areas in which laws and regulations are looked to for guidance even as the process is iterative, with market innovations pushing regulators to pass regulations that respond to market needs. However, the absence of a non-banking financial market until the 1990s due to state-owned banks dominating credit allocation meant that developments of the sector were at times entirely new but were closely related to the state's larger economic aims. But, after 2001 with WTO accession, China's financial markets were and will be shaped more than before by laws and regulations infused with international rules and expectations. This case study illustrates how in financial markets, laws and regulations may not be perfect and still exist in an underdeveloped overall legal system, but will shape the development of a crucial sector in China's economy.

1.3 Business in China

The concluding chapter that includes those two cases reflects on the ways in which business in China has changed during the post-1979 reform period, and how legal and economic policies have interacted to shape a new corporate landscape in the world's fastest growing major market. The book ends with some ruminations about how the evolving legal framework will affect business in China, and speculates that laws and regulations will become more important as its marketization develops.

The chapter contemplates the extent to which laws and policies have mattered for business and market development. For instance, it investigates whether the corporatization push to create shareholding companies and give them legal status starting in the 1990s has resulted in improved firm performance by the 2000s, and whether corporate laws have evolved sufficiently to support the market more broadly, such as the development of private firms. The chapter includes the two case studies discussed above assessing the effectiveness of laws in an underdeveloped legal system and how the post-WTO regime, which liberalized large swathes of China's services sector, is likely to further develop its financial markets.

With a fairly young system of corporate law and associated institutions, China may well need more time before its market environment is governed effectively. For instance, developing clinical legal education to produce lawyers and judges may take a generation. The existence of a non-independent judiciary poses additional challenges, reinforcing the lack of separation between laws and policies in many instances. Nevertheless, to support a market that requires innovation and industrial upgrading to sustain its growth momentum, a legal and institutional foundation must develop in order to manage the complexities of such a decentralized economy. China, moreover, has to contend with the expectations and demands of an international business community which operates within an increasingly formalized global rules-based system for trade and investment as well as financial regulation. Looking ahead, all of the indicators suggest that legal reform has to keep apace of economic initiatives or else risk derailing growth.

Going by the pace of legal reforms in the 2000s, this looks promising. For effective implementation of such laws, however, it may be some time yet before such an aim is achieved. What is evident though is that legal reforms are playing a growing role in Chinese markets. Their interactions with economic policies will shape the business environment in China. If these market-supporting institutional transformations proceed apace, then China has a better chance of realizing its potential as the world's fastest growing market as well as its most populous nation. Then, China's place as one of the major economic powers would be more assured.

2 Legal and Economic Reforms and the Development of a Corporate Sector

2.1 Introduction

The development of a corporate sector has followed the approach of China's broader economic and legal transformation: incremental, policy-led, market-oriented reforms are undertaken, resulting in complex economic system changes and legal reform. China's remarkable growth over the past three decades can be tied directly to its gradualist transition from a centrally planned economic system towards a market economy, while always facing the unique challenges of a developing country, as China's per capita income at the end of the first thirty years of reform only reached that of a lower middle income country. An understanding of contemporary business developments requires a detailed understanding of this wider context.

Corporate sector developments to date have evolved from policy-driven economic and legal reforms—generating China's astonishing growth while simultaneously maintaining relative social and political stability. These same business developments are accompanied or followed by (and sometimes led by) legal reforms that serve to incrementally confirm (and more rarely establish) the institutional bases for a transitional economy. This approach has permitted China to achieve very significant and far-reaching reforms based on economic necessity, while gradually filling out the substantive and institutional foundation needed to underpin the partially reformed system going forward. This progress in turn depends in part upon continued economic success, which then drives the need for a functioning legal system (including laws, regulations, and the institutions to apply them), particularly in a political–economic system where traditionally there have been poorly defined property rights and uneven enforcement of private contracts.

Reform and development of the corporate sector is characterized by the same principle apparent for the overall economic system—gradualism. China's transition has been experimental and incremental in nature, with only partial dismantling of the state sector. Although there is a common perception that a great deal of reform has been directed by top-down central policy dictates, there has at the same time been a large degree of decentralization of policymaking and enterprise-level decision-making, coupled with a covertly permissive attitude towards unbridled experimentation (see e.g. Naughton 1995). This latter aspect was seen at the inception of the reform era in the creation of Special Economic Zones (SEZs) which began in coastal areas but quickly spread nationwide. China also implemented a 'dual track' reform process which permitted the growth of the non-state sector alongside the state sector, via an initially limited allowance of private economic activity. The dual track resulted in transfers from the non-state sector which supported the state sector, so that partial reforms can eventually result in a melding of the two tracks without generating macroeconomic instability (see Fan 1994). In other words, the creation of a parallel track of private companies alongside mainly loss-making state-owned enterprises (SOEs) enabled transfers from the profitable enterprises to the state-owned ones that sustained economic and social stability, as SOEs provided the social safety net. This support of SOEs prevented large-scale unemployment from arising with the reform of the state-owned sector until the late 1990s after nearly a decade of reform. This has also led to a perception of China's reform path as being one 'without losers'—at least in its early stages (see e.g. Lau, Qian, and Roland 2001).

For China, the driver of reform was, and is, economic necessity, but not dire need because China did not experience the same dramatic declines experienced in other transition economies on the eve of reform in 1979. Accordingly, the maintenance of stability—societal and political—has long been a paramount requirement as the reforms went forward. The gradualist approach requires sufficient control over the process of liberalization itself so that the marketized or even private segments do not overwhelm the pre-existing state segment. If instability should occur, then the 'Big Bang' transition of the former Soviet Union might ensue, which has proved to be destabilizing, though perhaps theoretically more efficient (see Murphy, Shleifer, and Vishny 1992).

China has, since the inception of reform, faced a further challenge in establishing a market economy. From a theoretical vantage point, it is generally accepted that a market economy requires property rights and sanctity of contract (or enforcement of contract) in order to operate efficiently. Notwithstanding these anomalies in the case of China, part of the rationale for the development of a formal legal system in the late 1970s was to create the substantive and institutional basis for a well-functioning market economy, and enable commercial disputes to be resolved in an orderly and predictable manner. The inflow of foreign direct investment (FDI) starting in the early 1980s—and the perceived expectations of foreign investors—was a significant driver in the formation of a commercial legal system. This was exemplified by one of the first six major laws promulgated in 1979, the 'Law on Chinese–Foreign Equity Joint Ventures'. The influence of foreign expectations has become even more relevant with the phenomenon of Chinese corporate issuers seeking finance on international capital markets, fast-growing FDI after service sector liberalization with World Trade Organization (WTO) accession in 2001, and the notable interest in portfolio investment in China's stunning growth since.

These same themes of stability and economic necessity pervade first the policy-led reform applied to the state-owned sector and then the subsequent development of the corporate sector. While permitting reform as a vehicle for achieving growth, policy and law are used to maintain stability and offer the promise of predictability, with the new legal system providing a critical institutional basis for market behaviour, contract enforcement, and dispute resolution when necessary. For instance, township and village enterprises (TVEs) arose due to the need for light industrial goods after decades of heavy industry-biased central planning and as an avenue to absorb surplus labour in the agricultural sector, one of the key challenges for a developing country like China. Permitting the institutional form of TVEs pursuant to laws and regulations governing 'collectively-owned' enterprises allowed the economy to generate economic growth without incurring instability, since TVEs also served the dual purpose of reallocating labour. Similarly, the need for FDI and technology meant that China experimented with opening at the start of the reform period in 1979. Realizing that foreign investors needed investment vehicles, various joint venture laws were adopted to facilitate economic growth via opening to international trade/investment, all the while limiting the reach of FDI to SEZs and keeping the new institutional form out of the reach of private Chinese businesses. Similarly, the reform of the SOEs starting in the early and mid 1980s followed from the lack of competitiveness of the SOEs. Those policy reforms were only 'legalized' in 1988 with the promulgation of an SOE Law (Law on Industrial Enterprises Owned Wholly by the People), already somewhat out of date at the time of promulgation.

In the 1990s, permitting corporatization under the rubric of 'share experimental' enterprises was meant to make Chinese firms more efficient, and ameliorate the adverse internal incentives determining governance. These policy initiatives were supported first by local-level regulations governing local establishments of companies limited by shares, then national standards for the same legal form, and only rather late in the day by the promulgation of the Company Law in 1993, which was completely amended in 2006 to reflect a seriously altered environment with WTO opening in 2001. The reform of the Contract Law preceding it in 1999 subsumed the various corporate laws that had governed foreign firms separately from domestic ones, so that one legal regime governed all firms by the 2000s. Similarly, recognizing *getihu* or self-employment/sole proprietorships was necessary as a policy matter to ease the impact of the large-scale redundancies from SOEs, and facilitate the emergence of a dual track of private economic activity in the mid 1990s. Yet, the form only existed in regulation and often less formally, and was only later subject to codification with the 'sole proprietorship form' in 1999. The 1999 Contract Law also, for the first time, granted individuals, and not just legal entities, the right to contract and gain security in entering into economic transactions. Furthermore, after WTO accession and the promised opening of the service sector as well as the need to stymie non-performing loans in a weak banking sector that is often a source of macroeconomic instability in transition economies, China adopted a series of regulatory measures. These were overseen by a trio of agencies: the China Banking Regulatory Commission (CBRC), China Securities Regulatory Commission (CSRC), and China Insurance Regulatory Commission (CIRC), that provided an institutional base for the governance of the developing financial sector.

In each instance, economic necessity drove policy reform, while also requiring stability so that the market could come into being and develop. In turn, legal reforms generally followed to provide further symbolic (political) and then institutional support for already established market mechanisms under a partially reformed system. And yet, China has in recent years seen a change in this dynamic—when substantive and institutional (including regulatory) legal reforms beget further economic reform. The laws bolstered the foundation of the market which enabled further marketization to take place, particularly where regulations were enacted following the legislation so that implementation resulted in better governed markets. Not only the Company Law, but the Mergers and Acquisitions (M&A) Law of 2003, the Bankruptcy Law of 2006 (significantly revising the previous law of 1986 that pertained to SOEs), and the Anti-Monopoly Law passed in 2007 established the bases for more complex market development to bolster economic reforms that relied increasingly on governing a decentralized economy. For instance, after the passage of the M&A Law, China's first overseas commercial investments and acquisitions took place, for example TCL acquiring the RCA brand from Thomson in 2004, and Lenovo's purchase of IBM's PC business in 2005. Similarly, regulators like the CSRC, CIRC, and CBRC lead reform of capital markets by enacting regulations, such as the 2010 rules allowing shorting of stocks for the first time on the stock exchanges.

The interaction and reinforcing nature of economic (policy) and legal reforms serves as the premise for understanding business developments in China. Even though this approach may not be the most economically efficient or fastest, this type of gradualist transition accompanied by both economic and legal reforms allows the Chinese economy and political system to maintain a degree of stability. Stability, in turn, enables the partially reformed economy that results from a gradual approach to transition, and suits the policy aims of the Chinese government. Moreover, the adoption of laws hastens China towards a functioning market economy where the complexity of economic transactions requires an established legal system. In other words, laws and the legal institutional system are increasingly critical as China's economic reforms progress.

This chapter presents stages of business sector development in the reform period after providing an overview of the various legal forms that exist in the corporate sector. Each section illustrates the interactions between policy-driven economic changes and the more formalistic legal reforms that pervade the development of the corporate sector. Although the processes of reform, uneven market development, and astonishing overall growth observed are complex, business developments are both shaped by, and directly affect, China's unprecedented transition to an increasingly marketized economy under an evolving substantive and institutional legal system where even implementation has begun to improve. Appendix 2.1 (at the end of the chapter) lists the key commercial and civil laws in China, while Appendix 2.2 covers the securities and banking laws. It is evident in both appendices, particularly the latter, that there has been a speeding up of substantive reform of laws needed to govern the increasingly decentralized market, particularly with WTO accession in 2001 marking China's era of global integration.

With WTO membership, China subscribed to the rules-based international system governing trade which concurrently required transparency in domestic laws and regulations. More potently in many ways, it was not the formal aspects of international economic law which led to Chinese legal reforms, but the norms-based, voluntary standards such as the Basel Committee on Banking Supervision's standards for capital adequacy that governed expectations in global markets which led China to revise and thus to adhere to better governance requirements in its banks and financial firms. In other words, although the WTO did compel China to revise its intellectual property laws to become harmonized with the international trade law governing intellectual property rights, much of the legal and regulatory reforms were associated with China's greater integration with global markets where multinational firms had expectations as to how markets were to operate. Thus China's capital market reforms proceeded quickly to offer foreign (and also domestic) firms the regulatory guidelines to invest in China, such as the 2002 Qualified Foreign Institutional Investors (QFII) regulations that permitted investment in China's stock markets and improved corporate governance, such as the disclosure requirements for listed firms passed in 2004. It is possible that WTO and global demands hastened and perhaps even overcame domestic resistance to greater law-based marketization and offered a foreign impetus to more rapidly develop and move China towards a market economy with sound institutional foundations. By doing so, China's economic growth stands a better chance of being sustained.

2.2 **Overview of corporate sector development**

2.2.1 STATE-OWNED AND COLLECTIVELY-OWNED ENTERPRISES

In 1978, state-owned enterprises and collectively-owned enterprises were essentially the only firms in China, with SOEs accounting for 77.6 per cent of industrial output and collectives the remaining 22.4 per cent (see Table 2.1). SOEs were state-owned at the national and local levels, whilst collectives were predominantly smaller, communally-owned urban enterprises that were the sister firms to the later township and village enterprises in rural areas. The dominance of state-owned enterprises undoubtedly reflected the 'urban bias' that had existed in the pre-reform period from 1949–78 whereby agricultural food prices were kept low in order to fuel urban-based manufacturing undertaken by SOEs that industrialized China. Figure 2.1 shows how China was industrialized in 1978 on the eve of market-oriented reforms with industry constituting around half of GDP, a share that has been maintained throughout the subsequent 30 years of reform. In 2007, industry accounted for 48.6 per cent of GDP, a very slight increase from 47.9 per cent in 1978. In other words, China started its reform period with an industrial sector, but one that was devoid of privately-owned firms as is characteristic of administered economies under central planning.

However, gradually with market-oriented reforms introduced at the end of 1978 by Deng Xiaoping, the industrial sector experienced changes that began to diversify the corporate sector. The process, though, as evident from Table 2.1

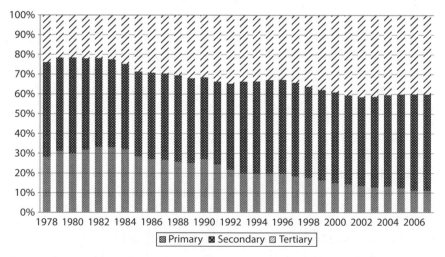

Figure 2.1. Sectoral composition of GDP

Source: China Statistical Yearbook Table 4–1.
Note: Primary refers to agriculture, secondary to industry and tertiary to services.

Table 2.1. Share of total industrial output by enterprise type

	1978	1979	1980	1981	1982	1983	1984	1985	1986	1987	1988	1989	1990	1991	1992	1993
SOE	77.6%	78.5%	75.7%	74.8%	74.4%	73.4%	69.1%	64.9%	62.3%	59.7%	56.8%	56.1%	54.6%	56.2%	51.5%	47.0%
Collective	22.4%	21.5%	23.8%	24.6%	24.8%	25.7%	29.7%	32.1%	33.5%	34.6%	36.1%	35.7%	35.6%	33.0%	35.1%	34.0%
Getihu	0.0%	0.0%	0.0%	0.0%	0.1%	0.1%	0.2%	1.9%	2.8%	3.6%	4.3%	4.8%	5.4%	4.8%	5.8%	8.0%
Other	0.0%	0.0%	0.5%	0.6%	0.7%	0.8%	1.0%	1.2%	1.5%	2.0%	2.7%	3.4%	4.4%	6.0%	7.6%	11.1%

	1994	1995	1996	1997	1998	1999	2000	2001	2002	2003	2004	2005
SOE	37.3%	34.0%	33.7%	29.8%	26.5%	26.1%	38.2%	35.1%	32.6%	30.1%	28.3%	27.2%
Collective	37.7%	36.6%	36.5%	35.9%	36.0%	32.8%	11.2%	8.3%	6.9%	5.3%	3.2%	2.8%
Getihu	10.1%	12.9%	14.4%	16.9%	16.0%	16.9%	0.0%	0.0%	0.0%	0.0%	0.0%	0.0%
Other	14.9%	16.6%	15.4%	17.4%	21.5%	24.2%	50.5%	56.5%	60.5%	64.5%	68.6%	70.0%

Source: China Yearbook of Industrial Economy Table 2–3.

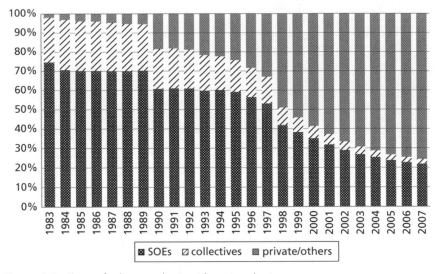

Figure 2.2. Share of urban employment by enterprise type

Source: China Statistical Yearbook Table 4–2.

Note: The 1987 and 1990 data were both affected by a census in that year.

and Figure 2.2, was slow in that SOEs continued to dominate both output and employment until the late 1980s and early 1990s, when losses at SOEs compelled greater liberalization which began the process of creating a non-state sector that included private and foreign firms. By contrast, urban collectives, unlike TVEs which had a niche in the absence of dominant SOEs in rural areas, quickly lost their economic clout during the reform period and contributed less than 5 per cent of urban employment by 2007, falling from their peak at the start of reforms in 1978 when they accounted for about 30 per cent.

2.2.2 PRIVATE FIRMS

There are numerous ambiguities in defining a private firm in China, particularly since the process of SOE reform has yielded some privatized SOEs, whilst others have become listed firms on the Chinese stock exchange but are still state-controlled, and still other shareholding firms which are also ultimately dominated by the state as majority shareholder. Privatized SOEs that underwent restructuring or *gaizhi* in the 1990s should be classified as private firms despite their state origins, though knowing that they were formerly SOEs is useful for some purposes. The 1994 'save the large, release the small' policy of keeping the large SOEs and privatizing small and medium-sized enterprises (SMEs) resulted in privatized SOEs, but mainly the SMEs. Those which undertook 'share issue privatization' (SIP) which began in earnest with the corporatization of SOEs in the early 1990s, and the conversion into publicly traded joint stock companies (after the establishment of the stock exchanges in Shanghai and Shenzhen in 1990 and 1991, respectively) were not so clearly privatized. State control was often retained; for instance, the listed firms were majority held by the state or legal persons (usually other SOEs). This would be the case even if the firm were listed on international stock exchanges, for example China National Offshore Oil Corporation Ltd (CNOOC) is listed on the New York Stock Exchange but is majority owned by the state-owned national oil company, CNOOC. Therefore, although SOEs have been privatized in numerous ways, the opacity of shareholding after only partial reform confounds their easy classification as private firms, even in the 2000s.

Nevertheless, there are *de novo* private enterprises, notably *getihu* or sole proprietorships, which are businesses started by entrepreneurs, including a growing number of the self-employed. Suffering from a lack of recognition of their institutional rights with only some acknowledgement in regulation in 1987, and suffering credit constraints even in the 2000s, private enterprises nevertheless developed in the 1980s and 1990s, and ultimately became recognized in law in 1999 with the Law on Individual Wholly-Owned Enterprises. However, their numbers are difficult to track. For instance, to manage in the difficult institutional environment, some private firms became 'red hat' firms. These *guahu* firms would pay a fee to a state-owned enterprise and borrow their name, bank account, and even their books for tax purposes, in order to operate in a system biased against private firms. Such masquerades were necessary, but confound an easy parcelling of state from non-state firms.

Getihu, which were recorded in official statistics in the 1980s and 1990s, disappeared from official classifications after the 1999 law on sole proprietorships when they were absorbed into the private sector, since they could then take on various legal corporate forms. From accounting for less than 5 per cent of industrial output in the 1980s, *getihu* rose to account for 16.9 per cent in 1999 before they were no longer separately counted. These are firms which employ fewer than eight people and had been thought to constitute much of the SME sector in China. From Figure 2.2, it can be seen that private firms (domestic and foreign) overtook SOEs as the larger source of employment in 1998 and had surpassed the urban collective sector much earlier in 1993. Undoubtedly the SME sector is important within the non-state sector as it is in most economies where small firms employing less than 250 people are the largest proportion of all firms. But, in China, the figures are imprecise.

For private firms (mostly after 2000) as well as privatized SOEs, there are numerous corporate forms that apply. They could be limited liability partnerships (LLPs pursuant to the revised 1997 Law on Partnership Enterprises), limited liability companies (LLCs as under the Company Law of 1993), joint stock companies (shareholding companies with shares constituting the equity of a company also under the Company Law), or shareholding companies that are publicly traded on either the Chinese stock exchanges in Shanghai and Shenzhen or Hong Kong (the 'H share' market) or internationally in New York, London, etc. The joint stock company is similar to the widely held public company with liquid shares in the West, while the limited liability company is a closely held corporation and is limited to fifty shareholders. Corporatization of a SOE, though, does not necessarily mean transfer of ownership or privatization, as the state can ultimately retain control. *Getihu* as a classification again disappeared in 1999 in the year of the passage of the Law on Individual Wholly-Owned Enterprises, transforming them into private firms, which could remain unincorporated as sole proprietorships under the new law, or take on one of the corporate forms discussed above.

These complications further underscore the difficulty of measuring the size of the private sector in China, which is why it is often (though not always accurately) calculated as the residual after the SOEs, collectively-owned (and foreign, where separately counted) firms are accounted for in output and employment. Nevertheless, private firms, along with foreign firms, constitute the important components of the non-state sector that has allowed China to gradually reform its SOEs and state-owned commercial banks (SCBs). By having a source of growth in the economy, China was able to maintain stability, as the non-state sector provided jobs and income whilst inefficient and loss-making SOEs were incrementally reformed.

2.2.3 FOREIGN FIRMS

Foreign firms form the final part of the corporate landscape in China, and have been present since the start of the reform period. Although the 'open door' policy was declared in 1979 and FDI began to flow into China in the 1980s, it wasn't until over a decade later in 1992 when Deng Xiaoping took his 'southern tour' of the provinces initially opened to foreign investment that the policy took off. Foreign firms in China were initially restricted to joint ventures (JV) with Chinese companies. In 1979, the Law on Chinese–Foreign Equity Joint Ventures allowed foreign investment to only lodge in a equity JV (EJV), defined by the respective equity contributions of the Chinese and foreign parties, with the Chinese partner retaining 51 per cent of control. Later on, in 1988, the Chinese–Foreign Cooperative Joint Venture Law was passed. It defined such JVs (CJVs) as based on contractually defined shares with more flexibility than EJVs.

The EJV is much like a partnership, although it has limited liability towards creditors and little of the flexibility associated with partnerships in many other countries. Profits are to be shared strictly in accordance with the proportionate investments of the parties, no matter when those investments are made. Parties may transfer their ownership stake only with the approval of the other parties. Directors owe their duties to the parties that appointed them, not to the EJV as a whole, and a number of matters require the unanimous approval of the board of directors, not just a majority.

A more flexible vehicle for foreign-invested firms (FIEs) is the CJV, also known as the contractual joint venture. This vehicle began as a relatively informal arrangement between Chinese and foreign firms that was structured entirely by the contract between them and was later formalized in the 1988 Law. Despite the flexibility offered by the CJV, due to approval difficulties, it remains relatively uncommon (see Figure 2.3).

Two years prior to the creation of CJVs, the Law on Wholly Foreign-Owned Enterprises was passed in 1986 permitting wholly foreign-owned enterprises (WFOEs), which were foreign firms, to operate without a Chinese partner.

For a number of reasons, from wishing to learn from the foreign partner in these foreign-invested firms to inhibiting the dominance of foreign multinational corporations in a fledgling Chinese market, JVs were the preferred FDI vehicle of the Chinese government. Unsurprisingly, the favoured JVs which dominated until WTO accession in 2001. As seen in Figure 2.3, only after then were WFOEs the predominant form of FDI in China. By 2006, WFOEs accounted for two-thirds of all inward FDI. The reasons for this growth have also to do with the nature of these investments as well as the shift in government policy related to WTO accession. JVs tended to be in manufacturing where a Chinese partner enabled access to land and labour, and the goods produced were destined for export.

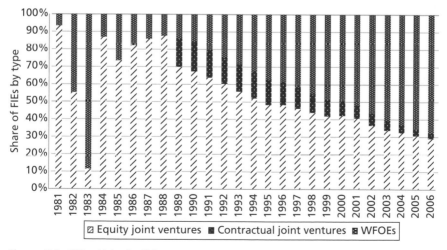

Figure 2.3. FDI vehicles in China

Source: China Statistical Yearbook Table 17–14.

WFOEs also sold for export, but many were in the retail or wholesale sector. Multinational firms such as restaurants and home goods replicate themselves to sell their goods and services around the world. This form of horizontal FDI depends on greater market opening which occurred after China joined the WTO and the associated loosening of government policy that has enabled greater penetration into China's vast domestic market. WFOEs are also less in need of a local partner if they are retail establishments rather than manufacturers, which can also account for the choice of FDI vehicle.

The export focus is evident in the 'open door' policy whereby Special Economic Zones were set up as akin to export-processing zones that attracted FDI by offering preferential terms and enabling China to become part of global production chains, also known as cross-border vertical FDI. For example, FIEs are exempt from income tax for the first three profit-making years, and pay only 50 per cent of what would normally be due for the following two years. Their shareholders also received a refund of 40 per cent of the tax paid on profits that, instead of being taken out of the country, are re-invested in another FIE. For many years, FIEs were also allowed to import necessary capital equipment duty-free, although that benefit was subsequently restricted to FIEs in the 'encouraged' categories. FIEs have also been encouraged to locate in the various special zones that the central and local governments have established, where preferential policies apply as well. By contrast, entry into the domestic market was prohibited and could attract

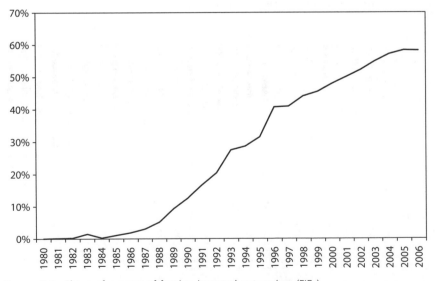

Figure 2.4. Share of exports of foreign-invested enterprises (FIEs)

Source: China Trade and External Economic Statistical Yearbook Table 4–26.

a 100 per cent tariff. It reflected a general restrictiveness of market access into China. Although, this had eased by the 2000s.

The contribution of FIEs to Chinese exports grew rapidly (see Figure 2.4). Accounting for around 5 to 10 per cent of Chinese exports during the 1980s, FIEs' share of exports grew rapidly with the take-off of the 'open door' policy, eventually accounting for more than half of all Chinese exports by 2001, the year of WTO accession, and they maintained that share unabated throughout the 2000s.

FIEs in China can take on the corporate forms outlined above, that is, joint stock company and LLCs (under the Company Law) or LLPs (under the Partnership Law). For instance, the various regulations passed after WTO accession, including the 2002 Securities Companies regulations and the Fund Management Companies regulations of the same year, permitted FIEs to operate in China's capital markets as either LLCs or JVs.

A foreign company can also establish a FIE holding company in China (typically a WFOE) to hold their interests in other FIEs. Although the holding company is technically a Chinese entity, it is deemed a foreign investor for purposes of its holdings in subsidiary FIEs. However, the establishment of such holding companies is difficult and provides few benefits, thus, this form is not commonly used.

Finally, foreign firms can establish a presence in China without investing, by setting up a representative office. They exist as a preliminary step before a foreign firm transacts business in China. It enables the Chinese government and the multinational corporation to begin the lengthy process of gaining permission to operate and the foreign firm to gain a better sense of the complexities of the Chinese mixed state/private market. Representative offices are also set up to provide support to the business of the parent company, for example providing after-sales service, but not to engage in business on their own. The exception is professional services, such as law firms and accounting firms, which are permitted to engage in business through representative offices.

2.2.4 THE COURT SYSTEM

The corporate sector in China is particularly complex, as the legal system in which it is at least partly situated is being developed alongside these reforms. China's court system consists of over 3,000 basic-level courts, hundreds of intermediate courts, thirty-one higher courts at the provincial level, and the Supreme People's Court, the highest court of the land. Under central planning, the state managed all economic matters, which left the courts the role of adjudicating civil and criminal, but not commercial, cases. The courts are part of the administrative system of the Chinese state, and its judges tend to be bureaucrats rather than legally trained practitioners as a consequence. The legal system is in dire need of structural reform to keep up with the pace of economic and increasingly with legal and regulatory reforms. This inadequate structure often leads to law makers and regulators as the source of guidance on commercial matters whilst bypassing the courts. Chapter 3 will analyse the issue of enforcement in China as part of assessing the interaction between laws and the market.

The changes in the evolving corporate sector are often driven by policy imperatives within the larger economy. To better situate the sector within that context, the following sections will tackle successive periods of China's marketization and identify the economic necessities that have arisen. This will form the backdrop to the focused analysis of the legal and economic reforms undertaken in each of the major corporate sectors in this volume.

2.3 **Rural and urban reforms in the 1980s**

The reforms of the 1980s were clearly propelled by economic necessity, with legal reforms coming afterwards in part to 'legalize' the policies which were already undertaken. These included the allowance of TVEs as part of rural reforms at the end of the 1970s which was only formalized with recognizing the TVE form in 1982 within the Constitution in the same year that the Household Responsibility System (HRS) which gave farmers incentives to produce was also recognized, some three years after these rural reforms had taken hold.

The 'no encouragement, no ban' approach to market-oriented reforms described by Naughton (1995) was nowhere more apparent than at the start of rural reforms. The HRS was initially banned until it was widely practised by farmers. TVEs arose to sell light industrial goods neglected by urban SOEs and also became a source of absorption of surplus labour in agriculture. In 1978, 82 per cent of the population was rural. Thus, with SOEs dominating industry in urban areas, agriculture accounted for only 30 per cent of GDP (gross domestic product) but employed 71 per cent of workers in the late 1970s (Figures 2.1 and 2.5). By 2006, agriculture's share of GDP had fallen to 11 per cent and yet, agriculture still accounts for some 40 per cent of employment, reflecting the 56 per cent of the population still dwelling in rural areas and who are constrained by the household registration system (*hukou*) from free movement to the higher income urban centres. The issue of surplus labour in rural areas, particularly in agriculture, was pressing, particularly before the gradual loosening of such migration controls in the 1990s. TVEs served to employ workers such that

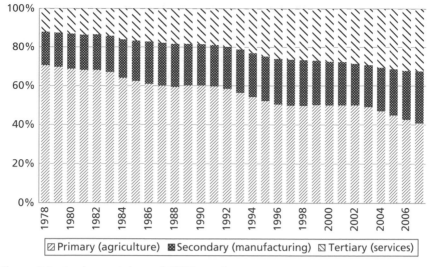

Figure 2.5. Employment share of GDP by sector
Source: China Statistical Yearbook Table 3–1.

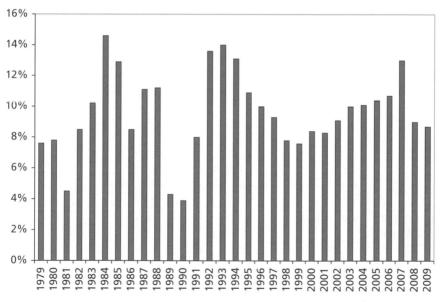

Figure 2.6. China's GDP growth, 1979–2009
Source: China Statistical Yearbook Table 2–1.

10 per cent of rural employment in the late 1970s and early 1980s was in those rural industries, which rose to one in five by 2006.

The combination of instilling incentives in farmers by allowing them to retain and sell at market prices output above the quota (the pre-determined amount to be remitted to the state), and rural industrialization with TVEs producing what SOEs were not mandated to produce helped generate remarkable growth in the early 1980s, such that China's take-off indeed started in the rural areas. Figure 2.6 shows the real annual GDP growth rate in China for the thirty years since 1979, with the spurt from the initial rural phase clearly evident.

The success of these initiatives, which modified the communal property precept in various ways, propelled the Chinese authorities to begin to improve the property rights system, albeit very gradually, to sustain the momentum of growth. In 1984, a land lease programme was trialled. Two years later, the Land Administration Law was passed that formalized the leasing system that had been negotiated in 1984 with farmers. It extended the leasing of land from five to fifteen years. This slowly enhanced land security to increase the incentive to improve the land and bolster agriculture production while keeping ownership in public hands.

This 'dual track'—whereby the administrative track exists alongside a new market track—became the model adopted in 1984, known as the 'Dual Track (Plan and Market) System' that was applied to SOEs to incentivize their output. The Third Plenum of the 12th Party Congress implemented the dual track pricing system and gave SOEs autonomy to sell above-quota output at market prices and retain the proceeds for profit. A profit tax was introduced to replace the remittance of profit to the state. This Contract Responsibility System (CRS) relied on managerial responses to the link between pay and firm output, and gave SOEs some leverage over managers, including the payment of bonuses. Interestingly, not only was the 'dual track' system modelled on the rural reforms, the managerial responsibility system adopted in 1985 and 1988 in urban areas was also trialled in rural areas. In 1982, the Ministry of Commerce issued regulations allowing farmers to participate in the selection of cooperative managers and to receive dividends from profits.

Urban reforms thus began in the mid 1980s and were initially considered to be successful in creating a profit incentive in SOEs that were otherwise used to producing to a plan (see e.g. Groves et al. 1995). Following on, the late 1980s also witnessed a trend of liberalization geared at supporting the partially reformed market. In 1985, direct banking was permitted. Bank loans replaced central government grants to SOEs to make investment decisions more responsive to market signals. Previously, SOEs would ask for funds with a tendency towards over-investment as the true cost of the capital was never realized. In 1986, the General Principles of Civil Law was passed. The statute was intended to provide the basic legal principles for operating in a market economy. However, it failed to provide for important areas of law, such as contract, tort, and property. There was a 1981 Economic Contract Law pertaining to transactions between SOEs, but it was largely ineffectual in governing beyond that narrow relationship. For instance, the Economic Contract Law did not apply to private firms like *getihu* until 1993 when it was amended. Instead, the Civil Law provided the principles under which sole proprietors operated. Also in 1986, the Bankruptcy Law was also passed, with the goal of improving SOE performance by instilling the threat of closure. However, this disciplining device was ineffective, since the state was the ultimate owner who would rescue a failing SOE for reasons such as preserving employment. The overhaul of the bankruptcy regime in 2006 when there were non-state enterprises which needed legislation governing bankruptcy was unsurprising.

The creation of a market track led to the recognition in the 13th Party Congress in 1987 that private economic activity was a necessary supplement to the state sector. The non-state track, which included foreign firms discussed in the next section, was the source of the growth that generated the transfers which enabled the gradual reform of SOEs. Otherwise, more dramatic steps would have been needed, given the extent of the losses within the inefficient state system. However, the recognition granted to private firms was grudging at best. In 1987, regulations were passed offering some acknowledgement of private firms. In 1988, the Constitution was amended to reflect the existence of a private sector. Alongside that amendment, the Provisional Regulations on Private Enterprises were passed that allowed certain persons (farmers, urban unemployed, retired) to form private enterprises. That law offered very little in terms of allowing private firms to develop, but rather viewed such businesses as supplementary to the primary state-controlled economy. Nevertheless, during the 1980s, although halting, China's economic transition was under way, and led by policy dictates which were weakly legitimized by laws and regulations. In 1989 at the end of that decade, an Administrative Procedure Law was passed which established the principle that government agencies must justify their actions by reference to published laws and regulations. This did not pertain to the law-making process, but marked a shift in the perception of how rules governing what was evidently an emerging market economy were to be executed. Two years later, the Civil Procedure Law was passed, adding further institutional development to the legal system that was evolving with the burgeoning market.

2.4 'Open door' policy (1978/1992–)

At the very start of reforms in 1978, China undertook gradual opening of its economy to international trade and investment, but specifically in the form of export-processing zones (known as SEZs) with a focus on long-term FDI and not short-term portfolio flows, sometimes called 'hot money'. The aim from the start was to attract more advanced know-how and technology from foreign firms to help develop export capacity and domestic innovation. It was not to allow foreign firms to dominate an under-developed market in China or to permit speculative capital from derailing the nascent capital market, which was still dominated by a state-owned banking system with virtually no financial sector to speak of. Unlike domestic firms, foreign investors required more certainty in contracting to plough their monies into factories in China. It could not take the same form as law later 'legitimizing' economic policy, as had happened with Chinese enterprises. Thus, the first piece of corporate law in China was the 1979 Law on Chinese–Foreign Equity Joint Ventures. In 1980, the two initial SEZs were created in Guangdong and Fujian provinces, with another two added a year later also in the south. Dramatic expansion of these export-processing zones which attracted FDI by offering concessions on tax and preferential treatment did not occur until Deng Xiaoping's southern tour of 1992, after which nearly all provinces had an SEZ by the end of the 1990s.

Perhaps unsurprisingly, given China's abundant and low cost labour, FDI poured in from the start. Multinational corporations sought out China for its low wages to give them a cost advantage, utilizing China's comparative advantage as would be expected by firms that range over the world seeking ways to specialize and divide their production chains across borders in order to maximize profit by taking advantage of what different globally linked countries have to offer. Straightaway in 1981, foreign-invested enterprises began to produce for export in China. Their share of exports rapidly grew, such that by the middle of the 1980s, they accounted for around 5 per cent of all exports and doubled that share to 10 per cent by the end of the decade. By 1992, their share had doubled again to 20 per cent and the jump after the creation of many more SEZs that year is evident from the export picture in Table 2.2 as well as in Table 2.3 which traces the inflow of FDI into China. FIEs produced 29 per cent of China's exports in 1994, 40 per cent in 1996, 50 per cent in the year of WTO accession in 2001, and shot up even further to nearly 60 per cent five years later. The average flow of inward FDI per annum of some $50–60 billion is fairly remarkable and reflects, in part the early adoption of laws geared at developing FDI vehicles.

With the launch and rapid success of the 'open door' policy, China passed the Foreign Economic Contract Law in 1985 which bears some passing

Table 2.2. Foreign invested enterprises' share of exports

1980	1981	1982	1983	1984	1985	1986	1987	1988	1989	1990	1991	1992	1993	1994
0.0%	0.1%	0.2%	1.5%	0.3%	1.1%	1.9%	3.1%	5.2%	9.4%	12.6%	16.8%	20.4%	27.5%	28.7%
1995	1996	1997	1998	1999	2000	2001	2002	2003	2004	2005	2006			
31.5%	40.7%	41.0%	44.1%	45.5%	47.9%	50.1%	52.2%	54.8%	57.1%	58.3%	58.2%			

Source: China Trade and External Economic Statistical Yearbook Table 4–26.

Notes: The figures were also calculated from China Statistical Yearbook, Tables 4–2, 17–1, 17–13. The FIE share of exports was computed from the value of exports from FIE in value terms as a ratio of total exports for each year.

Table 2.3. FDI in China (in US$billions)

1986	1987	1988	1989	1990	1991	1992	1993	1994	1995	1996
4.76	7.628	8.452	10.226	10.06	10.289	11.554	19.203	38.96	43.213	48.133
1997	1998	1999	2000	2001	2002	2003	2004	2005	2006	2007
64.408	58.557	52.659	59.356	40.672	55.011	56.14	64.072	63.805	67.076	78.339

Source: China Statistical Yearbook Table 17–15

resemblance to the Economic Contract Law promulgated the year before for transactions between SOEs. This statute governed contracts between Chinese and foreign firms to increase contracting security and legalize the terms of dealing between the foreign firms now entering China and the suppliers and distributors that they would transact with whilst operating in the domestic market. This legislation is part of the separate legal regime for foreign firms that operated until the 2000s, in which FIEs were granted more legal protection than domestic firms and became a source of discontent particularly among the private Chinese firms beginning to emerge at the same time with the implementation of the 'dual track' system (see e.g. Huang 2003).

Moving gingerly towards improving contracting security for foreign firms, in 1986 China joined the Convention on the Recognition and Enforcement of Foreign Arbitral Awards, which permitted arbitration as a way to resolve contractual disagreements that did not rely on China's under-developed legal system. However, in practice, the referral to arbitration was by no means automatic, particularly if the Chinese partner was a state-owned enterprise, which was always the case in the early part of the reform period. Nevertheless, this intention to try and improve the contracting system by offering arbitration was part of the overall aim to secure foreign investment by offering better legal protection than would be the case in a developing/ transition economy such as China's. In 1994, the Arbitration Law was set up, which led to the creation of the China International Economic and Trade Arbitration Commission (CIETAC) that has become the preferred channel as opposed to litigation for resolving contractual disputes. In this sense, the parallel legal regimes for domestic and foreign firms were ever evident.

Other legal vehicles had also been developed for foreign firms during this early period. In 1986, the Law on Wholly Foreign-Owned Enterprises was passed, which allowed foreign firms to organize as foreign subsidiaries. This was followed in 1988 by the Law on Chinese–Foreign Cooperative Joint Ventures, offering a triumvirate of vehicles for foreign investors. However, for reasons of technology and learning discussed below, JVs were the preferred vehicle in the early days of opening.

Around this time in 1984, Economic and Trade Development Zones (ETDZ) or 'Open Port Cities' (OPCs) were created. The OPCs were originally created to address the perceived shortcomings of the initial SEZs. These OPCs became ETDZs in 1985. These new zones aimed, and were considered, to be more successful than the SEZs in attracting investments beyond low-tech goods such as clothing/textiles and instead brought in particularly consumer electronics and computer goods. They are located along China's eastern coast and granted preferential investment terms as well as import treatment. There are officially twelve ETDZs sanctioned by the central government, but there are thought to be many more such areas under local authority governance (Lin et al. 2003).

The 1987 Technology Contract Law codified the terms of utilizing foreign technologies through provisions governing the technology transfer agreements signed by JVs that also allowed for dispute resolution when the need arose. The better articulated law governing technology contracts was needed to support the new phase of FDI policy geared ever more at attracting technology. The criteria for approval was guided by the aims of FDI policy, which is to attract technology and know-how in order to increase productivity, while at the same time controlling the market incursions of FIEs to allow domestic firms to develop and learn from the more advanced foreign multinationals. The Chinese authorities sought FDI that had superior technology and proven demand as an export product. This also resulted in a preference for JVs over WFOEs which stemmed from the desire to gain positive 'spillovers' from FDI, that is, benefits to China beyond what was internalized in the gains to the foreign firm. In JVs, the Chinese partner would usually contribute the factory and workers, while the foreign partner, the capital and technology. These partnering arrangements allowed for formal transfers of technology as well as informal 'spillovers' where learning occurs by Chinese employees working alongside foreign managers. This is less likely to occur with WFOEs.

Often, the JV contract included a technology transfer agreement that granted the Chinese party access and use of the proprietary know-how of the foreign partner as part of the consideration to form the joint venture. This was a cheaper form of gaining know-how than licensing the proprietary technology, and thus offered China the opportunity to 'catch up' by cheaply adopting existing advanced technology that would boost its productivity and therefore growth rate. This is before IPR regimes were tightened with harmonization of protection of proprietary knowledge with the formation of the WTO in 1995. This was not an uncommon practice among developing countries that had the leverage with foreign firms to extract such benefits in exchange for permitting multinational corporations to operate. Further liberalization followed.

In 1992, another iteration known as Free Trade Zones (FTZs) was created to facilitate the take-off of the 'open door' policy. FTZs are specially designated urban areas selected for receiving preferential trading privileges. The investment incentives in FTZs are extremely attractive since exports and imports are free of any taxes or tariffs so long as the goods are not sold in China. Items intended for re-sale in China were, by contrast, subject to high tariff rates. The best-known FTZs are Shanghai's Pudong district, particularly Waigaoqiao, Tianjin Harbour, Shenzhen's Futian, Dalian, and Haikou on Hainan Island.

China continued its push to attract more advanced technologies by developing High-Technology Development Zones (HTDZs) in 1995, just three years after the successful creation of FTZs that generated an influx of FDI, seen in Table 2.3. The intent of the HTDZs was to increase China's research and development (R&D) capabilities through fostering both domestic and foreign investment. With the exception of the three inner provinces (Xinjiang and the Tibet and Ningxia Autonomous Regions), every province has at least one of the fifty-three HTDZs. Each zone includes a number of 'industrial parks' and 'science and technology parks' open to domestic and foreign high-tech investors. The actual number is higher as numerous zones sprang up that have not been sanctioned by the State Council, as had happened also with the ETDZs.

HTDZs comprise cities or certain areas of urban China, such as the well-known 'Haidian' district in Beijing, often likened to Silicon Valley, particularly given its proximity to leading research universities such as Peking University and Tsinghua University. These zones are intended to promote industrial applications of technology and tend to be located in proximity to existing or planned research institutions, or research and development centres. A characteristic of the HTDZs is the '3-in-1' development system, whereby every zone must include a university-based or other research centre, an innovation centre to utilize applied technology for product development, and a partnership with a commercial enterprise to manufacture and market the products. Foreign investors continue to be offered preferential treatment as an incentive to establish high-tech joint ventures in these zones. The HTDZs are designed to contribute to China's science and technology infra-structure, though there is a question as to whether domestic firms have gained in innovative ability as a result of FDI. Although more than 50 per cent of China's exports have been produced by foreign-invested enterprises, an esti-mated 80 per cent of China's high-tech goods are produced by FIEs (see Yueh 2006). This mid 1990s' focus on technology was mirrored in innovation policies governing domestic firms, including the passage of intellectual prop-erty rights (IPRs) laws, to facilitate the absorption of FDI and develop indigenous innovative capacity.

The need for investment vehicles for foreign firms to invest in China, which was an important part of the 'catch up' growth strategy, led to the early passage of the JV laws. Much of what was promulgated in the FDI laws had no prior existence in Chinese commercial or enterprise law (legal personality, limited liability, contractual enforcement, dispute resolution, status as inves-tor/shareholder, board of directors, etc.). In order to attract foreign investors used to having legally specified contracts governing their investments, the FDI laws pre-date much of the development of Chinese corporate laws. Over a decade after the Equity JV Law, the Company Law was passed in late 1993. And it was not until 1999 that the three different contract laws (Economic Contract Law of 1981, Economic Contract Law for Foreign Parties of 1985, and the Technology Contract Law of 1987) were unified into one Contract Law offering a harmonized regime for domestic and foreign firms.

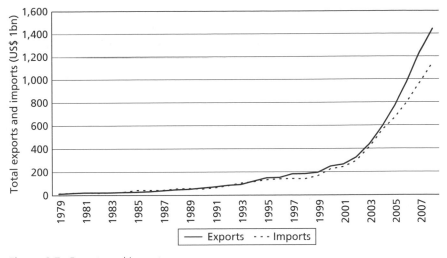

Figure 2.7. Exports and imports
Source: China Statistical Yearbook Table 17–3.

The policy aim of maintaining stability during economic transition meant that there would be a limit to the incursion of FDI into the domestic markets, while Chinese industries 'learned' and developed. Examining the carefully wrought trade liberalization that occurred throughout this period, the 'open door' policy was successful in boosting exports as well as imports, as seen in Figure 2.7. China quickly rose throughout the 1980s to increase its global market share in manufactured goods trade by sixfold in a decade, and to become the world's largest trader within another decade by 2009.

China started negotiating for entry into the WTO in 1986 and succeeded fifteen years later. Within seven years of first opening to the global economy, China aimed to join the global trading system, but the laws governing foreign trade did not exist until after it had already begun trading. Similar to the other laws of the early 1990s, the Foreign Trade Law of 1994 was promulgated more than a decade after China's launch of its 'open door' policy and two years after Deng Xiaoping's southern tour which marked its take-off. In other words, China was already exporting and importing based on detailed policies. But, the Foreign Trade Law laid the institutional grounding for trade liberalization and the eventual adoption of free trade agreements (FTAs) when it was amended in 2004. Immediately after WTO accession in 2001, China agreed two FTAs in 2002 —with Hong Kong and Macao (known as CEPAs or Closer Economic Partnership Arrangements). These were Special Administrative Regions (SARs) of China, so the early cementing of the trade relationship is not surprising. After amending the Foreign Trade Law in 2004, China entered into a total of sixteen FTAs involving twenty-eight countries by 2009, though these agreements tended to be only in traded goods (as with the ten nations of the Association of Southeast Asian Nations or ASEAN) and not 'deeper' integration of services and product standards as with the CEPAs. This was then followed by the articulation of a FTA strategy in 2007 by President Hu Jintao during the 17th National Congress of the CPC.

The economic necessity of opening led to the adoption of a law which in turn spawned a set of trade agreements which spurred the later amendments that helped to further market development as seen in China's first ever FTAs. And only afterward was a national strategy articulated. Whereas foreign firms were granted legal foundations from the outset, the overall process of opening is better characterized as part of the gradualist transition approach, where economic policies were only later effectuated through laws. Both sets of reforms of FDI and trade, though, were initially driven by economic needs, and then supported by laws when the strategies proved to be successful.

2.5 **Early 1990s' liberalization policies**

The push for a corporate law in China arose out of economic necessity in order to provide an institutional form for the corporatization of SOEs, transforming them into shareholding companies (some of which became publicly listed) as the preferred alternative to mass privatization by voucher or other means used largely unsuccessfully in other transition economies of the former Soviet Union in the early 1990s. The rapidity of those reforms was never to China's taste. China had started reforms in the previous decade and did not subscribe to the mass privatization adopted in those countries during that time, and thus avoided the subsequent decade of negative growth in Eastern Europe and the former Soviet bloc.

The creation of the stock markets in Shanghai and Shenzhen in 1990 and 1991, respectively, provided the bourses upon which 'share issue privatized' firms could list and become publicly traded. The particular nature of these reforms meant that the state did not give up all ownership; rather, the partial reform which permeates China's overall transition is also found here. But, there was urgent need as SOE inefficiency took a toll on the state-owned banking system funding their losses and resulted in significant amounts of non-performing loans (NPLs) in the banks, made worse by the increased competition from a burgeoning non-state (private, TVE, and FIE) sector.

The law legitimized policy reforms undertaken to stymie the losses of SOEs. In the early 1990s, an estimated two-thirds of all SOEs were loss-making (Fan 1994). The initial success of the CRS had faded. Although output had been stimulated by the 'dual track' system whereby above-quota output could be sold and retained as profit and generated higher wages for managers and workers, the lack of reform of inputs meant that inefficiency reigned. The 'soft budget constraints' which characterized SOEs under state ownership meant that, although output was incentivized, there was no curbing of the reliance on the government to provide cheap capital and allocate labour. To a large extent, the 'multi-tasking role' of SOEs where they aimed to maximize profit but also to maintain full employment in the economy meant that state support was expected (Bai et al. 2000). Instead, higher output growth created a perverse incentive to demand ever more inputs with which to produce output. In other words, SOE output might be growing but inefficiencies were worsening, leading to significant losses requiring state support that generated NPLs in the state-owned banking system which were estimated at some one-third of GDP in the 1990s (Fan 2003).

The corporatization of SOEs took two main forms: closely held and publicly traded companies. In 1992, two policy statements from the State Commission on Reform of the Economic System were issued that facilitated this corporate reorganization, which were later codified in the Company Law of 1993, effective from 1994. The Company Law was promulgated a year after two significant documents were issued by the State Commission on Reform of the Economic System. In May 1992, the Normative Opinion on Joint Stock Companies and the Normative Opinion on Limited Liability Companies were passed which essentially formed the two halves of the Company Law. The Normative Opinion on Joint Stock Companies provided a corporate form for enterprises that wished to restructure and list their shares on the newly formed stock exchanges. The Normative Opinion on Limited Liability Companies provided a new corporate form for those enterprises wishing to restructure into companies with investors holding equity shares but not to become listed companies.

Thus, in December 1993, the Company Law was passed and came into effect in July of the following year. It formalized and legalized the forms of the joint stock company (those shareholding companies which were publicly listed and traded) and the limited liability company (LLC) which covered those shareholding companies that were not listed firms. The Normative Opinion on Limited Liability Companies allowed SOEs to restructure as corporations, with investors holding equity shares, while the Normative Opinion on Joint Stock Companies served as the second half that provided an organizational vehicle for enterprises that wished to transform into shareholding companies and list on the stock exchange.

The stock exchanges in China were unusual institutions that reflected the partial reform tendencies of the state. As a compromise of sorts to retain state ownership, the stock market had several classes of shares: state shares, legal person shares, and common shares. State and legal person shares were not publicly tradable so that state ownership could be preserved. Legal person shares could only be held by legal person institutions or corporations, which referred to state institutions like the state pension fund or state-owned enterprises. The floating or tradable common shares were further divided into 'A' shares denominated in renminbi or yuan (RMB) for domestic investors and 'B' shares which are for foreign investors. Unsurprisingly in the presence of considerable capital controls as described in the last section in China's incremental 'open door' policy, the 'A' share market predominated while foreign investors were not allowed to participate in the main share market until after WTO accession. In 1997, with the handover of Hong Kong back to China from the British government, 'H' shares listed in the Special Administrative Region (SAR) of Hong Kong formed a further class of shares. All shares had the same voting rights, but two-thirds of the mainland market was non-tradable as a result of the state and legal person shares.

That was not the only anomaly of the exchanges. In 1993, the State Council issued the Provisional Regulations on the Administration and Issuance and Trading of Stocks. In effect, this was China's first securities law. The Provisional Rules on Stock Issuance and Trading established the framework through which SOEs could become publicly listed companies. As evident from Table 2.4, it was only SOEs which could list in the early days of the bourses and it was not until 1998 that the first five privately controlled firms were traded. Even those SOEs which undertook initial public offerings (IPOs) were chosen so that the emergence of publicly traded companies was gradual. Provinces were granted annual quotas to select SOEs for listing. IPOs meant the ability to raise capital and tap into the rapidly growing amount of household savings in China that was confined to domestic investment due to external capital controls. With the housing market not privatized until 1998, the stock markets became the preferred avenue for asset investment, rising steadily throughout the 1990s despite their rather odd complexion. Nevertheless, they served the purpose of facilitating SOE reform in that share issue privatization (SIP), including publicly traded corporations, was under way by the early 1990s.

Gradual reform of SOEs occurred during a period of greater market liberalization. Starting in the late 1980s and early 1990s, China's wholesale and retail markets were increasingly freed from state control. The growth of TVEs in this segment and increasingly of *getihu* (sole proprietors) operated alongside SOEs, leading to the 1993 revision of the Economic Contract Law. Previously, this law applied to SOEs transacting with each other, since there was not much in the enterprise sector apart from them. However, with the emergence of the non-state sector, there was a need to extend the Economic Contract Law to cover the contracts signed by *getihu* since there was a need to govern their transactions as well. *Getihu* as a rather loose form of economic organization had previously fallen under the General Principles of Civil

Table 2.4. Listed companies in China

	1990	1991	1992	1993	1994	1995	1996	1997	1998	1999	2000	2001	2002	2003	2004	2005	2006	2007
Listed firms	10	14	53	183	291	323	530	745	851	949	1092	1140	1204	1258	1355	1351	1434	1526
Private firms	0	0	0	0	0	0	0	0	5	67	97	120	185	272	353	374	456	532
% private	0%	0%	0%	0%	0%	0%	0%	0%	0.6%	7.1%	8.9%	10.5%	15.4%	21.6%	26.1%	27.7%	31.8%	34.9%

Source: China Securities Regulatory Commission.

Notes: According to the Measures for the Administration of the Takeover of Listed Companies, Article 84 states that the controlling right of a listed company is 'private' if a private shareholder meets any of the following: (1) The investor is controlling shareholder that holds more than 50 per cent of the shares of the listed company; (2) The investor can actually control more than 30 per cent of the voting right of shares of the listed company; (3) The investor can decide the election of more than half of the directors of the board of directors of the company by actually controlling the voting right of the shares of the listed company; (4) The voting right of shares of a listed company under the actual control of the investors is sufficient to produce significant effects on the resolutions of the general assembly of the shareholders of the company; or (5) Any other circumstance as recognized by the CSRC.

Law, so this marks the first time that their contracts were governed by corporate law.

The consumer market began to develop around this time. In 1992, food prices were no longer administered, and the end of the 'dual track' pricing system was evident. This stands in stark contrast to the food vouchers that had existed until then, for instance. In response, a 1993 Product Quality Law was passed to govern the emerging consumer goods market, though it was inadequate, as with most such laws from this period, which became evident during the much later scandals of the 2000s despite a revision of the law in 2000. The development of this market was undoubtedly related to the 'open door' policy taking off and the incursion of multinational firms into sectors such as the mobile and telecommunications market supplying phones and services to a burgeoning middle class in urban areas. The fast-growing domestic market further attracted a different type of foreign investment, with WFOEs as another FDI vehicle more geared at retail establishments like food stores (as compared with manufacturing JVs) gaining in importance.

However, maintaining stability and domestic industrial capacity meant that certain industries, such as automobiles, were still taking the form of JVs. This ongoing concern about technology and industrial strength permeated and percolated into a focus evident since the mid 1990s on technology and developing the institutional bases for competitive industries that increasingly included better legal protection of property rights and contracts.

2.6 Mid to late 1990s' focused marketization

By the mid 1990s, marketization and the legal reforms accompanying the developing market economy had begun to take hold. The government juggled several aspects of this process, including speeding up the reform of SOEs that included full privatization for the first time, as well as securing better property rights to foster innovation and develop a sounder legal footing for its expanding non-state-owned enterprise sector. At the same time, China was nearing the end of its fifteen-year negotiation to enter the WTO, which offered not just trade benefits but also required certain legal reforms such as transparency of laws and adoption of an international IPR system, adding even more urgency to the evident intent to promote more domestic capacity for innovation and industrial upgrading.

2.6.1 INNOVATIVE CAPACITY

As seen in the treatment of foreign multinational corporations, the mid 1990s was marked by a focus on developing innovative capacity, including strengthening property rights, which was important for developing better security for proprietary knowledge that could foster innovation. However, as the section on the 'open door' policy suggested, there was a dualist nature, in that imitation of more advanced technology from foreign firms was also sought as a cheaper alternative.

For instance, the technology-oriented SEZs known as HTDZs arose out of a feeling that China's growth was not sufficiently driven by technological advancement. The creation of these zones was intended to promote R&D and innovation, which led in turn to the need for better IPR protection. Patent laws and proactive industrial policies centred on fostering scientific personnel combined to increase productivity in the economy. For foreign investors wishing to guard against expropriation of their proprietary knowledge, the use of hybrid forms of FDI vehicles became part of the strategy, for example JV for production, but WFOE for R&D.

This was in spite of an IPR system that had been formally in effect since the mid 1980s. China's patent law was enacted in 1984 and promulgated in 1985. In 1992, it was revised to extend the length of patent protection from fifteen to twenty years for invention patents and from five to ten years for process patents, for example model and design patents. In 2000, it was further revised in anticipation of accession to the World Trade Organization which occurred a year later. In 2001, China adopted trade-related aspects of intellectual property rights (TRIPs) as part of its WTO obligations whereby its IPR standards were harmonized with international rules. Since the passage of the patent laws, there have been dozens of regulations and guidelines adopted to promote innovation. The patent law amendments also included conditions on the granting of compulsory licences and prohibiting the unauthorized importation of products which infringe on the patents.

China's copyright law was promulgated in 1991 and has been amended several times since and limits protection to works that do not harm China's 'public interest'. Enforcement of copyright laws was further strengthened to step up criminal prosecutions in 2004. To complete the IPR system, China's trademark law was promulgated in 1983 with significant revisions in 1993, which permit registration and provide protection for service marks and also criminal sanctions for trademark infringement.

By the mid 1990s, China had a nominal, though not widely regarded as effective, set of IPR laws intended to offer protection to inventions and therefore foster innovation. Because of the poor protection afforded to IPRs, patents in China grew slowly during the decade after the enactment of

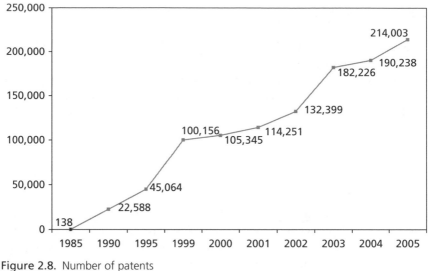

Figure 2.8. Number of patents
Source: China Statistical Yearbook Table 20–56.

the Patent Law (Figure 2.8). This prompted the focus on technology that was evident in FDI policy. Estimates of Chinese growth bolstered the fears of the government that the 9 per cent growth rate could not be sustained. Factor accumulation of capital and labour accounted for the bulk of Chinese growth and not productivity gains (see e.g. Borensztein and Ostry 1996). Although unsurprising in that many developing countries grow by capital accumulation in the early stages, the inability to sustain productivity advances will lead to a slowdown as the accumulation process reaches its limits. For China, the estimates that total factor productivity (TFP), which measures the productivity of the factors in the economy, was around 3 to 4 per cent before the mid 1990s but fell afterwards to less than 3 per cent, cemented the renewed technological focus (see e.g. Zheng, Bigsten, and Hu 2009 for reviews of studies of TFP).

The TRIPs provisions within the WTO articles have been subject to numerous critiques on account of their strict imposition of an IPR system into economies which are still aiming to imitate rather than innovate. Developing countries had previously been able to use tools such as compulsory licensing to obtain more advanced technologies cheaply because, prior to TRIPs, IPRs were not respected across national borders. After TRIPs, the international system became harmonized. Most least developed countries (LDCs) obtained a grace period to implement TRIPs and carve-outs were also made for pharmaceuticals and other sensitive items. China, by contrast, adopted TRIPs upon accession. At the same time, WFOEs began to dominate the FDI vehicles coming into China, while technology firms guarded their proprietary know-how through hybrid corporate forms increasingly available by the early 2000s. The avenues of previous technology transfers and cheap imitation were increasingly closed off. The result was a push to develop domestic innovation, particularly in light of the foreign competition after WTO accession. R&D spending rose from negligible amounts to rival the spending of OECD countries by the 2000s. All of this contributed to an explosion of patents in China, primarily driven by domestic firms filing for protection of their IPRs.

The mid 1990s focus on technology, coupled with forced improvements to its IPR system with WTO accession, reflect a convergence of policies and laws that may well allow China to achieve a sustained rate of growth. The development of the technology sector is in many ways revealing of how an imperfect legal system worked alongside economic necessity to realize an aim of the state.

2.6.2 PRIVATIZING STATE-OWNED ENTERPRISES AND IMPROVING THE CORPORATE LEGAL FOUNDATION

As with all other aspects of corporate development in China, this marketization process was focused but undertaken gradually and motivated largely by economic necessity. Following from the corporatization policy of 1992 (share issue privatization) and 1993 (restructuring into LLCs and joint stock companies), the *zhuada fanxiao* ('save the large, let go of the small') policy was enacted in 1994 and effectively privatized the small and medium-sized SOEs. Notable fiscal reform in the same year centralized finances such that the support offered by local governments and local state-owned banks towards local SOEs was diluted and aided the reforms.

From over 10 million SOEs in 1994, the total fell by a quarter a year later, as seen in Table 2.5. By 1997, SOE reform was truly under way when the state allowed redundancies to occur. From 1997 to 2001, a quarter of the urban labour force was laid-off, though the figures did not appear in the official urban unemployment rate due to the status of *xiagang* given to such workers, which designated them as nominally laid-off but still registered with their work unit so that they received small amounts of payment while they looked for work.

This significant reform meant that SOEs could be privatized once their employment role was diminished. In 1998, SOEs had shrunk from 7.9 million in the previous year to 165,000. The share of total industrial output did not register a similarly dramatic decline. SOE share of output fell from 33.7 per cent to 29.8 per cent, on account of the large remaining SOEs. These include energy and commodity companies, utilities, and state-owned commercial banks.

Table 2.5. Number of SOEs

1978	1979	1980	1981	1982	1983	1984	1985	1986	1987	1988	1989	1990	1991
348,400	355,000	446,300	494,500	566,600	712,500	869,200	5,185,300	6,706,700	7,474,100	8,105,600	7,980,700	7,957,800	8,079,600

1992	1993	1994	1995	1996	1997	1998	1999	2000	2001	2002	2003	2004	2005	2006
8,612,100	9,911,600	10,017,100	7,341,500	7,986,500	7,922,900	165,080	162,033	162,885	171,256	181,557	196,222	276,474	271,835	301,961

Source: China Statistical Yearbook Table 13–8.

Far from disappearing such that China would become a fully private economy, SOEs were consolidated and national (state-owned) champions like the National Oil Companies (NOCs) were promoted. In 1999, the NOCs were reorganized into three firms, each responsible for a specific segment of the oil market, such as CNOOC which was geared at offshore exploration. In 2001, the same occurred with the steel industry. The state-owned banks were reformed by a 1995 law and readied for IPOs, even whilst the state retained a majority share.

Thus, the SOE share of output hovered at 30 per cent of GDP throughout the late 1990s and 2000s, rather than disappearing altogether. However, as these are largely capital-intensive industries, the share of urban employment of SOEs declined continuously until they accounted for less than 10 per cent of urban workers, a far cry from the days when SOEs were maintained despite their losses to meet the government's goal of full employment.

This in turn has meant a growth of the non-state sector and increased marketization in the economy, which led to more legal and institutional measures to support an increasingly decentralized market in the mid to late 1990s. In 1995, the Negotiable Instruments Law was passed which made payments by cheque and other non-cash methods easier. However, as this was promulgated at around the same time as the Commercial Banking Law which furthered the reform of the state-owned banking system, there was not a sufficiently established central bank to guarantee the cheques of its member banks, among other problems. Also in that year, the Security Law was also passed which enabled secured lending to facilitate corporate development, but as property rights were opaque, the impact was limited.

Chinese corporate forms such as partnerships also began to develop during this period, which were also associated with the speeding up and refocus of economic policy geared at supporting growth driven by increased marketization. Completing the set of laws on economic entities, a Partnership Law was passed in February 1997 that granted the form of a partnership, and in August 1999, the Law on Individual Wholly-Owned Enterprises was also promulgated. Neither provided for limited liability but granted legal recognition to the standard corporate form of a partnership and sole proprietorship, the latter of which is notable in China, since the communal property state created uncertainty around self-employment. The 2006 amendments to the Partnership Law, which came into effect in 2007, rectified some of the misgivings surrounding the statute. The revised statute permitted organizations and not just individuals to be partners and also allowed for a modest degree of liability, creating LLPs (limited liability partnerships).

This large-scale move to corporatize or *gongsihua* therefore encompassed all firms in China, even the *getihu* or the self-employed and certainly the foreign and other domestic firms in China, including SOEs which underwent significant restructuring as corporations in the 9th Five Year Plan that was completed towards the end of the 1990s. The need for a legal framework to govern these corporatized firms was apparent from the efforts to create such a system.

In 1997, there was even a Price Law that was passed in an effort to establish the principle that the great majority of prices were to be set by the market, that is, to be decided by firms according to market forces of supply and demand. However, it contained provisions to prevent excessively high and low prices, indicating that the legacy of the administered economy remained. Much more importantly, in 1998, the Revised Land Administration Law was passed. It updated the 1984 and 1986 laws by extending the term of land leases from fifteen to thirty years. This allowed for much greater security in leasehold property rights that enabled land owners to invest and improve their holdings. It stopped short of privatizing land, but the longer leasehold offered greater security, particularly after the 2007 Property Law that granted equal protection to private and public property. For grassland and forest land, the leases were made even longer —to fifty and seventy years, respectively, by the 2002 Rural Land Contracting Law. However, the state retained ownership of land so this partial reform of an important property right was no different from the overall reform path.

The parallel decision to reform urban housing in 1998 eventually gave the owners of newly privatized housing similarly long fifty-year leaseholds. Housing had previously been allocated by SOEs as part of the benefits expected with the 'iron rice bowl'. That included a job for life and all social securities including pensions—to be provided by the work unit or *danwei*. The decision to significantly restructure SOEs led to the removal of the housing benefit by 1998. By 2001, SOE employees had largely purchased their flats at preferential prices. The security afforded by the leasehold system led to the rapid growth of the real estate market in China, later a source of concern, along with stocks as the main asset classes.

The passage of the Securities Law in December 1998 at this time completed the *de jure* set of corporate laws. The 1998 Securities Law effectively completed the set of corporate laws in China, Along with the Company Law, a legal regime now governed corporate formation, public offerings, and securities trading. It initiated the prolific set of regulations governing companies operating in capital markets evident in the 2000s (see Appendix 2.2). Although there had been lower-level regulations governing securities, allowing a very proscribed set of rules for listing since the early 1990s' establishment of the stock exchanges (see Du and Xu 2009 which describes the provincial quota system), the Securities Law marked the first national-level rules, and the start of significant securities regulation in China. At the same time, it established the securities regulator, CSRC, with the power to regulate and supervise securities issuers, as well as investigate and impose penalties for illegal activities.

The impetus for improved protection of property rights in the mid and late 1990s stemmed not only from the will of the state as part of its gradual marketization strategy, but also from those who now owned firms, stocks, and housing. As stakeholders, they formed an interested constituency to push for better protection of their property, which is a common phenomenon in the development of other corporate law jurisdictions such as the US and Europe (see Coffee 2001). This was most evident in the area of securities, where a series of frauds led to public outrage and the subsequent establishment of a regulator some eight years after the opening of the stock market (see Chen 2003). As such, the laws of the late 1990s and the 2000s were unlike those passed during the early part of the reform period. These statutes and regulations were not the sole instruments of the state in legitimizing the government's economic policies, but were also reflections of the demand for legal reform by interested constituents to increase the security and protection of their property.

Therefore in 1999, the Constitution was amended to recognize the rule of law as a necessary part of governance. In 1999, a unified Contract Law was passed, as was a law that established private businesses as sole proprietorships. By 2001, President Zhang Zemin welcomed entrepreneurs into the Communist Party. None of these measures established an effective rule of law and protection of private property overnight, but the enactments reflect the demands of society for better legal protection now that they had property to protect, and also mark a stage where laws are used to further develop markets by offering the necessary institutional support through improving contracting security and legitimacy of corporate forms of ownership. Thus, in 2007, the Property Law granted formal legal protection to private property, a struggle that dates to an attempt twenty years earlier to do so in the General Principles of Civil Law.

By the 2000s, China was on its way to having a modern corporate law system. The Company Law was fundamentally revised as the original statute was intended to provide a legal basis for the corporatization of SOEs, but subsequently was revamped to govern the emerged diverse set of firms. The 1999 and 2005 amendments to the Company Law created a statute that ran to 230 articles covering the establishment and organization of companies, bond issuances, accountancy matters, mergers, bankruptcy and liquidation, the responsibilities of branches of foreign companies, and other matters. The Company Law also imposes a number of corporate governance requirements, such as duties and process rules for company operations, and the constitution of boards and directors as well as company managers.

Finally, this period of intense marketization included China's industrial policies 'going global'. China's 'going out' policy was launched in 2000 with the aim of establishing Chinese firms as global players, including SOEs like the NOCs and the state-owned commercial banks. Chinese firms could learn by operating in more developed economies and benefit from the competitive pressures of selling in global markets. The benefits of economies of scale could also be realized as well as international specialization as Chinese firms locate their production and distribution chains worldwide in the same way that foreign multinationals have in China as part of global supply chains. The policy resulted in international IPOs of large companies such as the state-owned bank, ICBC, and also the flagship carrier, Air China, on the New York and London stock exchanges. It also generated the first-ever overseas commercial acquisition by a Chinese company in 2004, which was enabled by the Mergers and Acquisitions Law passed the previous year that set the legal parameters of such deals. China's TCL purchased the Thomson brand of France, while a year later and the largest deal at the time for a Chinese firm, a much better known, Lenovo (Legend pre-M&A), bought IBM's PC business. These deals were unlike the SOE-led overseas investments in energy and commodities which continued to take place. These were, in effect, the first overtures of domestic firms seeking to expand overseas, and a maturation of Chinese corporations aiming to become multinational firms.

Unlike previous legislation, the laws and regulations of the late 1990s and the 2000s seemed to establish the foundation to enable such further market development. The 1999 Contract Law unified the previously separate foreign and domestic legal regimes governing contracts, and offered for the first time, a contract law that governed contracting arrangements among SOEs and private firms, domestic and foreign. A slew of regulations and laws were passed in 2000 and 2001 to regularize the law-making process itself to meet the requirements of transparency mandated by the WTO, for example the Legislation Law of 2000, Regulations on the Procedure for Formulating Administrative Regulations in 2001, and Regulations on the Procedure for Formulating Departmental Regulations in 2001. Other examples include the aforementioned 2003 M&A Law and the 2005 amendments to the Company Law, which enacted 230 articles covering the establishment and governance of companies, including requirements for boards of directors and bond issuances. Significantly, the 2004 amendments to the Constitution offered greater assurances against the expropriation of property, which led to the 2007 Property Law. For the first time, private property was afforded the same legal protection as public property, moving towards establishing the principle of well-defined property rights that would enable the efficient development of a market economy. Other laws like the 2006 overhaul of the ineffectual 1986 Bankruptcy Law, the enactment of an Anti-Monopoly Law in 2007 and an Employment Law in 2008 offered further governance of an emerging, decentralized market. The implementation of these laws and regulations continues to be imperfect, but the trend is towards formal legislation which will enhance market development. In other words, by the 2000s, law did not seem to just be a way of making legitimate in some institutional form whatever the government wished to enact as a policy matter. Laws began to reflect the changing market and the demands of property owners for better security, both for domestic and foreign parties.

In short, the period of the mid to late 1990s was characterized by the historic downsizing of SOEs and required the development of the non-state sector to sustain economic growth which laid the foundation for the rapid market development and legal changes of the 2000s. Notable reforms were undertaken to both restructure SOEs and bolster the institutional foundations of non-state firms. The predominate corporate form that emerged was joint stock companies, through which small and medium-sized SOEs were 'let go', the more profitable parts of SOEs were spun off, and the large SOEs were consolidated and transformed into shareholding companies. At the same time, the needs of an increasingly decentralized market called for greater legal reforms that led to laws that enabled further market development such as M&As, as opposed to simply legitimizing the economic policies of the government. Nevertheless, the state sector remained a significant part of the corporate sector, evident in the establishment of SASAC (State-owned Assets Supervision and Administration Commission) in 2003 to manage SOEs and the effective exclusion of SOEs from provisions of the Anti-Monopoly Law.

With global integration, moreover, the demands of overseas listings in New York and London meant a further need for corporate governance measures and reforms. The incursion of multinational corporations into China after WTO accession, particularly in financial services, also called for legal reforms to govern the emerging capital markets. Whereas the mid/late 1990s were characterized by focused marketization, WTO accession in 2001 marked a new era where international rules and norms also came into play, particularly in the weakest sector in China's transition, which is the banking and financial system.

2.7 **Rapid market development in the 2000s**

WTO accession in December 2001 marked the start of rapid market development in China. It followed from the intense marketization efforts of the late 1990s which were characterized not only by seismic economic reforms, but also by legal reforms designed to respond to market needs. In a sense, economic necessity has been joined by market demands as the drivers of legal reform. Global integration via WTO membership, and the maturation of the 'going out' policy, also added urgency to formulating rules and regulations to govern the fast emerging market and non-state sector. The 2000s were characterized by legal reforms that were sequenced to some extent with economic reforms, and certainly were adopted alongside market-oriented changes to provide the institutional framework to support further development.

An example is the 2003 M&A Law which was enacted prior to the first overseas commercial deal by a Chinese firm. After a decade of fierce competition in the 1990s in the domestic consumer market, Chinese firms were seasoned and wished to expand overseas to seek new markets as well as acquire brands with which to compete on quality and not only price. The 'going out' policy nurtured since the period of marketization culminated in Chinese firms being granted permission to operate overseas. The M&A Law provided the legal framework for their activities, which enabled the further development of mergers and acquisitions that are a part of a maturing market, where firms are no longer growing organically (or according to the plan) but are expanding and restructuring their organizational forms. The complete revamp of the Bankruptcy Law in 2006 was also necessary as uncompetitive firms wound up and needed dissolution schemes, for which the original 1986 statute designed to close down SOEs was completely inadequate. With these laws in place, as well as the development of the securities law, China had for the first time a full panoply of corporate laws that could govern and evolve with the market; thus, law not only serving as a nominal vehicle but sequenced and adopted to enable further market development. The next step is developing regulations to effectuate the laws, which is most apparent in capital markets. China is no exception and the 2000s marked an unprecedented period of regulatory development, driven by both the securities scandals of the 1990s and also the requirements of WTO opening.

International trade liberalization was a significant but not the only part of what it meant for China to join the WTO. Opening its own markets and abiding by WTO principles were facets of WTO accession, which had notable implications for the development of China's business sector. To join the WTO, China agreed to reduce tariffs across the board on imports of manufactured goods to below 10 per cent and heralded a period where its own exports, particularly in labour-intensive products like textiles and clothing, could be sold worldwide as part of the multilateral trading system that covered the near totality of international trade and certainly vast swathes of manufactures which themselves accounted for over 80 per cent of world trade. Joining the global trade body, though, was more involved, as the rules-based organization mandated changes in China's governance of its business sector in a number of ways, some of which were due to the WTO's own principles such as non-discrimination, but some were also because of the concessions granted by China in negotiating with each of the existing WTO members for entry. For instance, China agreed to eliminate geographical restrictions such that foreign firms can operate in more than one province, whereas previously, it resisted such expansion, so that a firm with offices in Beijing could not transact in Shanghai. However, rules limiting the opening of foreign branches to one per year as in the case of foreign banks meant that the fulfilment of this principle to treat foreign and domestic firms on an equal footing still translated into slow expansion for foreigners.

In other areas, China is bound by its own terms of accession. One of the WTO's articles pertains to a harmonized intellectual property regime that caused China to significantly revise its own patent and related laws, particularly in terms of implementation. Again, China signed up to the TRIPs agreement upon entry, so it agreed to be bound by its tenets despite having an underdeveloped legal system when other developing countries, such as India, were able to defer the implementation of TRIPs.

These accession terms also characterize China's agreement to open its services sector (banking, financial, insurance, professional such as accountancy, law, and education) despite fragility in its capital markets. In one sense, the very backwardness of China's financial system meant that gradual opening of the sector by bringing in foreign expertise to aid its development was reminiscent of its previous strategy in creating manufacturing JVs in the 1990s. The result was rapid adoption of a series of regulations to govern the previously largely state-run banking system which simply had no need for corporate governance. Appendix 2.2 highlights the significant securities laws in China and shows how the void in the 1990s had been supplanted by rapid enactment of regulations governing everything from disclosure to derivatives trading. Indeed, the trio of regulators were all established at the end of the 1990s/beginning of the 2000s: CIRC in 1998, CSRC in 1999 (when it obtained national authority), and the CBRC in 2003. To understand the lack of regulation until the 2000s, the state-run banking system has to be assessed.

2.7.1 THE BANKING SYSTEM

At the start of the reform period, China's banking and financial system under central planning was essentially an arm of the state. The People's Bank of China (PBOC) was the sole bank since 1949 until the 1980s reforms, with responsibilities for both central and commercial banking operations. Cooperative banks existed to serve rural areas, but there was little else in terms of a financial system. The PBOC was the central bank in charge of monetary policy and oversaw all banking needs, which was primarily to serve as cashier for the state in the administered economy. However, with market reforms occurring successfully in the early 1980s, the banking system itself was reformed to be more market-oriented and to be able to serve a marketizing economy in need of commercial banking services.

In the mid 1980s, the commercial banking functions of the PBOC were split off into four state-owned banks (Bank of China, Industrial and Commercial Bank of China (ICBC), Agricultural Bank of China (ABC), and China Construction Bank (CCB)), and the PBOC was directed to serve as a central bank. These state-owned commercial banks, though wholly stated-owned, were to be independent and to operate on the basis of profitability and 'hard' budget constraints, that is, not expecting subsidies from the state. The Commercial Banking Law adopted in 1995 eventually established the legal foundations of the banking system and gave these SCBs much greater latitude to act on a commercial basis. However, interest rates were not fully liberalized (and only partially so in 2004), which placed a ceiling, and eventually just a floor, on lending rates. In addition, the SCBs continued to fund SOEs and accumulated non-performing loans throughout the 1980s and 1990s until the *gaizhi* policy was seriously implemented with the massive downsizing of the state-owned sector in the late 1990s. Following on from these reforms, in 1998, the PBOC underwent a major restructuring in which all of its provincial and local branches were abolished. The PBOC instead has nine regional branches, similar to the American central bank/US Federal Reserve System. Also in 2003, reforms sped up with the creation of the China Banking Regulatory Commission, which removed the role of regulatory overseer from the PBOC, moving it closer to the model of an independent central bank focused on monetary policy.

In addition to the SCBs, three policy banks, the China Development Bank, the Export–Import Bank of China, and the Agricultural Development Bank of China, were also established to perform the developmental role previously undertaken by the PBOC. They are charged with financing infrastructure projects and other state-supported or non-profit-making projects. The China Development Bank in recent years has also undertaken the investment functions of a sovereign wealth fund, acting alongside the official fund, the China Investment Corporation (CIC).

There is also a second tier of state-owned banks. They have become joint stock banks, which have shares owned by the government including private entities. There are approximately fourteen joint stock commercial banks, which were largely set up in the 1990s. They include the Bank of Communications, China Everbright Bank, CITIC Industrial Bank, Shenzhen Development Bank, Pudong Development Bank, China Merchant Bank, Fujian Industrial Bank, and Guangdong Development Bank. Several are listed on the domestic stock market, including the Shanghai Pudong Development Bank, the Shenzhen Development Bank, and the China Merchants Bank. At the local level, there were originally some 3,000 urban and 50,000 rural credit cooperatives which have gradually merged into banks. For example, the Shenzhen Cooperative Bank was created from sixteen urban cooperatives and the Shanghai City United Bank from ninety-nine urban cooperatives.

In the 2000s, in the midst of rapid capital market development, China gave permission for the establishment of private banks; the first was Minsheng Bank. China Minsheng Bank was then certainly unique in having mostly private owners and being publicly listed on the domestic stock market.

With WTO accession in 2001, China realized that it would be eventually competing with foreign banks, and a decision was taken to transform the SCBs into joint stock companies, with the state as the dominant shareholder. At the end of 2003, the Bank of China and the China Construction Bank were selected to be the first of the big four to undertake this transformation. All have had initial public offerings (IPOs) on stock markets, domestically and internationally.

In terms of foreign banks, there were nearly 200 operating in China in the 2000s, of which just under half have approval to conduct RMB business prior to the opening of the sector in December 2006, five years after WTO accession as agreed upon accession. Restrictions remained in terms of their operations, but foreign banks, particularly those which are locally incorporated, were able to increasingly undertake RMB business. Also, prior to the IPO of three of the four SCBs, minority equity stakes in the SCBs were sold to foreign banks to improve governance and help the SCBs to operate commercially. The shares were bought by a wide range of international banks who viewed China's high savings economy as an attractive market for developing financial services, and equity holdings in the SCBs gave them a foothold in the market. In the aftermath of the 2008 global financial crisis, though, a number of these foreign banks withdrew in order to re-build their balance sheets, shattered by their exposure to US subprime mortgages and the securitization of which that had led to part or whole nationalization of previously 'blue chip' banks. As a further consequence, China's SCBs became among the largest banks in the world.

For much of the reform period, there had been only one investment bank in China, the China International Capital Corporation (CICC). CICC was established in 1995 as a joint venture between China Construction Bank, Morgan Stanley Dean Witter, and several other smaller shareholders. Its remit includes underwriting domestic equities, taking equity stakes in foreign investments in China, undertaking mergers and acquisitions, organizing project finance, and handling foreign exchange transactions. The Bank of China was the only other bank which had provided investment banking services, although the other SCBs and one of the policy banks (China Development Bank) eventually set up investment banking services of their own. Foreign competition after WTO accession provided a further impetus for China's banks to develop in this area. However, the relative underdevelopment of the investment banking functions meant that China was not badly affected by the 2008 global financial crisis.

Chinese reforms of the banking sector have taken place in stages. The main focus of the first stage was to improve asset quality by reducing the amount of non-performing loans and increasing the responsiveness of lending to commercial signals. For instance, in 1998, the government issued special bonds to recapitalize the four big state-owned banks in order to improve their capital adequacy ratios. Further recapitalization also took place later on, using funds from China's vast foreign exchange reserves. In 1999, the most significant reform was undertaken: 1.4 trillion RMB worth of non-performing loans were offloaded to four newly established asset management companies (AMCs), each attached to a SCB. The Chinese government also abolished the credit quota policy so that banks could lend on the basis of returns rather than by political dictate.

The next two stages were to improve corporate governance and convert the SCBs into joint stock companies. The Bank of China and the China Construction Bank were the two selected SCBs to undertake the pilot programme, and they improved their accountancy standards and corporate governance. This was with an eye towards listing on domestic and foreign stock markets. And, the Bank of China's IPO to transform itself into a joint stock company was preceded by selling minority equity stakes to a consortium led by the Royal Bank of Scotland (RBS). The sale of minority equity stakes in the smaller banks had also been happening quietly for a number of years. And, when it was viewed as relatively successful, as with all such reforms in China, it was permitted with the requirement that foreign equity shareholding in a SCB must not exceed 25 per cent of the total, with no single foreign investor holding more than 20 per cent. Control, therefore, would remain with the Chinese side, though foreigners have been agitating to increase their control rights in a few of the smaller banks.

China's banking sector is still state-dominated, with an estimated 60 per cent of credit issued by the SCBs in 2009 (Shen et al. 2009). By the time of WTO opening and the IPOs of three of the four SCBs, non-performing loans were reduced to less than 5 per cent, suggesting that the efforts to ward off a banking crisis had worked. However, two disturbing developments cast some doubt onto this conclusion. In 2009, the AMCs which had taken on the bad assets from the banks in return for issuing bonds with interest payments of 2 per cent were struggling to make the payments, since the debt-for-equity swaps where such assets could be sold did not materialize and the NPLs were associated with loss-making SOEs that would never regain their value. The implication was that the Chinese government must then take on the liabilities of these offloaded bad debts, which could figure as a significant share of GDP. Also that year, the initial delay to launch an IPO for the last of the four SCBs, the China Agricultural Bank, further suggests the persistence of the NPL problem. Instead, China's sovereign wealth fund bought a 50 per cent stake in the China Agricultural Bank in a sizeable recapitalization effort prior to the planned IPO in 2010. Moreover, the 2008 global financial crisis led to the government using the state-owned banks to fuel around two-thirds of the four trillion RMB, two-year fiscal stimulus package. Around 9.5 trillion RMB of credit was issued in 2009, leading to a need for the SCBs to issue more shares in order to increase their capital base to cope with non-performing loans. Although NPLs became a concern at that time, the state-owned banks were still to fund the rest of the stimulus package in 2010. As a result of the crisis, troubled foreign banks reined back their non-core operations and some sold their shares in Chinese banks. For example, the Royal Bank of Scotland became part-nationalized by the British government, and sold its stake in the Bank of China in an effort to improve its balance sheet. The departure of a number of foreign banks, including investment banks, takes with them the knowledge that China had desired from foreign firms as it struggles with the reform of a sector that has derailed numerous other transition economies.

All of these factors point to a banking system that has been significantly reformed by policy dictates but also rules that have begun to set parameters for commercial banking operations including foreign banks, propelled by WTO-mandated opening of the sector after 2001. The two major laws (Commercial Banking Law of 1995 and the Regulations on the Administration of Foreign-funded Banks of December 2006) are landmark pieces of legislation—the former commercialized the domestic banking system, while the latter codified the presence of foreign banks. Because of the special place held by banks in China's transition economy, the laws are only the first step towards reforming this sector. Much of it is taking place under the guidance of the regulator, CBRC, established in 2003 to govern a sector that had become much more marketized after 2001. This interaction of law and policy is a harbinger of the future contour of Chinese reform.

2.7.2 CAPITAL MARKETS

Unlike the banking system, the non-banking financial sector did not exist until the 1990s and was hardly governed throughout its first ten years. The stock markets operated by government dictate, firms were listed by quotas granted to provinces, and trading was limited to the so-called common shares that constituted a mere third of the market. By the end of the 1990s, though, regulators were put in place, and the rapidity with which regulations were adopted in the 2000s attests to the speed of legal developments in China.

The financial sector in China is in its nascent stages. This was one of the reasons why China was shielded from the worst of the 2008 financial crisis, as its underdeveloped financial market did not trade in the complex securities which brought down large segments of the Western banking system. However, it is a quickly developing sector, particularly after WTO accession which saw China agree to open vast swathes of its services industries, including banking and finance.

As stated before, China's two stock exchanges were opened in Shanghai in 1990 and Shenzhen in 1991, with trades permitted in 1993. In late 2009,

Shenzhen launched a NASDAQ-style bourse called the Growth Enterprise Board, aimed at listing smaller companies, after a five-year trial period. Within a decade of its inception, China had one of the largest stock markets in terms of market capitalization in Asia, with a market value of half a trillion, and eventually, by 2009, it became the second largest in the world. The Shanghai Stock Exchange was valued at over $3 trillion in 2010, rivalling the largest bourses in the world in less than two decades of existence. However, this measurement is plagued with problems, as some two-thirds of all shares in the 1,500 listed companies on these exchanges are non-tradable, so their value is prescribed rather than market-determined. Table 2.4, however, shows that privately controlled firms rose to account for 30 per cent of all listed firms by 2007, reflecting a freeing-up of the quota system with the May 2006 regulations governing IPOs that sanctioned the listings of private firms and lately marked the abandonment of the previous system. Also, in 2005, the government announced plans to make all shares tradable and began experimenting with large SOEs like Baosteel to eventually remove this artificial element of the market (the April 2005 'Listed Companies Share Reform Experiments and Related Issues' notice promulgated by the CBRC).

Nevertheless, the stock markets are estimated to provide only 5 per cent of corporate financing in China, so their reach is limited despite the market capitalization (Riedel, Jin, and Gao 2007). The numerous designations of shares as individual, government, legal persons, 'A', 'B', and 'H', each with its own restrictions with respect to trading remain problematic. These restrictions further insulate listed firms from feeling the discipline of the market. Corporate governance has thus not been improved significantly by the corporatization of Chinese enterprises (see e.g. Sun and Tong 2003). Not surprisingly, returns to Chinese equities are volatile, rising during the 1990s and then losing an estimated 50 per cent of their value in the early 2000s before growing quickly (and falling) with the global financial crisis. In the first half of 2009, the Shanghai market was up over 80 per cent in seven months and then promptly lost 20 per cent of its value in three weeks, becoming a bear market with amazing speed, further displaying the roller-coaster trajectory evident throughout its short history.

The underdevelopment of the stock market is symptomatic of the state of the financial system. Chinese financial markets are 'thin' (Allen, Qian, and Qian 2005). This is not atypical of emerging economies; however, for China, it is exacerbated by a stock market with a significant portion of non-tradable shares belying the large capitalization of the Shanghai and Shenzhen stock exchanges. On the whole, Chinese firms do not meet many of the accounting practices or reporting requirements that permit assessment of risk. One danger, among others, is the transfer of risk from the capital market to the banking sector.

China's WTO obligations, however, have hastened the development of the financial sector. The expectations of international financial markets in terms of corporate governance and reporting requirements are fuelling reforms in China, particularly as its 'going out' strategy suggests that more firms will be seeking to establish themselves internationally. Reforms such as permitting the creation of fund management companies, developing investment banks, and liberalizing some aspects of the currency are all reforms that are aimed at strengthening the financial markets in China.

These regulatory improvements are evident since the 2000s (see Appendix 2.2). In January 2002, the newly established CSRC issued a code of corporate governance for listed companies, which was revised in November 2004, and further strengthened with rules in July and August of 2006 which increased transparency, strengthened risk management, and improved protection for minority shareholders. In January 2007, further measures regarding disclosure were adopted, reflecting a continuing effort, but also the challenge, of reforming the governance of majority state-controlled companies.

In 2002, the CSRC promulgated a series of rules granting access to foreign investors into China's financial sector in accordance with its WTO commitments. For instance, the Qualified Foreign Institutional Investor (QFII) system allowed foreign investors to trade on the Chinese stock markets up to a quota specified by the CSRC. The WTO-agreed Securities Companies Regulations of the same year permitted the creation of foreign-invested entities in the form of either a LLC or a JV to undertake: (1) underwriting of equity shares (including 'A', 'B', and 'H' shares); (2) trading/brokerage of 'B' and 'H' shares; (3) trading/brokerage of government and corporate bonds. Any FIE must apply to the CSRC for approval. The Fund Management Companies regulations were similarly formulated, with strict delineations that block the wholesale entry of foreign financial firms.

Similar restrictions pertain to China's small bond market, which comprises two markets: the inter-bank market and the stock exchange bond market. Commercial banks (both local and foreign) are only permitted to participate in the inter-bank market. The inter-bank bond market consists of government bonds, financial bonds, and People's Bank of China bills. Foreign banks are not allowed to participate in the issuance of RMB corporate bonds. But, as of January 2007, financial institutions domiciled in the mainland have been allowed to issue RMB bonds in Hong Kong. This is reflective of a larger trend of using Hong Kong as an experimental place for financial liberalization. 'Red chip' stocks, which are mainland companies incorporated and listed in Hong Kong, along with 'H' shares issued by mainland domiciled companies but listed in Hong Kong, link the Hong Kong Stock Exchange with the mainland, the SAR having become a conduit for trial policies such as the Qualified Domestic Institutional Investors (QDII) scheme, for example. The 2006 QDII permitted limited overseas investments by Chinese investors, which offered some loosening of China's capital account. By 2007, Chinese residents were allowed to make limited overseas investments in Hong Kong.

The currency market has also been reformed in the 2000s. The RMB is officially a restricted currency and therefore not tradable on foreign exchange markets in an attempt by the Chinese government to maintain its fixed exchange rate in place throughout the reform period, though with periods of it being a managed float. In 2005, non-financial institutions and enterprises were allowed to enter the foreign exchange market which had been previously restricted to the Bank of China. In that same year, non-deliverable forward contracts were traded over the counter (OTC) outside of China, and the following January saw the development of an OTC spot market.

The pace of regulation and the development of the capital market since WTO accession, though imperfect and incomplete, have been rapid. In September 2006, China's Financial Futures Exchange was established to allow derivatives trading, and regulations to manage this new exchange were passed by the State Council the following spring. In March 2009, China announced the creation of a NASDAQ-like bourse called the Growth Enterprise Board, for smaller, technology companies, discussed earlier. Within the span of a few years, China has developed new capital markets as well as begun to regulate them, in contrast to the previous decade where the bourses and banking system operated largely without a regulator.

The 2000s reflected a change of pace in the adoption of laws to support markets. Partly this was due to the creation of stakeholders of assets like property and stocks which demanded better protection of their rights. In part, it was also due to China's entry into the global trading system that propelled its markets to become more globally integrated and thus to meet the higher expectations of legal protection held by multinational firms. In this manner, it is not dissimilar to the early JV laws which afforded legal rights to foreign firms which were used to operating under rules and regulations. Perhaps the speeding up of legal reforms has simply to do with the market developing to a certain stage in China after three decades of market-oriented reform that warranted more formal guidelines to enable its further development. As examples, M&As require laws governing such mergers and acquisitions, particularly overseas involving foreign businesses, and minority shareholders want protection before investing further.

2.8 **Conclusion**

The corporate sector has evolved gradually since 1978 with the governance of business in China closely linked to its overall economic mandate, which is driven by necessity and formulated on the basis of measures that will instil stability. Each of the ownership forms in China (SOEs, collectives including TVEs, private firms, and FIEs) have been subject to different economic and legal regimes suited to how they are perceived to fit into China's overall transition and development strategy. Each will thus be investigated in separate chapters.

The overall pattern over the past three decades of growth can be summarized thus in a few key themes. The 1980s' reforms were truly experimental and many of them were informal as market forces were gradually introduced in farming and rural industry, and eventually via managerial incentives in SOEs. Laws, the few which were passed, were geared towards foreign firms and to realizing China's industrial policy aims of gradual opening to the world economy while bolstering its own manufacturing capacity. Very little was offered to domestic firms, and economic necessity to instil market incentives resulted in policies rather than anything more formal, and often the state remained uncertain about the treatment of the emerging non-state sector. The 1990s saw laws being used more as tools to legitimize the actions of the state. SOE restructuring through share issuance had been planned and executed but formalized by the Company Law taking effect towards the middle of the decade. Private firms had been operating and contracting since the 1980s but were not recognized in law until the 1999 law creating individually wholly-owned enterprises.

However, by the 2000s, legal and particularly regulatory reform sped up, abetted by WTO entry and the requirement for governing intellectual property rights and capital markets in particular. Laws began to rationalize market developments such as extending protection to private property and responding to market-determined needs, such as an operative bankruptcy law. The pace of legal reform was particularly significant in capital markets, and China went from having virtually no regulation to issuing several major rules per year to develop the financial sector.

Business in China is affected by a complex interrelationship between economic and legal reforms adopted to serve the twin aims of economic necessity and stability. Since 1978, the corporate sector has come a long way with a set of Company and Securities Laws and ensuing regulations that provide a legal framework, albeit one situated within an imperfect system of enforcement. The retention of a state-owned sector of firms, banks, and institutions shows the state's continued involvement in enterprise. Nevertheless, the dwindling of SOEs and SCBs has opened the way for a competitive private sector to develop, which includes domestic firms as well as foreign ones. Entry into the WTO and global integration of its economy also means that China faces increasing pressure to reform both its economic and legal systems. China's reforms have thus far generated impressive growth for thirty years. How it traverses the difficult final transformation into a market economy in which enterprises operate embedded within a sound institutional framework of laws and policies will determine whether China is indeed a rare success story of economic growth, development, and transition.

■ APPENDIX 2.1 KEY CHINESE COMMERCIAL AND CIVIL LAWS

1979   Chinese–Foreign Equity Joint Venture Law

1981   Economic Contract Law (revised 1993 and superseded by the Contract Law of 1999)

1982   Civil Procedure Law

1982   Constitution (revised 1988, 1993, 1999, and 2004)

1985   Economic Contract Law for Foreign Parties (superseded by the Contact Law of 1999)

1986   China Joins the Convention on the Recognition and Enforcement of Foreign Arbitral Awards

1986   General Principles of Civil Law (effective as of 1987)

1986   Enterprise Bankruptcy Law (revised in 2006)

1986   Law on Wholly Foreign-Owned Enterprises (revised in 2000)

1987   Technology Contract Law (superseded by the Contract Law of 1999)

1988   Law on Industrial Enterprises Owned by the Whole People

1988   Chinese–Foreign Cooperative Joint Venture Law (revised in 2000)

1989   Administrative Procedure Law (effective as of 1990)

1991   Civil Procedure Law

1993   Company Law (effective as of 1994, revised 1999 and 2005)

1993   Product Quality Law (revised 2000)

1994   Arbitration Law (effective as of 1995)

1994   Foreign Trade Law (revised 2004)

1995   Negotiable Instruments Law (effective as of 1996, revised 2004)

1995   Security Law

1995   Commercial Banking Law

1996   Administrative Penalty Law

1997   Price Law

1997   Law on Partnership Enterprises (revised in 2006)

1998   Securities Law (effective as of 1999)

1999   Contract Law (unifying Contract Law and superseding the Economic Contract Law of 1981, Economic Contract Law for Foreign Parties of 1985 and the Technology Contract Law of 1987)

1999   Law on Individual Wholly-Owned Enterprises

2003   Securities Investment Fund Law (effective as of 2004)

2003   Law on Mergers and Acquisition (revised 2006)

2007   Property Law

2007   Anti-Monopoly Law (effective as of 2008)

2008   Employment Law

■ APPENDIX 2.2 SECURITIES AND BANKING REGULATIONS IN CHINA

December 1990	Shanghai Stock Exchange opened.
July 1991	Shenzhen Stock Exchange opened.
October 1992	China Securities Regulatory Commission (CSRC) is established.
May 1995	Commercial Banking Law passed.
November 1998	China Insurance Regulatory Commission (CIRC) is established.
December 1998	Securities Law passed.
July 1999	CSRC granted effective authority under the Securities Law, which became effective in July 1999.
January 2002	CSRC issued 'Code of Corporate Governance for Listed Companies in China' jointly with the State Economic and Trade Commission (SETC).
July 2002	CSRC issues Securities Companies regulations.
July 2002	CSRC issues Fund Management Companies regulations.
December 2002	CSRC promulgates the 'Qualified foreign institutional investors in securities investment interim measures' or the QFII system.

April 2003	China Banking Regulatory Commission (CBRC) is established.
November 2003	Securities Investment Fund Law passed, which became effective on 1 June 2004.
November 2004	CSRC revised listing rules to improve on disclosure of information by listed firms.
December 2004	CSRC issued 'On the strengthening of social protection of rights and interests of the public shareholders of a number of provisions' and 'Listed companies classified voting system.'
April 2005	CSRC promulgated 'On listed companies share reform experiments related issues notice', indicating the beginning of the share reform pilot project.
May 2006	'Measures for the Administration of Initial Public Offerings and Listing of Stocks' took effect.
July 2006	CSRC promulgated 'Securities Companies Risk Control Indicators Management Approach'.
August 2006	CSRC promulgated 'Acquisition Management Practices of Listed Companies'. The five information disclosure criteria include Report of Changes in Interest, Report of the Acquisition of Listed Companies, Tender Offer Report, Report of the Board of Trustees of the Acquired Company, and Tender Offer Exemption Application Documents. It was aimed at strengthening control of listed companies, increasing transparency, safeguarding market order and protecting the interests of minority shareholders.
August 2006	Qualified Domestic Institutional Investors (QDII) scheme, permitting limited overseas investments by Chinese investors.
September 2006	China's Financial Futures Exchange established for derivatives trading.
December 2006	Regulations on the Administration of Foreign-Funded Banks promulgated.
January 2007	Financial institutions in the mainland were permitted to issue RMB bonds in Hong Kong.
January 2007	CSRC implemented the regulation: 'The Management of Listed Companies to Disclose Information'.
November 2009	Growth Enterprise Board as part of the Shenzhen Stock Exchange was launched.
April 2010	Stock Index Futures launched.

3 Law and Markets

3.1 Introduction

One of the enduring paradoxes in China's remarkable economic growth experience in the three decades since 1978 is the lack of a well-established legal system supporting the increasingly decentralized and marketizing economy (see e.g. Allen, Qian, and Qian 2005; Cull and Xu 2005). It is a notable puzzle in that robust institutions are thought to be required both in theory and in practice to support markets (see e.g. Acemoglu and Johnson 2005). For instance, in a Coasian or Walrasian sense, a market economy is predicated on well-defined property rights and low transaction costs that permit efficient exchange to take place (Coase 1937). The rapid transition experience of many other economies such as the former Soviet Union was in part predicated on the establishment of private property rights and removal of the inefficient state in the burgeoning market economy. In China's case, however, much of its reforms have been undertaken without an established rule of law and in the absence of a change in ownership from state to private. It raises questions as to how China was able to instil economic incentives in the absence of private property rights, and how an imperfect legal system could protect against expropriation that would normally limit investment and other private economic activities, particularly foreign direct investment (FDI).

The gradualist and evolutionary nature of both economic and legal reform provides a basis for understanding the relationship between law and growth in China. The Chinese legal tradition is distinct from that of common law (UK, USA) and civil law (Continental Europe) countries, although that does not negate the incrementalist nature of legal reforms which can exist in all legal systems (see Jones 2003 for the present-day influences of China's dynastic legal system). Perhaps most evident in common law countries, law develops from case law—judicial pronouncements which give meaning to, and shape, the interpretation of the statutory laws. Common law itself is premised on cases furthering common laws. *Stare decisis* and precedent naturally carry significant weight in judicial rulings and in shaping the development of the rule of law. Law, therefore, develops over time rather than appears as a wholly formed system of a 'rule of law'. Even in countries with a civil law tradition, laws are evolutionary, as comprehensive codification is not feasible and the state, including its administrative organs, largely takes on the interpretative role.

In the law and finance literature, this debate has started to take shape, including for China. Chen (2003) argues that China's financial development follows a 'crash-then-law' path proposed by Coffee (2001). From a legal perspective, Coffee (2001) argues that capital market developments precede—and not follow—legal protection for shareholders. This runs contrary to the view of economists such as La Porta et al. (1997, 1998) who posit that the rule of law causes financial markets to develop (see also Acemoglu, Johnson, and Robinson 2005 for a similar argument regarding institutions and economic growth). Coffee (2001) offers evidence from the historical development of the USA and UK, where ownership by dispersed shareholders arose with the establishment of their bourses in the nineteenth century, while legal protection for minority shareholders came afterwards, largely in the early twentieth century. His argument is premised on the creation of interested parties as instigators of market institutional development: legal reforms are enacted due to the agitations of a motivated constituency that believes that it will be protected by the proposed reforms. Therefore, he argues that the constituency must arise before it can become an instrument for legal change. Chen (2003) applies this approach to China's capital markets and shows that an interested constituency arose after the creation of the two stock exchanges in Shanghai and Shenzhen in the early 1990s which led to the Securities Law of 1999. La Porta et al. (1997, 1998), by contrast, draw a distinction between common law and civil law countries and argue that common law countries provide better shareholder protection which fosters the development of financial markets. Their argument is that legal protection allows markets to develop through providing protection against expropriation and improved contracting security; therefore, law creates markets. Allen, Qian, and Qian (2005) compare China with the La Porta group of countries and conclude that informal institutional arrangements, such as trust based contracting, supplanted the role of law in fostering capital markets.

Aside from the question of the sequence of law and market development, there remains a further conundrum as to how markets developed in China in the absence of private property rights, which are typically established in law. Unlike the US or Europe and even other transition economies which adopted private ownership early in their transition, China's lingering communal property system should have impeded market development. Without clearly defined property rights, transactions should have been hampered and the market stifled.

Therefore, this chapter will propose that legal and economic reforms give rise to, and reinforce, each other in China. Also, institutional reforms through administrative dictates, such as the Contract Responsibility System that injected market forces into state-owned enterprises (SOEs), were sufficient to instil incentives to create markets in the absence of strong legal protection. Therefore, once a market is created by law or more informally such as through institutional reform (e.g. administrative dictate or absence of notable prohibition as with the Household Responsibility System that incentivized agricultral production), then interested constituencies and stakeholders will push for more formal and explicit legal reforms to protect their interests. Better legal protection in turn promotes market development by providing greater security of economic transactions. Informal, trust-based relationships supplant the incomplete legal system, particularly in terms of enforcement. In this way, the complementary processes of legal, institutional, and economic reform in China can explain the paradox of remarkable growth within an underdeveloped system of law.

3.2 **Law and markets**

3.2.1 THEORETICAL AND EMPIRICAL RELATIONSHIPS BETWEEN LAWS AND MARKETS

There are both theoretical and empirical perspectives on the relationship between law and markets that both affect economic growth. At first glance, it may appear that some laws are less relevant to economic growth, such as the workings of the criminal law system. However, crime may well deter investment, and social stability can be a determinant of location for risk-averse firms (see e.g. Brock 1998). Thus, the functioning of the legal system across its various dimensions may well be relevant for economic growth, though the focus here will be on civil and commercial legal developments.

From a theoretical perspective, the 'invisible hand' of the market works efficiently when there exist optimizing agents transacting in a framework of well-defined property rights and sufficiently low or zero transaction costs (see Coase 1937). Law establishes those conditions. A legal system defines the property rights and the costs of transacting and exchange. For instance, ownership recognized by law establishes the security of the private property to be exchanged. A well-functioning legal and regulatory system can ensure that transactions involving those properties take place at non-prohibitive costs, that is, provide contracting security. For China, one element of the paradox is the lack of legally protected private property rights (see e.g. Jefferson and Rawski 2002). It was not until the Property Law of 2007 that equal protection was granted to both private and public property. Instead, much of China's growth and reform has taken place with the state retaining ownership of enterprises, land, and housing. Privatization of SOEs only occured gradually over the three decades of market-oriented reforms since 1979 and remains incomplete. The private housing market was only recently established, concurrent with the conclusion of the housing privatization reforms in 2001, and the creation of long-term rights of use rather than freehold ownership resulted. Land remained largely in state hands (see e.g. Ho 2006).

From an empirical standpoint, these theoretical insights have been incorporated into the literature advocating the importance of laws and institutions in explaining persistent economic growth differences (see e.g. Rodrik, Subramanian, and Trebbi 2004; Acemoglu and Johnson 2005; Acemoglu, Johnson, and Robinson 2005; Dam 2006). La Porta et al. (1997, 1998) emphasize the importance of legal origin, for example whether a country had a common or civil law system, in influencing financial sector development and consequently economic development. China did not fit well within these frameworks, particularly because legal origin was largely based on the externally imposed legal system of the colonial powers on developing countries in these studies. But, for countries such as China which did not adopt a legal system from a particular colonial power, the legal formalism hypothesis would have minimal explanatory power. Studies of other transition economies conclude that the effectiveness of laws is more important than the completeness of the written formal law for economic growth, further reducing the force of the legal origins school. One significant conclusion is that legal systems 'transplanted' into neophyte transition economies—whereby the wholly formed laws of developed countries which would presumably encompass the necessary elements for a 'rule of law'—have not worked (Pistor, Martin, and Gelfer 2000). Building on the earlier La Porta et al. (1997, 1998) work, Glaeser et al. (2004) emphasize the functional rule of law as relevant for growth. Therefore, the elements of a well-functioning legal system would include an independent judiciary, freedom from executive branch interference, and low risk of expropriation (Pistor and Xu 2005; Fan et al. 2009).

Institutional development was therefore considered to be important, and the focus has shifted away from legal formalism and legal origin to some extent (see e.g. Rodrik, Subramanian, and Trebbi 2004). For instance, Acemoglu and Johnson (2005) emphasize two types of market-supporting institutions which are important for economic growth: property rights institutions which protect against expropriation by government, and contracting institutions which ease contract enforcement. For China, these institutions also do not measure up well when compared with its impressive growth rate, giving rise to the 'China paradox' of strong growth within a 'weak' legal system (see Cull and Xu 2005; Lu and Yao 2009).

3.2.2 THE CHINA PARADOX

Various measures of the rule of law and institutional development in China all suggest that its formal legal system is underdeveloped (see e.g. Allen, Qian, and Qian 2005; Cull and Xu 2005 for a range of indicators). Using the World Bank's Worldwide Governance Indicators for 2006, Table 3.1 shows that China ranked in the bottom 50th percentile of all countries surveyed for rule of law. It is also evident from Table 3.1 that China grew more rapidly than economies of comparable size (largest ten economies in the world) in the top half of the table and out-paced the growth of other transition economies in

Table 3.1. Rule of law

Country	Percentile rank (0–100)	Rule of law score (−2.5 to +2.5)	Average annual growth rate of real per capita GDP, 1990–2003
China	45.2	−0.40	7.61%
Brazil	41.4	−0.48	0.96%
France	89.5	1.31	1.47%
Germany	94.3	1.77	1.43%
India	57.1	0.17	3.95%
Italy	60.0	0.37	1.25%
Japan	90.0	1.40	0.95%
Russia	19.0	−0.91	−1.27%
United Kingdom	93.3	1.73	2.03%
United States	91.9	1.57	1.75%
Select Eastern Europe and former Soviet bloc countries			
Albania	48.8	−0.14	2.58%
Bulgaria	66.3	0.54	1.03%
Croatia	61.5	0.35	0.25%
Czech Republic	79.5	0.95	0.92%
Estonia	92.2	1.42	2.45%
Hungary	85.9	1.1	1.72%
Poland	69.3	0.64	3.23%
Romania	62.0	0.37	0.19%
Slovakia	83.4	1.08	1.65%

Source: World Bank Worldwide Governance Indicators, 2006.
Notes: Rule of law measures the extent to which agents perceive that the rules of society, in particular the quality of contract enforcement, the police, and the courts, as well as the likelihood of crime and violence, are enforced. The percentile rank places the country on a scale of 0–100 where 100 indicates a country that scored the highest possible value on the rule of law indicator. The governance score is normally distributed with a mean of zero and a standard deviation of one. Governance is better as the value increases. See Kaufmann, Kraay, and Mastruzzi (2007) for a complete definition and discussion. The growth rate of per capita GDP is in 1990 US dollars and calculated from Maddison (2001).

Table 3.2. Regulatory quality

Country	Percentile rank (0−100)	Regulatory quality score (−2.5 to +2.5)	Standard error
Russia	35.0	−0.44	0.17
China	45.6	−0.24	0.17
India	46.1	−0.22	0.17
Brazil	53.4	−0.04	0.17
Albania	55.8	0.09	0.18
Croatia	64.1	0.43	0.17
Romania	66.0	0.48	0.17
Bulgaria	69.9	0.61	0.17
Poland	72.3	0.71	0.17
Italy	74.3	0.81	0.21
Czech Republic	80.1	0.96	0.17
Slovakia	81.1	0.99	0.17
Japan	83.5	1.05	0.21
France	85.9	1.15	0.21
Hungary	86.4	1.15	0.17
United States	90.8	1.45	0.21
Estonia	92.2	1.50	0.17
Germany	92.7	1.50	0.21
United Kingdom	98.1	1.86	0.21

Source: World Bank Worldwide Governance Indicators, 2008.
Notes: Regulatory quality measures the ability of the government to formulate and implement sound policies and regulations that permit and promote private sector development. The percentile rank places the country on a scale of 0–100 where 100 indicates a country that scored the highest possible value on the indicator. The indicator score is normally distributed with a mean of zero and a standard deviation of one. Quality improves as the value increases. See Kaufmann, Kraay, and Mastruzzi (2007) for a complete definition and discussion.

the bottom half of the table from 1990 to 2003. Its growth in per capita GDP exceeded 7.6 per cent over this period and was substantially higher than Brazil's, which ranked close to China in the rule of law indicator, and also Estonia, which had a rule of law indicator that was higher than that of the USA. No proxy for rule of law will be perfect; however, nearly all studies conclude that China has an underdeveloped legal system (see e.g. Yao and Yueh 2009). When measured in terms of regulatory quality, a counterpart to an effective legal system, China fares even worse. Table 3.2 ranks countries in terms of regulatory quality, measuring the ability of the government to formulate and implement sound policies and regulations that permit and promote private-sector development. Whereas China ranked better than Russia and Brazil on rule of law, it ranked only better than Russia on the composite index for regulatory quality.

Tables 3.3–3.6 provide more disaggregated measures of different dimensions of the rule of law in China as compared with other countries, namely, investor protection, contract enforcement, security of property rights, and freedom from corruption. Table 3.3 proxies the extent of investor protection as measured by the World Bank Doing Business Survey from 2008, where China's rank out of 175 measured countries was 86, placing it just above the bottom half of all nations. In particular, it had the poorest rating on the transparency of related-party transactions (extent of disclosure index), which reflects the lack of arms-length dealing and opacity in its enterprises. By contrast, China ranks relatively well for contract enforcement (Table 3.4). The number of procedures and days as well as the cost of enforcing a commercial contract places China no worse than European countries. The composite indicator, though, may be biased by the low cost of enforcing contracts in China and the relative speed with which courts operate which is picked up by the first two indicators. However, the effectiveness of the legal system depends not only on speed and cost, but on the extent of the proffered

Table 3.3. Investor protection

	Rank	Investor protection index	Disclosure index	Director liability index	Shareholder suits index
Brazil	64	5.3	6	7	3
Canada	5	8.3	8	9	8
China	*83*	*5*	*10*	*1*	*4*
France	64	5.3	10	1	5
Germany	83	5	5	5	5
India	33	6	7	4	7
Italy	51	5.7	7	4	6
Japan	12	7	7	6	8
Poland	33	6	7	2	9
Romania	33	6	9	5	4
Russia	83	5	6	2	7
Slovakia	98	4.7	3	4	7
South Africa	9	8	8	8	8
Ukraine	141	3.7	1	3	7
United Kingdom	9	8	10	7	7
United States	5	8.3	7	9	9

Source: World Bank Doing Business Survey, 2008.
Notes: The investor protection index (measured from 1–10) calibrates the strength of minority shareholder protection against directors' misuse of corporate assets for personal gain. The indicators, also out of 10, distinguish three dimensions of investor protection: transparency of related-party transactions (extent of disclosure index), liability for self-dealing (extent of director liability index), and shareholders' ability to sue officers and directors for misconduct (ease of shareholder suits index). Countries are ranked out of 175.

Table 3.4. Contract enforcement

	Rank	Procedures (number)	Time (days)	Cost (% of debt)
Brazil	106	45	616	16.5
Canada	43	36	570	16.2
China	*20*	*35*	*406*	*8.8*
France	14	30	331	17.4
Germany	15	33	394	11.8
India	177	46	1,420	39.6
Italy	155	41	1,210	29.9
Japan	21	30	316	22.7
Poland	68	38	830	10.0
Romania	37	32	537	19.9
Russia	19	37	281	13.4
Slovakia	50	30	565	25.7
South Africa	85	30	600	33.2
Ukraine	46	30	354	41.5
United Kingdom	24	30	404	23.4
United States	8	32	300	9.4

Source: World Bank Doing Business Survey, 2008.
Notes: Contract enforcement measures the efficiency of the judicial system in resolving a commercial dispute. The data are built by following the step-by-step evolution of a commercial sale dispute before local courts. The data are collected through study of the codes of civil procedure and other court regulations as well as surveys completed by local litigation lawyers and by judges in some instances. Countries are ranked out of 183.

Table 3.5. Protection of property rights

United States	90
Canada	90
United Kingdom	90
Germany	90
Japan	70
France	70
Slovak Republic	50
South Africa	50
Italy	50
Poland	50
Brazil	50
India	50
Romania	30
Ukraine	30
Russia	30
China	*20*

Source: Heritage Foundation Index of Economic Freedom, 2008.
Notes: Property rights are an assessment of the ability of individuals to accumulate private property, secured by clear laws that are fully enforced by the state. The index is from 1–100 with 100 as the highest value.

Table 3.6. Freedom from corruption

United Kingdom	86
Canada	85
Germany	80
Japan	76
France	74
United States	73
Italy	49
Slovak Republic	47
South Africa	46
Poland	37
Brazil	33
India	33
China	*33*
Romania	31
Ukraine	28
Russia	25

Source: Heritage Foundation Index of Economic Freedom, 2008.
Notes: Freedom from corruption is based on quantitative data that assess the perception of corruption in the business environment, including levels of governmental legal, judicial, and administrative corruption. The index is from 1–100 with 100 as the highest value.

protection of contracting security. Indeed, when the quality of contract enforcement as perceived by the respondent is considered as in Table 3.1, in contrast to the more objective measures of the number of procedures and days and costs of enforcement, China ranks rather worse. Interestingly, India fares badly on objective measures of contract enforcement, ranking well below China in Table 3.4, and yet it is better rated than China in Table 3.1 on the overall measure of rule of law that takes into account the quality of the legal system. A comparable measure by the Heritage Foundation is that of enforcing property rights, and China fares among the worst of selected countries, as seen in Table 3.5.

Table 3.5 measures the security of property rights, both to obtain and to enforce. China has one of the least secure systems of property rights, probably due to its underdeveloped private property system that has only ostensibly existed since the notion was recognized in the Constitution in 2004 and with the passage of the Property Law in 2007, which extended equal protection to private and public property for the first time. China performs better in Table 3.6 which measures the extent of corruption. China's degree of corruption is comparable to India and Brazil, while it fares better than Russia and the Ukraine. Overall, though, China ranked 126 out of 157 countries based on these indicators produced by the Heritage Foundation's 2008 Index of Economic Freedoms.

In summary, although no indicator is perfect, across various measures of legal/institutional development, China ranks in the bottom half of countries despite being the fastest growing major economy in the world. The accumulated evidence suggests that the paradox of fast growth and a poor legal system remains after three decades of reform.

3.2.3 A COMPLEMENTARY VIEW OF LEGAL AND ECONOMIC DEVELOPMENT

This chapter will argue that legal development in China should be viewed as an evolutionary process that took place alongside incremental economic reforms undertaken during its transition from central planning. This is not dissimilar to the experience of rich countries at a similar stage of development when their legal systems developed concomitantly with their markets. What makes China unusual is a confluence of factors. First, it was able to establish markets within a communal property system, which highlights the importance of administrative measures and institutional reforms. Second, its transition and therefore its marketization were gradual, such that markets were not always established by laws at the outset but developed over time with experimentation of various market mechanisms, such as the 'dual track' pricing system and the export-oriented Special Economic Zones (SEZs). Third, it is undertaking reform and global integration at a time of international economic laws and norms which extend beyond trade and range into financial regulation and intellectual property rights. The external influence of laws and rules will affect expectations within and without China, particularly in terms of regulatory transparency and the enforcement of laws.

3.2.4 STRUCTURE OF THE CHAPTER

After the introduction in Section 1, Section 2 examined the law and markets literature and how China appears to be an outlier, and set out the outlines of a view of complementary legal and economic reform. Section 3 will review the literature on the experience of other countries in fashioning a corporate law framework: specifically, a comparative view of market development and legal reform will be made of China and the US. The comparison will aim to shed light on the extent to which it is feasible to establish a comprehensive legal system at an early stage of economic development. Section 4 will propose a framework of complementarities between laws and markets in lieu of the sequential argument of one necessarily preceding the other. Some limited econometric evidence will be brought to bear on this approach for China. Section 5 will focus on China's particular sequence of legal, institutional, and economic reform. In the case of the early reforms of the late 1970s and early

1980s, the context of Chinese gradualist transition meant that institutional reform—through creating an expectation of property rights—was sufficient to instil the necessary incentives for the development of markets. However, as markets developed, more formal and explicit legal reforms were needed, and thus China began to rapidly adopt laws during the 1990s and 2000s, particularly with the additional pressures of international economic laws with WTO accession in 2001. Enforcement will be examined in Section 6, notably in respect of foreign-invested enterprises (FIEs) and the reliance on informal relational contracting as official enforcement is weak. The final section will conclude with an assessment of the relationship between law and economic growth in China, and posit that China's experience is unusual in the post-war period where the transition and development models are heavily tilted toward formal legal rules, but is not atypical of the experience of developed countries' legal and economic development during their industrialization at the turn of the twentieth century. The conclusion will also assess the influence of international laws and rules, particularly in shaping the enforcement of laws in China.

3.3 A comparative perspective of legal development and markets

3.3.1 CHINESE LAW

The legal system in China is modelled after the Japanese civil law system (Jones 2003). The Japanese legal system was itself fashioned after the German civil law tradition during the nineteenth century period of the Meiji Restoration. However, strong elements of China's own legal tradition persist, notably in terms of the emphasis on administrative law and the lack of separation between the legal and administrative systems. Adjudication was undertaken by administrative officials who acted on behalf of the emperor in all matters of state, including deciding lawsuits. The judicial system in China today is still part of the administrative system and hence there is no effective independent judiciary (Alford 2000). As a result, procedural laws are comparatively underdeveloped, whilst administrative law is at the core of the Chinese legal tradition, with criminal and administrative sanctions preferred for enforcement. Jones (2003) argues that this stands in contrast to the tradition of Roman law from which many Western legal systems are derived. As Roman law was developed primarily to resolve civil disputes amongst individuals and groups in a largely agricultural society, civil matters are central to Western laws by contrast.

This mixed legal tradition renders it difficult to situate China in the comparative law and finance literature, which emphasizes the distinction between common law (US, UK) and civil law (Continental Europe) countries. In particular, the La Porta et al. (1997, 1998) perspective views civil law countries as less effective in promoting financial sector development than common law countries, due to the latter's ability to offer better protection for investors. La Porta et al. (1998) draw the further distinction that civil law countries such as German and Scandinavian nations provide better protection than French civil law countries, though not as much as common law jurisdictions in a survey of forty-nine countries. Strong protection of shareholders and security holders is associated with more liquid capital markets and more dispersed share ownership. This seminal work has led to the 'law matters' thesis whereby effective legal protection is concluded to cause financial sector development (see also Levine 1997, 1998). This thesis has been challenged by Coffee (2001). Coffee (2001) disputes the significance of the difference between the two sets of legal traditions and goes further in arguing that market development leads to better legal protection, as evidenced by the historical pattern of laws following security market developments in the US, UK, and Continental Europe. He argues that the chief difference between the two types of legal systems is the extent of state involvement in the market. In the US and UK, in contrast to Continental Europe, the state did not actively intervene in capital markets and instead relied on private stock exchanges to self-regulate in their own self-interest. In France, and to some extent in Germany, the state intervened frequently in the market, which left no room for what he calls 'enlightened self-regulation' (Coffee 2001: 9).

More generally, Coffee (2001) reiterates the pattern observed by legal scholars that laws tend to follow from market developments historically (see also Banner 1997 who surveys 300 years of legal developments to conclude that securities regulations are consistent with this pattern). Pistor, Martin, and Gelfer (2000) come to a similar assessment after surveying shareholder rights in twenty-four transition economies during the 1990s. They conclude that legal reforms tend to be responsive to economic changes rather than precede them.

China does not fit the paradigm of common versus civil law countries, particularly as these cover only roughly forty-nine, or less than a third of the countries in the world, virtually all of which are former European colonies (see Acemoglu, Johnson, and Robinson 2005). China's case is much closer to other transition economies as they had to re-initiate the market during the 1990s after decades of central planning (see e.g. Pistor and Xu 2005). However, unlike these countries, China did not adopt a legal system transplanted from developed economies (see e.g. Pistor Martin, and Gelfer 2000; Berkowitz, Pistor, and Richard 2003). Instead, it developed its own legal system which, however, has been influenced by the legal codes of other countries, for example Chinese civil law has elements of German law. Nevertheless, the appropriate sequence of law and markets would remain relevant and gives rise to the China puzzle. The paradox casts doubt on the 'law matters' thesis and has implications for the progress of reform in China some three decades since starting the marketization process.

Undoubtedly there has been a push for legal reform in China. This pressure has derived in part from its global integration and membership in the multilateral rules-based trading system (World Trade Organization or WTO), as well as in response to domestic pressures, which led to the recognition of the existence of a 'rule of law' in the Constitution in 1999. Although on its face, the amendment appears symbolic, Clarke (2007) argues that it formally incorporates the legal system into China's system of governance. Legal reform, therefore, became prominent at the same time that the private sector was also recognized as part of the socialist market economy in the amended Constitution. The latter shift culminated in the 2001 embrace of entrepreneurs in the ruling Chinese Communist Party. This symbolic move also occurred in the midst of ongoing legal and economic reforms which had taken place since 1978 (see Appendix 2.1 for the key legal reforms accompanying the period of marketization), adding more credence to the view that legal and economic reforms did not progress in a particular sequence but developed alongside each other.

3.3.2 LAWS AND MARKETS IN CHINA AND THE USA

Although there are pitfalls with a comparative perspective, an examination of whether markets precede or follow laws in China and the US can inform the debate over whether the rule of law is necessary before markets can develop. Examining the respective legal developments at similar stages of economic development for these two countries would be informative.

Table 3.7 outlines the key pieces of commercial law for the US and China as compared with the level of economic development, but there are notable differences as between the two countries to consider in drawing any conclusions. The first is that the US common law tradition means that cases rather than legislation shape the law, though laws can certainly be amended, such as the Bankruptcy Act of 1898 which was entirely superseded by the Bankruptcy Code of 1978 which still governs corporations in the twenty-first century. Legal developments can take place in federal or state courts, and much of US corporate law is state law, with notable exceptions such as bankruptcy and patents which remain under federal jurisdiction. The corporation law identified in Table 3.7 refers to the statute of the State of Delaware, which accounts for some half of all US incorporations, due to its favourable provisions for corporate governance.

Table 3.7. A comparative perspective of US and China economic and legal developments

	US		China	
	Year	GDP per capita[a]	Year	GDP per capita[a]
Start of industrialization period	Industrial Revolution of 1820	$1,257	Start of industrialization under central planning in 1950	$448
End of industrialization period	Industrial Revolution concluded in 1870	$2,445	End of planned economy in 1978	$978
Anti-trust legislation	Sherman Act of 1890	$3,392	Anti-Monopoly Law of 2007	$8,788[b]
Bankruptcy law	Bankruptcy Act of 1898[c]	$3,780	Enterprise Bankruptcy Law of 1986[d]	$1,597
Corporate law	Delaware General Corporation Law of 1899	$4,051	Company Law of 1993	$2,515
Securities regulator	US Securities and Exchange Commission (SEC) of 1934	$5,114	China Securities and Regulatory Commission (CSRC) of 1992	$2,132
Patent law	Patent Act of 1790	$1,257[e]	Patent Law of 1985	$1,519

Notes:
[a] Per capita GDP is adjusted for PPP and in 1990 US dollars (Maddison 2001).
[b] This figure is from the IMF *World Economic Outlook* (2007).
[c] The Nelson Act was superseded by the Bankruptcy Code of 1978.
[d] Substantially revised in 2006.
[e] The figure pertains to 1820 (Maddison 2001).

China, by contrast, has elements of civil law and a strong administrative component, as compared with the common law and judicial review emphasis of the US. Its laws, moreover, have to contend with the transition of its economy from being dominated by SOEs to a market with private domestic and foreign enterprises. For instance, the United States was confronted with the 'robber barons' of US Steel and other monopolists at the conclusion of the industrial revolution, which raised concerns about anti-competitive practices. The 'trust busters' of the late nineteenth century, therefore, enacted the Sherman Act of 1890 which was geared at dismantling monopolies. China, however, did not pass an anti-monopoly law until 2007, quite late in its market transition, due to the unique dominance by state-owned enterprises, which accounted for over 90 per cent of GDP in 1978 and gradually declined in importance throughout the next three decades. With the creation of a more competitive market after the large-scale SOE reform of the late 1990s, as well as the incursion of foreign firms after WTO accession in 2001, there was then a need to ensure that monopolies did not distort the market.

Other differences included the separate legal regimes for foreign and domestic firms. There were numerous laws geared at attracting and also controlling foreign investors to prevent dominance in the domestic market, for example Chinese–Foreign Equity Joint Venture Law of 1979. Then, there was a need to govern the later emergence of domestic private firms, for example Law on Individual Wholly-Owned Enterprises in 1999. Parallel laws for foreign and domestic firms resulted. Therefore, there was subsequent unification of various pieces of law governing the same issue, such as the Contract Law of 1999 which unified the three forms of contract law that had governed domestic and foreign enterprises separately (see Appendix 2.1).

Examining the periods of adoption of key commercial laws harkens back to the age of industrialization. At around the start of the industrial revolution in 1820, the US had a per capita GDP (adjusted for purchasing power parity or PPP) of $1,257, which doubled by the end of that period in 1870 (see Maddison 2001 for the historical global GDP per capita measures reported in 1990 US dollars). If China's industrialization is considered to have taken place between 1950 and 1978 under the command economy, when it was transformed from an agrarian economy to one whose GDP is generated largely by industry, then both countries experienced a doubling of incomes during the industrialization process (see Table 3.7 for US incomes doubling between 1820 and 1870, and China's incomes doubling between 1950 and 1978). However, China's GDP per capita was half of that of the US at the start as well as at the end of the industrialization period.

The US had a per capita GDP of around $3,000–4,000 at the time of the adoption of a key body of corporate laws at the turn of the twentieth century, such as anti-trust legislation, bankruptcy law, and the Delaware General Corporation Law, which were all passed between 1890 and 1900 (see Table 3.7). The comparable set of laws for China was adopted when market-oriented reforms were implemented in the mid 1980s to mid 1990s, when its per capita income was around $1,500–2,500. Focusing on the main pieces of corporate law for these countries, the Delaware General Corporation Law of 1899 was adopted when US per capita GDP was $4,051,[1] while China's Company Law was promulgated in 1994 when its GDP per capita was $2,515. The adoption of commercial laws at an earlier stage of economic development by China is also evident when comparing the establishment of the securities regulator in both countries. The US Securities and Exchange Commission (SEC) was founded in 1934 when US income was $5,114, while the China Securities and Regulatory Commission (CSRC) was created in 1992 when Chinese income was $2,132 (though it did not gain effective powers until the 1988 Securities Law). China's commercial laws came into existence at an earlier point of its economic development than did those in the US.

A number of reasons for this earlier adoption include the imperfect parallel of industrialization which in the US was founded on technological breakthroughs that transformed industry and led to a need for laws, while China undertook industrialization under quite different circumstances within a centrally planned economy but in a context where there were established corporate laws on global markets. China's laws were further adopted at a time of global trade and financial rules stemming from the WTO and the international financial institutions (IFI) such as the Financial Stability Forum (FSF) of the Bank for International Settlements (BIS), for example the TRIPs or trade-related aspects of intellectual property rights agreement of the WTO which harmonizes intellectual property regimes across countries and the Basel standards of banking regulation from the BIS. Due to this trend of harmonization of international laws, there are proponents of a view that there is convergence of corporate governance systems worldwide (see Hansmann and Kraakman 2001). Therefore, the expectations of the actors in the global economy include rapid implementation of commercial laws and rules to facilitate cross-border transactions, which form an external impetus for China and other developing countries to create a legal framework at an earlier stage of development. The areas where China lags behind, for example antimonopoly and bankruptcy laws, reflect a lack of market need because of the SOEs, which made it less relevant to be concerned with competition policy or bankruptcies. Overall, China appears to have adopted legal reforms at an earlier stage of economic development than the US, making the Chinese paradox—growth without legal development—less of one.

A comparison of the key commercial laws—patent law designed to foster innovation, corporate law to enable commercial activity, and financial regulation to safeguard capital markets—will highlight the complex interaction, rather than present a clear sequence, of how law and markets evolved in both the US and China. A distinction that appears is between the *de jure* 'law on the books' and the *de facto* effectiveness of the law. The relationship of the latter to markets is where the disagreement between the two schools of thought lies. Lawyers such as Coffee (2001), as well as economists such as Chen (2003), would argue that the laws follow markets, while others like La Porta et al. (1997, 1998) believe that effective laws (such as providing better shareholder protection) precede market development. In the comparative analysis that follows, laws appear to largely follow some economic developments and play a market-supporting role in other areas. Although, overall, the pattern appears to be that of a complementary process whereby laws or other institutional forces create markets, in turn, markets foster a need for more and better laws, the adoption of which leads to more robust market development.

3.3.2.1 Patent laws and economic growth

Where there is some correspondence between the level of income and legal reform between the US and China is in the area of patent law and the protection of intellectual property rights (IPRs). As seen in Table 3.7, the US Patent Act of 1790 was adopted when US per capita GDP was about $1,257, and China's Patent Law was first promulgated in 1985 when its GDP per capita was $1,519. It is often thought that international pressures persuaded the Chinese to better protect intellectual property within their borders against the risk of expropriation and thus safeguard the incentive to invent (and invest in China). Interestingly, both the US and China adopted their laws preceding that of the development of international IPR laws under the WTO established in 1995; however, the US was a leader of international norms, whereas China revised its IPRs to comply with those laws.

US patent law preceded the Paris and Berne Conventions of 1867 and 1871, respectively. By that time, the US had completed its industrial revolution, incomes had doubled, and technological progress, such as the invention of the steam engine, had occurred. The breakthroughs of the two industrial revolutions of the UK during the late 1700s to early 1800s, and the US and Germany during the slighter late period from 1820 to 1870[2] provided a strong motivation for protecting inventions. This, of course, continued in the twentieth century with the promulgation of TRIPs and cross-border harmonization of IPR laws for WTO members, which encompass the near entirety of trading nations.

China's patent law also preceded the adoption of the global IPR regime but under a very different context. IPRs are governed by the WTO TRIPs agreement which came into effect in 1995 and bound China upon accession to the global trade organization in 2001. TRIPs governed IPRs on the dual premises of sovereignty and independence, whereby recognition and enforcement of such rights had previously been within a country's control (Yuch 2007). TRIPs increased both the scope of the protection of IPRs and harmonized such protection worldwide among WTO members. This runs contrary to the previous regime and led to several revisions of Chinese laws.[3] As such, enforcement at the level of that of the developed countries is expected of China.

Interestingly, China grew faster than the US after the passage of the IPR regime, despite complaints of weak enforcement in China as compared with the strong protection in the US. In the decade or so after passage of the law, US per capita income grew at an average of 0.9 per cent per annum from 1820 to 1830,[4] while China's grew at 6.6 per cent from 1985 to 1995. The fact that it preceded the industrial revolution may explain the lower American growth rates, or the different context of these laws could also play a role. The common law tradition of the US would result in the effective development of the law only over time. Therefore, the patent law not generating as strong growth in the US could be due to the lack of case law affording the magnitude of protection that is evident at present. By contrast, China's patent law was promulgated after it industrialized and during a period of initial transition from central planning, when China experienced 'catch up' growth, that is, developing from a low level of income and 'catching up' to the economies at the technology frontier like the US. Inventions, moreover, require time. Unlike the US, China is growing during a period when general purpose technologies like computing have already been invented by more developed countries, and thus it can manage a faster process of technological adoption through imitation and incremental improvements on existing inventions.

The adoption of IPR protection at a similar level of economic development, though under very different contexts, could reflect a number of factors. The first is that when a society undergoes industrialization (the US in the 1800s) or marketization (China in the 1980s), there is a push for protection of commercial interests to be able to profit from invention. It could also reflect the belief of government that innovation needs to be fostered in order to promote the commercialization of invention, to deepen markets and to generate the technological progress needed to fuel economic growth.

The adoption at a similar period of economic development could reflect the same impetus for promoting growth, though the contexts were rather different, as were arguably the outcomes as a result. IPRs indeed create a market for invention, which fuels clamours for better protection within a country and across borders as global integration progresses. The process is therefore one in which property rights are created by laws, but the market itself generates the constituency to agitate for more legal protection that meets the needs of that emerging sector, which in turn fuels the development of that market. The early government focus is undoubtedly due to the importance of innovation in fuelling long-run economic growth, which is evident in both the US and China which turned to protecting IPRs at roughly the same level of economic development, albeit with rather different contextual drivers.

3.3.2.2 Corporate law and economic necessity

Corporate law in the US and China both developed in response to their respective economic needs.[5] In the US, corporation law was left to the states after the US federal constitution adopted in 1789 did not explicitly govern incorporation, thus paving the way for states to adopt their own laws during the early nineteenth century.[6] New York was the first in 1811, followed by New Jersey, both of which pre-dated the US industrial revolution. The industrial revolution, however, led states such as Delaware, which has come to dominate corporate law in the US, to pass its general corporation law in 1899 to govern and attract a growing number of companies, with the resultant fiscal benefits to the state (see Hamermesh 2006).

In China, the corporatization process began in the early 1990s when SOEs were in need of reform. By 1992, an estimated two-thirds of all SOEs were thought to be loss-making (Fan 1994). By creating shareholding companies out of SOEs, the corporatization process transformed these enterprises into joint stock companies owned by shareholders, and therefore began the gradual process of privatization, as many SOEs retained the state as their majority shareholder even as they underwent reform (see Clarke 2003c). The passage of the Company Law in 1993 and promulgation in 1994 provided a basis in law for defining the rights and obligations of shareholders. Subsequent laws created other corporate forms, such as partnerships through the Law on Partnership Enterprises in 1997 and the Law on Individual Wholly-Owned Enterprises in 1999 which sanctioned privately-owned firms. The coincidence of laws with economic necessity is expected insofar as laws arise to address a specific development in the market, whether it is the growth of firms in the Industrial Revolution or the creation of companies defined by shares to reform an inefficient state-owned sector.

A common perception is that the US has, and has had, a well-defined and highly functional rule of law. However difficult that is to measure during the late nineteenth century, the US common law system is developed through case law which occurs over time and was unlikely to have existed as a fully fledged and effective 'rule of law' at the start of the era of the corporation. In examining ten countries of different legal origins (common law, civil law, and 'transplanted' countries such as Malaysia and Spain), Pistor et al. (2003) argue that the corporate laws at the time of adoption tend to be simple and concerned with establishing the corporation, but do not address more complex issues concerning corporate governance that demarcate an effective legal system, such as shareholder lawsuits. They find that countries, even after adopting similar corporate laws, will diverge and follow their own paths. Therefore, they conclude that the indicators of effective corporate governance which are typically relied upon as indicative of a well-functioning legal system, tend not to exist at the outset, including in the United States which was encompassed in their study.

The evolution of corporate law is further complicated in China by its distinct legal tradition which does not rely on courts as the main institutional source of development of the legal system. Instead, legislative enactments will have a larger role, in line with civil law countries such as Germany, although the administrative law tradition in China also plays a part. Nevertheless, its Company Law has been in existence for less than two decades and its poor scores on the corporate governance indicators, which are seen as representing the effectiveness of a legal regime, probably reflect the nascent stages of its legal development.

However, China's economic development has sped up, particularly with global integration after the 'open door' policy accelerated in 1992. The rapid passage of laws and regulations during the 1990s following the Company Law, such as the unified Contract Law of 1999, and the M&A Law and Securities Investment Fund Law both of 2003, reflect the push to legislate and thus improve the effectiveness of the commercial laws to govern the fast growing market economy. In a country with a civil law tradition, laws are developed through legislative action which in turn reflects the needs of the market, much as in a common law system where case laws arise from litigants seeking adjudication of disputes arising from market transactions. For instance, WTO-mandated liberalization of capital markets led to the passage of the Securities Investment Fund Law to govern the foreign and domestic firms expected to operate in the newly opened sector. Similarly, the 'going out' strategy of Chinese firms since 2000 culminated in permission being granted to private firms to invest overseas, as witnessed by TCL's purchase of the Thomson brand in 2004, which was followed by Lenovo's purchase of IBM's personal computer business a year later. The acquisition and mergers associated with these commercial transactions led to a need for an M&A law. Since the first deals were dated right after the passage of the law, it is unlikely that the law provided a strong basis for M&A transactions, as its scope would not have been immediately evident, though it is plausible that the same forces pushing for permission to operate in international financial markets are the same firms and government officials who viewed the 'going out' strategy as sufficiently mature to take this step, and thus create the need for a governing statute (see e.g. Sun and Tobin 2009 for the argument that innovative Chinese firms can enter and learn from international capital markets, which in turn can induce market-level improvements through regulatory competition and industry demands for a more standardized system of economic regulation in China).

3.3.2.3 Regulatory reform supporting markets: China's CSRC (China Securities Regulatory Commission) and the US SEC

Regulation plays a role in a legal system through providing the measures often necessary to implement laws, and the apparatus with which to enforce the same. Regulatory agencies, therefore, oversee markets and are the source of regulations governing markets under their remit. Regulatory systems differ significantly across countries, with one key difference between rules-based and principle-based systems which is evident in the US and UK respectively, though both are common law countries. In a rules-based system, the adherence to the letter of the law takes precedence whereas a principle-based system relies more on self-regulation to fulfil the spirit of the law. In both systems, however, there is a strong contrast with civil law countries where these systems are characterized by much greater state interference in markets. Coffee (2001) describes the late development of regulatory agencies in the US and UK after the establishment of the market as the reason that such markets governed in their self-interest as a result of a lack of government involvement. He describes it as 'enlightened self-interest'. In terms of the sequence of law and the development of capital markets for China, this ground has been well covered by Chen (2003), who argues that capital markets are the most evident place for the 'crash-then-law' hypothesis because this sector generates a powerful political constituency to lobby for legal change, given the high degree of commonality of interest among the interested parties and the ability to obtain immediately measurable benefits. Chen (2003) details the scandals and shortcomings in the Chinese stock market during the 1990s which led to better regulation and protection of shareholders by the end of the decade.

Examining capital market development in a comparative perspective, there is evidence of regulatory reform adopted to better govern markets in both the US and China. The stock markets in Shanghai and Shenzhen were established prior to the regulatory agency, the CSRC, in 1992, which is a pattern that is evident in the US as well (see Appendix 2.2 for the key securities and banking laws of China). The US Securities and Exchange Commission (SEC) was established in 1934 in the aftermath of the 1929 stock market crash and subsequent Great Depression of 1929 which lasted until 1934. The bourse pre-dates the regulator. The New York Stock Exchange (NYSE) was created in 1792 when a group of stockbrokers gathered together to trade securities on Wall Street in New York City. For the next 142 years, the NYSE operated without a central regulator until the stock market crash of October 1929. It triggered the Great Depression which was characterized by real output falls, deflation, and widespread banking failure in which half of all US banks failed or merged between December 1930 and March 1933 until President Roosevelt was forced to shut down the entire US banking system (Bernanke 2004). Prior to the SEC which was created by the Securities and Exchange Act of 1934, securities trading was governed by states with decentralized supervisory authority that did not extend beyond their boundaries. Following the stock market crash in 29 October 1929 (known as 'Black Tuesday'), a plethora of laws as well as the SEC came into existence in order to safeguard markets. The plight of consumers, who had lost money in the stock market and their bank deposits due to widespread banking failure without deposit insurance for savers, heralded the need for a regulator to govern and restore confidence in the financial system. The SEC, therefore, was established in response to a crash in the market and was charged with implementing laws to safeguard the financial sector, such as corporate governance reforms like the much later Sarbanes-Oxley Act of 2002, passed in the aftermath of the Enron scandal.

China's CSRC was established just a year after the creation of the two exchanges, but lacked the central authority to govern effectively until the 1998 Securities Law. And, China did not have a banking regulator until 2003 (see Appendix 2.2). Both were empowered to regulate the financial sector, alongside the insurance regulator, following the establishment of the capital, banking, and insurance markets, largely in the 1990s. As discussed earlier, China scores poorly on corporate governance indicators, reflecting the lack of effectiveness of the law and the imperfect oversight of China's trio of regulators (CSRC, CBRC or China Banking Regulatory Commission and CIRC or China Insurance Regulatory Commission). The late establishment of the CBRC in particular suggests that the banking sector had developed in the absence of regulation, which would be paradoxical except for the dominance of state ownership and therefore state control in bank lending. As the banking sector became increasingly liberalized and the dominance of the state banks receded, then there was a push—particularly with the post-2001 WTO-mandated opening to foreign banks—for a regulator and improved governance. Thus, the CBRC was established sixteen months after WTO accession but prior to the entry of foreign banks in December 2006, consistent with the agreed schedule for opening. The insurance market was also lately developed. Since before the 1990s SOE reforms, insurance was provided by the SOE *danwei* or work unit, so a market hardly existed. With reform, the market developed and the CIRC undertook a corresponding governance role.

Regarding the CSRC, Chen (2003) documents the ways in which securities regulations were passed in response to the demands of interested constituents in the burgeoning capital market (see also, Sun and Tobin 2009). Despite the relatively early establishment of the CSRC soon after the bourses and comparatively early in relation to the United States, there were no significant securities laws passed for six years until the Securities Law of 1998. Prior to its enactment, the stock markets operated under administrative direction. Provincial governments selected firms to become listed firms and they in turn were allocated a certain quota to do so. As a result of the incentives of the quota system, provincial authorities selected the better performing firms for initial public offerings (IPOs) so that the stock market grew throughout the 1990s (Du and Xu 2009). In this way, China's capital markets functioned prior to the establishment of the relevant laws and in the presence of a passive regulator. However, WTO accession in 2001 changed the picture. As part of its WTO terms, China agreed to open its financial sector to foreign firms. Before then, the Securities Law completed the set of corporate laws for China, alongside the 1993 Company Law.

The anticipated opening led to a series of securities laws passed after 2001 (see Appendix 2.2), which rapidly reformed China's financial sector. Foreign firms and governments interested in accessing China's market as well as the *de novo* private sector would be among those clamouring for better defined rights. The Chinese government's desire to foster its own state-owned enterprises as well as safeguard the market from foreign dominance would be among other drivers, for example the State-owned Assets Supervision and Administration Commission (SASAC) was established in 2003 to oversee state-owned assets as SOEs continued to exist and a 25 per cent ceiling on foreign equity ownership in Chinese firms prevented takeovers.

The result was a large number of regulations passed since 2002 that are geared at improving transparency, increasing disclosure requirements, reforming the non-tradable shares in the stock markets, extending protection to minority shareholders, forbidding insider trading, and monitoring mergers and acquisition activity. All of which address the needs of shareholders, investors, debtors, and firms in the market (see Chen 2003). In turn, the growth of the market led to the need for regulation and regulators. And the regulatory apparatus can support the further development of the financial sector. After the establishment of the SEC in 1934, the NYSE experienced its longest bull market of eight years from 1949. Although the same cannot be said of the effect of the CSRC in its first decade and a half, the numerous securities laws passed since greater market opening after WTO accession herald significant reform of the stock market in China, though more needs to be done to remove the distortions posed by the controlling shares held by the state.

In China's financial sector, the sequence seems to be one of markets preceding effective laws. Laws appear to develop alongside, and in response, to market needs. As in the United States, laws and regulations were not established in a vacuum to predate markets. Instead, some laws (and administrative dictates in China such as the provincial quota system for IPOs) create markets, which gives rise to a need for further laws and regulatory bodies, which in turn govern and establish new segments of the market. Therefore, it seems that whether it is 'crash and pass' like the US SEC and the late reforms of capital markets in China, or a more evolutionary process to accompany economic reform—such as the Company Law and corporatization movement in China and the Delaware Corporation Law after the US industrial revolution, or the passage of IPR laws to promote technological advancement, the process is better characterized as complementary rather than sequential or cause and effect.

3.4 **Complementarities between law and markets**

There appears to be a complementary process between law and markets, where law neither entirely precedes market development nor vice versa. Formal written law creates property rights in intellectual property, legitimizes corporate forms, and establishes capital markets. Markets can also be created more informally via administrative dictates or due to a lack of prohibition, the latter of which is seen in the Household Responsibility System described further in the next section. Once the markets are established, then in both common law and civil law traditions, there is a process of interpreting and revising the laws respectively through judicial or legislative avenues. This iteration is driven by interested constituents vested in the markets, which can include holders of IPRs, owners of private firms, and shareholders (see Coffee 2001; see also, Sun and Tobin 2009), as well as governments wishing to reform state-owned enterprises (e.g. China in the 1990s) or restore confidence in markets (e.g. US SEC). Countries which produce more effective laws and regulations will have better functioning markets, which in both the common and civil law traditions occur over time (see La Porta et al. 1997 for the finding that better shareholder protection is associated with higher growth rates; see Cull and Xu 2005 for the finding that provinces in China with better legal protection is associated with improved firm performance). Evaluating the US at the time of the adoption of its corporate laws, the indicators of effectiveness of laws are unlikely to be as strong as they are at present, since key protections are not specified in statutes when they are passed, but develop over time with judicial and legislative review (see Pistor et al. 2003 for a historical review of common and civil law countries that finds that the countries do not have a strong rule of law at the inception of the laws but effectiveness as measured by shareholder protection develops over time; see a contrary argument by Acemoglu, Johnson, and Robinson 2005 that countries which inherited better institutions, that is, those that protected against risk of expropriation, from colonial powers, enjoyed subsequently higher growth rates).

For the US and China, key commercial laws were adopted at comparable levels of development, with China having done so more often at an earlier stage and with seemingly more impressive subsequent economic growth rates. However, the speed of setting up a market or adoption of laws does not equate to effectiveness of the legal system. China also had the advantage of being a late developer so that it could learn and imitate legal best practices in the same sense that countries do in economic terms, such as not having to 'reinvent the wheel' in technological improvements. Undoubtedly, the transition and globalization context increases the difficulty of a comparative analysis. The short period of time since the creation of China's corporate law system and its establishment of capital markets also makes it challenging to disentangle the sequence of law and markets dispute. The next section analyses the limited evidence from this short time span and finds some limited support for the argument of this chapter that there is no sequential order as between legal and economic development.

3.4.1 A TEST OF GRANGER NON-CAUSALITY

The methodology used is a time-series estimator (VAR or vector autoregressive model) that tests for Granger causality. It is a particular form of causality used not to establish causal relationships per se, but rather to rule them out.

In other words, econometricians rely on the Granger concept not to prove causal relationships, but to establish when they do not exist and the variables under scrutiny are found to be exogenous. In this case, the relationship to be tested is between legal development and economic growth. The law and finance position would suggest that laws establish markets so that legal development should lead to better economic growth. By contrast, the lawyers argue for the opposite, whereby markets lead to legal reforms. The position in this chapter is that it is a complementary process as between legal and economic development. In Granger terminology, this chapter hypothesizes that the lagged values of legal development have no explanatory power as to later economic development and the true holds vice versa. The law and finance position would argue for lagged values of law explaining economic growth, while their opponents would seek to find that prior economic growth has explanatory power with respect to subsequent legal development.

Technically in this specification, Granger causality is inferred when lagged values of a variable y have explanatory power in a regression of a variable x on lagged values of both variables (Granger 1969, Sims 1972). If the lagged values of a variable y have no explanatory power for any of the variables in a system, then y would be viewed as weakly exogenous. A simple VAR to test whether changes in the rule of law cause movements in GDP growth in the Granger sense would be as follows:

Let $x_t = $ [GDP, rule of law]$_t$.
Then,

$$x_t = \begin{bmatrix} \mu_1 \\ \mu_2 \end{bmatrix} + \begin{bmatrix} \alpha_1 & \alpha_2 \\ \beta_1 & \beta_2 \end{bmatrix} x_{t-1} + \begin{bmatrix} \epsilon_{1t} \\ \epsilon_{2t} \end{bmatrix}.$$

The parameter α_2 must not be zero to find a causal relationship. This is, however, insufficient to establish causality as the estimation is unable to discard other variables that could affect these movements. However, this approach can be used to establish exogeneity, such that if lagged values of y_t add no information to explanation of movements of x_t beyond that provided by lagged values of x_t itself, then y_t can be viewed as exogenous:

$$f(x_t|x_{t-1}, y_{t-1}) = f(x_t|x_{t-1}).$$

Wald F-tests can be used to test this relationship in a VAR model (see Sims 1980; Stock and Watson 2001). If previous measures of the rule of law do not help explain changes in GDP even in the presence of lagged values of GDP, then the null hypothesis that the rule of law does not 'Granger-cause' GDP growth is not rejected. As the unrestricted equations have identical regressors, the opposite relationship can also be tested, that is, the null hypothesis that

GDP movements do not cause changes in the rule of law. If this null hypothesis is rejected, then previous lags of GDP 'Granger causes' changes in the rule of law. Granger non-causality is inferred when a variable adds no information to the movements of another one, such that the null hypothesis is not rejected and there is no consistent statistical feedback loop.

3.4.2 THE EMPIRICAL RESULTS

Figure 3.1 shows that China has made halting but generally positive progress in improving its rule of law from 1996 to 2008. GDP growth over the past decade, though, has been more consistently positive. With twelve years of data such that $n \geq 10$, the appropriate small sample adjustments can be made in the VAR. A small-sample degrees-of-freedom adjustment is used when estimating the error variance-covariance matrix such that 1/(T-average number of para-meters) is used instead of the large-sample divisor. Also, t- and F- statistics are computed instead of the large-sample normal and chi-squared ones. The estimations use two lags of each explanatory variable. Too few and too many lags both cause problems. The former could potentially omit important

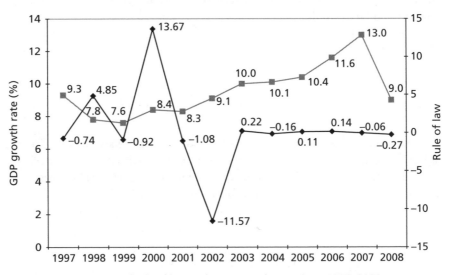

Figure 3.1. Evolution of rule of law and GDP growth over time, 1997–2008

Sources: World Bank Worldwide Governance Indicators, and Chinese Statistical Yearbook Table 2–1.
Notes: Rule of law measures the extent to which agents perceive that the rules of society, in particular the quality of contract enforcement, the police, and the courts, as well as the likelihood of crime and violence, are enforced. The percentile rank places the country on a scale of 0–100 where 100 indicates a country that scored the highest possible value on the rule of law indicator. For 1997, 1999, and 2001, the values are imputed from a simple average of the preceding and following years. Governance is better as the value increases. The rate of change is plotted in the figure. Real GDP growth is reported annually.

variables which lead to biased estimates, while the latter wastes observations and will increase the standard errors of the estimated coefficients and thus cause a loss in the precision of the results. The decision typically reflects whether the additional lags add explanatory power to the model. The R-squared from the model where rule of law is the dependent variable estimated with one lag were 0.3597 and 0.0250, which increased to 0.4130 and 0.1270 with two lags, which suggests a two lag model. As a robustness check, the model was also run with one lag, which did not change the results. An augmented Dickey–Fuller unit root test was undertaken in which the null hypothesis of non-stationarity was rejected, which suggests the variables are stationary, for example GDP growth (*p*-value of 0.0381), change in rule of law (*p*-value of 0.0171), change in regulatory regime (*p*-value of 0.0000).

Estimating two lags of the variables over the period, the coefficients (with standard errors in parentheses) from the VAR model are as follows:

$dGDP = 5.929288$ (4.329681) $+ 0.7112655$ (0.7273891)$dGDP_{t-1} - 0.3230709$
(0.9589954)$dGDP_{t-2} - 0.064735$ (0.0931301)$dlaw_{t-1} - 0.0078928$ (0.0968869)
$dlaw_{t-2}$,

$dlaw = 8.473367$ (19.31648) $- 0.1276195$ (0.4154917)$dlaw_{t-1} - 0.3322019$
(0.4322521)$dlaw_{t-2} - 0.6983353$ (3.24518)$dGDP_{t-1} - 0.1646832$ (4.278471)$dGDP_{t-2}$,

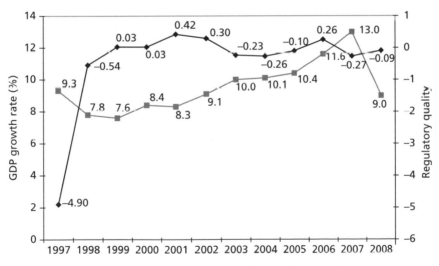

Figure 3.2. Evolution of regulatory quality and GDP growth over time, 1997–2008

Sources: World Bank Worldwide Governance Indicators, and Chinese Statistical Yearbook Table 2–1.
Notes: Regulatory quality measures the ability of the government to formulate and implement sound policies and regulations that permit and promote private sector development. The indicator score is normally distributed with a mean of zero and a standard deviation of one. Quality improves as the value increases. For 1997, 1999, and 2001, the values are imputed from a simple average of the preceding and following years. Regulation is better as the value increases. The rate of change is plotted in the figure. See Kaufmann, Kraay, and Mastruzzi (2007) for a complete definition and discussion. Real GDP growth is reported annually.

where *dGDP* represents annual real GDP growth, *dlaw* is the per annum change in the rule of law index, and *t* represents the year.

The Wald tests reveal that neither of the two null hypotheses (law does not cause movements in GDP growth; GDP growth does not cause changes in the rule of law index) are rejected (*p*-values: 0.7939 and 0.8734). Both variables are likely to be exogenous, and thus Granger non-causality can be inferred. Neither past GDP movements nor changes in the rule of law have any explanatory power in terms of determining subsequent legal development or economic growth, respectively. As the hypotheses relate to changes in the variables of growth and law, the differenced values capturing annual growth are used in the estimations. Using the levels forms of the variables does not change the results.

A second formulation tests the potentially more important regulation in governing capital markets, and thus a more potent regulatory system could have a more direct impact on economic growth than the rule of law measured more generally. Figure 3.2 shows the gradual improvement in regulation in China. Using an alternative formulation of regulatory quality (*dreg* which represents the annual change in regulatory quality) to substitute for the rule of law index yields the same results. Again estimating two lags of the variables over the period, the coefficients (with standard errors in parentheses) from the VAR model are:

$$dGDP = 2.338485 \ (4.53868) + 0.0790054 \ (1.303295)dGDP_{t-1} + 0.7347871$$
$$(1.623732)dGDP_{t-2} + 2.703518 \ (2.363902)dreg_{t-1} + 0.1122766 \ (0.7315255)dreg_{t-2},$$

$$dreg = 0.49603 \ (0.8781) + 0 \ .0063742 \ (0.457345)dreg_{t-1} + 0.0540213 \ (0.1415285)$$
$$dreg_{t-2} - 0 \ .1522005 \ (0.2521489)dGDP_{t-1} + 0.108675 \ (0.3141441)dGDP_{t-2}.$$

The R-squared for this set of equations are respectively 0.5237 and 0.2160. The Wald tests find that the two null hypotheses (regulatory quality does not cause movements in GDP growth; GDP growth does not cause changes in regulatory quality) are again not rejected (*p*-values: 0.4708 and 0.6168). Both variables are likely to be exogenous, and thus Granger non-causality can be inferred. The alternative and narrower measure of legal reform also supports the conclusions of the general measure of rule of law that past changes in GDP and regulatory quality do not have explanatory power respectively for regulatory reform and latter growth in the economy. When the VAR is estimated on yet another measure of government effectiveness, which is sometimes argued to be a substitute in China for legal development (see Fan et al. 2009), measured in the same World Bank survey of governance indicators, it is similarly found to indicate Granger non-causality.

This empirical evidence provides some limited support for the thesis of the chapter that the relationship between law and economic growth in China is unlikely to be determinative as argued by the proponents of either laws preceding or following markets. Although these measures of legal reform are crude, a growing number of papers utilize these proxies, particularly over time, so as to capture the trend of change as in this chapter, to attempt to add some evidence on the dynamics of legal reform and economic growth in China and elsewhere to the largely qualitative debate (see e.g. Kaufmann, Kraay, and Mastruzzi 2007).

3.5 **Institutions and transition in China**

The sequence of law and markets is not the only paradox of China's economic success. Markets were created in the absence of private property rights as China's transition has been largely undertaken whilst maintaining a communal property system. Laws therefore did not play the sole role in creating markets during much of China's reform period; instead, administrative dictates and institutional reform were often more crucial. For instance, the passage of the Company Law in 1993 occurred after the start of the transformation of SOEs into shareholding companies, just as private firms emerged prior to the passage of the Law on Individual Wholly-Owned Enterprises in 1999 (see e.g. Du and Xu 2009 for the argument that administrative arrangements took the place of laws in creating China's capital markets). In numerous respects, markets started with institutional reform in China.

Harkening back to the agricultural reforms of the late 1970s and early 1980s, the 'institutional innovations' of the Household Responsibility System (HRS) created property rights by allowing farmers to retain a portion of their earnings under the still communal land system (see e.g. Lin 1992). Much of China's reform of SOEs has occurred without an explicit change in ownership from state to private, as the gradual corporatization and the share issue privatization process are ongoing after three decades.

China's approach has been to pass laws or administrative dictates to support a successful experiment. The Household Responsibility System, responsible for raising agricultural productivity during the early 1980s, was initially banned, then permitted (see Naughton 1995 for a description of this 'no encouragement, no ban' approach). The same occurred with land tenure rights which led to farmers selling their freeholds in rural areas, which was initially banned until it became widespread and also predated the passage of the Property Law in 2007. Many attribute this flexible approach to 'experimentation' as the source of China's success (see e.g. Qian and Xu 1993).

The notable 'institutional innovations' were the Household Responsibility System for rural residents in the late 1970s and early 1980s, the Budgetary Contracting System (BCS) allowing decentralization of state-owned banks and local authorities in the early 1980s, and the Contract Responsibility

System instigated at around that time for state-owned enterprises. A more formal set of legal property rights was created for foreign investors in the form of joint venture laws.

The operation of China's 'dual track' transition, in which one part of the market was liberalized while another was kept under administrative control, depended on generating growth from the marketized part of the economy which could then subsidize the faltering state-owned sector, with the overall outcome of maintaining economic stability (Lau, Qian, and Roland 2001). Prior to the 'institutional innovations', collectivization meant that there was little incentive for farmers to produce output as their work points were allocated on the basis of a day's labour irrespective of effort. Adopted by households gradually in the early 1980s amidst a move to de-collectivize agriculture, the incentives generated from receiving some returns from own labour caused agricultural output to increase substantially (Riskin 1987). A significant part of China's growth in agricultural productivity and the overall rural economy can be traced to both the HRS and de-collectivization (Lin 1992; Huang and Rozelle 1996).

Whereas the HRS refined the incentives facing households, the creation of township and village enterprises (TVEs) is a striking example of how China created a new institutional form whose parameters were defined by policy and not by private ownership or outright transfer of the ownership to individuals. Yet, the reliance of the Chinese rural workers on this newly recognized institutional form of enterprise was sufficient to instil market-driven incentives to fuel rural industrialization whereby TVEs grew rapidly and accounted for an impressive one-third of China's total output in the mid 1990s. The evidence of growth stemming from these reforms is notable, as rural industrialization helped remove surplus labour from the farms and contributed significantly to the remarkable poverty reduction in the reform period (see Ravallion and Chen 2007).

With respect to the urban economy, the CRS in 1981 permitted state-owned enterprises to pay a fixed amount of taxes and profits to the state and retain the remainder (Koo 1990). In principle, so long as the SOEs delivered the tax and profit remittances specified in the contracts, they were free to operate. This resulted in increased production of SOEs in the 1980s through the re-orientation of incentives of managers (Groves et al. 1995). However, the decline of SOEs in the 1990s illustrated the limits of relying on the so-called institutional innovations as 'soft budget constraints', whereby the enterprises are not bound by the constraints of profit and cost due to the support of the state, continued to plague SOEs. This is in spite of the positive incentive effects of the CRS, and eventually led to the transformation of many SOEs into stock-holding companies in the 1990s with ownership changing into private hands (Choo and Yin 2000).

Reform of the state sector was also important. Decentralization has occurred in nearly all areas of decision-making in production, pricing, investment, trade, expenditure, income distribution, taxation, and credit allocation through the BCS (Riskin 1987). Since 1980, under the BCS, the central government shares revenues (taxes and profit remittances) with local governments. For local governments which incur budget deficits, the contract sets the subsidies to be transferred to the local governments. It allowed regional experimentation by local governments, a key element to China's gradualist path because it permitted market-oriented activity while limiting the possibility of instability through enabling the fairly autonomous actions of different provinces to act relatively independently. This was instead of a top-down approach where a mistaken national policy could reverberate throughout the country (see Qian and Xu 1993).

Since 1985, state grants for operating funds and fixed asset investments have also been replaced by bank loans. Local governments and SOEs are allowed to borrow directly from banks. Six years later, they could access funds from other institutions. Rapid changes in the banking and financial system followed. The sole bank, the People's Bank of China (PBOC), became a central bank and was divested of its retail banking functions and was reformed to focus on monetary policy formation in the mid 1980s. Its banking functions were in turn divided into four state-owned commercial banks (SCBs), each initially with a specialized remit that was reflected in their names: Industrial and Commercial Bank of China (ICBC), China Construction Bank (CCB), Bank of China, and the Agricultural Bank of China (ABC). Three further policy banks were also formed in 1994 to take over the developmental aims of the state banking system: China Development Bank (CDB), Export–Import Bank of China, and the Agricultural Development Bank of China. There is also a second tier of state-owned banks, which have shares owned by the government as well as by private entities. There are approximately a dozen or so of these joint stock commercial banks, which were largely set up in the 1990s. A commercial banking law was passed in 1995, though these reforms pre-date the law and are driven by governmental institutional reform. Other financial institutions, such as investment banks and other financial intermediaries, made little headway until liberalization sped up in the 1990s with anticipation of accession to the WTO.

Therefore, across all sectors of the economy, marketization, though imperfect, has gradually taken hold in transitioning China (see e.g. Young 2000). Given the gradual reform over three decades whereby the market developed over time, the legal system supporting the market economy was likewise underdeveloped for most of this period. Instead, the development of the market in China can be traced to governmental administrative dictate and institutional reforms (see e.g. Du and Xu 2009 for the argument that administrative measures creating a quota system across provinces produced a successful stock market in China during the 1990s). Not all of these were initiated by the state, but the system was adaptable, and included economic experiments which often led to the passage of law and regulations by the government, such as the Property Law of 2007. Individuals and firms, moreover, responded well to the incentives generated by administrative measures. China's strong administrative law tradition is perhaps one explanation of the willingness of the populace to rely upon such administrative arrangements instead of clearly defined property rights established in law.

3.6 Enforcement of laws

3.6.1 FOREIGN FIRMS

China's treatment of foreign firms, by contrast, was governed by formal laws which nevertheless suffered from imperfect enforcement. Gauging their development sheds some light on how China's imperfect enforcement of laws, which is viewed as being as important as the written law itself, has not deterred its marketization process.

Since the 'open door' policy reforms of China's external sector were adopted in the late 1970s and sped up in the early 1990s, China has rapidly become one of the world's top destinations for foreign direct investment. The first significant commercial law passed in China was the Chinese–Foreign Equity Joint Venture Law of 1979. This, and its counterpart laws establishing cooperative JVs and wholly foreign-owned enterprises (WFOEs) passed in 1986 and 1988 respectively, pre-date laws granting corporate legal forms and protections to Chinese domestic firms which were passed a decade or so later. The better delineated rights of foreign investors have been a source of contention amongst Chinese private firms, whose rights were less clearly protected during most of the reform period (see e.g. Huang 2006).

Especially prior to WTO accession in 2001, after which legal reforms were targeted for improvement, the predominant form of FDI was Chinese-foreign joint ventures, where the Chinese and foreign partners set up either equity or cooperative joint ventures. Both forms of joint ventures were vested in contracts that legally specified the rights and obligations of both parties and were subject to judicial enforcement. The same could be said of the law governing WFOEs. The uncertainty that might have been generated by the lack of adequate protection of private property due to a weak legal system, though, did not seem to serve as a deterrent to FDI, which is another puzzle in China's growth narrative. Indeed, China is a competitive destination for FDI, even measured against developed economies, such as the US and the UK, despite its underdeveloped legal and institutional system (see e.g. UNCTAD 2006).

One explanation is that China recognized early on that foreign firms from developed economies operating in a global context needed laws to govern their rights, even if the enforcement of those rights was imperfect. Unsurprisingly, it generated an interested constituent of private Chinese firms who sought a similar level of legal protection of their property and transactional security, which led to the passage of laws on partnerships and sole proprietorships in the late 1990s and early 2000s. Whereas Chinese firms can accept administrative rule in lieu of judicial enforcement or an open legislative process to effect change, the puzzle is that the lack of effectiveness of laws, particularly in the area of enforcement, did not deter foreign investors (see Clarke 2003a for the argument that rights in China are interpreted differently from property rights in developed countries). However, since WTO accession, the clamour for better protection, in particular of IPRs from foreign firms and governments has increased.

One potential explanation has to do with the rise in alternative dispute resolution (ADR), notably arbitration, in China, which sought to supplant an incomplete legal system. The China International Economic and Trade Arbitration Commission (CIETAC) is relied upon by international investors, for instance, as is resort to international arbitration based in Europe or elsewhere (see Bosworth and Yang 2000 for the importance of CIETAC and arbitration in resolving commercial disputes in China). Alternative dispute resolution has become more popular even in countries with well-developed legal systems such as the United States due to its lower costs. There is also the Chinese reliance on relational contracting, that is, transacting on the basis of trust and known relations, which is in part cultural, as it is evident even in overseas Chinese diasporas, that affords foreign firms another avenue of information. Finally, there is a degree of risk in investing in any developing country so foreign firms have a greater appetite for uncertainty when dealing in China or other emerging markets such as Russia than in the United States. In their calculus of making the investment decision, they would have measured the risks of expropriation and lesser contracting security against the rewards of efficiency, cost saving, and market access.

3.6.2 INFORMAL INSTITUTIONS

The issue of enforcement further points to the role of informal institutions, such as reliance on relational contracting or trust-based relationships in China. There is undoubtedly a cultural element in that interpersonal relationships, such as *guanxi*, play a notable role in economic transactions within and without China, even among the overseas diasporas situated in countries with strong legal systems. Within China itself, this was also perhaps reinforced by the reliance on administrative dictates—a legacy of China's administrative law tradition.

Due to the absence of a well-established legal system, developing countries tend to rely on informal institutional arrangements, such as utilization of social capital or relational-based contracting, whereby contracting is undertaken with people on the basis of trust. Even developed countries at the start of their marketization relied on such relationships (see e.g. Franks, Mayer, and Rossi 2009 who studied the development of the UK capital market and found that ownership dispersion relied initially more on informal relations of trust than on formal systems of regulation). Enforcement, which is often a challenge in an underdeveloped legal system, can be by means of activating social capital instead of courts. For instance, social sanctions and norms account for the success of micro-finance institutions such as the Grameen Bank in Bangladesh. The high repayment rate of loans is not due to the threat of legal action, but on account of social capital in the community, whose norms act to enforce the terms of the loan. By overlooking informal institutional arrangements which support the rule of law and other formal institutions, the extent of legal and institutional reform can be misjudged and developing countries could suffer from misfashioned policies as a result. In other words, as countries are increasingly judged on the quality of their institutions, poor legal systems are a common area of criticism of developing countries, and aid or technical assistance can hinge on legal reform and so lead to the adoption of laws that may not suit the country. At the extreme, 'transplanting' legal systems into less developed countries has not been successful (see Pistor, Martin, and Gelfer 2000 for the conclusion that legal systems transplanted into newly transitioning economies did not foster economic growth).

Enforcement can be easier within communities, but the judicial system needs improvement as the number of arm's length agreements increase with market development, and this makes informal enforcement less feasible. Legal reforms in the West followed a similar pattern, suggesting that greater marketization will require more legal reform to govern relationships that can no longer rely on trust alone (see Franks, Mayer, and Rossi 2009). However, relational contracting, that is, dealing with trusted parties, is much cheaper than litigation if a relationship goes sour, and this also explains the continued reliance on social capital by small businesses, even in developed economies with more complete but expensive legal systems, such as the United States. China is at a stage where its entrepreneurs can still effectively utilize informal institutional arrangements for enforcement alongside a set of evolving formal reforms.

Given the necessarily slow pace of creating an independent judiciary, it is likely that informal arrangements, as well as arbitration in particular when the transactions are at arm's length will remain in place for some time to come. But, this can also help explain how China has been able to grow and marketize with a legal system that suffers from weak enforcement and thus lacks effectiveness.

3.7 Conclusion: China's legal and economic reforms in an era of global integration

China's experience over the past thirty years has been the envy of many developing and transition economies, as well as being an 'outlier' with its poor legal system and rapid growth. A final aspect is the influence of the international economic system. Whilst China has gradually integrated itself into the global economy during the 1990s, the world economy also underwent a transformation with the emergence of a growing body of international economic laws and rules. Although global trade rules in particular have existed previously, the creation of the WTO in 1995 brought into prominence a number of laws, rules such as those governing intellectual property, and a dispute resolution mechanism (dispute settlement understanding or DSU) with influences on China's legal reforms with accession in December 2001. Clarke (2003*b*) asserts that the main effect of WTO-related changes is to increase the transparency of laws in China. Other rules that China accepted, such as the TRIPs provision, led to further revisions of its intellectual property rights regime in order to comply with the harmonized global laws governing IPRs. Moreover, the DSU provides a forum for countries to bring actions against other WTO members who are thought to have violated a precept of the WTO rules. For instance, China was the largest target of anti-dumping actions before the DSU in the late 2000s. Threatened action alone can at times discourage the behaviour, such as the US rescinding tariffs on steel imports under the prospect of a WTO action. Moreover, legal protection and enforcement of IPRs as provided for under the TRIPS agreement can also be actioned before the DSU, as seen in the 2007 US case brought against China for inadequate protection of IPRs.[7]

Aside from trade rules, the past decade has also witnessed the development of greater integration among financial markets, which has led to the creation of financial codes such as the Basel accords specifying the prudential capital adequacy ratios of banks, promulgated by the Financial Stability Forum of the Bank of International Settlements (known as the central banks' central bank). In particular, the Asian financial crisis of the late 1990s highlighted the linkages among banking and financial systems, which prompted the need for coordination of financial regulation and commonly understood standards. Unlike the WTO-related rules, countries voluntarily adopt these standards to signal their management of risk and financial soundness to global capital markets. In a similar vein, Sun and Tobin (2009) argue that Chinese firms that list overseas and operate in international financial markets do so to signal their quality when capital could be otherwise raised in China's high savings economy. The more rigorous standards of overseas listings are borne as a sign of a robust enterprise that a Chinese domestic listing could not provide. Other examples include the voluntary code of conduct adopted by Sovereign Wealth Funds (SWF), that is, state-owned funds investing foreign exchange reserves overseas. Although there are no rules which compel a SWF to do so, those from countries such as Singapore declare their activities and their intent to invest as passive, minority shareholders in the companies of other countries in an attempt to avoid political interference in their overseas investments. All of these factors suggest that China's legal reforms will not be advanced in a vacuum, particularly given its prominence in the global economy.

This chapter has examined several aspects of the relationship between law and economic growth in China. It assessed the theoretical and empirical relationships between laws and the development of markets across countries, spanning developed, developing, and recently transitioned economies. The relationship between law and markets appears asynchronous for China. This perspective reconciles the existing views in the literature by arguing instead that laws both precede and follow markets. Thus, this chapter posits that the studies in the literature in some respects are describing different facets of an evolving picture (see e.g. Chen 2003 who subscribes to the 'crash-then-law' hypothesis versus La Porta et al. 1997, 1998 and Acemoglu, Johnson and Robinson 2005 who argue that the existence of market-supporting institutions is the cause of subsequent robust growth). Some limited empirical evidence in support of this chapter's position was also presented.

It is difficult, if not impossible, to fit China into the paradigm given its history and context. However, China's experience suggests that there are more parallels than would at first appear between its legal and economic development with the United States. The argument that laws and economic development reinforce each other was made through an examination of the experience of the United States at a similar stage of economic development. By comparing three facets of Chinese and American legal reforms—intellectual property protection, corporate law, and securities regulation—the pattern was seen to be largely evolutionary in that laws may have created a market in the case of IPRs and established corporations, but regulations which gave substance to the law and therefore its effectiveness were largely passed after there was an evident economic necessity, such as abuse of monopoly power or financial sector scandals. Therefore, although a law or administrative dictate (or absence of strict prohibition) may create a market (or an informal one), this alone is insufficient to argue that the sequence must be laws preceding markets. Even innovation can happen without IPRs. By the yardstick of whether an effective rule of law exists, which goes beyond just the provisions that create an IPR or a corporate form, laws appear to develop in response to market demands and needs, which in turn leads to more marketization and economic development. Specifically, China's legal development is similar to the US at a comparable time in their respective economic development, and often pre-dated American laws in governing evolving markets.

A further paradox in China's growth model was explored, which is the development of a market within a state-controlled communal property system. Administrative measures and ensuing institutional reform complete the picture for China, whereby its several decades-long economic transition has been driven by a series of experiments, trials, and a 'no encouragement, no ban' policy. Given the context, the lack of laws establishing clearly defined property rights appears not to be as pertinent as was thought.

Finally, the chapter concludes by accounting for the influence of the global rules-based system that is gradually emerging, and gained prominence around the same time as China's integration into the international system after years of inward-focused development. There are numerous limitations in the reach of the fledging international legal system, but certain rules such as IPR protection will influence the course of China's domestic reforms. The system, though, is two-way. Particularly in the area of voluntary adherence to standards and norms, China and its firms will seek to shape international rules as they increasingly operate in the evolving global financial system. The picture may be more complex, but looks ever more evolutionary as countries gather at various meetings to negotiate and agree everything from liberalization of trade to rules governing risk assessment of banks.

China may continue to be viewed as a paradox, but its path will be enticing for many developing countries for which it is not unusual to have a nascent legal system that will not rate well in terms of either effectiveness or enforcement. The success of China, and the prospect of it strengthening laws alongside robust economic growth, has the possibility of its being a model to emulate, though it has a way to go before its legal system and economy reach the standard of that of the advanced countries.

■ NOTES

1. There had been corporation law prior to the Delaware Act, though the dominance of Delaware as a preferred state for incorporation lends itself to be identified as the key article of US company law (see e.g. Hamermesh 2006).

2. The steam engine, spinning and weaving machines, cast iron, and electric battery were among the major inventions of the 19th century industrial revolutions. By the 20th century,

the international conventions on patents occurred during a time of inventions such as the telegraph, telephone, and electricity, which saw a fivefold increase in per capita incomes in Western Europe as compared with the threefold increase between 1700 and 1800 (Maddison 2001).

3. The 153 members of the WTO in 2010 account for nearly the totality (97%) of world trade.

4. Per capita GDP for the US is not available in 1790, so the nearest in time available data from 1820 is reported.

5. See e.g. Horwitz (1992) on the evolution of US contract law during the late 19th and 20th centuries in response to the economic and social conflicts of the time.

6. The presumption of the US federal system is that unless explicitly claimed in the Constitution or Act of Congress, an area of law was to be governed by state law. The 'state's rights' doctrine is embodied in the 10th Amendment concluding the Bill of Rights to the US Constitution, which states: 'The powers not delegated to the United States by the Constitution, nor prohibited by it to the States, are reserved to the States respectively, or to the people.'

7. WTO Dispute DS362, initiated on 17 April 2007: http://www.wto.org/English/tratop_e/dispu_e/cases_e/ds362_e.htm.

4 State-Owned Enterprises: Law as Instrument of Economic Policy

4.1 Introduction

State-owned enterprises (SOEs) dominated the Chinese economy throughout the centrally planned period from 1949 to 1978. But, SOEs suffer from the inefficiencies associated with 'soft budget constraints' whereby state owner-ship meant that they were not subject to a 'hard' or actual budget, since they received their inputs (labour, capital) directly from the state. There was no incentive to minimize cost and instead there was overinvestment, as SOEs did not have to take account of the actual cost of their inputs (Kornai 1992). They were characterized by surplus labour for similar reasons but also because SOEs were the state's vehicle to sustain urban employment. As a result, most were loss-making and subsidized by the state, whose aim was to use SOEs not only for production but as vehicles for delivering social securities and main-taining full employment. Even throughout the post-1979 reform period, the 'multiple objectives' of SOEs meant that they were not only maximizing profit, but were also providing public and social goods to the urban popula-tion (Bai et al. 2000).

The state funded SOEs directly through subsidies and indirectly through the state-owned banks. The funnelling of credit to SOEs from state-owned banks resulted in significant accumulation of non-performing loans (NPLs) in the banks, which were themselves plagued by the same inefficiencies due to also being state-owned enterprises characterized by inefficient levels of capi-talization and an inability to shed labour. This system of supporting SOEs led to inflationary episodes whereby loose monetary policy was used to fuel credit to the state-owned banks and SOEs (Brandt and Zhu 2000). This was worsened by the 'dual track' transition where the state-owned banks had been allowed to undertake direct lending as of 1985 and preferred to lend to the more efficient non-state sector. However, they were still directed to lend to the SOEs. Therefore, episodes of rapid credit expansion followed the trajectory of growth, while non-performing loans lent to SOEs built up at the same time.

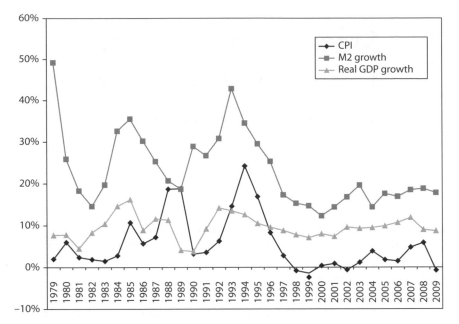

Figure 4.1. Inflation: CPI and M2 growth, 1979–2009

Source: China Statistical Yearbook Table 8–1, People's Bank of China Statistical Yearbook.

Figure 4.1 shows the rapid growth of broad money (the M2 monetary aggregate) that accompanied real output growth. When the consumer prices index (CPI) followed, and reached double digits during the early swings of the business cycle, the government would rein back those policies and impose austerity measures which drove fairly dramatic upturns and downturns in China's business cycles in the mid 1980s, late 1980s, and early 1990s, in which GDP growth would fall dramatically from year to year, for example from over 16 per cent to some 8 per cent (1985–6), 11 per cent to 4 per cent (1988–9), and a milder but nevertheless evident drop in GDP in the early 1990s (see Figure 4.1). The late 1990s and 2000s were not characterized by such volatility, and could be attributed in part to the decline of SOEs as well as benign global conditions during the Great Moderation of the decade from the late 1990s when the world experienced strong growth and low inflation. Even when the Great Recession followed in 2008 with the onset of the global financial crisis, China's low point was still an impressive 9.2 per cent growth rate in 2009, suggesting that its economic fluctuations during the latter part of the reform period were better managed than the previous 'stop-go' cycle.

At the same time, state-owned enterprises still had claims on credit from the banking system, distorting the efficient allocation of capital away from the more efficient non-state sector due to their linkages with the state that owned both these enterprises and the banks. This was not only a central government feature but was found throughout the provinces as local governments, local state-owned banks, and local state-owned enterprises replicated the arrangement.

There was an evident need to reform SOEs for both macroeconomic stability as well as microeconomic efficiency reasons. The transformation of state-owned enterprises in China has been analysed from many angles, particularly the early 'dual track' transition where managerial incentives were instilled through the 1980s' Contract Responsibility System (CRS) whilst preserving state ownership (Groves et al. 1995). Later reforms in the 1990s identified features of the partial reform strategy that left SOEs with multiple objectives, such as maintaining employment instead of only the usual commercial motive of profit-maximization (Bai et al. 2000). In the 2000s, debate continued over the role of SOEs as the sector has been largely restructured into shareholding companies (*gongsihua*), but large state-owned enterprises remain, with no suggestion of mass privatization to come. Thus, this lingering issue of policy-directed lending associated with the retention of 'soft budget constraints' that provide SOEs with cheap inputs of investments and also raw materials from the state which allow for inefficiencies to remain in the reformed sector. Also, NPLs and the stability of the banking system remain as lingering concerns.

Government policies towards retaining state ownership in the economy, political economy motivations such as the 'multi-tasking' role of SOEs, and the conflictual principal–agent problems that arise with 'soft budget constraints' have been explored in a vast literature on SOEs (see e.g. Garnaut et al. 2003). What has been less emphasized is the interaction between SOE reforms and legal developments.

Not much noted with respect to the reform of SOEs but happening nevertheless with rapidity, particularly throughout the 1990s, was the establishment of a corporate law system. Key laws, such as the Company Law of 1993 and the Securities Law of 1998, accompanied by a myriad of regulations passed in the 2000s, set up the corporate law system in China.

This system was initially instigated coincident with the main reform policy since the CRS of the 1980s, which was the 1990s' restructuring of SOEs. Starting in the early 1990s with the establishment of the stock exchanges in Shanghai and Shenzhen, these bourses allowed the public listing of SOEs that had been transformed into shareholding companies starting in 1993 and to be governed by the Company Law of the same year. This form of 'share issue privatization' or SIP was favoured over other forms of privatization which had resulted in instability in the former Soviet Union's 'big bang' reforms from 1989 onwards. SIP was also consistent with a partial reform strategy that did not involve wholesale privatization as it enabled the state to preserve its ownership of enterprises since shareholding allowed it retain control, for example two decades later, the stock market still comprises of mostly non-tradable shares held by the state and legal persons (mostly other SOEs). The aim was to transform SOEs into corporations, that is, shareholding companies that could be run on a commercial basis to increase their efficiency through distilling the incentives gleaned from having shareholders, including publicly traded stocks. Not only would this transformation be viewed as important to increase productivity and stymie the expanding non-performing loans in the state-owned banking system on account of inefficient SOEs, it would help establish the perceived viability of Chinese firms on the global stage, and therefore acceptance in world markets. For instance, the 'going global' policy launched in October 2000 was intended to make Chinese firms multinational corporations that were competitive internationally. Listing on global bourses such as the New York Stock Exchange (NYSE) and London Stock Exchange (LSE) followed when the 'going out' policy ripened with the first commercial outward foreign direct investment (FDI) permitted in 2004.

Without the legitimization of laws, regulations, and other governance measures, the transformation of SOEs would be baseless in the eyes of a global system accustomed to well-defined strictures for corporations. Therefore, although not the forerunners or the main instrument for SOE reform and corporate development, the laws governing SOEs legitimized the *gongsihua* or corporatization policy that was the main goal to be achieved by restructuring (*gaizhi*) the sector throughout the 1990s and 2000s. Far from being insignificant, corporate laws in China embodied a public dimension of the SOE reform policies. They provided the institutional grounding for the restructured SOEs to operate domestically and globally as delineated corporations.

Therefore, corporate laws in China could be viewed in part as legitimizing tools for SOEs. Indeed, in spite of lacking many of the characteristic features of an effective rule of law such as an independent judiciary, China has and continues to pass laws to govern the behaviour of its SOEs and later on, other enterprises. This promulgation of law begs the question of exactly why China would pass these laws when reforming SOEs is more a matter of policy dictate than legal formality. This chapter posits that this process is best understood through viewing laws as legitimizing what has already become common practice for SOEs. The focus of this legitimacy appears to be with an eye towards the international community as much as for domestic consumption. China's corporate laws were passed fairly quickly starting at the inception of its decision to enact significant SOE reforms. Laws and regulations provided the system by which restructured and corporatized SOEs would be governed in an increasingly marketized economy. Laws did not dictate policy, but should be viewed as instruments for legitimizing the policy aims of the state in a form that is familiar to those used to operating in markets.

This chapter will focus on the major pieces of legislation in conjunction with primary reform policies, to highlight the importance of laws in SOE reforms. Laws act not as governance mechanisms controlling SOE behaviour, but rather as signifiers of a Chinese government keen to establish greater legitimacy amongst international arenas and investors.

4.2 **Early reforms: Incentivizing state-owned enterprises in the 1980s**

4.2.1 SOE LAW

The use of law as a legitimization tool was evident even in the initial stages of reform of the late 1970s and early 1980s. China's economic and SOE reform process officially began with the Third Plenum of the Eleventh Central Committee of the Communist Party of China (CPC) in December 1978. The Plenum put forward suggestions to set up an independent and complete industrial system and national economic system from 1978 to 1980. The session emphasized that economic development would be the measure of the success or failure of such policies. The proposed 'reform and opening' were specifically geared at readjusting the industrial sector dominated by SOEs.

Prior to 1979, the Chinese central government was solely responsible for the operation and management of what were referred to as 'state-run enterprises,' and the sale and distribution of goods were conducted largely through a quota system. Following the Fifth Plenum, certain powers and decision-making rights were slowly given to state-run enterprises and comprised the initial step to reform. It is generally acknowledged that the most important of these was the *fangquan rangli* or 'relaxation of authority and allowance of profit-making' policy which began in 1979, although it clearly took time to spread through China (see Naughton 1995).

The major goal of the programme was to institute administrative decentralization and profit retention. A pilot reform programme on the expansion of enterprise autonomy was started in late 1978 in Sichuan and then extended to the rest of China. SOEs were allowed to retain 3 per cent of their profits, so that there were incentives to improve productivity and efficiency (Huang and Woo 2004).

Quantity targets were retained but were kept low, and enterprises were encouraged to sell any quantities produced in excess of the plan at market prices, thus encouraging the response of production to some form of market pricing, the so-called 'dual track', where an administered segment existed alongside a market segment of the economy. Naughton (1995) argued that this process meant that the share of an enterprise's activity based on centrally planned goals of outputs and inputs would fall, and the share based on autonomous decision-making and market prices would steadily increase (see also Fan 1994 who argued that the 'dual track' would eventually lead to a convergence between the two tracks allowing reforms to proceed without the instability associated with introducing market prices into a command economy with repressed inflation). Indeed, in 1984, the government specified nine particular areas where SOEs' decision-making autonomy must be guaranteed. These were later expanded to fourteen in 1992. China would thus, consciously, 'grow out of the plan' (Naughton 1995).

A major part of the policy was what was not reformed at this time: ownership. This was whilst the 'dual track' was creating a market economy that operated alongside the existing administered economy.

In 1981, the State Council established the provisions governing private investment by individual household firms (*getihu*) in cities and towns, limiting the number of employees to seven. The 1982 Constitution declared that the basis of China's economic system was socialist public ownership of the means of production, and that the state sector was to be the leading sector in the economy. The non-state/individually based economy was declared to be a 'complement' to the socialist public economy. Article 15 of the Constitution declared: 'the State practises economic planning on the basis of socialist public ownership.' This socialist ownership and control was seen as extending throughout the economy. Article 11, for instance, also argued that the state (and not the rule of law) should protect the legitimate rights and interests of the self-employed and private enterprises, and China should also exercise guidance, supervision, and management over them according to the law, which was hardly in existence for the emerging non-state sector.

Central Party Document No. 1 of 1983 extended the provisions on the individual economy to rural areas. This was the most legitimization accorded to the private sector at that time. Neither policy nor law provided an organizational vehicle for larger private enterprises. The only way for such enterprises to exist was as 'red hat' enterprises: businesses formally registered as collective instead of private in exchange for a fee paid to the local government for protection against predation and to qualify for various benefits available only to the public sector.

Moreover, as Schipani and Liu (2002) argue, SOEs in the period of the planned economy were not regarded as independent legal persons. SOEs, as in the centrally planned period, were simply an arm of the state for which government policies provided guidance, without need for a separate system of corporate governance. This began to change with the 'Decision of the Central Committee of the Chinese Communist Party on Several Issues Concerning the Reform of the Economic System' in 1984. This decision outlined why traditional SOEs should become legal persons and gain additional managerial powers to make them more competitive and less inefficient. The Law on Industrial Enterprises Owned by the Whole People (or SOE Law) was then passed in 1988, providing a statute-based organizational form to state-owned enterprises. As SOEs had of course existed prior to the passage of this law, the real change was the implementation of the idea that business organization should be governed by statutes from the National People's Congress (NPC).

The SOE statute, therefore, was out of date at the time of its passage since SOEs already existed as a vehicle, but significantly served as an indicator of the change in direction of the Chinese reform path by the mid 1980s. With the early success of the 'dual track' in the early part of the decade, growing marketization warranted a statutory recognition that SOEs were legal entities separate from the state that were governed by statute and should be considered public enterprises. Of course, the statute itself governed little, and SOEs were still dictated by policy. However, the rudimentary beginnings of corporate law were taking shape, no doubt hastened by the passage of like corporate laws governing foreign-invested enterprises at that time. In spite of its nominal seeming nature, the SOE law played a legitimizing role in the Contract Responsibility System (CRS) discussed later.

4.2.2 BANKRUPTCY LAW

One of the critical problems of transition economies is the ability of public officials to 'rent seek'. For example, managers set up small businesses and cooperatives within their factories, which are used to strip state assets. Under the 'dual price' system, production was diverted from the planned to the cooperative sector where they could sell at higher prices. Easy profits can be made by buying inputs (often from oneself) at fixed state prices, diverting them to cooperative production, and then selling at much higher prices.

As part of the broader programme of reform, enterprise financing was shifted from the old system of government grants to a new system of reliance on bank loans repayable with interest, with the hope of signalling the real cost of capital. However, these policies brought the undesirable consequence of motivating SOEs to bargain with, or to hide profits from, the government, causing government revenue to decline. The government implemented two new measures to combat this problem in the 1980s. First, SOEs were required to pay taxes instead of turning in profits in order to reduce bargaining. This policy was known as *ligaishui*. Second, the funding for SOE capital investments, instead of being allocated directly from government financial reserves, had to come through bank loans (*bogaidai*). These policies relieved the government's financial burden and placed incentives to restrict wanton lending of capital.

However, they also proved somewhat ineffectual. SOEs used their money to pay interest to the bank instead of taxes to the government. In Chinese accounting, interest (or financial charges) is paid before operating income. SOEs now had an incentive to declare no profit or low profits. The government ended up again with lower revenue (Sun and Tong 2003). This also had a major impact on SOE debt and produced non-performing loans in the state-owned banking system which was exacerbated by a difficult macroeconomic period. The mid 1980s witnessed a glut of goods entering the market, causing market prices to fall below that of administered ones as well as a serious bout of inflation triggered by the repressed inflation in a system that was characterized by shortages under central planning. In turn, this caused the government to tighten delivery contracts and other requirements (Sicular 1988).

A remedy for 'rent-seeking' and these assorted agency problems is bankruptcy. The Enterprise Bankruptcy Law (passed in 1986 but not in effect until 1988) was mostly a procedure for closing down SOEs. Specifically, losses due to bad management, not adverse changes in the market, were to be the basis for closure. It was, however, a major shift for state-owned enterprises. In another instance of the law signifying policies that had been enacted, two years before the formal promulgation of the Bankruptcy Law, the first ever Chinese bankruptcy occurred when Shenyang Explosives went out of business.

The Bankruptcy Law had to be fundamentally revamped in 2006 as it was designed to be narrowly applied to SOEs and was inadequate to govern the largely marketized economy that subsequently developed. As the requirements for bankruptcy had to do with poor management instead of balance sheet reasons as in most market economies, the law was largely inadequate, as its later fundamental overhaul suggests. But, importantly, it served as an indicator of the sea change in SOE reform attitudes. Before then, no SOEs were shut down: as they provided the social security, housing, and the 'iron rice bowl' for urban residents on behalf of the state, their existence was secure. However, the shift in policy was made concrete through the Bankruptcy Law that served, like the SOE Law, as largely symbolic but nevertheless was an instrument for the effectuation of government policy regarding SOE reform.

4.2.3 CONTRACT RESPONSIBILITY SYSTEM (CRS)

The next phase of reform was marked by the introduction of a managerial incentive system in an attempt to achieve those elusive reforms but still without ownership change. Companies began to transform from state-run enterprises to state-owned enterprises with the introduction of the responsibility system of contracted management and lease systems (Contractual

Management System also known as the Contract Responsibility System or *chengbaozhi*). The contract system suited the aims of partial reform because it maintained state ownership and because of the success of similar 'institutional innovations' in rural China (see e.g. Li and Putterman 2008).

The CRS was a shift away from what could be referred to as the state-owned-and-managed model. Under this model, state ownership was generally assumed to be the only legal form available to provide a safeguard for state property. Not only did the state have ownership of all the property of the SOEs, but it also enjoyed managerial powers. The backbone rationale behind this model was paramount state ownership of property, and this was central to the tenets of a centrally planned economy where the state administered all of the economic decisions for a communal property system.

The new reforms retained state ownership of property, but made SOEs act as 'legal persons' responsible for their own gains and losses in the market. The CRS provided that SOEs should become legal persons that enjoy full management authority and full responsibility for their own profits and losses. This, in effect, separated ownership and control (Schipani and Liu 2002).

In April 1987, the Central Committee of the Chinese Communist Party and the State Council adopted a contracting system (*chengbaozhi*) to govern the relationship between the state and an appointed manager (factory director) in SOEs nationwide. The 'manager contract responsibility system' was then enacted in the 13th National Party Congress in October 1987. Then, the State Council enacted the Provisional Regulations on Contracting Management System in SOEs in February of 1988 to govern this relationship, based on separating state ownership from control of SOEs.

These changes culminated in the SOE Law adopted in 1988. The SOE Law recognized that: 'The property of the enterprise shall be owned by the whole people (equivalent to the notation of "State"), and shall be operated and managed by the enterprise with the authorization of the State in line with the principle of the separation of ownership and managerial authority.' The SOE Law, therefore, effectuated the main policy reform of the time and legitimized the new governance structure in statute.

The corporate governance structure introduced by the SOE Law changed the incentives for SOEs. According to the contracting system, the two parties to the contract are the appropriate level of government and the SOE, as represented by its chief executive officer (CEO) or what is more commonly called 'factory director'.

As noted by Schipani and Liu (2002), the CEOs of SOEs were selected through a competitive process. They acted as the legal representatives of the SOEs and took full responsibility for their management. Thus, the major shift of this law was that the factory director (manager), rather than the state, assumes overall responsibility for management of the enterprise, and for the performance of the firm.

To stimulate managers' interest in profit generation, profits were given an important place among the criteria for judging managerial success. Importantly, enterprises were permitted to retain a portion of profits, some of it for managerial bonuses, and a succession of arrangements to raise the proportion of marginal profits retained were tried (Yusuf, Nabeshima, and Perkins 2006).

It had a dramatic effect on the nature of the relationship between the SOE and the workforce. New hiring began to be done on the basis of shorter-term contracts, to last only five years instead of the implicit lifetime contract. The 'iron rice bowl' which was the heart of the work unit or *danwei* system became far less secure.

Crucially, the policy to retain state ownership but separate the rights of ownership from control, in an effort to instil efficiency-oriented incentives, was effectuated through the SOE Law. Although not strictly necessary since the same policies can be enacted without law, particularly in the absence of a commercial law system, and the state retained ownership, the SOE Law was passed, and used to first establish the organizational form of SOEs and then to specify their governance structure. As such reforms can be undertaken without law and corporate governance measures, the question as to why the law was passed must be considered within the wider context. By the late 1980s, the set of laws governing foreign-invested enterprises (FIEs) had been passed, as well as a rudimentary system of civil and administrative laws. China was beginning to open up to the global economy, and the entry of FIEs increased the integration of China with world markets generally underpinned by legal structures, particularly the sort of foreign investors from more advanced countries that China aimed to attract to help it upgrade its productive capacity. By situating its reform of SOEs within statute, this approach began to pave the way towards establishing their legal and organizational entity vis-à-vis the foreign firms in China. Reading the laws in conjunction with policy sheds more light on the intent and aim of the Chinese reform path.

4.2.4 PROBLEMS WITH THE CRS

As with the reforms in the rural sector, SOE profit retention seemed to have a beneficial early impact. For instance, Groves et al. (1995) found that managerial incentives generated initial efficiency gains. Most studies of total factor productivity (TFP) growth during the 1980s find evidence of positive growth rates for SOEs. For example, Jefferson, Rawski, and Zheng (1992) estimate TFP growth of 2.4 per cent for state-owned enterprises for the period between 1980 and 1988.

However, the widely observed phenomenon of the 'soft penalty' undermined managerial incentives and the resultant firm performance (Choo and Yin 2000). Due to output being incentivized while budget constraints remained 'soft', the CRS did not impose market discipline on the cost side, and SOEs continued to require subsidies even as managers responded by increasing production.

The hypotheses of Kornai (1992) in regard to SOE property rights appeared to manifest itself more greatly in SOEs than in the countryside. As the SOE managers' obligations were largely on the profit side of the balance sheet, it was difficult to make SOEs fully responsible for their losses. For instance, Sun and Tong (2003) argued that hard budget constraints could not be strictly imposed on SOEs due to their relatively unfavourable operating conditions, and that 'soft budget constraints' gave the SOEs enough leeway not to improve their efficiency.

Others believed that the contracting system and the transitional model it represented failed to provide much in the way of SOE reform (see Schipani and Liu 2002). However, their argument was based more on an inability to correctly calculate the initial boundary conditions under which contract responsibility could operate. First, it was very difficult to identify a reasonable minimum amount of profit for the SOEs to pay to the state. Second, although most SOEs enjoyed benefits when they were profitable, they were unable to pay the fixed amounts required to the state when they sustained losses. Third, there was a fair amount of exploitation of the assets of SOEs for personal use. Finally, too little SOE profits were retained for development purposes, leaving insufficient resources for future expansion.

Lin, Cai, and Zhou (2003), on the other hard, point to the problems of SOEs as stemming from the prior structure of the Chinese economy. As a result of decades of central planning and forced industrialization, SOEs were typically capital-intensive. Heavy costs of capital and capital obsolescence were resultant problems. Second, they often made products of strategic importance and product prices were heavily suppressed to facilitate national development plans, making it harder to expand into more efficient product lines. Finally, they needed to bear the cost of all the social benefits of their employees such as medical insurance, social welfare benefits, housing benefits, and education for their children. Given the political consequences of a redundant workforce, real and binding budget constraints for SOEs appeared unlikely.

Finally, Naughton (1992) argues that the biggest challenge facing the SOEs during the first decade and a half of China's reforms came from the fact that increasingly competitive market conditions were eroding profits and undermining the ability of SOEs to generate revenues for their government owners and to repay the loans with which they met their financing requirements.

As detailed by Naughton (1992), even as output per unit of input was rising, the average rate of profit earned by SOEs was falling, from 25.2 per cent in 1980 to 16.8 per cent in 1989. Heading into the 1990s, the picture worsens. Holz (2003) puts profit per unit of equity for the SOE sector at 7.7 per cent in 1993, 6.7 per cent in 1994, 4.1 per cent in 1995, and 2.2 per cent in 1996.

Industrial profits had fallen from 14 per cent of GDP in 1978 to only 2 per cent of GDP in 1992, with only about half of that decline expected as a result of the declining SOE share of industrial output. Government revenues, which had overwhelmingly come from SOE profits, had fallen correspondingly.

Meanwhile, SOEs had gone from obtaining 62 per cent of their investment in fixed capital from government grants in 1978 to obtaining less than 3 per cent by 1997, with bank credit making up most of the difference. As SOEs' ratio of debt to equity climbed from 12 per cent to a soaring 211 per cent between 1978 and 1994 (Naughton 2007), these estimates suggest that upwards of half of the loans outstanding in the banking system—the bulk of it loaned to SOEs—could be considered non-performing.

Naughton (1992) argued that the falling rate of profit in the SOE sector—and by the mid 1990s in the TVE sector as well—was largely a sign of the erosion of the monopoly profit rates that had been built into the pre-reform system as a way of financing the state's capital-intensive investment programme. Letting local governments start new SOEs, collectively-owned enterprises (COEs), and township and village enterprises (TVEs), and letting enterprises compete with each other and determine their own prices, was bound to reduce profit rates if real competition emerged.

These trends were unsustainable. The NPL issue added further pressure to accelerate SOE reform. By the early 1990s, some two-thirds of SOEs were either explicitly or implicitly loss-making (Fan 1994). As a result, NPLs were estimated to be some one-third of the banking system's assets, causing China to be in danger of a banking crisis. Official estimates are that the ratio fell to just over 5 per cent for the big four state-owned commercial banks in the 2000s as a result of recapitalization and the creation of Asset Management Companies (AMCs) to remove the NPLs from the balance sheets of the banks in 1999 in anticipation of IPOs and share-issue privatization. These figures are debatable and exclude the Agricultural Bank of China (ABC), whose position was so poor that China's sovereign wealth fund purchased a 50 per cent stake in 2009 in advance of an IPO. This lingering and ongoing problem of NPLs highlights the need for significant reform that took shape in the late 1980s/early 1990s.

The mounting stock of non-performing loans indicated that neither the state-owned banks nor the SOEs had yet grasped the concept of commercial debt, or, to put it differently, been given sufficient incentives to do so. Failure of new entry to be balanced by exit of less successful firms, another symptom of soft budget constraints, also contributed to the decline in profits. And, real labour costs were rising, in part due to the SOEs' burden of unfunded pension payouts to a growing number of retirees produced by an ageing demographic.

Moreover, in the late 1980s and early 1990s during the period of the Contract Responsibility System, the economic conditions were volatile. Market-oriented reforms attempted to liberalize prices, starting from the premise of a shortage economy. Significant price rises and heady investment growth led to a series of actions by central government, including price caps on major industrial inputs, reduced expenditure, strictly controlled credit, and at one point even cessation of lending to township and village enterprises. As a result, economic growth plummeted to 3.8 per cent in 1990 from 11.3 per cent in 1988.

This was followed by another episode from 1991 to 1995 when the central government pursued loose and then tight fiscal and monetary policies. It first reduced interest rates and expanded money supply to stimulate the economy following the 1990 downturn, but then reversed course when a record high inflation rate of 21.7 per cent was reached in 1994. The government managed to curb price hikes by keeping the growth of money supply and fiscal outlays within a moderate range.

These were the considerations that lay behind the central government's decision to allow local governments to privatize their small state-owned enterprises and to seek ways to harden the budget constraints of the medium and large state enterprises by means of a more radical new set of reforms (Li and Putterman 2008). The next step was corporatization, which was, as with all Chinese reforms, pushed ahead by the decreasing effectiveness of the Contract Responsibility System. However, it required a wholesale invention of a corporate legal system.

4.3 *Gongsihua* and ownership reform in the 1990s

4.3.1 CORPORATIZATION

The 14th Party Congress in October 1992 announced the target of constructing a socialist market economy and establishing a modern corporate system. This spearheaded the next stage of SOE reforms, corporatization (*gongsihua*). The goals of this process were to provide legal rights for different ownership structures and clearer property rights.

A new and first ever Company Law was adopted in 1993, providing a framework largely to allow for ownership restructuring that was to include the conversion of SOEs into corporations. SOEs would be transformed into limited liability and joint stock companies by means of corporatization (*gongsihua*). More evident than the previous statutes (SOE Law, Bankruptcy Law), the Company Law was intended to be the instrument through which the most far-reaching SOE reforms would be legitimized. Instead of being non-consequential, the reform process culminated in the promulgation of corporate law to govern the restructuring of SOEs. Again, if the law was unnecessary to achieve that goal, then its use must be through a desire to establish in a recognizable fashion the wholesale adoption of corporate forms in China. Of course, these reforms proceeded gradually and took the entire decade for SOEs to be 'corporatized'.

With the earlier problems in mind, this latest stage of the reform process reflected a desire to build a modern enterprise system compatible with the market economy, but to retain the state's role within it. To achieve this goal, Chinese policymakers began to look to the modern corporation model in the Western world for possible solutions. The 1993 Company Law is the first comprehensive piece of legislation on business corporations since the founding of the People's Republic of China in 1949. It provided the legal foundations for the transformation of SOEs into different business corporations, including wholly state-owned corporations, closely held corporations, and publicly held corporations. The Normative Opinion on Joint Stock Companies was also passed almost simultaneously by the State Commission on Reform of the Economic System in May 1992. This served as one half of the general Company Law, and provided an organizational vehicle for enterprises that wished to restructure and list shares on the stock exchanges. These corporate laws, though, were intended largely to facilitate restructuring by SOEs, not to facilitate the formation of new enterprises. The laws, therefore, existed to serve the needs of SOE reform and were only later extended to govern non-state enterprises, whilst foreign firms were governed by a separate legal regime, including their own corporate statutes and contract laws.

Despite the facially wide-reaching nature of these reforms, as the authorities retained controlling shareholdings, they had the effect largely of nominally changing ownership rather than altering much of the running of the companies (Dougherty, Herd, and He 2007). This was also the case in the publicly listed firms under these statutes.

The Shanghai and Shenzhen Stock Exchanges were established in 1990 and 1991, respectively, to enable the public listing of SOEs. In 1993, the informal ability to list SOEs on the stock market changed to a formal quota-based listing procedure (Du and Xu 2009).

As a political compromise to retain state ownership and control, the reformers proposed to have several classes of shares: state shares, legal person shares (only owned by legal person institutions and corporations which were SOEs), and floating common shares ('A' shares for domestic citizens and 'B' shares for foreign investors). In particular, the state shares and legal person shares would not be publicly tradable, so that no loss of state ownership and therefore control would occur. However, regardless of share type, the holder of a share is entitled to the same cash flow and voting rights.

Not unexpectedly, this required regulations to govern the now publicly traded shares. The Provisional Rules on Stock Issuance and Trading of 1993 issued by the China Securities Regulatory Commission (CSRC) proscribed various miscreant practices and provided for civil compensation for those who were financially injured as a result (Hutchens 2003). But, the courts were not ready for private securities litigation, and hence these administrative provisions did not amount to significant protection for private investors. Penalties based on the Provisional Rules of 1993 could only be enforced either administratively by the CSRC or through criminal litigation by the Public Security Department. This led to widespread shareholder protests throughout the 1990s which culminated in the significant reforms of the financial sector in the latter part of the decade, including the 1998 Securities Law that gave the CSRC the necessary authority to regulate capital markets (see Chen 2003).

This part of the regulatory reform process would be familiar in markets undergoing development that required legal guidelines to operate. In this sense, the corporate law system operated as expectedly. Share issue privatization, in turn, heralded significant ownership reform in the 'save the large, let go of the small' privatization push in 1994 and the subsequent *gaizhi* policy that restructured and privatized most of the SOEs by the 2000s. China, in the twenty-first century, embraced corporatization under laws designed for SOEs to serve as instruments of reform which eventually became a system of corporate law that governed not only the eventually privatized SOEs but the enterprise sector (domestic and foreign firms alike) as a whole.

4.3.2 'GRASPING THE LARGE, RELEASING THE SMALL'

A significant part of this thematic shift away from old ownership forms came in December 1994 when the State Council proposed a pilot scheme for a few large SOEs. From this, the *zhuangda, fangxiao* or 'grasp the large and release the small' policy was unveiled. The large SOEs were to be retained, but the smaller ones were effectively privatized.

'Grasping the large' meant that large enterprises in industries viewed as strategically important for the government to control, including petroleum, metallurgy, electricity, military industry, and telecommunications, remained under state ownership and control. Other relatively large SOEs, although not clearly slated for lasting government control, were also not liquidated or privatized outright. Rather, these companies were converted to joint stock corporations, some shares of which were sold to workers and managers, others of which were made available for purchase and trading by individuals on the stock exchanges. Corporatization or SIP, thus, did not necessarily result in privatization.

'Letting go of the small' meant allowing provincial and lower-level governments to dispose of their loss-making enterprises, and between 1995 and 2000 some 82 per cent of a total of 59,410 small- and medium-sized SOEs, which together accounted for about 33 per cent of overall SOE sector

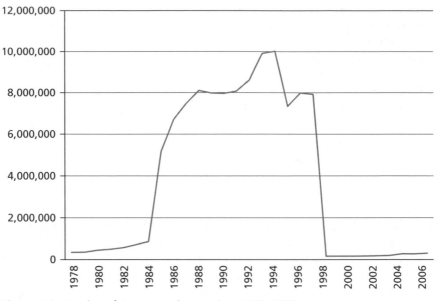

Figure 4.2. Number of state-owned enterprises, 1978–2006

Source: China Statistical Yearbook Table 13–8.

output,underwent restructuring. By the end of 1998, more than 80 per cent of state and collective firms at the level of the county or below had gone through fundamental restructuring, involving direct privatization in most cases. Figure 4.2 shows the notable drop in SOE numbers in the late 1990s.

The government kept a firm grip on 100 central and 2,600 local, large SOEs, which were eventually placed under the overview of the State-owned Asset Supervision and Administration Commission (SASAC) when it was created in 2003. But, numerous weak enterprises were sold off through auctions and corporate transformation while some large- and medium-sized SOEs were transformed into publicly listed firms on the stock market. Only relatively strong SOEs were eligible to go public. At the end of 2000, there were about 1,080 firms listed on China's two national stock exchanges (see Figure 4.3). Almost all these firms were former SOEs.

This process, called *gaizhi* (change of system), affected almost all SOEs. According to a retrospective panel survey of 683 firms in 11 cities analysed by Garnaut et al. (2003), 86 per cent of all SOEs had been through this process by the end of 2001. It took various forms, including internal restructuring, corporatization and public listing of shares, sale, lease, joint ventures, and bankruptcy. Among the surveyed mid- and large-scale SOEs that were restructured, 13 per cent had gone through bankruptcy or debt-equity swaps, 28 per cent were sold or leased out to private owners, 27 per cent

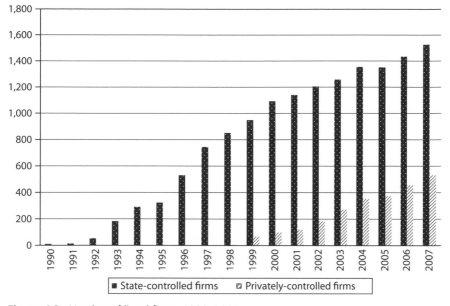

Figure 4.3. Number of listed firms, 1990–2007

Source: China Securities Regulatory Commission.

introduced employee shareholding, 20 per cent underwent internal restructuring, 8 per cent had ownership diversification, including public offerings and private placement to outside investors, and the remaining 4 per cent became joint ventures. In more than 70 per cent of these cases, *gaizhi* involved the transfer of at least a portion of ownership from the state to private hands (Garnaut et al. 2003). Case study 1 of the former SOE, white-goods producer Haier, provides an illustration of the stages of SOE reform that culminated with the restructuring of most SOEs.

However, this also meant that a new 'reform with losers' (Naughton 2007) phase began as millions of employees lost their previously protected jobs in SOEs, urban collective enterprises, and government and public service units. Layoffs began to surge in 1995, and in the four-year period from 1996 to 1999, some seven million workers were laid off annually (Dong and Xu 2008). Between 1993 and 2004, in excess of 50 million employees had been made redundant from the SOE sector.

By the end of the process in the early 2000s, China had become a system dominated by non-state ownership in need of governance. The old corporate laws formulated for SOEs were adapted to govern the newly privatized SOEs as well as the fast growing private firms in a market increasingly characterized by diversified and dispersed shareholders. Laws became paramount, and the 2000s was characterized by a slew of laws and regulations which were facially neutral. Still, though, in some respects, they reflected government policy, including towards SOEs. In other words, although China was no longer an economy dominated by the state-owned sector, it retained control over the development of enterprises and the corporate sector. The evidence is once again found in the laws which enacted and embodied state dictate.

4.4 **Dispersed ownership and the enactment of securities laws**

With the opening of the Shanghai and Shenzhen stock exchanges in the early 1990s, listed companies were, with considerable restrictions, able to raise funds from domestic and foreign investors. The primary initial purpose of opening the two stock exchanges was to raise funds for SOE restructuring and to foster a more effective management system. They also illustrated how securities regulations were used to facilitate SOE reform, but were also a vital part of the emerging corporate law landscape.

Perhaps the seminal decision in this process was the edict in 1999 of the Central Committee that SOEs should attempt to diversify their shareholders. In this sense, the role of a non-public-owned economy with a private sector was formally confirmed. Undoubtedly, at the conceptual level, the reform's emphasis on leasing SOEs to legal identities, and the diversification of ownership, raised a fundamental question of what form of economic system China actually is.

A pertinent example of this is the ability of SOEs to undergo IPOs. Before 2001, the question of whether a Chinese company could undertake an IPO was determined largely by administrative fiat. The functioning of regulatory decentralization depended upon the administered system of stock issuance. The process of listing in the 1990s was based on a quota system (see e.g. Du and Xu 2009). Provincial governments and ministries conceived annual plans for issuing shares and then submitted them to the central government for approval. The central government determined the total number of shares to be issued in the country and then allocated stock issuance quotas. As part of this process, regional governments or ministries negotiated the size of the quotas for their regions or ministries with the central government. When they reached an agreement, the central government and the CSRC then decided on the allocation of quotas to different provinces and ministries within the bounds of the total stock issuance quota.

Thus, when an SOE wanted to go public, it had to seek permission from the local government and/or its affiliated central government ministries, which receive an IPO quota from the CSRC. There are no explicit rules governing quota allocations. This process opened SOE reform to considerable political economy influences. In this sense, the quota system of share issuance was designed by the central government to control the size of financial markets, to maintain balance among the regions, and to preserve the dominant position of state ownership in listed companies.

Critical to the idea of how this worked was the concept of 'legal persons' in China. The share structure of China's listed companies is quite unique as for most companies only a small part of the shares can be traded on the stock exchange. Again, the shares of listed companies are typically divided into state, legal person, and public shares. As state and legal person categories of shares cannot be traded on the stock exchanges, their transfer required special approval from the China Securities Regulatory Commission.

Public shares are tradable shares issued to the public and are mostly held by individual shareholders. Legal person shares are owned by domestic institutions, most of which are partially owned by the central or local government. There can be several legal person shareholders in a listed firm. 'Legal persons' are typically business agencies or enterprises of local governments that helped in starting up the public company either by giving permission to operate or by allowing resources under their control to be used for the start-up.

Thus, in the stock issuance process, the state is usually represented by a provincial branch of the state asset management bureau, which represents the state in numerous other companies. This significantly reduces the state government's monitoring ability. Moreover, unlike state ownership, many legal persons have close business connections to the 'share issue privatized' firms. Many legal persons are the SOEs from which these firms were carved out, and some have come about through a debt-equity swap. As part of the restructuring policy to solve the SOE debt problem, the government allowed SOEs to settle debts among themselves by swapping debts for company shares.

As the problem of SOE debt became more entrenched, and, even though the market was immature, the number of listed companies, trading volume, and the total market capitalization grew quickly during the 1990s, and the impetus for the government to act grew significantly (see Figure 4.4).

The central government promulgated the Securities Law at the end of 1998. Although China had previously had lower-level regulations on securities, this statute finally provided national (or NPC-level) rules. Moreover, with the 1993 Company Law, the Securities Law marked the completion of the 'laws-on-the-books' concerning corporation formation, public offering, and securities trading in China. However, injured investors could not rush to court to file lawsuits for damage recovery or to force a corporation's board and/or management to take shareholder-interest-maximizing measures (Clarke 2003c). Although numerous restrictions were outlined by the Securities Law, including a segregation of securities, banking, and insurance businesses,

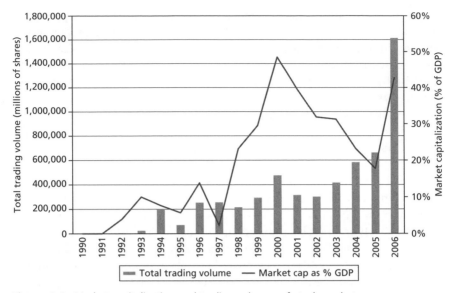

Figure 4.4. Market capitalization and trading volumes of stock markets

Source: China Securities Regulatory Commission.

a prohibition on the over-the-counter market sales, and prohibitions on the widespread use of financial derivatives, it was still a considerable legal step forward.

Like most laws, it also required a regulator to issue the implementing regulations. The Chinese Securities Regulatory Commission was granted 'teeth' at the same time. The CSRC has the power to regulate and supervise securities issuers, as well as to investigate, and impose penalties for, illegal activities related to securities and futures. The CSRC is empowered to issue Opinions or Guideline Opinions, non-legally binding guidance for publicly traded corporations. In other words, it held the authority expected of a securities regulator to oversee the markets, such that the Securities Law cannot be viewed as negligible, though it clearly embodies the policy aims of reform.

Accompanying this was a considerable shift in the government's attitude towards ownership. During most of the 1990s, the limit on the private ownership stake in China's listed firms stood at one-third. In 1999, the Ministry of Finance permitted the state-owned shares to be reduced to 51 per cent. In 2000, the government decided to abandon the quota system for listing. The first non-quota IPO appeared in 2001, heralding the first appearance of private firms on the stock market.

In 2005, the Chinese authorities announced the gradual floating of non-tradable state-owned shares for all domestically listed companies, paving the way for privatization through SIP. All listed companies were required to propose a reform plan to transfer the status of non-tradable shares and to develop a compensation package for existing tradable shareholders. In addition, the authorities announced plans to allow foreign firms to acquire substantial holdings of tradable shares through the market, up to an initial limit of 10 per cent of the target's stock. The central purpose of this reform is to convert non-tradable shares to tradable shares at a price acceptable to minority investors. By the 2010s, it is expected that most of the shares on the Chinese bourses will be tradable and the plethora of regulations passed in the 2000s begin to provide the type of governance expected for publicly traded firms. By 2009, the number of tradable shares outweighed non-tradable shares. Although both increased, the expansion of the former in 2009 was notable as seen in Table 4.1. Nevertheless, the opacity of the ultimate shareholding structure of the listed firms, many of which are subsidiaries of SOEs, continues to cast a shadow over the stock exchange.

The securities regulations adopted to facilitate the share issue privatization policy were a significant step towards using laws, even governing SOEs, to regulate firms and issue guidance for shareholders and investors. In many respects, the securities laws were not symbolic or instrumental but could be viewed as serving the more usual functions of law, that is, to establish the institutional guidelines for the market. The choice of SIP led the Chinese government to adopt significant corporate laws and regulations, which in turn legitimized the corporatization reforms.

International listing took this a step further and also addressed the issue of opacity among listed Chinese firms. The importance of signalling that they are well-governed firms has been argued to be the reason as to why SOEs list abroad in stock exchanges in New York, London, and Hong Kong. With higher disclosure and transparency requirements, 'blue chip' firms like Air China and the Bank of China undertook dual listings in China and overseas, perhaps to signal that they are competitive and can meet the quality expectations of international investors and therefore raise capital on global markets. This, in turn, argues Sun and Tobin (2009), further pushes Chinese domestic regulations along. In any case, the diversification of ownership and the increasing utilization of securities laws developed concurrently with the first significant ownership reform in China.

Table 4.1. The dual system of shares (in billion RMB)

	2005	2006	2007	2008	2009
Tradable shares	1,063	2,500	9,306	4,521	15,125
Non-tradable shares	2,180	6,440	23,407	7,615	9,268
Total	3,243	8,940	32,714	12,136	24,393

Source: CSRC.

4.5 **Governance by corporate laws in the 2000s**

The 2000s witnessed two competing forces. On the one hand, foreign competition and the growth of the non-state sector cried out for effective corporate laws. On the other hand, the state-owned enterprises remained the privileged vestibules for China's industrial growth strategy to underpin its continuing economic development. This meant that significant and much-needed laws were passed in the areas of mergers and acquisitions (M&A), corporate governance, bankruptcy, and anti-trust, but SOEs were often privileged, and active industrial policies were undertaken to ensure the continuing reach of the state.

For instance, SASAC, a State Council body, takes the role of beneficial owner of all state assets and is responsible for the supervision of the very largest SOEs. Exercising direct control over about 100 large SOEs from Beijing, it has branches throughout the country. SASAC was given a remit, and the promise of considerable public funds, to ensure that these SOEs became 'globally competitive' businesses. This led to some tensions. The foundation of these acts and the creation of SASAC showed the 'two-tier' strategy utilized by the Chinese government. The first part in this strategy was the encouragement of greater utilization of the stock market by Chinese enterprises. The second tier of this strategy was the promotion of the 'national champion' strategy, and the cementing of the status of SOEs in the Chinese economy. In 2004, SASAC noted that of the fourteen mainland Chinese enterprises listed in the Fortune 500, eight were under its direct supervision, mainly in the heavy industry and telecommunications sectors. The first mention of an overt policy to lift this number occurred in 2006.

Although the policy was as yet unmentioned on SASAC official documentation, in 2006, SASAC announced that it would maintain controlling positions in some crucial SOEs (the so-called 'national champions'). These sectors included armaments, power generation/distribution, oil/petrochemicals, telecommunications, coal, aviation, and shipping. SASAC's goal is to maintain 'between thirty and fifty internationally competitive conglomerates with intellectual property and famous brand names'. Case study 2 of the national oil companies (NOCs) highlights the state ownership and consolidation of a strategic industry that has become global. By contrast, case study 3 presents the case of the aviation industry as an instance of the challenges of promoting a high-tech sector despite active industrial policies for economic development.

Alongside this retrenchment of state control, governance by corporate laws and not just policies was gathering pace in an increasingly decentralized and commercial enterprise sector. The aims of the state, though, continued to be manifested in the laws. In 2002 after WTO-related opening, the CSRC announced the guidelines for takeovers and mergers of listed companies, including a 10 per cent limit on the stake that a group of foreign investors can hold in a Chinese company. This was later raised to 25 per cent. Nevertheless, increasing quantities of state-owned shares were sold to non-state entities, including, since 2002, qualified foreign-based institutional investors such as Goldman Sachs, Deutsche Bank, and Merrill Lynch. Accordingly, China's first M&A law was passed in 2003 to provide guidelines. The restriction on foreign control, limiting foreign shareholding, would be enacted through the M&A law for non-listed firms, just as the CSRC rules govern listed ones. They would, in effect, protect SOEs from hostile takeovers whilst promoting the policy of learning from foreign firms but not allowing them to dominate the Chinese market.

The government was often deliberate in targeting these well-known institutional investors, noting that they were 'strategic partners' designed to bring knowledge of corporate governance techniques with them. Many of the larger investors were given seats on the board, such as Goldman Sachs with the float of ICBC, the biggest of the four state-owned commercial banks. Bringing them in highlighted the need for laws to govern the increasingly competitive corporate sector, especially after greater opening with China's WTO accession in December 2001. Case study 4 illustrates the corporatization and listing of ICBC as an instance of the retained and restructured SOEs, namely, the largest of the SCBs.

The year 2005 further saw considerable reform to the Company Law and the Securities Law. The two laws were originally enacted with the purpose of facilitating the reform of financially troubled SOEs. Very little of this legislation covered private companies or offered investor protection. In this sense, the role of these two laws has changed from serving the corporatization of SOEs to providing a legal framework for all market participants and encouraging investment.

These revisions caused the Company Law to become a more general corporate statute by deleting many, but not all, of the provisions of the 1993 law that gave special privileges or protection to SOEs. As Wu (2007) observes, about fourteen Articles in the old law specially designed for SOEs were aborted by the new law, although the special section on wholly state-owned companies remains. The reforms were notable. For instance, the 1993 Company Law allowed only SOEs to issue corporate bonds, a regulation removed in the 2005 iteration.

The 2005 reforms also saw a considerable softening in attitude towards individual firm autonomy. The law includes relaxed incorporation requirements and the initial capital requirements for new firms. It gave to all firms more discretionary and enabling rules, and expanded corporate power.

The 2006 Enterprise Bankruptcy Law perhaps best illustrates China's two-tier strategy. Its promulgation means that for the first time bankruptcy of all legal persons in China is governed by one uniform bankruptcy law. Previously, the 1986 Interim Enterprise Bankruptcy Law applied only to SOEs, and the bankruptcy of private enterprises and foreign-invested enterprises was governed by a different body of often contradictory or inconsistent laws. This law finally provided an exit strategy for foreign investors. Notably, the Chinese government exempted approximately 2,100 SOEs from the new law, forcing them to close following policy-arranged bankruptcy procedures instead. Law, in this sense, reflected market developments but it also embodied policy by exempting SOEs once again.

The same can be said for the 2007 Anti-Monopoly Law, another pillar of the corporate legal system. It is facially neutral and follows general competition policy principles found in the European Union and the United States in limiting the exercise of undue monopoly power, limiting market concentration, and promoting competition. However, as with the other statutes, it exempts SOEs on the grounds of public interest in some instances.

Therefore, the dual purposes of preserving SOEs and governing a competitive, corporate sector are evident in the laws passed in the 2000s. The various laws are designed to govern a market economy but have carve-outs for SOEs so that China can simultaneously maintain its industrial policies geared at achieving economic growth. Laws, as instrumentation to legitimize policy, have morphed into laws as the indicators of policy mandates. In essence, laws that have been enacted alongside SOE reform are not only significant but also reveal telling signs of where reforms are headed and the limits of market development at each stage of China's transition. It seems as true in the 2000s as it was in the 1980s and 1990s for SOEs even as the laws and regulations are evolving into a rule of law for the non-state sector.

4.6 Conclusion

Legal reforms legitimized SOE reform, rather than create property rights and contract rights to dictate the restructuring of such enterprises in the classic economic mode. Such rights were rather assumed through the political structure, but a growing market economy requires further signals. Thus, legal reforms can be viewed as signposts as well as present an understandable façade to investors, including in world markets. They embodied SOE reform in the 1980s through dictates that operationalized some of the policy goals of injecting market-based incentives by creating 'legal persons'; in the 1990s, they effectuated the corporatization policy as the instrument for governance of a mixed state/economy; and in the 2000s, they served as tools to promote SOEs whilst at the same time supporting the burgeoning corporate sector.

Rather than overlook laws, missing them in the picture of SOE reforms leads to incompleteness. The corporate transformation in China was not built on policy and administrative measures alone. Laws do not dictate SOE reforms, but they do legitimize the transformation of SOEs into corporations—albeit some remain in state ownership—but all are operating in an increasingly commercialized economy with a need for well-defined legal forms that are governed by a corporate legal system.

Case study 1

THREE DECADES OF STATE-OWNED ENTERPRISE REFORM—HAIER

The decade of the 1980s witnessed a significant effort to reform SOEs. It was also the beginning of an infusion of foreign direct investment (FDI) into China, much of it in the form of Chinese-foreign joint venture (JV) enterprises as China began to open its economy to foreign capital after decades of isolation. During the initial wave of investment, FDI was closely regulated by the government and, for the most part, JV contracts between Chinese and foreign firms were the predominant form of FDI. Early FDI policy was thus part of the SOE reform effort at the very start.

These early JVs were between Chinese state-owned enterprises (SOEs) and foreign firms. The partnership allowed China to develop a non-state sector and inject profit incentives into SOEs during a time when their inefficiencies were increasingly evident. The control over the FDI vehicle allowed the Chinese government to limit the incursion of foreign firms into China's market and prevent their dominance in the domestic economy at a time when Chinese firms were not as competitive due to lack of efficiency and economies of scale.

This intertwining of FDI policy and SOE reforms can be seen in the case of one of the most successful state-owned enterprises to emerge from this process, Haier. This case study will outline the development of Haier from a provincial, state-owned factory dependent upon German technology to its current iteration as a major global home appliance player. Much of Haier's early success was due to its ability to capitalize on the market incentives proffered to SOEs, including the ability to utilize foreign investment and technology. Its future, though, will be dependent on becoming a market innovator, rather than an imitator with its own branded products and no longer a homogenous seller of white goods like refrigerators. In other words, the same trajectory that all reformed SOEs must follow.

History of Haier

The 1920s saw the private construction of a factory to build refrigerators in China's coastal city, Qingdao. Following the Communist revolution in 1949, the factory was taken over by the government during the 1950s. Under government control, however, the factory went into a long period of decline. By the early 1980s, its production had slowed to a trickle. The company, then known as Qingdao Refrigerator Company, had been losing money and was close to bankruptcy. As Haier itself later said, the company, where production struggled to top eighty refrigerators a month, consisted of little more than 'a row of shabby buildings containing several lathes'.

The early 1980s also marked the first opening of the Chinese economy to the international market. A large number of foreign companies travelled to China seeking investment opportunities. One of these was Germany's Liebherr Haushaltgerate, a leading appliance maker in that country. Liebherr proposed a partnership with the Qingdao Refrigerator Company, including the sale of Liebherr's refrigerator technology. The owner of the Qingdao Refrigerator company, the city of Qingdao, agreed to the partnership, under a typical JV agreement whereby the foreign partner provides technology and capital, while the Chinese partner supplies labour, land, and the plant.

Technology alone was not enough to rescue the company, however. Instead, the Qingdao company's rebirth relied on the arrival of a new managing director, Zhang Ruimin, in 1984. Zhang, the son of a Qingdao textile worker, had joined the municipal government in the 1960s, when the Cultural Revolution had shut down the country's school system. Zhang, an avid reader, studied on his own, focusing particularly on Japanese and Western management techniques (Wen 2007). After the Qingdao plant's managing director left the company in 1984, Zhang became the factory's leader.

Zhang was given considerable freedom by the Qingdao government to introduce his own policies, typifying the mid-1980s reforms which were geared at granting managers more discretion to incentivize performance (the Contract Responsibility System). Zhang was granted latitude by the government due firstly to the sheer precariousness of the situation as Haier had large amounts of debts and was a drain upon the state. Zhang's previous status working for the Qingdao municipal government for 20 years also endowed him with credibility with the local government.

In 1986, the plant made a loss of 1.47 million RMB. Zhang then had to find loans in order to pay the salaries of 600 employees. As a loss-making local but not key enterprise, it was impossible to get credit from regional state-owned banks. But, perhaps due to his previous service with local government and connections there, he was allowed to use his own contacts to bring in external capital (Young and DeWoskin 1998). One of Zhang's first moves was to turn to friends in Qingdao's outlying and cash-rich agricultural cooperatives for loans in order to pay some of the back wages owed to the company's workers. Zhang also bought a company bus and began providing transportation to workers in order to relieve commuting costs.

Zhang recognized that simply introducing Liebherr's technology would not be enough to turn the company around. He introduced his own management system (6S, an adaptation of the Japanese 5S model with an added inducement to improve safety). The installation of Liebherr's equipment and technology was accompanied by a new and rigorous commitment to quality. Workers were expected to follow the protocols, at the risk of being exposed to public criticisms—and ultimate dismissal, once a rarity in China. To improve product quality, Zhang also ruled that if defective products were produced, 20 per cent would be deducted from the salaries of all the employees involved.

Growth of the Haier mythology

This introduction of a quality system was the formalization of an already instituted commitment to building quality and a brand, a concept new to socialized economies. In 1985, of the 400 or so finished refrigerators at the factory, nearly 20 per cent had failed inspection. Taking the seventy-six flawed refrigerators, he ordered the names of the workers who were responsible to be placed on them, and demolished them with sledgehammers. Zhang punished himself as well, foregoing a month's salary to take responsibility for poor management. The entire process was photographed and recorded, and the sledgehammers kept as a reminder to employees. Perhaps more significantly, the incident was widely publicized.

Similarly, when a farmer in Sichuan province was said to have broken his Haier washing machine by using it to scrub his yams, Haier engineers not only fixed the machine, but also, to ensure customer satisfaction, created machines that could wash yams and shrimp (Wen 2007).

Policy environment creating opportunities

These changes occurred during the late 1980s at a time of when businesses began vying for the top spot in China's refrigerator market. As China's economy began lifting living standards and developing a consumerist middle class, an era of price competition was slowly beginning.

Concomitantly, the government's industrial policy began to change. A cluster of policies increased the autonomy of enterprise managers, reduced emphasis on planned quotas, allowed enterprises to produce goods outside the plan for sale on the market, and permitted enterprises to experiment with the use of bonuses to reward higher productivity (Naughton 1995).

The most significant of these for Haier was that enterprise managers gradually gained greater control over their work units, including the right to hire and fire, although the process required endless struggles with bureaucrats and Party cadres. Other measures were introduced to improve worker incentives: instead of the permanent employment enjoyed by most urban employees, contracts were introduced which could, at least in theory, be terminated.

The practice of remitting taxes on profits and retaining the balance became universal by the 1980s Contract Responsibility System, increasing the incentive for enterprises to maximize profits and substantially adding to their autonomy. A change of potentially equal importance was a shift in the source of investment funds from government budget allocations, which carried no interest and did not have to be repaid, to interest-bearing bank loans around 1985. As of 1987, the interest rate charged on such loans was still too low to serve as a check on unproductive investments, but the mechanism was in place.

Haier was in the right place at the right time. It was a good time to be in consumer durables, as shown by the 20 per cent industry annual growth from 1986 to 1999. Moreover, as an early market entrant, Haier was able to reap the benefits of cheap access to capital from local governments looking to stimulate production. It was then able to start making profits just as the government was taking that away and starting to check unproductive investments. Moreover, when the central fiscal crisis hit, Haier's remittances to the government became all the more useful.

With its success, the municipal government asked it to take over some of the city's other ailing appliance makers. In 1988, the company assumed control of Qingdao Electroplating Company (making microwaves) and in 1991, also took over Qingdao Air Conditioner Plant and Qingdao Freezer. In conjunction with this horizontal expansion, Haier also began to expand its operations within the refrigerator industry, including making its own refrigerators.

This consolidation period was also a time when Haier's production techniques became more flexible and when they began to use a rapid product turnover to build a competitive advantage. In 1989, for instance, sales of one model of refrigerator were high in Beijing but underperformed in Shanghai. Through market research, Haier discovered that Shanghai residents then had crowded living conditions, and that there was little space for a large refrigerator. As a result, Haier designed a smaller refrigerator only for the Shanghai market, and sales subsequently surged (Liu and Li 2002)

At the same time, foreign trade procedures were greatly eased, allowing individual enterprises and administrative departments to engage in direct negotiations with foreign firms. A wide range of cooperation, trading, and credit arrangements with foreign firms were legalized so that China could enter the mainstream of international trade.

Haier, seizing this opportunity, then utilized its growing connections to the Party and reputation for quality to make a major push for expansion through building far greater capacity. In 1992, Qingdao expropriated 800 mu (15 mu = one hectare) of land in the high- and new technological zone in the eastern part of Qingdao and set up a modern industrial park there. This park, named the 'National-level High and New Technology Industrial Development Zone of Qingdao' (one of the early HTDZs or High-Technology Development Zones that sprang up in the 1990s) was established with the approval of the State Council in May of 1992. Haier itself then set up four industrial parks in Qingdao, including the 49 hectare Haier Industrial Park which was considered sufficiently high-tech that leading Japanese technology firms, Sanyo and Mitsubishi, set up factories within it.

This push for expansion was aided by an influx of capital. Although Haier, as a government-controlled body, was barred from the stock exchange, it found its way onto the Shanghai Stock Exchange in 1993 through the listing of its subsidiary, Qingdao Haier Refrigerator, as part of the quotas extended to provinces where local authorities chose SOEs to become publicly traded. The listing of a subsidiary of a SOE was common practice and political links facilitated IPOs during a time when the state controlled the entrants onto the stock markets. The company raised nearly 370 million RMB in the offering, which was used to increase its production capacity and to produce refrigerators destined for the export market.

This overt desire for export market growth was stimulated partly by a changing domestic market. Although it is estimated that the annual sales of refrigerators grew by rapidly until 1994 (reaching 28.1 per cent annual growth in 1994), the industry immediately faced the problem of over-capacity once domestic retail consumption growth slowed. Production capacity of all refrigerator manufacturers in China was estimated to be 20 million units, whilst in 1995 total domestic sales were 13.1 million units. By 1997, Haier and other manufacturers found themselves sitting on escalating inventories of finished goods, which began to erode their new found economic viability.

The saturation of the Chinese home appliances markets with intensifying competition during the period of market liberalization of the late 1980s was a major impetus for this export focus. Following diminishing margins in the early to mid 1990s, price wars broke out one after another in various home appliance markets. At the end of 2000, Haier's domestic market shares of refrigerators, freezers, air conditioners, and washing machines had reached 33 per cent, 42 per cent, 31 per cent and 31 per cent, respectively. The potential for further development in the domestic market was seen as being highly limited.

This growingly precarious competitive domestic environment led to Haier engaging in a diversification drive during the 1990s in order to protect itself from downturns in any of its core product categories. Part of the company's diversification came through a series of acquisitions of struggling Chinese companies, often at the request of the municipal governments. Such was the case with the company's acquisition of its chief rival in Qingdao, Red Star Electric Appliance Factory, in 1995. That purchase was followed in 1997 by the takeover of failing Huangshan Electronics Group, a maker of televisions, in 1997.

By the end of the 1990s, Haier's diversification, for the most part, was completed. With an array of products ranging from its core white goods to mobile telephones and personal computing systems, the company faced the reverse possibility of having diversified too widely. Nonetheless, the company continued to play a role as one of China's fastest-growing firms, with sales topping $2.3 billion in 1998. By then, the company had captured 40 per cent of refrigerator sales, nearly 36 per cent of washing machine sales, more than 47 per cent of all freezer sales, and nearly 37 per cent of air conditioners sold in China.

This domestic stability allowed Haier to begin to devote increasingly more focus to export activities. Haier described this process as 'after lighting up the East, then turning around to light up the West' (Haier 2008). Haier drew up an export development strategy, known as 'taking on the difficult one first and then the easy one': this meant going first to countries that follow the strictest standard requirements, then to developing countries. First, Haier went to Germany to sell its refrigerators branded 'Made in China'. In 1992, the result of a performance comparison between Haier refrigerators and German-made refrigerators was so positive that Germans signed contracts right on the spot for 20,000 Haier refrigerators. Moreover, the increasing, though controlled, entry of global home appliance manufacturers into the Chinese market also compelled Haier's international expansion. Since China joined the WTO in 2001, almost all of its international competitors have invested in China, establishing wholly foreign-owned companies. In 2007, Panasonic, Siemens, LG, Sanyo, Whirlpool, and Samsung all entered the 'Top 10' in market sales in washing machines in China. All of these brands now have Chinese offices. Many of these brands also have long histories of dealing with the Chinese market. Panasonic, Siemens, and Samsung also had high profile joint venture projects prior to selling their own branded products (Young and

DeWoskin 1998). The best defensive strategy for Haier would be to have a presence in its competitors' home markets.

It would have been highly difficult to embrace these export opportunities without a permissive and indeed encouraging stance from the central government. The reward for excellent performance in China was the opportunity to enter overseas markets. Haier's initiative in internationalization was encouraged and supported by the Chinese government. Being an international player gained Haier some special conditions that other Chinese companies could not obtain. For instance, Haier had already been approved to establish a financial company, to be the majority shareholder of a regional commercial bank, and to form a joint venture with an American insurance company. Without its active pursuit of internationalization as well as a dominant position in home appliance sectors, it would normally be impossible for a manufacturer to get approval to enter the financial sector.

This push for international markets was matched by a push for greater levels of research and development (R&D) in an effort to create a company with the capacity to develop its own products. In 1998, Haier invested 500 million RMB to build the Haier Research Institute to develop 'ahead-of-time' new products. This was again sanctioned by the central government. In 1999, President Jiang Zemin himself came on an inspection tour of Haier, after seeing the Haier Research Institute. Externally, Haier has set up overseas development design branches in Tokyo, Lyons, Los Angeles, and Amsterdam and four other cities, whilst signing cooperation and technological cooperation agreements with well-established multinational corporations such as Toshiba, Philip, Motorola, and Sanyo.

This R&D push is clearly seen by Haier as being seminal to its future ability to grow, largely due to shrinking margins in the domestic market. An example is the fall in the prices of air conditioners, a mainstay product sector for Haier. Data from 2005 showed that the sales breakdown by product across the entire Haier group of companies was air conditioners 50.0 per cent, refrigerators 29.6 per cent, and freezers, showcases, etc., accounting for 7.1 per cent. Yet, in 2005, Haier's gross profit ratio for its mainstay air conditioner line was 11.1 per cent, which was low compared to average profit margins such as 16.3 per cent for refrigerators, 15.7 per cent for freezers, etc., and 18.9 per cent for rice cookers and other small consumer electronics.

Samsung, in contrast, enjoys high profitability and is supported by its semiconductor division. Viewed by non-consolidated settlement data, the overall ratio of operating profit to sales is 20.8 per cent. Semiconductors, however, which account for 31.6 per cent of sales, generate 62.2 per cent of the company's operating profits, with the semiconductor division's ratio of net profit to sales rising to 41.0 per cent. For Samsung, the source of this profit stream lies in the ratio of R&D spending to sales, which at 8.0 per cent is higher than both Haier (4.8 per cent) and Sharp (6.9 per cent) (Muroi 2005).

To rectify this problem, along with setting standards, Haier quickened its pace in obtaining patents. In 2005, it applied for 241 patents, which was an increase of over 100 per cent compared with the previous year. Take the company's detergent-free washing machine, a high-tech product developed by Haier itself. The company holds thirty-two patents, where seventeen are patents for the more innovative category of invention as opposed to process or design patents. Then, in September 2006, it started a two month marketing campaign in more than 100 cities to promote the concept of a detergent-free washer, which has been rolled out worldwide, though with limited impact.

Hence, Haier has utilized IPRs as a tool to compete in the global market. In line with the company's strategy, Haier set up its own IPR management department in 1992. Apart from this boost in R&D, Haier began to leverage its links to capital markets in order to prepare for overseas expansion. With the support of the Chinese government, Haier entered into the financial sector, and acquired majority shareholding in a regional bank. This, however, has proved to be highly controversial. Other problems can be seen in the failed bid for the US's Maytag in 2004. Maytag had originally agreed to be acquired by Ripplewood Holdings, a New York investment firm. But, in a statement a month later, Maytag said it was considering a preliminary bid from Bain Capital, Blackstone Group, and Haier America of $16 a share, $2 a share more than the offer from Ripplewood. However, in doing so, Haier clearly ruffled a number of feathers. The unsuccessful bid for Maytag was reminiscent of the also failed, and highly controversial, bid for the US oil company Unocal, by China's CNOOC Ltd. Some of the problems with this bid were associated with Haier's corporate structure. Haier has two listings on stock exchanges; however, both of these are subsidiary companies, of which Haier has over 280. The importance of each of the subsidiaries to Haier's total business is unknown, and as Table 1 shows, Haier's total market capitalization is thus impossible to ascertain.

Table 1. Haier's listed companies as of 2007

	Stock code	Stock market number	Initial sale price (RMB)	Shares released	Market capitalization (RMB)
Qingdao Haier Co., Ltd	SHA	600690	12.65	1.3 billion	16.93 billion
Haier Electronics Group Co., Ltd	HKG	1169	1.2	2 billion	2.23 billion

The reason for this opacity is also indicative of the SIP process for SOEs. Listed company groups in China are usually headed by a holding company (*jituan gongsi*, directly translated as 'group company'). These holding companies are usually controlled and majority-owned by a state-controlled company, which are given names such as a government asset management company, an investment company, etc. The listed companies are usually majority-owned by the holding company directly, and thus, are indirectly controlled by the government. This distortion comes from the separation of ownership rights and control rights, and the holding company or the asset management company is thought to be the channel for the government. Moreover, there were suspicions that Haier inflated the profit and revenue numbers of a Shanghai-listed subsidiary by shifting assets between the parent and the subsidiary. The group's finances were viewed as a black box. The Haier Group is government-owned, but Zhang runs it with a free hand. It is made up of dozens of companies, only one of which is listed on the Shanghai stock market. Haier's culture of secrecy may hurt it as it moves overseas and pursues a US stock listing.

In spite of the failure to buy Maytag, the idea clearly showed Haier's strategic direction. In the US, Haier's inexpensive refrigerators and washing machines have generally been sold only by discount chains such as Wal-Mart. Taking over Maytag would have bought it a household brand name and given it a nationwide distribution network that could vastly expand its sales. Like the rest of Haier's trajectory, this strategic move again typified China's 'going global' strategy, where the state aims to create Chinese multinationals, granting permission to select companies to expand overseas.

Much of this centres on a belief in the power of brands. Branding, to Zhang, remains the critical factor, which in China has to be achieved not only in economic but also political terms. Zhang himself has an unusually high profile compared to other business leaders. He was an alternate member of the 16th National Congress of the Communist Party of China, and enjoys the privileges of a deputy minister. Zhang has received more international press and attention than any other large enterprise manager in China. He has sought this, having read the works of high-profile international CEOs and recognized the importance of putting a 'face' on a global company. This interest in external exposure is itself a sharp turn from normal Chinese manager behaviour. From his building of a semi-cult of personality around his obsession with quality, to the modern-day use of his public profile to discuss the need for internationalism in his workers, Zhang clearly believes that his ability to intertwine his own personal characteristics and message with that of the brand gives Haier a competitive advantage commensurate with the risk of being caught in the shifting sands of Chinese politics.

Conclusion

Haier's story epitomizes SOEs reform since 1979. It is a state-owned enterprise that has become a successful firm amidst a competitive market that started off with an injection of foreign technology. Its board has considerable Communist Party influence, and its CEO is well connected politically, yet the company undertakes highly commercial strategies, such as branding and R&D.

There are, however, a number of problems with such a reformed SOE. Haier's links with the government and opaque financial status caused considerable tension within foreign investors, as shown by the failed Maytag bid. In spite of Haier's commitment to research and branding, its products still suffer from low profit margins. It competes in largely niche or low-price overseas markets and has not established itself as a leading brand outside of China.

Haier demonstrates how SOEs have managed to become profit-oriented without becoming privatized. Its development will be a harbinger of the future of partially reformed SOEs.

Case study 2

STATE OWNERSHIP AND CONSOLIDATION—NATIONAL OIL COMPANIES

Dr Kun-Chin Lin, King's China Institute and School of Social Sciences and Public Policy, King's College, London

As one of the world's largest oil producers, China remained self-sufficient in domestic supply of crude oil from 1965 to 1993. The Chinese oil industry has been nationally owned and administered by agencies of the State Council in the post-Mao era.[1] This case study provides an overview of industrial policies, enterprise reforms, and pricing policies that have affected the performance and organization of oilfields. Increasingly in the 1990s, macroeconomic fluctuations and external price shocks had prompted shifts in government–industry relations and interindustry relations between the upstream (crude oil exploration and production) and downstream (refining, sales, and distribution) sectors. The current market structure and corporate organization is derived from the 1998–2000 radical restructuring of the national oil companies, which represented a particular conception of marketization based on the centralization of the state's ownership and financial controls.

China National Petroleum Corporation as an administrative company: 1978–1998

The oil industry received top billing in reform policies as the cash cows that would earn the foreign exchange and supply energy inputs for the heavy industrialization programmes of Mao's immediate successor Hua Guofeng.[2] While Deng Xiaoping and other reform leaders attempted to strike a balance between energy conservation and exploitation, they did not fundamentally alter the politicized role of domestic oil producers as a revenue generator for the government and as a primary source of cheap inputs for petrochemical production and energy necessary for rapid economic growth. Through the 1990s, the upstream sector experienced slow productivity gains but steady output increases.

The China National Petroleum Corporation (CNPC) was established in 1988 as a nominally independent, wholly state-owned 'administrative company' (*xingzhengxing gongsi*) upon the abolition of the Ministry of Petroleum. It represented an organizational façade that extended command economic planning into separating functions of onshore oilfields, refineries and petrochemical plants, offshore oilfields, and foreign trading. With the dismantling of the short-lived Ministry of Energy in 1992, CNPC and China Petrochemical Corporation—more commonly known as Sinopec, the administrative company for downstream operations—were left in a formal, freestanding status.[3] Coordination of interministerial interests and resource exchanges in a bureaucratic landscape of overlapping jurisdictions effectively left the final authority in the hands of the State Planning Commission, which set investment and quantity targets for the Five Year Plans as well as the bandwidth of domestic prices for crude oil and finished oil products.[4] In practice, industrial governance was far messier than a top-down affair. First, no different than other Chinese state-owned enterprises, oilfields were accountable to provincial and local governments. These governments held leverage in daily decision-making, personnel decisions, land and input allocation, and access to regional product and labour markets. In addition, provincial governments operated cartels in the distribution, wholesale, and retail of finished oil products.

Second, CNPC showed weak capacity in coordinating its subsidiary oilfields and affiliated production and technical service units. The central institutions affecting managerial incentives were: 1) the cadre appointment and promotion systems of the Chinese Communist Party, and 2) the managerial contract responsibility system (CRS) that started in the mid-1980s. CRS devolved microeconomic decisions from central planners to state-appointed directors of petroleum administrative bureaus, resulting in the latter experiencing enhanced autonomy, entrepreneurialism, and sensitivity towards local political and economic imperatives. The decentralized approach to industrial governance worked better for the downstream producers which pursued an aggressive expansion of production capacity for mass petrochemicals. The oilfield executives remained frustrated by administratively depressed crude prices and heavy taxation, and channelled their energy towards developing sideline businesses, exploiting arbitrage opportunities availed by the multi-track pricing system, and padding the wages of their workers. As a result, investment in oilfield exploration and equipment upgrades lagged, and oil-fields ran up heavy debt burdens.[5]

Impact of marketization on investment and competition

External market shocks triggered rounds of organizational reform in the Chinese oil and petrochemical sectors.[6] In 1993 and 1998, global crude prices crashed, leading to massive losses for the upstream, with dire implications for the central government's coffers and for domestic price stability. In 1993, as China made the transition to a net crude oil importer, Beijing adopted a series of adjustments to the plan, including lifting the ceiling on oilfields' produc-tion for sale at the market price, adjusting the administrative prices of finished oil products, and unifying retail prices across the nation.[7] These measures did not address the worsening problems of domestic market fragmentation from various price distortions and barriers to entry thrown up by protectionist local officials, as well as from the regulatory segregation of the upstream and the downstream businesses. Eyeing the seemingly insatiable domestic demand for petrochemicals, CNPC subsidiaries sought administrative permission to diversify into oil refining and distribution and marketing. Concurrently, Sinopec refineries lobbied for decreased dependence on CNPC through im-porting cheap and better quality crude from abroad. These pressures from the administrative companies led reformers to draft plans for integration based on models of multinational oil companies.

As the Chinese government initiated divestitures of state-owned enterprises in the mid 1990s, oil and petrochemical industries were identified as 'strategic sectors' with economies of scale, to be restructured into modern corporate forms under close state supervision, ownership control, and policy support.[8] However, early efforts at corporatization amounted to no effective change in industrial structure and operations, as oilfields and refineries railed against vertical and horizontal integration that would undermine their autonomy and networks.[9]

The perfect storm in 1998 and the restructuring of NOCs

When the Chinese Premier Zhu Rongji set about to restructure the oil and petrochemical industries in preparation for the WTO accession in 1999, he capitalized on the paralysis of industrial interests to engineer a top-down overhaul of the market and corporate structures. The depressed global crude prices in 1998—for the first time in the reform history, domestic prices of crude exceeded global prices—erased the thin profit margin of upstream producers.[10] Simultaneously, Chinese refineries that were already suffering from overcapacity at home faced an import surge of petrochemicals from neighbouring economies suffering from the Asian financial crisis. South East Asian and Korean producers had witnessed capacity build-up in the second half of the 1990s, and their exports became even more competitive with currency devaluation.[11] The Chinese government stepped in with radical reforms to bail out the domestic producers.

Unlike prior efforts at enterprise reform, this round of organizational reform aimed to establish new and comprehensive rules for market competition, government–business relations, corporate governance, and labour relations.[12] Zhu Rongji ordered all state-owned assets and operations in the oil and petrochemical sectors to be consolidated into two onshore national oil companies (NOCs)—CNPC and Sinopec—with each containing oilfields, refineries, and distribution channels (i.e. vertically integrated) within protected territories (horizontally integrated).[13] In principle, the China National Offshore Oil Corporation (CNOOC)—founded in 1982 with relatively modern corporate governance structures and managerial practices—would also aggressively expand and diversify away from its niche in offshore specialization to compete with CNPC and Sinopec.[14] The asset reallocation aimed to overcome market fragmentation in two ways. First vertical integration would reduce transaction costs across the entire chain of oil and petrochemical businesses. Second, by taking economic decision-making away from local governments and managers of petroleum administrative bureaus and placing them in the hands of powerful corporate headquarters, the Chinese government enabled the oil corporations' effective exercise of their property rights across administrative jurisdictions. The NOCs were turned into shareholding concerns in which the central state held the dominant controlling share, and subsequently listed in domestic and international stock markets, starting in 2000.

The Chinese government expected oligopolistic competition between CNPC and Sinopec to create incentives for more efficient production and product upgrades, without causing fiscal disruptions and potential waste of resources from competition among excessive numbers of new entrants. To encourage NOCs to respond more directly to price signals in the domestic and global markets, the State Council replaced the multi-track pricing system that distinguished between various 'within-plan' and market prices with a mechanism of centrally administered crude oil prices pegged to various global indices.[15]

Coordination of firm-level decisions would be dealt with henceforth by direct corporate oversight by the parent company of the subsidiaries, rather than through the plan, with the implementation of a centralized, 'multi-divisional' form of industrial organization. At each production site, the former petroleum administrative bureau was divided into a 'core' company with a lean workforce and ample capital, and a 'non-core' company heavily saddled with the least profitable aspects of the socialism legacy, such as social goods and services and the bulk of the workforce. This asymmetry in asset and employee allocation directly reflected Beijing's aim to maximize the value of public listings of NOCs. In financial accounting terms, core subsidiaries of NOCs have turned into 'profit centres', while non-core subsidiaries were became 'cost centres' responsible for offering an agreed-upon level of cost reduction.[16] Both statuses represented a serious loss of autonomy for managers as compared to their role under CRS.[17] Oilfield managers were placed under new contracts pegged to simplified criteria of profit attainment and lay-off targets. Financial centralization extended deeply into all aspects of corporation, including the corporate headquarters assumption of the subsidiaries' cumulative debt and centralized approval of bank loans and all other major sources of capitalization. NOCs also directly negotiate with the State Council's asset management companies on sharing of dividends and divestiture of state-held shares.[18]

The organizational legacy on government–business relations

The restructuring of China's national oil companies in 1998–2000 illustrates the possibility of the central government strengthening its ownership control over key SOEs, effectively reversing the trend of attenuated ownership rights under the decentralized approach to industrial governance in the reform period. However, this shift from administrative to corporate hierarchy in production relations and marketization has left a mixed legacy in the NOCs' conflicting relationship with the central regulators.

Since restructuring, NOCs have faced three policy-enforced organizational constraints on their growth strategies. First, CNPC and Sinopec are locked in their respective protected markets demarcated along the Yellow River. Early efforts to penetrate each other's territories led to freefalling prices of oil products, compelling the government to impose a 'freeze' on domestic turf wars. The government's insistence on fixing the prices of finished oil products has undermined Sinopec's profitability in recent years of high global crude prices.[19] In response, NOCs those Beijing's attempts at price controls and tax reforms, and leveraged their oligopolistic power to stifle nascent private refineries.[20]

Second, the asset restructuring of 1998–9 has not produced significant efficiency gains at the firm level. In any given production locality, the core and non-core companies continue their operational partnership through service contracts. To realize the profitability of the core company, the corporate headquarters of NOCs have held down the value of services performed by the non-core subsidiaries. This practice places the burden of adjustment squarely on the shoulders of the non-core companies, reducing incentives for the core units to adopt more efficient technologies and production methods.[21] Foreign shareholders have yet to exercise a significant voice in corporate governance—with the possible exception on the matter of workforce reduction—for reasons of their minuscule shares in Sinopec Listed as well as strategic considerations. For Western oil majors such as BP and Royal Dutch/Shell, equity investment has been tied to privileges in market access. In supporting the Chinese NOCs' listings, they have obtained exclusive market access via joint ventures in the profitable sectors of refining and retail petrol and service stations in China.[22]

Third, top executives of NOCs lack the decision-making autonomy that comes with the institutionalization of the ownership role of the Chinese state. Politicization of the corporate boardroom is prevalent with the State Council's ad hoc interventions in key decisions and appointment of career politicians as top executives of NOCs.[23] At the same time, the state's ownership and regulatory roles often come into contradiction. For example, it has held back from further selling off of state shares, concerned that that act would bring instability to the domestic stock markets. Apprehensive of grassroots discontent among workers and managers in failing non-core firms, it has cross-subsidized non-core subsidiaries with profits from the core-listed company.[24]

The government leadership seems to have recognized that strong corporate headquarters are not adequate substitutes for ministerial management of the oil business. In 2005, the State Council established a National Energy Leading Group to serve as the highest political forum for addressing China's energy security issues, and also to provide a formal, unified governmental interface with the emerging corporate interests of the NOCs. These developmental strategic and industrial governance functions have become disarticulated in March 2008 upon the State Council's establishment of a National Energy Commission and a National Energy Bureau. The former serves as a formally independent policy forum, and the latter a supra-ministerial agency housed in the National Development and Reform Commission.[25]

In short, a deep dissatisfaction with the limitations of existing market structure and corporate governance framework has haunted both the oil corporations and national reformers in the past decade. In the next few years, the government would be under tremendous pressures to liberalize domestic prices of finished oil products while protecting the profitability of NOCs. Further reform steps under discussion include the application of the existing anti-monopoly law to promote a more level playing field among the NOCs and with foreign and domestic private firms, corporate governance and disclosure requirements in domestic stock markets, tax and dividend payout adjustments, and asset redistribution between parent holding companies and the listed subsidiaries to enhance the global competitiveness of the latter.[26] To manage these complex issues that involve multiple bureaucratic interests, the State Council would need to invest in the authority and capacities of a national energy regulatory framework. The return of an energy ministry would not necessarily suggest backsliding into the socialist planned economy, as the establishment of NOCs in late 1990s has fundamentally reshaped the domestic market and government–business relations in the oil and petrochemical sectors. In place of mediating sectoral conflicts by allocating subsidies and manipulating the political incentives of its local agents, the new ministry will face as its primary challenge the reconciliation of national priorities with the coherent commercial interests of NOCs competing and colluding within an oligopolistic market. The new and contentious politics of governing big businesses lies at the heart of continued state ownership in China.

Case study 3

HIGH-TECH GOODS/R&D SECTOR—THE AVIATION INDUSTRY

Aircraft manufacturing has been a long-term priority sector of the Chinese government. The industry is important to China and other countries given its strategic significance, but the technological capacity required to develop this sector means that it is out of reach for most developing economies. But, China's desire to become a notable major economy places it in its sights. Its track record highlights the difficulties involved in building the domestic innovative/R&D capacity that is needed to develop a high-technology sector such as aircrafts.

Historically, China had devoted much of its political energy and fiscal resources to the production of military aircraft. During the era of Mao Zedong, aircraft production was the responsibility of the Third Ministry of Machine Building, which was controlled by the Central Military Commission and mainly geared towards military production. Until 1978, civilian aircraft production accounted for only 6.5 per cent of total aircraft manufacturing, and the total inventory ratio between military and civilian aircraft was 19:1 (Jane's Information Group 1997). With the onset of economic reform, China has channelled more and more resources to the development of non-combatant aircraft for civilian use. Yet this fraction of the industry remains intricately linked to the country's military concerns and defence capabilities.

China's determination to nurture its own aircraft industry is also motivated by technological and economic reasons. This high-tech sector lies at the apex of a country's industrial superstructure and is a crucial indicator of its overall level of economic and technological development. The ability to produce an entire aircraft in one country requires a 'broad-based industrial infrastructure of considerable depth and sophistication' (Dougan 2002: 25). In this regard, civil aviation is really an 'amalgamation of many different types of economic activities and associated industries' (Dougan 2002: 25). The Chinese government has therefore been keen to develop its fleet of domestically produced aircraft and acquire the technical capacity for supplying its own equipment. As part of the economic reform, the government has designated a group of large industrial enterprises as its 'national team' to compete on the global market. Aircraft manufacturing has clearly been one of the sectors in which the country aspires to become globally competitive (Nolan and Zhang 2003).

Despite the lofty ambitions, China's attempt to develop its own aircraft industry has not been straightforward. The global production of civilian aircraft is dominated by Western manufacturers with the US accounting for 75 per cent of the market. The rest is supplied mainly by Western European firms with a minor share taken up by Russia and Canada (Dougan 2002). Leading manufacturers, such as Boeing, Airbus, and Rolls-Royce, were quick to tap into China's emerging market. With the rapid growth in demand for civil aviation transport in China, it is predicted that, over the next twenty years, the country will require around 1,800 new commercial jet aircraft at a cost of over $120 billion (Dougan 2002). If China is unable to produce aircrafts of a comparable quality to those manufactured by foreign firms within a relatively short span of time, the prospects of gaining a foothold in the market would become increasingly slender. It would also mean that the country will continue to buy foreign aircrafts at notable cost to serve its rapidly growing airline industry.

The aircraft manufacturing sector is a good case for the study of China's industrial and technological development at the high-tech end where R&D is essential. The case study will examine how the country has sought to acquire technology from foreign manufacturers to enhance its domestic capabilities and the limited progress that it has made in the reform period.

Developments in China's aircraft industry

The early years of the economic reform were marked by efforts on the government's part to transform the almost purely military production structure of the aircraft industry to one that supports both military and civilian aircraft production (Jane's Information Group 1997). The Third Ministry of Machine Building became the Ministry of Aviation Industry, which eventually came under the control of the State Council in 1986. Another government agency, the Civil Aviation Administration of China (CAAC), is in charge of administering civilian air transport and services. With increasing emphasis on the development of aircraft for civilian and commercial uses, a more diverse array of bureaucratic interests had also entered into the picture. For instance, the China Aviation Industry Import/Export Corporation was set up in 1979, which, in coordination with other state bodies such as the Ministry of Foreign Trade and Economic Cooperation, were to handle matters of foreign trade in relation to the sector. Throughout the 1980s, resources were devoted to consolidating and expanding existing factory bases for the aviation industry.

The 1990s saw a range of attempts by the Chinese government to enhance the country's capacity in civilian aircraft manufacturing. In 1993, the Ministry of Aviation Industry became the Aviation Industries of China (AVIC). The agency was formally turned into an experimental 'State holding company' in 1996 (Nolan and Zhang 2003). This change in status was perceived as an attempt to divest AVIC of its planning and administrative duties and focus its energy on business management functions (Dougan 2002). A new direction for reform of state-owned enterprises, namely 'corporatization,' was established under the Third Plenum of the Communist Party's 14th Central Committee meeting. Pursuant to the plan, some of the larger aviation manufacturers in the country were transformed from factories into legal person companies (Dougan 2002). Except for the Xian Aircraft Manufacturing Company, which made an 'A' share offering on the Shanghai stock exchange in 1998, most domestic manufacturers became limited liability companies, with AVIC being the sole shareholder (Dougan 2002).

In 1999, AVIC was split into two entities, commonly known as AVIC I and AVIC II. After the restructuring, the new AVIC I took over businesses in manufacturing interceptor, interceptor-bomber, tanker, transporters, trainer, and reconnaissance aircraft, while AVIC II focused on helicopter, transporters, trainer, and general aircraft (Nolan and Zhang 2003). The same period also saw the government pursuing the 'grasping the big, releasing the small' policy. The first track of this policy entails the formation of *jituan* (integrated corporations) and condensing the industry down to around a dozen major corporations. The second track is concerned with dismissing employees of the former AVIC or transferring them to other businesses (Dougan 2002).

However, despite all of these attempts at corporate and commercial reforms, the Chinese aviation manufacturing industry was thought to be still fraught with problems of inefficiency. For instance, in 2000, the combined total sales of AVIC I and AVIC II were less than one-tenth of Boeing's. Yet AVIC I and AVIC II together employed over 400,000 people, more than twice as many as Boeing (Nolan and Zhang 2003).

Challenges in the development of domestic civilian aircrafts

The Chinese aircraft industry did not develop as rapidly and successfully as the government had intended. Most of China's general transport aircraft used to be copies of Soviet aircraft acquired in the 1950s and 1960s (Dougan 2002). Both prior to and during the economic reform period, China sought to develop indigenous civilian aircrafts, notably the 'Yun series', but progress was far from smooth. By 1995, China had produced various models such as the Yun 5, 8, 11, and 12. Yun 12 was the only domestically manufactured aircraft to receive airworthiness certification from the US Federal Aviation Administration (FAA), meaning that the aircraft can fly in US airspace and in other countries where FAA standards are recognized. In 2000, a Yun 7 aircraft exploded in mid air. Following the conclusion of the crash investigation, CAAC decided to remove all Yun 7 aircraft from service in June 2001 (Nolan and Zhang 2003).

Most civilian aircrafts produced in China are delivered to the military, the airline companies under CAAC, or exported to developing countries (Dougan 2002). As of 2006, there were around thirty airline companies in China and they were predominantly controlled by the state (Björkell 2006). For example, China's largest commercial airline (in terms of traffic volume and company assets), the national flagship carrier, Air China, is a subsidiary of CAAC. The other two major airlines, China Southern Airlines and China Eastern Airlines, are both state-owned.

But, like all other industries in China, the landscape of the airline industry has changed during the economic reform. First of all, control of the industry has become more decentralized, with local governments increasingly taking charge of domestic airline companies (Dougan 2002). Secondly, the state has permitted the establishment of some private airline companies. In 2005, the CAAC declared that it will open China's aviation sector and encourage private and foreign investment in Chinese airlines (Björkell 2006). In that year, for example, CAAC issued a total of 14 air operating certificates to private domestic airlines (Björkell 2006). The new private airlines like Beijing's

Okay Airways, Chengdu's United Eagle Airlines and Shanghai's Spring Airlines are seeking a slice of the market with their low-cost services, although the airline industry is still very much dominated by the three state-owned giants (Björkell 2006).

However, the airlines—including the state-owned ones—have not added many domestic aircrafts to their inventories (Dougan 2002). For instance, China's attempt to build its own indigenous large passenger aircraft, the Yun 10, ultimately failed as the country's airlines refused to buy the plane (Nolan and Zhang 2003). The Yun 10 model is extremely heavy compared to the Boeing 707, with high fuel consumption and a very limited range (Nolan and Zhang 2003). Instead, domestic airline companies mainly purchased their commercial jet aircraft from North American and Western European producers, such as Boeing and Airbus (Dougan 2002).

Foreign cooperation and technology transfer

Along the lines of its over-arching industrial and FDI policies geared at technology transfers, the Chinese government has been keen to obtain the necessary technological capacities for its aircraft industry from foreign companies as a basis to build its own domestic capacity. Since the early 1980s, Chinese companies have made parts for both Boeing and Airbus (Kingsbury 2007). And, Boeing had been enlisted to assist with the manufacture of complex areas of aero engines and avionics on all of the Yun-series aircrafts to try and learn through foreign cooperation (Dougan 2002).

After abandoning the Yun 10 production in 1985, a 'three-step plan' was devised by the then Ministry of Civil Aviation in the quest to manufacture a domestic commercial jet aircraft. These steps include: (1) cooperating with a foreign partner to assemble medium-sized long-haul aircraft within China; (2) with a foreign partner, jointly designing and manufacturing a 100-seat short-haul aircraft in China; and (3) amassing all the relevant technologies to provide the industry with the ability to design and build an entire 180-seat long-haul aircraft independently (Dougan 2002).

The relatively low production costs in China are no doubt attractive to the world's leading aircraft manufacturers, which have endeavoured to integrate and develop their global supply chain under increasingly competitive pressures in the industry (Nolan and Zhang 2003). Moreover, foreign manufacturers have also been eager to supply their aircraft to the Chinese market in light of the rapid growth of China's aviation transport sector. The Chinese government has sought to take advantage of this by making foreign suppliers' sales to China contingent on their willingness to engage in technological transfer (Dougan 2002). Generally speaking, foreign presence in China's aircraft industry has indeed expanded considerably. Dougan contrasts the situation in the 1980s, when no Western manufacturers had an active presence in China, to that of the 2000s, where 'over a dozen of the world's leading companies are involved in varying types of parts manufacturing and technology transfer deals' (Dougan 2002: 130).

However, instances of Chinese–foreign cooperation in aircraft manufacturing suggest limited success. Back in the late 1970s, the US manufacturer, McDonnell Douglas was already involved in co-production of the MD-80 model with the Shanghai Aircraft Manufacturing Company. Yet the project was later downgraded to some basic assembly work because Chinese materials and overall quality control could not pass the required FAA standards (Dougan 2002). Co-production projects with McDonnell Douglas were launched again in the 1980s and 1990s. However, despite the intention of having Chinese-made components total 25 per cent of the finished aircraft, this was not achieved, again because of quality control problems (Dougan 2002). The 1990s saw the Chinese industry engaging in active negotiations with foreign manufacturers. For example, in mid 1997, a contract was signed for joint production of the AE-100 aircraft. The Airbus group was to take a 39 per cent share, a Singaporean company 15 per cent, and AVIC the remaining 46 per cent, with the final assembly to take place in China (Dougan 2002). However, the project was stalled by the end of 1998 and sidelined by 1999. At that time, this was perceived outside China to 'deal a severe blow to China's nascent aviation industry' and 'throw into doubt its plans to become a substantial aircraft manufacturer' (*Financial Times*, 5 August 1998 and 6 October 1998, cited in Nolan and Zhang 2003: 296). It appeared that each of the objectives under the 'three-step plan' had fallen by the wayside (Nolan and Zhang 2003).

The less than auspicious development in China's quest for foreign aviation technology has been attributed to a number of factors. First, it could have stemmed from the unwillingness of foreign manufacturers to share their core technologies, for technological advancement on the Chinese side would enhance the industry's competitiveness vis-à-vis foreign manufacturers. The termination of the AE-100 project was seen to result partly from China's demands for access to core technologies which Airbus did not wish to share (Dougan 2002). Second, control of the airline industry became more decentralized and increasingly fell into the hands of local governments during the reform period. To forge deals with foreign manufacturers and attract their investments, local authorities and/or individual airline companies may not be inclined to bargain intensely for technological transfer (Dougan 2002). Third, as discussed above, many domestic airline companies were not keen on purchasing domestic aircrafts. The lack of demand by domestic airlines contributed to the failure of projects like the MD-80 and AE-100, and thus the 'three-step plan' policy (Dougan 2002).

Furthermore, although foreign technology transfer is generally recognized as crucial to the development of China's aircraft industry, there are also reservations as to whether foreign cooperation is wholly desirable or necessarily effective. For example, China's reliance on foreign technology gives foreign partners the power to determine which technologies to share and transfer and, in the long run, to influence the agenda of China's aircraft manufacturing (Dougan 2002). It is questionable as to whether Chinese partners in joint production projects have been able to make major inroads, in the sense of fully absorbing foreign technologies—especially in relation to 'soft' but crucial technologies like production coordination systems, modern quality control, and inspection procedures (Dougan 2002).

And, since the 1980s, China's aircraft manufacturing companies have greatly diversified their production to include a range of 'non-aviation related' products, such as turbines, generators, automobiles, and even kitchen appliances. By 1997, the production of 'non-aviation related' products accounted for as much as 80 per cent of the industry's total output (Dougan 2002). While these diversified product fields have been able to generate strong revenues, they may also become an undesirable distraction if too many companies were lured away by these more lucrative businesses in the short term from making long-term investment in aircraft production (Dougan 2002). Yet, despite the government's aims, manufacturing domestically developed aircrafts was challenging and not necessarily cost-effective to these companies in view of the aforementioned obstacles.

Developing China's aircraft industry

Despite the previous setbacks, however, the Chinese government's determination to develop its aircraft industry has not waned. The 2000s was characterized by a host of new developments. In March 2007, the Chinese government pledged to invest at least $6 billion to produce a 150-seat jetliner (Kingsbury 2007). In May 2008, the country launched its first jumbo jet company in Shanghai—the Commercial Aircraft Corporation of China Ltd—which is responsible for researching, developing, manufacturing, and marketing a large passenger aircraft. The primary goal of these steps is to produce a commercial jumbo jet which by 2020 could compete with global manufacturers like Boeing and Airbus (Kingsbury 2007). This is clearly no easy task given China's so far largely unsuccessful endeavour.

The formerly split AVIC I and AVIC II were merged again into one entity in November 2008, along the lines of other state-owned enterprises which were merged around this time. This policy was prompted by the perceived need for a consolidated state agency to oversee the development of a globally competitive aircraft industry, which is not a dissimilar strategy in view of the support given to Boeing and Airbus by the United States and Europe, respectively. Some progress had appeared by that time. In November 2008, the ARJ21—China's first home-grown regional jet—completed its maiden flight in Shanghai, after six years of research and development. This time, the CAAC seems to be determined to court the customer base of domestic airlines, announcing that it would block the creation of any new Chinese airlines until 2010—unless the new carrier flies the ARJ21 (Kingsbury 2007). The country has also sought to improve its supporting infrastructure by building more regional airports, particularly in western provinces. Response to ARJ21 appears to be positive thus far, with the Canadian manufacturer, Bombardier, announcing plans to invest $100 million with CAAC in designing additional versions of the model.

Of course, many challenges still lie ahead. First and foremost, China would need to ensure that its aircrafts must be up to global standards so that they can be used in other countries, especially the US and Europe, to which China wishes to sell its new jets (Kingsbury 2007). Chinese planes will also be facing intense competitions from manufacturers abroad, most of which have established extensive global networks to ensure parts availability and provide operators with support (Kingsbury 2007). China, in contrast, will need to build its own global support system 'virtually from scratch' (Kingsbury 2007).

Not entirely typical, the aviation industry is one that is clearly driven by high levels of technological content. China's strategy of learning from foreign investors has not so far produced a viable high-tech industry in 30 years. Thus, it underscores the challenges of developing such a high value-added sector despite massive amounts of government support. Although the regional aircraft ARJ21 is seen by some as being China's 'best bet' under immense global competition (Nolan and Zhang 2003), the success is regarded by China as just the beginning of its aerospace ambitions. As China becomes more innovative with economic development, it may yet achieve its global ambitions.

Case study 4

CORPORATIZATION OF STATE-OWNED BANKS: ICBC

In 2006, the Industrial and Commercial Bank of China (ICBC) initiated the world's largest ever Initial Public Offering (IPO) to date, raising some $22 billion. As one of the four large state-owned commercial banks (SCB), ICBC spearheaded the push by the Chinese government to use the listing of China's largest state-owned enterprises (SOEs) on stock exchanges to restructure these enterprises. As part of the strategy of commercializing the state-owned banks following the overall policy of corporatizing state-owned enterprises, listings were one facet of the share issue privatization reforms. Also, before the IPOs, minority equity stakes in SCBs were sold to foreign investors. The aim was to improve corporate governance and instil market incentives: in a sense, preparing the banks to become shareholding companies and remove them from the inefficiency necessarily engendered by state-ownership deriving from a planned economy.

In undertaking this float, ICBC became the first major Chinese firm simultaneously to list on mainland Chinese and overseas stock markets. Previously, Chinese blue chip firms listed first on overseas markets before going public on domestic exchanges. ICBC, however, simultaneously priced 'A' (mainland) and 'H' (Hong Kong) shares and released them for trading on the same day. A Goldman Sachs-led consortium (including Allianz and American Express) had acquired a 10 per cent stake of the company for $3.8 billion a year before ICBC went public. Of this, Goldman ended up owning a (relatively) small strategic stake in ICBC of 5 per cent, which it agreed not to sell for three years. By the time of the float, Goldman Sachs had made a profit on that single deal of $3.9 billion. As of 2008, its profit on the ICBC deal was in the region of $6–7 billion.

At the close of the float, overall subscription to the offer closed in excess of $500 billion. As with most listings of SOEs, all this investment was for only a minority share (14.8 per cent) of ICBC's enlarged share capital, in a company where the Chinese Ministry of Finance (MOF) and Central Huijin Investment Co., a state-owned holding company, both own 36.2 per cent of the company respectively and have control of its operations.

In spite of the fact that 'A' shares were priced in Chinese currency and available only to mainlanders (and selected foreign investors), there was enormous demand, at almost thirty times over subscription. More than $81.5 billion of demand came from retail investors in mainland China, while institutional investors chipped in another $16.3 billion. Individuals from Hong Kong ordered $54 billion. However, the real push came from overseas investors, who attempted to order a phenomenal $345 billion worth of shares, an oversubscription of some 1,500 per cent.

The state-owned bank, ICBC, had clearly arrived on the world stage.

STATE-OWNED ENTERPRISES 145

History

Perhaps the most remarkable thing about this process is that ICBC was only established in 1984, and in many ways its development is inseparable from that of the Chinese banking sector as a whole. It is only in recent years that ICBC has begun to develop commercially. In the pre-reform period, the People's Bank of China (PBOC) combined all the roles of central and commercial banking and was the only bank in China. However, in the early years of economic reform, the PBOC was divested of its commercial banking functions. Four state-owned banks were then instituted in four specialized areas: the Agricultural Bank of China (ABC), the Bank of China (BOC), the China Construction Bank (CCB), and ICBC.

These four state-owned banks were granted limited autonomy with respect to their commercial operations and permitted to slowly expand into other banking businesses beyond their specialized functions. Enterprise financing was shifted from the state budget to the banking sector. State-owned enterprises were allowed to retain after-tax profits at that time, and rapid economic growth triggered a flood of savings channelled into the banking system, especially since capital controls kept the funds within the country.

However, China's banking system continued to be tightly restricted by governmental plans and policies, and the state-owned banks did not operate on an independent or entirely commercially oriented basis. The four banks were allowed to expand their scope of business and to compete with each other in providing loans and deposit services; however, they served mainly as policy-lending conduits for the government, and lacked the requisite autonomy to seriously compete with each other. As a result, their activities remained closely tied to their areas of specialty (as indicated in their nomenclature), particularly notable in the case of ABC which supported the agricultural sector.

In the mid-1990s, the Chinese government accelerated its financial reforms and began to encourage the state-owned banks to operate on a more commercial basis. In 1994, three policy banks were established to assume substantially all of the policy-lending functions of the state-owned banks. These were the China Development Bank, the Export–Import Bank of China and the Agricultural Development Bank of China. Accordingly, the four state-owned banks were transformed into state-owned commercial banks. The rules governing the new commercial banks were laid out within the Commercial Bank Law, which was passed in March 1995. The most important feature of the law is that it grants all commercial banks operational independence except in the case of a national emergency.

Another crucial part of the reforms was to increase the level of competition by allowing the entry of new competitors. In 1995, the first private bank, Minsheng Bank, was established. Although the four large state-owned banks dominate China's banking sector, the emergence of smaller national and regional commercial banks has made the system more diverse and competitive. These were mainly wrought from rural and urban credit cooperatives which began banding together. The market for bank loans has also been made more competitive and there has been a steady decline in the dominance of the four large state-owned banks. In 1986, they accounted for about 90 per cent of the share of loans (Pei 1998). A decade later, their share fell to about 78 per cent; the strongest competitors to the largest state banks were rural credit cooperatives and urban trust and investment companies (with a combined share of 15 per cent). However, still another decade later, by 2006, the 'big four' still accounted for about 60 per cent of all bank lending. By the late 2000s, ICBC and three of the four SCBs were among the largest banks in the world. SCBs show no signs of disappearing and epitomize the corporatization strategy of enterprise reform: commercialization through restructuring into shareholding companies but not necessarily privatization.

Structural problems

Throughout this time, the predominance of bank credit going to SOEs remained even as the SCBs became commercialized. In 1995, 84 per cent of their loans were made to SOEs while only 5 per cent went to non-state firms. In this way, the big four SCBs, despite a mandate to behave like commercial entities, were still heavily intertwined with elements of the planned economy.

This was exacerbated by government funding requirements. In spite of the reforms, the separation between policy banks and state-owned commercial banks was far from neat and complete. The policy banks lacked sufficient branch networks or capital to engage in the level of policy lending previously provided by the SCBs, so the commercial banks continued to engage in policy lending in one form or another in response to pressures from central and local governments.

The SCBs were politically too weak to resist the demands placed by the government on their activities. This was particularly true even for the central bank, the People's Bank of China, the supposed guardian of monetary policy. Before the passage of the Central Bank Law in 1995, the PBOC continuously financed the central government budget deficits in the form of overdrafts. Moreover, before the passage of that reform, the PBOC was also heavily influenced by provincial politicians who were eager to obtain extra credit to accelerate local economic development. Such local political interference was considered a major cause of inflationary pressures (Pei 1998).

The Chinese banks were also financially weak. The accumulation of policy loans and government-directed lending to non-viable SOEs inevitably led to the rise of sizeable non-performing loans (NPLs) in their portfolios. The capital of these banks was eroded by the state's failure to inject new equity capital into them due to the government's own fiscal difficulties. This instead meant that the SCBs took on funding obligations for SOEs, while the deteriorating earnings caused by the accumulation of non-performing loans worsened their positions.

The single most important obstacle on the banking reform path was a gargantuan proportion of non-performing assets. After several rounds of pre-2002 bail-outs, the NPL ratios for the SCBs were reduced, but were still between 15 and 25 per cent of loans. There was no plausible scenario that Chinese banks could 'grow out' of these losses without external financial assistance. State-orchestrated bail-outs were necessary.

ICBC Vice President Wang Lili told senior officials in a speech she delivered at the Central Party School on 8 January 2002:

Currently, we have inadequate bad debt reserves and can only use profit to write off NPLs. Also, the Ministry of Finance says that we can at most use 1 per cent of our assets to write-off NPLs. We have to think of another way—ICBC currently has 250 billion (RMB) in policy loans and 160 billion of it is NPLs, so if the state can take it off our hands, our NPL ratio would decrease by 6 per cent. In 1998, MOF recapitalised the Big Four banks with 270 billion (RMB), which gave them a 5 per cent capital adequacy ratio. However,... the state will need to recapitalise another 400 billion in 2003. IPOs are not the answer since the Chinese market is not ready to raise this kind of money. (Imam 2004: 21)

ICBC acknowledged the situation in a 2004 report:

Although the Industrial and Commercial Bank of China's profits kept rising quickly from 2000 to the first half of 2004, chalking up a combined 190 billion RMB, nearly 90 per cent of the profits were used in risk provisions and write-offs of historical financial burdens... But, capital will still be seriously inadequate, and bad loan provisioning coverage will remain fairly low... Since the gaps are too huge, we are still far from meeting the requirements of a public stock offering.

One year later, they engaged in the largest public stock offering in history. Understanding the reasons behind this unusually public change of mind by both ICBC and the Chinese government requires an assessment of the policy environment of the time.

Push for reform

In addition to the pressing problem of NPLs, the extent of bank dominance itself became a reason for structural reform. Due to the nascent nature of equity and bond markets in the banking system, the dominant player in

China's financial sector and the entire Chinese economic system are the state-owned banks. Over 60 per cent of Chinese financial assets are in the banking system, compared to less than 20 per cent in the US and just below 30 per cent in the Euro Zone. Even India, a country with a significantly lower GDP per head has only just over 40 per cent of its financial stock in the form of bank deposits. A 60 per cent ratio is unusual for a country at China's stage of development.

As Table 1 shows, the implication of this is that most credit is extended through bank loans, which represented 78 per cent of funds raised in 2005. Normally, by this stage of development the equity and bond markets would account for a larger proportion of the financing of companies. The international financial institutions typically recommend that developing countries seek to diversify their funding sources and to develop healthy bond markets. Otherwise, far too much of the burden of financing development falls on the banking system, and the financial system is in turn more vulnerable.

Thus, reform of the banking sector became more and more pressing as the Chinese economy continued to grow. Any sign of banking instability or crisis would have had serious repercussions on the economy as a whole.

The other critical challenge was that banks, including ICBC, were organizationally inefficient since their governance derived from the state's administrative system rather than on commercial principles. Thus, every bank had a branch in each administrative unit, regardless of business conditions. Staff were poorly trained, and their equipment and use of modern technology were backward. However, the most striking weakness of Chinese banks was the degree to which the organization of their business activities produced conflicts of interests, irregularities, and corruption (Pei 1998).

In the 1990s, reform-minded technocrats came up with the idea of selling stock to foreigners, partly as a means of attracting capital and management know-how, but mainly as a counterweight to mismanagement and rampant corruption. In theory, domestic banks would clean up their act as they felt the pressure of foreign scrutiny and competition. Simultaneously, strategic

Table 1. Funds raised in China, 2001–2005 (as percentage of total funds)

	2001	2002	2003	2004	2005
Bank loans	75.9	80.2	85.2	82.9	78.1
Government bonds	15.7	14.4	10.0	10.8	9.5
Corporate bonds	0.9	1.4	1.0	1.1	6.4
Stocks	7.6	4.0	3.9	5.2	6.0

Source: People's Bank of China reports, 2002–6.

partnerships with foreign investors would strengthen the management and IT capacity of the institutions.

The remedy

The solution for the Chinese government and ICBC appeared clear. As Liu Mingkang, Chairman of the regulator, the China Banking Regulatory Commission (CBRC), said in a 2004 speech:

In my view, strategic investors in the state-owned banks, foreign strategic investors in particular, can play a catalytic role in changing the corporate behaviour of the state-owned banks. Foreign partners will not only supply capital but also better governance.

ICBC, grasping the nettle, indicated their plans for an initial public offering, arguing that they would not only raise badly needed capital, but help the bank improve corporate governance. As a 2004 ICBC report stated:

Although a stock listing is not the ultimate goal, for a bank with huge historical burdens like the Industrial and Commercial Bank of China, a financial restructuring enabled by a stock listing will undoubtedly give a strong push to its ongoing construction of corporate governance mechanisms and a comprehensive risk management system.

The then vice governor of ICBC, Yang Kaisheng, cleverly took the opportunity to link ICBC's success with China's desire to create national champions, noting in an interview:

As long as we firmly grasp the historical opportunity of joint-stock reform, and build up a perfect governance structure and policy management system, we can prove that China can also establish modern commercial banks with good service and profit.

The government response was twofold. It first moved to essentially write off the major banks' bad debts and reshuffle them into shareholding companies. It then invited strategic foreign investors and let the banks go public. Foreign investment thus came before the IPOs. This allowed the Chinese government to 'cherry pick' the early investors in the banks, establishing considerable international credibility pre-float. ICBC's use of Goldman Sachs as the initial investor on the condition that it had to hold onto its shares for a period shows how the Chinese government attempted to use the well-known investment bank as a form of reassurance for other investors.

The process

The first stage was the creation of asset management companies (AMCs) to bail-out ICBC's and the other SCBs' debts. The importance of this cannot be underestimated. With the pre-existing large NPL portfolios, ICBC needed to earn sufficiently high interest margins on the loan business to finance its operational costs. As recently as a decade ago, non-performing loan ratios at China's largest banks were estimated to be more than 40 per cent, denying ICBC the ability to become profitable.

Since 1998, Beijing has spent more than $400 billion on a series of ambitious capital injections and bad-loan removal schemes to put the banks on a solid footing. The equivalent of 22 per cent of 2004 GDP has been spent on bail-outs of the three largest SCBs since 1998, when the East Asian crises put banking reforms high on the agenda (OECD 2005). It must be noted here that there is considerable debate over the exact sums spent on these non-performing loans; hence all of these sums should be seen as indicative. The Asian Development Bank (ADB) notes that in April 2006 Ernst & Young, ICBC's auditor—released a Global Non-performing Loan Report, arguing that the Big Four Chinese banks had about $358 billion of NPLs on their books. This contrasted with the official figure of $133 billion. Following protests by Chinese officials, Ernst & Young withdrew the report.

Officially, a total of $15 billion of the country's foreign exchange was allocated to the ICBC for its reform in 2003. Given the bank's huge size and its bad loan ratio of nearly 20 per cent, the amount of capital injection required to be provided by the government, even aside from this official allocation of foreign exchange into the ICBC, was substantial. Although the actual numbers are uncertain, the total amount of capital injections and bail-outs handed out to ICBC by the mid 2000s has been estimated to be some $162 billion. To put this sum into perspective, the entire value of ICBC post-IPO was $130 billion. However, as Table 2 shows, the measures were effective.

Table 2. Non-performing loan ratios of the three largest Chinese state-owned banks, 2002–2006

	2002	2003	2004	2005	2006
ICBC	25.34	21.24	18.99	4.69	3.90
BOC	23.37	15.92	5.12	4.90	4.00
CCB	15.05	9.25	3.92	3.84	3.40

Source: Annual Reports of the banks and Fitch Ratings reports.

The debt then was transferred to the Central Huajin Holdings Company, an asset management company set up solely to recover some of ICBC's debts. The average write-off of debt was 70–90 per cent (Kudrna 2006). This allows them to have a single-minded focus on debt recovery without being concerned about a continuing banking relationship with the SOEs in default. Huajin attempted to sell the NPLs. It managed to sell some of the debt to joint venture funds but at less than face value and the funds did not receive the debt-for-equity swaps that were expected; thus, that avenue dried up, and the AMCs remain a source of contingent liability for the government.

But, for ICBC, having written off most of its NPLs, the second leg of the strategy was the introduction of strategic shareholders. In one sense, these transactions look surprisingly unattractive for foreign investors. A foreign institution can only own up to 20 per cent of the equity of a Chinese bank, and the total ownership of foreign equity investors is restricted to 25 per cent, which prevents control shifting to the investor from the Chinese government.

However, such minority shareholding provided a way for foreign banks to enter the vast market. In 2002, China imposed working capital requirements that were substantially higher than international standards: more than fifteen times higher than those required in the European Union, for example. The requirement that banks wishing to carry out RMB business must have operated in China for three years with two fiscal years of profitability was also a significant barrier to entry. Foreign bank representatives overwhelmingly identify the complex regulatory environment as the most difficult aspect of the Chinese banking industry. Though relaxed in 2006 in accordance with post-WTO opening, the barriers remain in the banking sector.

Clearly then, the Chinese government was relying on the promise of future relationships and entry into China's burgeoning financial services market to make ICBC a particularly attractive investment. As Table 3 shows, the float was indeed attractive, as investment banks Credit Suisse and Merrill Lynch became the two major overseas investors purchasing ICBC shares.

Table 3. Ownership of ICBC

Chinese state shareholders (%)	Non-state shareholders (%)
Ministry of Finance 35.3	Goldman Sachs 5.1
Central SAFE 35.3	Allianz 2.2
Social Security Fund 5.3	Credit Suisse 6.9
	Merrill Lynch 6.9
	American Express 0.8

Source: ICBC Hong Kong (2006b)

Thus, from a position in 2004 when ICBC was suffering from 'gaps (that) are too huge' and were 'still far from meeting the requirements of a public stock offering', ICBC was able only two years later to become instantaneously one of the biggest firms in Asia, overtaking the $100 billion valued Samsung and trailing just behind Toyota (whose market capitalization at the time was around $185 billion).

Furthermore, ICBC's post-IPO performance has been highly impressive. It reaped after-tax profits of 64.88 billion RMB in the six months of 2008, a year-on-year growth of 56.75 per cent, making it the most profitable bank in the world at the time. Its non-performing loan ratio fell to 2.41 per cent by then. ICBC remained China's leading corporate and retail bank, mortgage lender, and online bank, and had more than 18,000 branches, 2.5 million corporate customers, and 150 million individual clients in 2008.

Moreover, ICBC began to expand internationally. In 2007, it bought a 20 per cent stake in Africa's biggest bank, Standard Bank, for $5.5 billion. It had also acquired a 90 per cent stake in Bank Halim Indonesia in 2006, with an option to purchase the remaining 10 per cent.

Short-term gain, long-term questions

However, as recently as December 2005, when Goldman Sachs, Alliance, and American Express bought a 10 per cent stake in ICBC, the bank had an implied value of just $37 billion. This rapid rise has yet to be reflected in ICBC's bond ratings, particularly regarding financial strength. Yet this is not reflected in ICBC's stock price, which has fluctuated between price-to-earnings (P/E) ratios of 21 to 27, about twice the P/E ratio of elite Western banks.

This is probably due to continuing doubts over the viability of the Chinese banking system as the state retains control. On the one hand, the 'big three' SCBs hold over 50 per cent of all deposits in a society where the savings rate is an astounding 45–50 per cent of GDP. Families rely on their savings to cover any emergencies as well as their housing, pensions, healthcare, and education needs. But, there is no deposit insurance; therefore, any loss of savings in the SCBs would translate to loss of elementary security for a large proportion of the Chinese population. Corporate savings in China are also exceptionally high because retained earnings are a major source of investment funds. Therefore any form of banking crisis would threaten livelihoods and jobs on massive scale. Either of these events would cause major crises in legitimacy for the government.

Moreover, the performance of a bank depends on many other factors, such as the quality of the borrowers, the rule of law, and the regulatory system. This problem is exacerbated by the question of property rights. When an SOE forecloses, what happens to the assets, including land, can be highly variable. In some cases, the assets have reverted to municipal or provincial governments rather than to the banks which had a valid claim. Until China can improve these matters, using IPOs as the vehicle for banking reform is shortsighted in the view of some (Jia 2007).

On the other hand, Chinese banks are spending billions on state-of-the-art IT systems, and executives at ICBC, BOC, and CCB claim that foreign partners have been given broad sway to review their books and establish modern credit-control procedures. But, the challenge is non-trivial. ICBC, for example, has 18,000 branches and 335,000 employees. Senior executives acknowledge that at most branches, loan officers wouldn't necessarily be aware of a potential borrower's credit history, even if they had an account across town at another branch of the same bank.

Finally, Chinese banks will face considerably greater levels of competition in the future, particularly with the entry of foreign banks. Although they were still facing nominally restrictive policies, 2007 still witnessed a rapid growth of foreign banks, either locally incorporated or as foreign bank branches. By the end of 2007, the total assets of overseas banks stood at $171.46 billion, 47 per cent up from a year earlier and accounting for 2.4 per cent of total assets of all financial institutions. Outstanding loans of overseas banks stood at $95.16 billion, a year-on-year increase of 54.7 per cent. The outstanding value of deposits increased 68.8 per cent to $60.66 billion.

Thus, enormous questions remain about ICBC and the listing strategy as the main line of reform. Will this bank with a hitherto huge captive domestic market have the genuine incentive to become globally competitive? Can a bank majority owned and controlled by the state overcome problems of political influence and policy-directed lending that led to NPLs? Can a bank of such enormous size modernize quickly enough to beat off growing competition?

This is, of course, an enormously difficult task, especially as capital account liberalization looms on the cards such that savings can not only go into foreign banks but overseas. How ICBC fares will indicate not only its own progress, but the corporatization strategy at the heart of Chinese enterprise reform.

■ **NOTES**

1. China's domestic administered prices for crude oil were set significantly below global levels until 1998 when the domestic price actually exceeded the global price. Kun-Chin Lin, 'Macroeconomic Disequilibria and Enterprise Reform: Restructuring the Chinese Oil and Petrochemical Industries in the 1990s'. *The China Journal*, No. 60, July 2008, 55.

2. From 1981 to 1985, oil export represented 23.2% of the value of total exports. Qiu Baolin, *Zhongguo shiyou tiaozhan WTO* [*China's Oil Industry Takes on the WTO*]. Beijing, PRC: Shiyou Gongye Chubanshe, 2000, 233.

3. Thomas Fingar, 'Implementing Energy Policy: The Rise and Demise of the State Energy Commission', in David Lampton, ed., *Policy Implementation in Post-Mao China*. Berkeley, CA: UC Press, 1987.

4. Not surprisingly, these companies inherited many 'mothers-in-law' who imposed multiple subordination: the Planning Bureau of the State Council continued to set production-related quota; the Ministry of Finance gave strict guidelines on tax contributions and profitability levels; the Pricing Bureau enforced administered price stability; and the Ministry of Foreign Trade controlled import–export volumes and demanded foreign currency earnings, etc. The NOCs at the time had neither the institutional resources nor the political status to challenge meddling by various agencies. Interview with the State Council Development Research Center (SC DRC), Beijing, June 2002.

5. CNPC, '*Guojia shiyou gongsi jiben kuangjia de yanjiu*' [A Study of the Basic Framework of the National Oil Company]. Beijing, PRC: Unpublished company research report, 1994, 148–54. CNPC, '*Zhongguo shiyou gongye guanli tizhi gaige yanjiu*' [A Study of the Reform of the Governance Structure of the Chinese Oil Industry]. Beijing, PRC: Unpublished company research report, 1998, 54–5.

6. For the full argument on external market impact on oil industry restructuring, see Kun-Chin Lin, 'Macroeconomic Disequilibria and Enterprise Reform', 49–79.

7. Zhang Nianyu, *Zhongguo nengyuan jiage* [China's Energy Prices]. Guangzhou, PRC: Guangdong Jiaoyu Chubanshe, 1998, 363. Wang Haijing, 'China's Oil Policy and Its Impact'. *Energy Policy* 23(7), 1955, 630.

8. For domestic analyses of Beijing's preferential treatment of the 'strategic sectors', see Jin Pei (ed.), *Guoyou qiye genben wenti* [Root Problems of State-Owned Enterprises]. Beijing, PRC: Beijing Chubanshe, 2002; Liu Xiaoxuan, *Zhongguo qiye fazhan baogao 1990–2000* [A Report on the Development of Chinese Enterprises, 1990–2000]. Beijing, PRC: Shehui Kexue Wenxian Chubanshe, 2001; Yin Wenchuan and Zang Yaoru, *Qiye gaizu yu jiegou tiaozheng* [Enterprise Reform and Economic Restructuring]. Beijing, PRC: Zhongguo Jihua Chubanshe, 2001, and *Zhonggyo qiye jituan tizhi muoshi* [The Organizational Framework of China's Enterprise Groups]. Beijing, PRC: Zhongguo Jihua Chubanshe, 1999; State Economic and Trade Commission (SETC) Qiye Gaige Si, *Zhongguo guoyou dazhongxing qiye gaige yu fazhan rougan zhongda wenti yanjiu* [Research on the Major Problems in the Reform and Development of Large- and Medium-Size State-Owned Enterprises in China]. Beijing, PRC: Renmin Chubanshe, 2001); Liang Zuchen, *Chuangjian zhongguo gongsi zhi* [Establishing Chinese Corporate Governance]. Beijing, PRC: Zhonggyou Jingji Chubanshe, 2000.

9. Zhongyang caijing lingdao xiaozu bangongshi, *Zhonggong zhongyang guanyu guoyouqiye gaige* [Study Guide for the Major Decisions on Problems of SOE Reform and Development, made by the Central Committee of the CCP]. Beijing, PRC: Renmin Chubanshe, 1999, 36; Zhang Yixiang, Wang Qiming, and Wang Baoxi, *Guoyou konggu gongsi lilun yu shixian* [Theory and Practice of State-Controlled Shareholding Companies]. Beijing, PRC: Jingji Kexue Chubanshe, 1999, 68.

10. By the end of 1997, 11 CNPC subsidiaries had lost a combined 6.47 billion RMB. Some 3,700 wells were capped, scaling back production by 1.47 million tons and contributing to 18.9 billion RMB in loan payment arrears. Jingji Ribao, *Dajubian: '98 zhongguo shiyoushihua dachongzu zishi* [The Great Transformation: A Documentary of the '98 Restructuring of the Chinese Oil and Petrochemical Industries]. Beijing, PRC: Jingji Ribao Chubanshe, 1998, 281. The external shock was comparable in 1993, but the domestic alignment of interests was different. The upstream sector was growing, and resisted Premier Zhu Rongji's proposals to restructure the industry towards vertical integration. Kun-Chin Lin, 'Macroeconomic Disequilibria and Enterprise Reform', 58–67.

11. Kun-Chin Lin, 'Finding the Right Chemistry? The U.S. Chemical Industry in Asia'. *Business and Politics* 3(2), 2001, 185–202.

12. Kun-Chin Lin, 'Disembedding Socialist Firms as a Statist Project: Restructuring the Chinese Oil Industry 1997–2002'. *Enterprise & Society* 7(1), March 2006, 59–97; K. C. Lin, 'Class Formation or Fragmentation? Allegiances and Divisions among Managers and Workers in State-owned Enterprises', in T. Gold, W. Hurst, J. Won, and L. Qiang, ed., *Laid-Off Workers in a Workers' State: Unemployment with Chinese Characteristics*. London: Palgrave MacMillan, 2009; Zhang Jin, *Catch-up and Competitiveness in China: The Case of Large Firms in the Oil Industry*. London: Routledge, 2004.

13. CNPC and Sinopec are roughly demarcated along the territorial boundary of the Yellow River. See Jingji Ribao, *Dajubian*, 400–10, for a detailed chronology of reform policy implementation. The offshore oil company CNOOC is omitted in the discussion.

14. However, CNOOC was not allocated sufficient onshore assets to establish a significant foothold in the national market. It is, though, in the process of building up refineries and pipelines in Shanghai and a handful of other coastal cities near CNOOC's offshore production sites.

15. 'China's Oil Price Reforms a Major Step in Deregulating its Petroleum Sector', *Oil & Gas Journal*, 10 August 1998. The pegged pricing mechanism was revised in October 2001 to reduce transparency and thus predictability for arbitrage players. The new mechanism lets the State Council adjust the crude price based on the price variations in New York, London, and Singapore; the exact formula for adjustment is not publicized. The liberalization of prices for finished oil products is a considerably more complicated affair, with the National Development and Reform Commission exercising direct controls over diesel and gasoline prices.

16. Robert F. Freeland, 'The Myth of the M-Form? Governance, Consent, and Organizational Change', *American Journal of Sociology* 102(2), 1996, 483–526, and Patrick Bolton and Joseph Farrell, 'Decentralization, Duplication, and Delay', *Journal of Political* Economy 98 (4), 1990, 803–26, for definitions of these organizational concepts.

17. See Kun-Chin Lin, 'Disembedding Socialist Firms as a Statist Project' and 'Class Formation or Fragmentation?' for managers' and workers' reactions, respectively.

18. *State Council Development Research Center Research and Study Bulletin*, 2/19/01; Edward S. Steinfeld, 'Free Lunch or Last Supper? China's Debt-Equity Swap in Context', *China Business Review*, July–August 2000.

19. 'Sinopec and PetroChina: Still Refining at a Loss', *Seeking Alpha*, 12 August 2008. The official reasons for keeping petrochemical prices down refer to anti-inflation and general consumer welfare considerations.

20. 'China Alters Fuel Pricing and Taxation', *Xinhua*, 6 December 2008; 'China Oil Cos Apply to Regulator to Raise Fuel Prices', *AFX UK Focus*, 9 July 2007; 'China's Top Oil, Gas Producers Call For Higher Prices', *Asia Pulse*, 29 November 2005; 'China's top three oil giants pay 16 bln yuan to government', *People's Daily*, 7 September 2006; 'China Looks at Tax to Profit from Record Earnings of its Oil Majors', *Bloomberg*, 14 November 2005; 'Non-State Enterprises May Sue Oil Giants', *China Daily*, 13 October 2008; Winnie Zhu, 'China Orders CNPC, Sinopec Group to Supply Non-State Refiners', *Bloomberg*, 28 November 2007; 'China's Shandong Seeks Crude for Small Refineries', *Reuters*, 16 October 2007; 'China to Let Non-state Firms Import Oil', *China Daily*, 18 April 2007; Karen Teo, 'Oil Giants in Push to Snuff Out Tiny Rivals', *The Standard* (HK), 20 January 2005.

21. Kun-Chin Lin, 'Class Formation or Fragmentation?'

22. Michael Harrison, 'BP and Shell Invest $1.2bn in Chinese Petrol Station Expansion', *The Independent*, 12 May 2004; 'PetroChina, BP Launch Gas station Venture', *China Daily*, 19 November 2004.

23. The lasting influence of the 'oil clique' in Chinese elite politics was identified by Kenneth Lieberthal and Michel Oksenberg in *Policy Making in China*. Princeton, NJ: Princeton University Press, 1988. One only needs to examine the recent career trajectories of Ma Fucai (former head of CNPC who resigned in 2004 to take the blame for deadly explosions in CNPC's Sichuan gas fields, but subsequently returned to influence in the National Energy Leading Group), Chen Tonghai (former head of Sinopec who has been sentenced to death for corruption), and Su Shu (former head of Daqing Oilfield, current head of Sinopec and an Alternate Member of the 17th Central Committee of the Chinese Communist Party) to observe the continuing politicization of managerial roles in the Chinese NOCs.

24. Kun-Chin Lin, 'Disembedding Socialist Firms as a Statist Project', 86. In 2007, the State-owned Assets Supervision and Administration Commission (SASAC) started asking large, non-financial, publicly listed SOEs, including the national oil companies, to hand over a portion of their post-tax profit as dividends. This demand ended a decade-long no-dividend policy for government-owned companies. 'SOE Dividends Should go to State Coffers', *China Daily*, 8 December 2006. The payout rate for the NOCs is 10 per cent of post-tax profits. Jing Ulrich, 'Dividends from China's State-owned Enterprises', *Financial Times*, 21 January 2008, 31. This new resource base could potentially further support cross-subsidization with the parent holding companies.

25. Erica S. Downs, 'China's "New" Energy Administration'. A Commentary for *China Business Review*, November–December 2008, 42–4.

26. Shi Dan, 'Energy Restructuring in China: Retrospects and prospects', *China & World Economy* 16(4), 2008, 82–93; Bi Xiaoning, 'State Firms Urged to do more Dividend Sharing', *China Daily*, 2 July 2009; Barry Naughton, 'SASAC and Rising Corporate Power in China', *China Leadership Monitor No. 24*, Spring 2008: Economic Policy. Available online at: http://www.hoover.org/publications/clm/issues/16610761.html.

5 Collectively-Owned Enterprises: Hybrid Ownership Form and the Partial Reform Strategy

5.1 Introduction

The leading force of China's departure from central planning came from market-oriented collectively-owned enterprises under the purview of local governments. This was particularly true in rural areas where township and village enterprises (TVEs) played a large role in rural industrialization. But, urban collectives also contributed, albeit in a smaller capacity, notably in providing around one-quarter of urban employment in the 1980s. The focus of the chapter will largely be on TVEs as the major collective sector, but the evolution of urban collectively-owned enterprises will also be briefly explored.

Together, the collectively-owned sector grew from accounting for around 22 per cent of GDP on the eve of reform in 1978 throughout the 1980s and 1990s, peaking at generating nearly 38 per cent of industrial output in 1994 before declining to 11 per cent by the end of the decade, and shrinking to less than 3 per cent in 2005 (see Figure 5.1). In the 1980s and early 1990s, the collective sector benefited from the liberalization of China's wholesale and retail markets and made forays into the new sectors not dominated by state-owned enterprises (SOEs). As they were not saddled with the 'plan', collectives had 'harder' budget constraints which meant that they were more efficient and competitive than SOEs and helped to create the market element of the 'dual track' transition. Their subsequent decline reflects a number of factors to be explored in this chapter.

TVEs were the larger part of the sector, but urban collectives were also important early on in the urban areas (Table 5.1). In 1980, of the 423 million strong labour force, TVEs employed 30 million (or 7 per cent) whilst urban collectives employed 24 million (or 5.1 per cent) of workers. But, as a percentage of their respective rural and urban labour forces, TVEs accounted for some 9 per cent of employment while urban collectives accounted for 23 per cent, making them a much larger employer. However, employment in

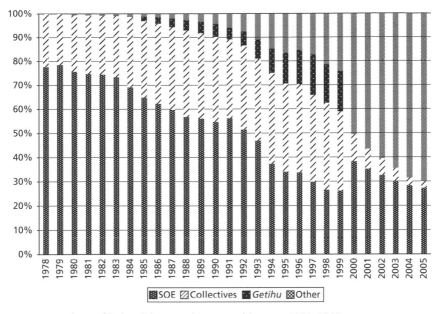

Figure 5.1 Share of industrial output by ownership type, 1978–2005

Source: Chinese Yearbook of Industrial Economy Tables 2–1, 2–3, 2–6.

urban collectives peaked in the early 1990s at 36 million or about one-quarter of the labour force, but TVE employment continued to expand even as the rural labour force remained stable due to migration. Employment in TVEs rose to around 100 million in the early 1990s and reached 150 million by 2007. This made TVEs the second largest employer in the 2000s in the entire (rural and urban) economy after the private sector.

This chapter outlines the origins of TVEs and how they came to be a significant sector in the rural economy. It analyses the puzzle as to how TVEs, which may be profit-oriented but are collectively-owned and therefore were characterized by poor property rights, flourished during the early part of the reform period. Subsequently, TVEs began to decline in output terms but retained their importance as a source for rural employment. This paradox gives rise to a theory that TVEs have multiple objectives, similar to SOEs in urban areas, where their aim is not only to maximize profits, but also to serve other public or social functions, such as providing employment. In many ways, TVEs epitomized the pragmatic reform approach of the Chinese transition, normally associated with SOEs. They are partially marketized enterprises but remain collectively-owned. When this hybrid form poses problems, then piecemeal reforms are adopted, including improving their legal position. Although a number of TVEs have been privatized as with SOEs, they have

Table 5.1. Employment in the collective sector, 1978–2007

Year	Labour force (millions)	Urban (millions)	Collectives (millions)	Rural (millions)	TVEs (millions)
1978	401.52	95.14	20.48	306.38	28.27
1980	423.61	105.25	24.25	318.36	30.00
1983	464.36	117.46	27.44	346.90	32.35
1984	481.97	122.29	32.16	359.68	52.08
1985	498.73	128.08	33.24	370.65	69.79
1986	512.82	132.93	34.21	379.90	79.37
1987	527.83	137.83	34.88	390.00	88.05
1988	543.34	142.67	35.27	400.67	95.45
1989	553.29	143.90	35.02	409.39	93.67
1990	647.49	170.41	35.49	477.08	92.65
1991	654.91	174.65	36.28	480.26	96.09
1992	661.52	178.61	36.21	482.91	106.25
1993	668.08	182.62	33.93	485.46	123.45
1994	674.55	186.53	32.85	488.02	120.17
1995	680.65	190.40	31.47	490.25	128.62
1996	689.50	199.22	30.16	490.28	135.08
1997	698.20	207.81	28.83	490.39	130.50
1998	706.37	216.16	19.63	490.21	125.37
1999	713.94	224.12	17.12	489.82	127.04
2000	720.85	231.51	14.99	489.34	128.20
2001	730.25	239.40	12.91	490.85	130.86
2002	737.40	247.80	11.22	489.60	132.88
2003	744.32	256.39	10.00	487.93	135.73
2004	752.00	264.76	8.97	487.24	138.66
2005	758.25	273.31	8.10	484.94	142.72
2006	764.00	283.10	7.64	480.90	146.80
2007	769.90	293.50	7.18	476.40	150.90

Source: China Statistical Yearbook Table 4–1.

retained their importance as an employer in rural areas, making them a more important government tool for maintaining social aims than SOEs, which had largely been restructured to shed their welfare functions by the 2000s. TVEs, by contrast, have taken on larger shares of rural employment as the rural economy lagged behind urban areas which are racing ahead in terms of income growth.

The situation of urban collectives will be presented by contrast. The sector has steadily lost its share of both industrial output and employment. In other words, there is not a similar set of impetuses for urban collectives to be maintained as a source of employment when the private sector in urban areas has expanded rapidly in the latter part of the reform period. The other public or social goods aims are served by maintaining a small number of large SOEs amidst a significant effort to create a welfare state to absolve such enterprises of those functions during the 2000s. Thus, the inherent inefficiencies of the collective form of enterprises have led to the virtual disappearance of the collectively-owned sector in urban areas when competing against private firms and privatized SOEs. The chapter will conclude with an assessment of the performance of the future of collectives as an organizational form in a rapidly marketizing China.

5.2 Origins of township and village enterprises (TVEs)

TVEs are economic units which are either collectively owned or mainly owned and controlled by the local residents in the rural areas of China. TVEs are nominally owned by local community citizens and under the direct control of local government leaders. Before economic reforms began in 1979, TVEs, known then as Commune and Brigade Enterprises, were completely subordinated to, and an invisible part of, the People's commune system in rural China. At that time, TVEs were physical entities but not recognized economic units, for example they had no balance sheets. Assets were moved in or out of a TVE, or even of the community in which it was based, at the will of the community or government authority. Hence, ownership and the entity itself were ambiguous.

TVEs experienced a significant expansion in the 1980s and early 1990s, specializing in the production of labour- or resource-intensive products neglected by the dominant state-owned enterprises focused on capital-intensive industries stemming from the pre-reform period of the administered economy focused on heavy industrialization. The contribution of TVEs, alongside the incentives offered to agriculture in the early 1980s, caused the rural economy to be widely viewed as the original engine of China's remarkable transformation (see e.g. Oi 1999).

The growth of rural industry is closely related to conditions in agriculture. Restrictions on farmers' non-agricultural activities were greatly relaxed after the Third Plenum of the Eleventh Central Committee in December 1978, which marked the start of market-oriented reforms in China. Unfavourable agricultural sector prospects were the initial force behind the development of TVEs. The adoption of the Household Responsibility System introduced market-oriented incentives, greatly enhancing the production enthusiasm of farmers and increasing their income, thereby at the same time providing capital for the development of TVEs. Undertaking industrialization in agrarian areas absorbed surplus labour from agriculture and so served to create non-farm employment, of particular value when farming was characterized by inefficiency, and the household registration system (*hukou*) prevented rural–urban migration.

In their early period of reform, TVEs were discriminated against by the central government because of their competition with state-owned enterprises for raw materials and markets. Nevertheless, this sector expanded rapidly under the promotion of local leaders. Shortly afterwards, the Chinese central government realized that setting up rural enterprises to absorb surplus rural labour was a preferable way to solve the rural unemployment problems than by allowing rural labour to search for employment opportunities in urban areas.

TVEs in the late 1970s depended heavily on financial support from the agricultural sector. Initially, the accumulation of funds for investment in non-agricultural activities was related to the unusual growth of agricultural incomes, which stemmed partly from the growth of agricultural production and partly from procurement price increases that returned industrial profits to agriculture. During this period, the saving rate of rural residents climbed by seven percentage points. The growth of rural deposits helped expand local banks' supply of funds and fund the development of TVEs.

Conversely, TVEs also raised rural incomes. During 1980–5, average per capita rural income jumped from 191 Yuan in 1980 to 397 Yuan in 1985. Combined with the growth in agricultural productivity, the early 1980s accounted for half of China's impressive poverty reduction during the reform period (Ravallion and Chen 2007).

Given this success, the Chinese government throughout much of the 1980s and the 1990s took a series of steps to make TVEs recognizable production units run like business enterprises. In 1983, the central government issued a policy document to make clear that the property and assets of the TVEs should be protected, those who contributed to TVE growth should receive the benefits in the forms of profit sharing and enhanced wages, and small-scale family production of some items should be encouraged. In 1984, the 'Horizontal Economic Alliances' policy was established. The role of TVEs was elevated making them an instrument of the government to achieve agricultural modernization, absorb surplus labour from agriculture, and alleviate poverty.

This government policy, combined with other shifts in stance, created considerable incentives for TVE growth. The fiscal decentralization of the early 1980s gave greater decision-making power to local governments, and linked fiscal revenue to the career potential of local officials, creating strong incentives for them to promote these enterprises. TVEs were also given privileged access to capital and were helped by massive loans from the state banking system. The Agricultural Bank of China (ABC) held nearly 80 per cent of all rural deposits and loans, about half of which were provided to TVEs (Brandt, Giles and Park 2003).

Under the purview of the Agricultural Bank of China until the mid 1990s, the township branches of the ABC and the rural credit cooperatives controlled much of the lending. In 1985–6, tight fiscal and monetary policies due to inflationary pressures in the macroeconomy meant that bank loans replaced grants, with the goal of making investment decision-making more market rational. Lower levels of the Agricultural Bank of China are responsible to the Ministry of Finance but are also responsible to local governments. This allowed provincial authorities to apply pressure on provincial bank branches to extend loans, even during periods when the central authorities were urging credit tightening. Capital thus flowed to TVEs ahead of others. Local governments had incentives to ensure that TVEs were profitable, as this gave government greater revenue. They also had influence over credit provision. TVEs were thus explicitly preferred in industrial policy and allowed greater access to capital.

As a result, TVEs developed quickly throughout the 1980s and in the early 1990s. In the late 1980s, over 18 million rural enterprises provided employment (sometimes seasonal or part time) to over 90 million people, some

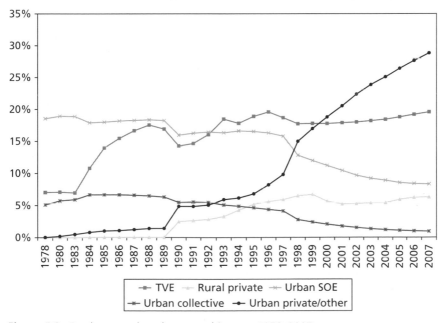

Figure 5.2. Employment share by ownership type, 1978–2007

Source: China Statistical Yearbook Table 4–2.
Note: Figures do not add to 100 per cent as select ownership types are shown.

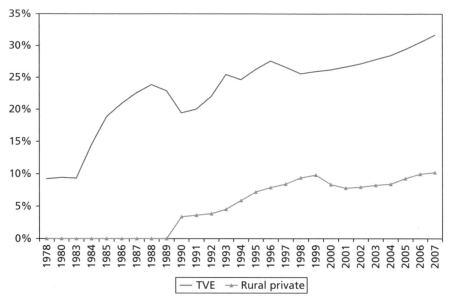

Figure 5.3. Rural employment shares by ownership type, 1978–2007

Source: China Statistical Yearbook Tables 3–5, 4–1, 4–2.
Note: Figures do not add to 100 per cent as classifications of rural employment have undergone changes, so only the shares of TVEs and private enterprises in the rural labour force are shown.

17 per cent of the national labour force, which rose to peak at 20 per cent in the early 1990s. At that time, their gross value of output was about 21 per cent of the national total even though TVEs constituted fewer than 10 per cent of all enterprises. Industry was the largest single rural enterprise sector, accounting for 60 per cent of employment and 70 per cent of the value of output. Within industry, TVEs accounted for 20 per cent of all enterprises, 60 per cent of employment, and 80 per cent of gross output. Figure 5.2 shows how TVEs were the most important non-public sector employer in China until 2000 when it was overtaken by the urban private firms. The numbers for rural employment are even more striking. Figure 5.3 indicates that TVEs accounted for between a quarter and a third of all rural employment, increasing their share even throughout the 1990s and 2000s.

The annual growth rate of value-added in TVEs from the mid 1980s to the mid 1990s was an impressive 25 per cent (Liu and Yu 2008). At the end of 1992, there were 48,200 townships and 806,000 villages. On average, each township with a population of about 18,000 had 8.2 township enterprises with 66 employees per enterprise, and each village with a population of about 1,000 had 1.4 village enterprises with 23 employees per enterprise. By the middle of the 1990s, TVEs accounted for approximately a quarter of China's

GDP, two-thirds of total rural output, and more than one third of China's export earnings. However, the picture changed dramatically by the end of the 1990s (Figure 5.1). TVEs accounted for less than 5 per cent of industrial output by 2005. Nevertheless, TVEs made up a steady and growing share of rural employment even as the rural labour force fell by 9 million between 2000 and 2006. Correspondingly, the TVE share of rural employment shot up to account for nearly one in three workers in 2006.

5.3 **The rise and fall of TVEs**

Jefferson (1993), analysing a panel of 204 state-owned enterprises and 132 TVEs covering the years 1984, 1988, and 1990, estimated that total factor productivity was higher in the TVEs than in the SOEs both at the beginning and the end of this period, with the gap growing over time. The differences attributable to ownership type largely disappear, however, when factors such as scale, management system, and proportion of output sold under state plan, are simultaneously considered. Management surveys reveal widespread agreement that state-owned enterprises, not TVEs, are leaders in the introduction of new technology, but also that TVE output is generally of lesser quality.

This initial out-performance has been attributed to a number of factors. Che and Qian (1998) and Walder (1995) are of the view that it is because local leaders have 'hard' budget constraints, as compared with the 'soft' budget constraints of SOEs which have access to cheap inputs of capital and raw materials. Another comparison is between TVEs and private enterprises. Private enterprises failed to out-compete TVEs until the 1990s. Chen (2000) points out that, relative to private firms which have been hampered in their development for much of the reform period, TVEs have better access to resources, such as land, bank loans, raw materials, and labour. Furthermore, TVEs' managers did not have to bear investment or operation risks, while private enterprises faced frequent and unpredictable bouts of uncertainty. Thus, the success of TVEs could be attributed to various factors such as local governments' financial incentives, their relatively hard budget constraints, managerial incentive contracts, and market competition (Naughton 1995).

However, TVEs began to decline for a number of reasons by the 1990s, culminating in their dramatic relative shrinkage in the 2000s. Notably, there is the issue of property rights. The property rights of a collectively-owned TVE are assigned to the whole of the residents in a community that runs the enterprise. However, due to dispersed ownership rights, it cannot be operated under the direct control of every owner of the firm, but has to be operated by the township or village government. Many view the *de facto* owners of TVEs as local government leaders as they are the public agents of local residents (Che and Qian 1998; Zhu 1998).

The inefficiency of public enterprises is often traced to their ill-defined property rights. Weitzman and Xu (1994) argue that TVEs are best viewed as vaguely defined cooperatives with weak property rights. The outstanding performance of TVEs appears to present a paradox or challenge for traditional property right theory. It could be that TVEs are basically quasi- or disguised private enterprises (Nee 1996).

The government, in any case, responded by trying to improve the property rights of TVEs, so piecemeal reforms were undertaken, very much in the spirit of China's gradualist transition that adopted institutional reforms alongside economic marketization. There are parallels between the approach taken for SOEs and TVEs, including marketization without an initial change in ownership from public to private but eventually with a move toward corporatization or transformation into shareholding companies where the government, at the local levels in this instance, can retain control. But, the legal reforms—more accurately described as policy reforms—adopted for TVEs could also be viewed as being more like 'stop-gap' measures in response to particular failings, and intended to boost production in a sector that appeared to be more efficient than SOEs but still suffered from organizational frailties. By having 'harder' budget constraints, TVEs did not become the burden on the state-owned banks that SOEs did, nor did they manifest the nation's industrial ambitions. Instead, they served a purpose in rural areas, to provide employment in particular. TVEs, in other words, are the embodiment of the gradualist transition, perhaps even more so than SOEs, since these smaller collectives could serve a simple function that did not raise the prospect of generating macro-level instability. Laws and policies for TVEs were simply pragmatic—the very essence of China's partial reform strategy that retains a role for the state in a largely marketized economy. Thus, in many ways, the piecemeal measures taken to reform this sector are truly reflective of the pragmatic policy of the overall incrementalist transition, that is, enactments to respond to problems, but without an overall aim in mind.

During the mid 1980s, local governments and firms started experimenting with joint stock ownership. In 1988, the government officially sanctioned private ownership in the TVE sector. In June 1990, the Regulation on Township and Village Collective Enterprises was issued by the State Council to establish their legal standing. By 1996, most of the steps taken to protect property rights and provide better incentives in the TVEs were confirmed through legislation when the country's highest legislative body, the Congress of People's Representatives, passed the TVE Law. The TVE Law states that '[n]o organisations or individuals shall illegally and administratively interfere with the production and operation of a TVE, including changing the individuals responsible for the firm, or illegally take or use the property of a TVE without compensating for it.' It also establishes the principle of simultaneous development of different forms of ownership in the sector, which eventually led to the sactioning of privately-owned firms that eroded the competitiveness of TVEs and also opened the way for them to undergo privatization.

Having started out producing consumer and light industrial goods neglected by SOEs geared toward heavy industry, the market niche of TVEs was eroded with SOE reforms allowing diversification of production. As competition intensified from domestic as well as foreign firms with greater opening in the 1990s, and credit became increasingly hard to obtain, the collectively-owned TVE sector began to shrink and there was a trend toward privatization. Falling growth rates and deficits came to characterize TVEs.

Also, TVEs were highly geared towards exports. The average annual real growth rate of their exports over the ten-year period from 1988 was as high as 28 per cent, exceeding that of China's total export growth of around 13 per cent over the same period. However, after WTO accession in 2001, there was greater competition from foreign firms which contributed to the decline of TVEs. As part of its WTO terms, China has lowered tariffs. Moreover, in 2000 in anticipation of accession, the Law on Wholly Foreign-Owned Enterprises was revised. This law now allowed wholly foreign-owned enterprises to sell their own products in China, or to appoint other business organizations to sell their products under certain conditions. Indeed, from 1992 onwards, the TVE sector undertook significant privatization. More than 930,000 TVEs had been fully privatized, and more than 461,000 have been partially privatized by the mid 2000s. Township and village governments almost always sold majority shares to insiders, mainly in the form of sales of control rights to managers and employees or to foreign investors. In some cases, the community governments continued to hold a minority stake in the partially privatized former TVEs (Che and Qian 1998). Case study 5 on the toy industry, where China is the world's largest exporter, illustrates the story of TVEs.

Finally, part of the argument for the decline in TVEs relates to the theory that greater competitiveness will probably result in a decline in the attractiveness of TVEs as a form of ownership. China instituted a number of policies designed to increase competition, an important factor in stimulating efficiency improvements in transition economies. For instance, in 1999, the State Development Planning Commission instituted regulations imposing fines for companies found to have cut their prices below cost, or to have offered hidden discounts (Wedeman 2003). Private firms were also accorded greater rights. A 1999 constitutional amendment redefined the private sector. It was recognized that private enterprises play 'an important part in the economy' and that 'private property rights should be protected'. This was followed by the 2007 Property Law providing equal protection to private and public property for the first time. The constitutional change also acknowledged that the self-employed, private, and other non-public sectors constituted an important component of the socialist market economy, whose lawful rights and interests would be protected by the state. These developments underscore the growing importance of new and private forms of ownership. TVEs as an opaque hybrid ultimately defined by collective ownership began to lose their lustre with the rise of the private sector. However, the sector prevails and TVEs, as mentioned at the start, have become more, and not less, important as a rural employer.

5.4 **The multi-tasking role of TVEs**

TVEs are a hybrid form—having harder budget constraints than SOEs, which explains their initial success but not the strong market incentives of private ownership which led to their subsequent decline—that is reminiscent of SOEs in transition. For SOEs, in spite of staggering levels of losses, the motivations for the gradual reform and retention of such enterprises have been well explored. Influential among these is the work of Bai et al. (2000) and their application of the Hart, Shleifer, and Vishny (1997) model of property rights and contracts to SOEs. With multiple objectives associated with public ownership that span not only profit-maximization but governmental aims such as maintenance of full employment and provision of social security, SOEs are viewed as 'multi-tasking', and therefore preserved in an economic as well as political sense. Nevertheless, effective privatization has taken place for most SOEs, and their role in the economy has lessened.

TVEs, despite their differences from SOEs in terms of budget constraints and the lack of historical provision of social securities, can be viewed in similar terms. Collective ownership also causes TVEs to have multiple objectives. They are a provider of rural employment at a time when the rural economy has fallen behind the growth of the urban sector, whilst the household registration system (*hukou*) prevents migration. The shrinking agricultural sector puts pressure on TVEs as the engine of rural industry to provide employment even if surplus.

The unique duality of TVEs and their ability to have a 'foot in both camps' makes them a telling embodiment of the pragmatic reform attitude of the Chinese government in rural areas. The laws and policy pronouncements, as with SOEs, are signposts of needed reforms, such as when property rights need to be shored up to contend with a growing private sector. Perhaps even more so than SOEs, whose inefficiencies threatened the stability of the macroeconomy, TVEs being smaller in scale do not run that risk whilst being an important element of rural industry, such that the multi-tasking theory ascribed to SOEs could be just as, or even more, applicable to TVEs.

Their preservation serves a similar role as SOEs, but their plight is in some ways more difficult as the resources of rural governmental authorities are limited. Serving the dual purpose of having a public function as a generator of employment, but with the realities of constrained budgets, puts TVEs in a hard-to-reconcile situation. Nevertheless, their multi-tasking role offers an explanation for the continued maintenance of TVEs in an economy characterized rapidly expanding private sector and a privatizing by a state-owned sector in the 2000s.

5.4.1 WHY PUBLICLY-OWNED ENTERPRISES MULTI-TASK

The multi-agent theory of reform outlined by Bai et al. (2000) explains the role played by SOEs during China's transition. They argue that there are two types of theories of public ownership: the efficiency theory and the political patronage theory. The political patronage theory (Shleifer and Vishny 1994, Boycko, Shleifer, and Vishny 1996) considers the personal interests of government officials and explores the implications for public ownership. One of the most important objectives of government officials is to maintain their own employment. To achieve this objective, they need to cultivate political support among their constituents by creating jobs for them or protecting their jobs. The value of an SOE as a base for political support is partially determined by the specific industries involved. In labour-intensive industries, the cost of employing one worker in terms of required capital resources is low, and therefore firms in such industries offer better value as bases for political support.

The efficiency theory argues that public ownership is needed to achieve social objectives that are considered to be important by the government and may not be provided otherwise. Traditionally, this theory emphasizes public goods and the information problem in regulating market failures. The more recent development of this theory, which Bai et al. (2000) call the multi-task efficiency theory, focuses on the incentive problems when firms perform multiple tasks, and one of the tasks has externalities.

In the multi-task efficiency theory of public ownership of Hart, Shleifer, and Vishny (1997), the provider of a good or service can choose to invest in quality improvement and/or cost reduction. It is assumed that cost reduction has an adverse effect on the quality of the goods or service. Under private ownership, the provider can benefit more from cost reduction and therefore invests more in doing so than under public ownership. Given the adverse effect of cost reduction on product quality, and the assumption that quality is enjoyed mostly by the consumer of the good or service, quality is lower under private ownership than under public ownership, thereby offering a rationale for public ownership when product quality is deemed more important than cost.

Bai et al. (2000) model the multi-task efficiency theory of public ownership for China. Central to their approach is the assumption that, due to the legacies of the planned economy, there is a lack of an efficient and independent social security and sound financial systems in China. According to their theory, some activities of the firm have negative externalities for the society as a whole, and the incentives for the manager of the firm to engage in the negative-externality producing activities are weaker under public ownership than under private ownership. In China, given the strong legacy of central planning, such negative-externality producing activities take the form of laying off workers and getting debt written off by banks. It is thus optimal to have some firms be publicly owned and others privately owned, with the former choosing lower levels of the negative-externality producing activities than the latter.

Moreover, various levels of governments may have different incentives to privatize SOEs. According to the multi-task efficiency theory of public ownership, state-owned enterprises with higher level of government affiliation are less likely to be privatized. They also postulate that the cost of privatization increases with the amount of surplus labour, and the increase is faster for higher-level than for lower-level governments. Thus, they argue that there may exist a government-affiliation level below which SOEs with more surplus labour are more likely to be privatized, but above which the opposite is true.

Another cost of privatizing SOEs in China is related to the large amount of debt the SOEs carry. When SOEs are privatized, they often have a significant amount of debt written off by the banks with the help of the local government. The write-off is not just for solving the debt overhang problem as discussed by Myers (1977) but is a result of strategic default; many firms use privatization as a pretence to evade their debt obligations. This activity not only costs the central government by reducing the profitability of the banks it owns, but also threatens the stability of the financial system.

Bai et al. (2000) argued that the phenomenon of debt-obligation evasion implies lower-level governments have stronger incentives to privatize their affiliated SOEs for two reasons. One is that lower-level government pays less attention to the negative effect of privatizing local SOEs on the stability of the financial system, which is more of a national matter, and the other is that central government directives are less effective in preventing lower-level governments from pressuring the banks to write-off debt for their affiliated firms in the process of privatization.

5.4.2 THEORETICAL BASIS OF TVEs

This theory can be extended to explain the retention of TVEs. As labour-intensive industries owned by localities, the political patronage theory would point to the preservation of TVEs in a stronger sense than SOEs. As collectively-owned enterprises, the land, labour, and capital used in production by TVEs all rest upon political 'contracts'. In terms of the multi-tasking efficiency theory, public ownership rather than privatization would reduce the negative externalities in terms of layoffs. Without the 'soft budget constraints' of SOEs, the second externality of 'strategic default' is not pertinent, further implying that retention of TVEs does not jeopardize financial stability, or that lower-level governments should have a stronger incentive to privatize in any case. Thus, the prevention of layoffs as the overriding public incentive, coupled with political patronage, would suggest that TVEs will be preserved and held in public hands. This is not, though, without cost, as TVEs found it increasingly difficult to compete against a growing private sector.

Local officials in reform-era China have an overriding interest in promoting economic development. This interest stems from two features of the institutional environment. The first is the cadre evaluation system that sets criteria for the performance of Party cadres and government officials, monitors their performance, determines their remuneration, influences their tenure in office, and shapes their opportunities for advancement. The cadre evaluation system has an influence on the behaviour of officials because these officials seek to maintain their positions of power and advance within the system. The second is the fiscal system that finances their activities and generates the revenues that are essential at the local level.

Che and Qian (1998) interpret local government ownership of TVEs as such a mechanism. Owned by local residents, nominal ownership guarantees that most benefits are retained locally. In their model, the central government finds that surrendering property rights to the local authorities is better than centralization. They argue that total revenues flowing to the central government can actually increase when the centre surrenders its property rights under this institutional set-up, and that this can account for the observation that the property rights of local levels of government have been quite robust against possible infringements by superior levels of government. Thus, their argument is that most strategic control rights of TVEs are exercised by community government rather than by enterprises themselves. The autonomy of the enterprise was limited to daily operations.

To examine this more thoroughly requires an examination of the legal status of TVEs. Assets of TVEs legally belong to residents of the township and village: 'Assets (of a TVE) are owned collectively by the whole of rural residents of the township or village who run the enterprise; the ownership rights over the enterprise assets shall be exercised by the rural residents' meeting (or congress) or a collective economic organisation that represents the whole of rural residents of the township or village. The ownership rights of the enterprise assets will not change when the enterprise is under a managerial contract responsibility system, leasing, or joint operations with enterprises of other types of ownership' (Article 18, Chapter 3).

This means that the owner has control rights, delegated to agents representing the whole of the community, typically an 'Economic Commission' or 'General Corporation for Development' of community government. 'The owner of a TVE, according to the law, determines the direction and formats of its business operations, selects managers or determines the method of such selection, determines the specific distribution ratios of after-tax profits between the owner and the enterprise, and has the rights over the enterprise concerning its spin-off, merger, relocation, stop-operation, close-down, application for bankruptcy, etc.' (Article 19, Chapter 3).

Chang and Wang (1994) similarly describe the operational form of TVEs in its early iterations. The contributions of township–village government to TVEs were considerable: their political connections provided security for long-term development; they provided managerial inputs, especially when markets were suppressed; they provided access to outside resources like bank loans; and finally, they became the interface between the agency problems of central mandates. This control of the local government then interacted with local citizens providing labour (in abundant supply), and occasionally pooling financial resources together through *jizi* contributions at the initial stages of TVEs.

This led to a situation where residual profits from the TVEs were divided into three parts. The centre required 60 per cent be retained by the firm for production expansion, with a particular focus on labour-intensive expansion rather than capital-intensive expansion. The remaining 40 per cent was not regulated by the centre. Chang and Wang (1994) argued that usually a small portion was paid as bonuses to workers, and the larger portion was paid as fees to township–village government. This fee payment was then used for two purposes: to support communal social programmes and infrastructure projects, and to support the maintenance of township–village government operations.

Furthermore, the Regulation on Township and Village Collective Enterprises of the People's Republic of China issued in 1990 spells out, among other things, the ownership rights of a TVE's assets, the allocation of control rights, and the rules concerning distribution of after-tax profits. Revenues were used for two purposes: reinvestment and local public goods provision. 'The part retained by the enterprise should be no less than 60 per cent of the total and should be arranged under the enterprise's autonomous decision. The retained after-tax profits for the enterprise should be mainly used for the increase of the funds for production development in technological transformation and expansion of reproduction, and also for the appropriate increase of welfare funds and bonus funds.' And 'the part remitted to the owner of the enterprise should be used mainly for the support of construction of agricultural infrastructure, agricultural technology services, rural public welfare, renewal and transformation of enterprises, or development of new enterprises' (Article 32, Chapter 5).

In most cases, cadres acting as representatives of local governments effectively exercised property rights over local firms, including the right to make decisions about operations and personnel, to control residual income, and to dispose of assets. In areas with little legacy of state investment, by contrast, some local officials actively courted private investment, from which they could extract tax and fee revenue, thereby developing an interest in protecting private property rights. Thus, private investors could find pockets in which they could gain a foothold in the local economy and exercise effective property rights over their assets, including the rights to make decisions about operations and personnel, as well as to control residual income and dispose of assets. The changing fiscal environment and the motives of the cadres led to reform of TVEs.

5.4.3 SHIFTING POLICY BASE

Following the end of the communes, a system of fiscal responsibility (the Budgetary Responsibility System) was introduced in the early 1980s which lasted until 1994. This reform mainly pertained to the relationship between the central and provincial governments. Each province signed a contract with the central government, stipulating the amount of funds to be forwarded to the centre annually. Revenues generated over and above this stipulated sum could be retained in whole or in part for the provincial usage. Under this system, the provinces have more resources at their disposition should they successfully create more revenues. This system encouraged provincial-level hoarding of funds, whilst reinforcing existing vertical and horizontal inequalities (Wong and Bird 2008). Moreover, it led to the near bankruptcy of the Chinese state as its tax revenue dwindled and social spending withered (Figure 5.4). Due to incentives to stimulate local industry, provincial-level governments focused funds almost solely on doing so.

In 1994, a 'tax sharing' system, which formally delineates local and central taxes, was introduced to replace the Budgetary Responsibility System. The main aim was to strengthen the centre's financial position and sever the direct link between the revenues of the local government and those of the enterprises located within their respective geographical jurisdictions. The system theoretically enabled the central government to play a redistributive role through

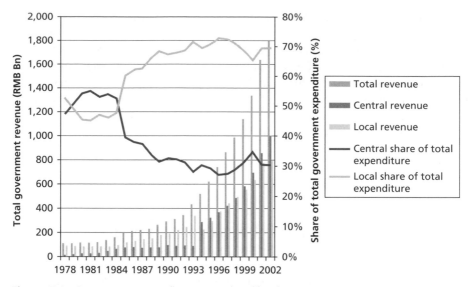

Figure 5.4. Government expenditure, central and local, 1978–2002

Source: China Finance Yearbook Tables 1–2, 1–3.

Notes: Total expenditure by central government was left out of this calculation as government price subsidies were listed as negative revenue items prior to 1986, but they have been listed as expenditure items in government accounts since 1986. For comparison purpose, budgetary price subsidies before 1985 were adjusted by the National Statistical Bureau and listed as expenditure items. Also, government expenditures include the interest payment on domestic and foreign debts since 2000. From 1988-2000, debts were taken out of the calculations (see the comparison between table 7.4 in the 2008 Chinese Statistical Yearbook and table 6.18 in the 1990 Chinese Statistical Yearbook). Thus, this table instead uses revenues solely.

the usage of fiscal transfers, ensuring that adequate funds were available throughout all levels of the Chinese political system. Enterprise profits no longer accrued to local governments, but rather to local financial institutions that then transferred income to the central government in the form of taxes rather than profits. There was also a new value-added tax (VAT) introduced to be collected by local bureaus of the central tax authority, in contrast to the previous VAT system that was administered locally, with the revenues then split between the centre (75 per cent) and local (25 per cent) governments. The new tax base thus relaxed some of the grip on local enterprises held by local government. The consequences of this shift in public finance were clear: horizontal and vertical inequities in revenue-raising capacity would be exacerbated. But, it ensured that the need for local enterprises to generate revenue becomes greater.

Local tax reform in 1994 was matched with banking reforms that changed fundamentally the way banks deal with local governments (Brandt and Zhu 2000). Before then, local branches made 70 per cent of the loans. Bank reform centralized the lending authorities to upper-level banks, which reduced the local government's influence on the bank's lending decisions. The shift in tax reforms and the introduction of 'harder' budget constraints made township governments responsible financially for bad projects and enterprise losses. Because it is more difficult for township governments to influence banks at an upper or county level, local governments faced a much harder budget constraint after the banking reform. Financial reform limited local governments to small-scale capital-raising. This was via internal fundraising or external sources, for example the Agricultural Bank of China or rural credit cooperatives, the use of community assets as collateral, or the provision of loan guarantees. As a result, inefficient firms were less valuable to these governments. Because township governments no longer had any advantage in the credit market, transferring ownership to managers became preferred.

Therefore, the 1997 Law on Township Enterprises then defined TVEs as 'different types of enterprises that are established in townships (including the villages under their jurisdiction) with the bulk of the capital being invested by the rural economic collectives or farmers'. This reform formalized the fact that, although they are publicly-owned, TVEs are subject to harder budget constraints.

The 1997 legislative changes concentrated on the selection and rewarding of TVE managers. Local government's ability to provide incentives for managers became more limited. For instance, these changes included restrictions on the use of after-tax profits for public expenditures, limited direct control over 'management fees' (portion directly remitted to community government), and profits retained for public expenditures, and less influence over profits for reinvestment. The result, similar to the overhaul of SOEs in the late 1990s, restructured TVEs and eventually led to privatization. Though, again, the incomplete privatization of the sector attests to the multiple roles played by TVEs in the rural economy, similar to SOEs, but arguably without the significant, macroeconomic downsides associated with 'soft budget constraints'.

5.4.4 TVEs IN TRANSITION

What rendered TVEs increasingly unable to contain or respond to a more competitive environment was that the key players—local officials and enterprise managers—were not the true owners of TVEs, yet they were able to use TVEs as vehicles for the maximization of their self-interest without having to bear full responsibility for the costs involved—especially hidden and/or long-term ones. It is not surprising that, when such costs reached a critical threshold that could no longer be justified and/or sustained by the pertinent benefits, only one viable option remained, that is, to privatize poorly performing TVEs.

Table 5.2. Rural enterprises, 2004

Ownership form	Number of firms		Employment		Value-added		Fixed assets (net)		Employees per firm	Value-added per firm (RMB 000s)	Fixed assets per firm (RMB 000s)
	000s	%	000s	%	000s RMB	%	000s	%			
Collectives	241	34.33	9,979	29.16	283,152	21.14	319,046	19.74	41.4	1,175	1,324
Collective and partially privatized firms	702	3.17	34,224	24.68	1,339,215	32.03	1,285,956	38.37	48.8	1,908	1,832
Joint stock co-operatives	97	13.82	2,665	7.79	100,811	7.53	95,068	5.88	27.5	1,039	980
Jointly-run firms	31	4.42	600	1.75	17,736	1.32	20,558	1.27	19.4	572	663
Limited liability firms	242	34.47	11,281	32.96	465,656	34.77	558,155	34.54	46.6	1,924	2,306
Shareholding firms	36	5.13	2,032	5.94	122,656	9.16	160,907	9.96	56.4	3,407	4,470
Joint venture firms	55	7.83	7,667	22.40	349,204	26.08	462,338	28.61	139.4	6,349	8,406
Private firms	2,771	12.52	42,491	30.64	1,365,521	32.66	1,159,433	34.60	15.3	493	418
Household-run firms	18,660	84.31	61,946	44.67	1,476,800	35.32	905,887	27.03	3.3	79	49
Total rural firms	21,326	100.00	132,876	100.00	3,238,581	100.00	2,691,227	100.00	6.3	189	151

Source: Category-match is based on Yearbook of China's Township and Village Enterprises, 2003, 130–1, 420, 422, 424. Figures are from Yearbook of China's Township and Village Enterprises, 2005, 108 and 110.

Although TVEs may well serve multiple objectives in the rural economy, the erosion of their contribution to industrial output stands in contrast to their continuing role as employment providers in rural areas. Their restructuring has led to a dwindling of numbers. Table 5.2 indicates that by 2004, about two-thirds of the TVEs in terms of both number of firms and employment, and some 80 per cent in terms of value-added and fixed assets had been restructured into a variety of ownership forms. These included joint stock cooperatives, jointly run businesses, limited liability companies, shareholding companies, and Chinese–foreign joint ventures, in which local governments typically had a minority shareholding stake or had exited completely. However, around one-third of TVEs remained in the narrowly defined collective category, which refers to those firms in which the local government holds a majority stake. Table 5.2 also shows how significant the scale of privatization had been. While TVEs, private firms and household-run firms each contributes about one-third of the total value-added in the rural enterprise sector, some one-third of firms in the private category are in fact fully privatized small TVEs. In contrast to SOEs, where the largest firms are in firm control of the state, the largest enterprises in the TVE sector are typically Chinese–foreign joint ventures and shareholding companies. The average employment in a joint-venture firm is typically three times that of a collective TVE. If comparing their sizes using value-added per firm and net fixed assets per firm, the multipliers become 5.4 and 6.3, respectively. While, on average, shareholding firms are similar in size to collective TVEs in terms of employees per firm, the former typically possesses two times more net fixed assets and produces two times more value-added than that of the latter.

By the 2000s, TVEs had been largely privatized and those which remained were small and less subject to the forces of decline. This makes their contribution to employment all the more remarkable, and the maintenance of the sector reflects the multi-tasking role that TVEs have taken on in the rural economy. As SOEs had been maintained for multi-tasking reasons in urban areas, TVEs appear to serve a similar purpose in rural ones.

5.5 Urban collectives and the performance of the collective sector

The fate of urban collectives stands in contrast. Figure 5.5 shows the decline in employment in urban collectives during the reform period. Having accounted for a smaller proportion of the urban workforce, their decline is less dramatic than SOEs. Nevertheless, by 2007, urban collectives accounted for 2 per cent of urban employment and less than 1 per cent of total employment in China,

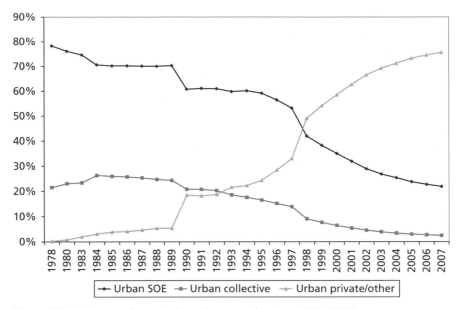

Figure 5.5. Urban employment shares by ownership type, 1978–2007
Source: China Statistical Yearbook Tables 4–8, 4–10, 4–13.

shrinking steadily each year since peaking at one-quarter of the urban labour force in 1984.

Similar to TVEs, urban collectives are enterprises communally owned by localities. They face harder budget constraints than SOEs, but their dwindling number suggests that the multi-tasking role ascribed to TVEs does not apply to collectives in urban areas. Private firms serving the fast-growing urban sector provided employment, and government revenues stemmed from a diverse enterprise sector, not burdened by the problems of a declining agricultural sector. Also, the dominance of SOEs, which were the 'multi-tasking' vehicle in urban areas, meant that urban collectives never played a central part. Rapid economic growth lessened their already peripheral role, and their hybrid, communal ownership form did not allow them to compete effectively against private firms and privatized SOEs.

Thus, the collective sector in 2007 numbered only 13,000 firms (Table 5.3) out of 336,000 above-designated size firms tracked by the National Bureau of Statistics. These are firms with annual revenue exceeding five million Yuan, but the figure gives an approximation of the relative size of the collectively-owned sector which comprise about 4 per cent of all large firms.

Correspondingly, the industrial output of the sector was only 2.5 per cent of total industrial output. In terms of assets, profit, and employees, the collectively-owned sector is much smaller than the others. Compared with

Table 5.3. Industrial output by ownership type, 2007

	Number of enterprises	Gross industrial output (100 million Yuan, current prices)	Total assets (100 million Yuan, current prices)	Profit (100 million Yuan, current prices)	Average average number of employees (10,000 persons)	Capital per worker	Output per worker	Profit per worker
Total	*336,768*	*405,177*	*353,037*	*399,717*	*7,875*	*44,829*	*514,498*	*448,290*
State-owned enterprises	10,074	36,387	54,723	2,630	646	84,687	502,608	464,801
Collectively-owned enterprises	13,032	10,170	5,739	640	246	23,275	412,466	232,752
Private enterprises	177,080	94,023	53,305	5,054	2,252	23,660	417,341	236,605
Foreign-invested enterprises from Hong Kong, Macao, and Taiwan	31,949	42,418	34,071	2,516	1,108	30,730	382,587	307,298
Foreign-invested enterprises	35,507	85,211	62,296	5,011	1,244	50,065	684,801	500,645

Source: China Statistical Yearbook Table 13–1.

Notes: The NBS only classifies industrial firms with annual revenue above 5 million Yuan. The figures do not add up to the total because only select categories are reported.

SOEs, it has one-third of the output, one-tenth of the assets, less than one-fourth of the profits, and one-third of the employees. In other words, collectives are less capitalized and profitable but manage to produce more output relative to assets. As these are likely to be labour-intensive rather than capital-intensive like the remaining SOEs, this is not unexpected. What Table 5.3 also shows is that in terms of capital per worker, output per worker, and profit per worker, the collective sector is below the average across all ownership sectors, but has a profile that is remarkably similar to private firms. These are the least capitalized and profitable as compared with SOEs and foreign firms, but the profile of the 13,000 collectives is similar to the 117,000 private firms among these larger-scale enterprises.

When production function is estimated, this observation is confirmed in Table 5.4. Using a nationally representative enterprise survey of around 1,200 firms for 2000–5, the productivity of the large-scale collectives is seen to be similar to that of private firms, both of which are more productive than SOEs (the omitted category), and more so than reformed SOEs, but not as productive as foreign-invested firms. The value-added of collectives is 0.294 log points higher than SOEs, translating into an almost 30 per cent higher productivity differential. When the wage bill which proxies for skills of the workforce is substituted for the simpler measure of employment, the coefficient increases, suggesting that the productivity differential is not a result simply of the skill base of the firm. This is, of course, relative to SOEs which have 'soft budget constraints' and are inefficient but preserved for other reasons. The remaining collectively-owned enterprises, therefore, likely still operate because they are as efficient as other domestic firms, including reformed SOEs and private firms. The inefficient ones have been privatized. But, foreign firms remain more productive and listed firms as well, so therefore there are a growing number of sources of competition in the economy.

Accounting for only 4 per cent of all large-scale industrial firms in China, the collective sector has shrunk dramatically in urban and rural areas. The sector's share of industrial output is even smaller. In rural areas, however, TVEs still number some 240,000 (Table 5.2). Among small and medium-sized enterprises (SMEs), they are estimated to constitute over 90 per cent of these typically employment-generating firms in rural areas, though these estimates are difficult to make precisely (Liu and Yu 2008). Nonetheless, TVEs accordingly provide a significant portion of rural employment.

The situation in urban areas is different. The urban collective sector has shrunk to account for only 1 per cent of the urban workforce in the 2000s. Without the additional public goods rationale associated with the preservation of TVEs, urban collectives, facing growing competition from firms with better defined legal rights—not just private and foreign firms but also privatized SOEs and listed ones—and without the cheap inputs of SOEs,

Table 5.4. Productivity of collectively-owned firms in the 2000s

Dependent variable: Value-added	(1)	(2)
Capital	0.291***	0.211***
	(0.019)	(0.021)
Labour	0.585***	
	(0.028)	
Wage bill		0.343***
		(0.018)
Collectives	0.294**	0.370***
	(0.120)	(0.111)
Reformed SOEs	0.264***	0.298***
	(0.090)	(0.082)
Private firms	0.215**	0.278***
	(0.091)	(0.084)
Foreign-invested firms	0.428***	0.378***
	(0.103)	(0.093)
Listed firms	0.263***	0.227***
	(0.097)	(0.083)
Constant	2.581***	1.867***
	(0.305)	(0.259)
Industry (35)	Yes	Yes
Province (11)	Yes	Yes
Year (5)	Yes	Yes
Adjusted R-squared	0.734	0.774
Firms	1169	1169
Observations	4253	4254

Source: NBS enterprise survey

Notes: All values for inputs are in logs, while ownership types are dummy variables. Reformed SOEs are state-owned enterprises which have been restructured into joint ventures or shareholding companies. Control variables include whether the firm is publicly listed, age of firm, first appearance in data set, city/province, industrial sector, outlier, and part of multi-plant firms. The 12 cities (province in parenthesis) are Beijing (municipality), Changchun (Jilin), Chifeng (Inner Mongolia), Dandong (Liaoning), Hangzhou (Zhejiang), Shijiazhuang (Hebei), Shiyan (Hubei), Shunde (Guangdong), Wujiang (Jiangsu), Xian (Shaanxi), Zibo (Shandong), Chongqing (municipality). Omitted categories are state-owned enterprises, year 2000, coal industry and Hubei province.

*** indicates significance at the 1 per cent level,

** at the 5 per cent level, and

* at the 10 per cent level.

have suffered. Interestingly, estimations using a firm-level data set for the first half of the 2000s, show that the remaining larger-scale collectives are as productive as other domestic firms. The implication is that the most efficient ones survived. Their dwindling numbers, though, indicate that their position may well be less tenable as other firms gain improved legal and organizational forms. And, urban collectives, in particular, lack the political support granted to TVEs, making their existence dependent on competitiveness that is undoubtedly hampered by their communal property status that stands increasingly at odds with the growing private sector with better property rights and the large SOEs whose state ownership can often be a source of advantage.

5.6 **Conclusion**

Township and village enterprises were the early engine of growth in China, but have struggled throughout the latter part of the reform period. With the growing employment pressures in urban areas and lagging incomes in the rural sector, there is a renewed attention paid to rural industrialization. By lifting rural incomes which have fallen behind urban ones and with the majority of the population still resident in rural areas, the revival of rural industry—perhaps in the form of TVEs—has become a policy priority (Figures 5.6 and 5.7).

Understanding the reasons for their decline and the prospects for rural industrialization has taken on a new urgency in China. However, as with most

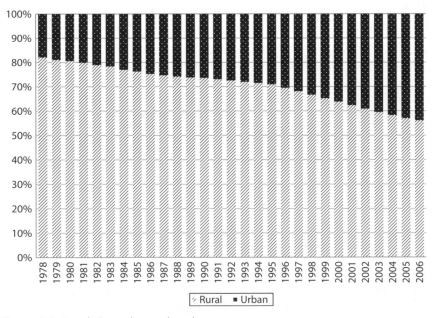

Figure 5.6. Population: urban and rural

Source: China Statistical Yearbook Table 3–1.

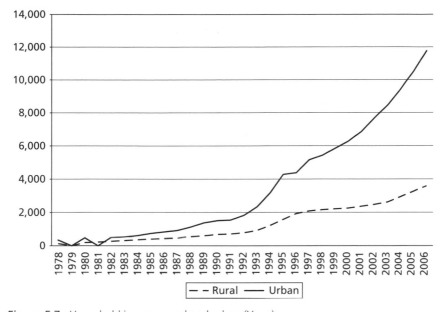

Figure 5.7. Household income: rural and urban (Yuan)

Source: China Statistical Yearbook Tables 9–2 and 9–7.
Notes: Household income is measured as consumption in urban areas but income in rural areas.

developing countries, the challenges of sustaining rural industry are not simple ones to contend with. China's early success with TVEs may be due to the surplus labour in agriculture which became a ready workforce that exploited a niche in consumer goods neglected by the dominant SOE sector. With competition and marketization, it is not apparent where the competitiveness of TVEs or other rural industries will lie vis-à-vis reformed SOEs and a burgeoning private sector. The continuing ambiguity over their property rights, particularly in the midst of an overall trend of corporatization in China, does not bode well. Nevertheless, as providers of employment with multiple objectives in addition to profit maximization, TVEs serve a public function in the countryside. The unknown question is: how long can they continue to do so even as rural industrialization is understood to be crucial to the process of growth.

By contrast, urban collectives have virtually disappeared as competition has exposed the weaknesses in their organizational structure. Without additional mandates to preserve the sector such as with TVEs due to the preferred SOEs in urban areas, there is no policy imperative to support these firms. This is particularly true as the private sector has grown rapidly in the 1990s and particularly the 2000s and come to dominate the urban economy. The remaining large-scale collectives are few in number but these have seemingly survived by being as efficient as other domestic firms.

TVEs may well have a future whilst China copes with the difficult question of the lagging rural economy by providing employment during ongoing reforms. No such rationale exists for urban collectives. The multi-tasking role of TVEs is similar to the reason for maintaining SOEs. But, the harder budget constraints of the collective sector, coupled with communal property ownership, raises serious doubts about the long-term prospects for these firms. Although they have operated largely outside of the legal structure created for firms in China, their continuation may well require that they are reformed in accordance with the corporatization trend, or else these communally-owned firms will find themselves increasingly at odds with the marketizing economy in China.

Case study 5

EVOLUTION OF TVEs—THE TOY INDUSTRY

The toy industry of China is a dynamic sector that has been an important driver of growth, especially in respect of the country's export sector, since the onset of economic reforms in the late 1970s. China became the biggest toy exporter in the world. In 2006, exports from the toy industry accounted for 20.26 per cent of the country's total exports (China Toy Association 2009). In 2007, China exported over 20 billion pieces of toys, which was about 60 per cent of the global total (Chung 2009). More than 70 per cent of those toys were manufactured in Guangdong province (Chung 2009). This case study of Chenghai will illustrate that the toy industry is one of those whose growth has been significantly driven by the development of TVEs. Chenghai District of Shantou City in Guangdong province is located in the Hanjiang Delta of southern Guangdong and the neighbouring Shantou Special Economic Zone (SEZ). Chenghai has an area of 345.23 square kilometres with a population of 710,000 and is known as a locality containing stories of successful TVEs in the toy industry. Historically, Chenghai was a rural agricultural area, but it eventually began to industrialize after the start of economic reforms in 1979 (Information Center of Chenghai Shantou 2009b). Chenghai now focuses on light-processing and developing sectors such as toys and handicrafts manufacture and the processed foods industry. But, it is especially renowned for being a major toy producing and exporting base in China, and is called the 'Chinese toys and gifts city'. Chenghai has over 3,000 enterprises specializing in the production of toys. In 2004, the industrial output in the sector amounted to 10.1 billion RMB, accounting for 40 per cent of Chenghai's total industrial output and 70 per cent of its exports. In 2005, total toy exports from Chenghai accounted for more than half of the total toy exports from Guangdong province (Li 2009). Over the years, Chenghai has seen the transformation of its small TVE toy factories into large corporations with exports to major international markets (such as Japan, the United States, Europe, and the Middle East) and offices operating outside of China (Li 2009).

A notable example of one such corporation is the Guangdong Huawei Toys Craft Company Limited, which is a joint stock company headquartered in Chenghai (Guangdong Huawei 2008). The company prides itself in an annual output of 60 million toys and revenues of 800 million RMB. Recognizing its achievements, it has been named as one of the nation's major TVEs with a successful brand name (Hong Kong Commercial Newspapers 2009). Its Quality Control (QC) Group was also recognized as an 'Excellent QC Group for a TVE system in 2003' (License Union 2008). Huawei's developments over the years epitomize the factors that make TVEs an important engine of rural industrialization and exports in China.

Huawei has its origin as a toy factory in Chenghai in the late 1970s. Although it was then the district's 'head toy factory', it lacked manufacturing premises, production facilities, capital, and technical skills. It was also plagued with problems of inefficiency. The turning point came when the local government decided to appoint a new manager for the factory, Guo Zhuocai, who was a leader in one of Chenghai's township committees (Hong Kong Commercial Newspapers 2009). From then on, the factory was run in a much more market-oriented and entrepreneurial fashion, shedding the strictures and inefficiencies commonly associated with state-owned enterprises (SOEs). This is telling as to why many TVEs in the 1980s started to outperform state-owned enterprises. One year after Guo took over the management, the factory was starting to turn losses into profits. It actively expanded its business base, explored new markets, and strived to meet customers' needs. For example, when approached by a Hong Kong import and export company with an order of 160,000 units of toys for export to West Germany, Guo managed to mobilize workers to work overtime for two months. It was this kind of flexibility and focus on customers' needs that enabled the factory—and other similar TVEs in China at that time—to venture into the export market. The factory also became the first electrified toy factory in Chenghai and a driver behind China's rural industrialization.

It should however be noted that, while TVEs generally differed from SOEs in having to operate under tighter budget constraints and take responsibility for their own finances, they did benefit, sometimes substantially, from their close affiliation with local governments. The toy factory under Guo, for instance, was able to borrow land from local authorities and set up manufacturing premises. It also managed to obtain loans from government departments when it was short of capital in the early years. Guo himself was, after all, appointed by the local government to be manager of the factory. Furthermore, the Chenghai authorities had been supportive of the development of TVEs and industrial activities at the township and village levels. By 1994, about fifteen years into economic reforms, Chenghai had a diverse set of industrial enterprises, including TVEs, SOEs, other collectively-owned entities and even some private enterprises.

As the operation and reputation of the toy factory grew, it underwent several major changes in the structure of its ownership and business strategy. In 1985, it was approached by a Hong Kong company (specializing in the production of plastics and ironware), turning the factory into the second ever Chinese–foreign equity joint venture in Chenghai since the start of the reform period. In 1997, Huawei was formally established as a limited liability company with registered capital of 66 million RMB and fixed asset investment of 200 million RMB. In 2000, Huawei announced plans to build an industrial park. Again, the company managed to secure government support, and its plan was listed as one of Shantou's major industrial projects in 2000. In 2007, Huawei was further restructured to become a joint stock limited liability company, transforming into a corporation. Huawei's development was in line with the policy direction of the Chenghai authorities, which, since the mid 1990s, began to encourage enterprises to pursue new corporate forms such as shareholding and partially privatized companies. Huawei's evolution into a limited liability company was also reflective of the development trend of some TVEs during the late 1990s and 2000s. In light of the country's increasingly marketized environment, that period saw some TVEs turning themselves into corporations and pursuing more modern forms of management.

Huawei is not the only success story in Chenghai. Another major toy company in the locality that has its origin as a TVE is the Guangdong Auldey Toy Industry Company Limited. Audley has been recognized as a 'famous brand' and an 'advanced private enterprise' in Guangdong (*People's Daily* (South China) 2001a, 2001b). There are also a significant number of TVEs that never transformed into large corporations like Huawei and Audley. They remain relatively small scale in their production and focus on the lower segment of the market. An important factor that set companies like Huawei apart and made its success possible is probably the emphasis on brand building and quality control. By the late 2000s, Huawei was reported to be devoting 4 to 5 per cent of its annual profits to research and development, but the future of the TVE sector is uncertain. The large ones have been corporatized, but the smaller firms remain linked to local governments and lack the scale to develop. Huawei and Audley typify the corporatization of the sector. The numerous smaller ones will need to be competitive in order to survive in an economy with greater marketization. Whether the TVE organization form allows them to do so is unclear.

6 Private Firms: Law Ex Post and as Obstacle

6.1 Introduction

The standing of privately-owned firms in China had always been less than certain during the reform period as it clashed with the notion of communal property pervasive through much of the economic reforms. However, by the 2000s, private firms in China were better established insofar as they were granted improved legal recognition, though most were small and medium-sized (SMEs) which still suffered from insecure property rights protection, credit constraints, and a lack of a level playing field with respect to state-owned enterprises (SOEs). The non-state sector, nevertheless, has been a strong driver of China's growth and started to outweigh the importance of SOEs in generating industrial output by the late 1990s. As such, private firms eventually benefited from the corporatization transformation of enterprises, such that they could become shareholding companies under the Company Law and operate as limited liability partnerships and incorporated firms.

Thus, private firms have largely operated without much guidance from laws or policies, and often at a disadvantage to SOEs. Their ability to manoeuvre the incomplete legal system is a familiar tale for private firms in developing countries, but the extent of financial repression whereby the banking system is dominated by state-owned banks adds a further layer of difficulties in developing *de novo* private firms. Private firms and entrepreneurs had grown rapidly, though, with the first stirrings of market liberalization. Although the numbers are difficult to nail down, particularly before 1990, official statistics began to measure the number of self-employed in the 1990s as one gauge of the size of the private sector (see Figure 6.1). By these figures, the number of the self-employed peaked at the end of the 1990s at the height of the large-scale *xiagang* policy which accompanied the restructuring of SOEs that led to the layoff of around one-quarter of the urban labour force. Many of those who became self-employed would have been involuntarily self-employed (Knight and Yueh 2004). Thus, the self-employed accounted for one-eighth of the total employment in urban areas and about 9 per cent nationally. The proportion fell afterwards, but remained on an upward trend even in rural areas. Given the constraints on self-employment, a survey conducted in 1999 found that most self-employed did not wish for their children to follow in their footsteps (Yueh 2009a). Therefore, when the private sector began to receive more accommodation, wage employment remained the preferred route. However, the same developments would have bolstered the prospects of entrepreneurship, which also explains the increasing proportion in urban areas back towards the 1999 peak. In rural areas, the loosening of the household registration system (*hukou*) in the 2000s due to reported labour shortages in the coastal provinces such as Guangdong would have propelled more migration in search of higher paying jobs. Thus, self-employment as a share of national employment does not trend as sharply upward as in urban areas. Nevertheless, those who have started their own firms still account for one in sixteen workers nationally in the 2000s.

Official statistics of private firms are often difficult to interpret as many will be privatized SOEs or collectives, and a number will also be joint stock companies which again include partially privatized SOEs or collectives. The truly private sector, therefore, is hard to assess. Nevertheless, the self-employed or *getihu* (sole proprietorships with fewer than eight employees) can be classified as the *de novo* private sector which comprises entrepreneurs starting their own businesses. Unsurprisingly, what determines and affects entrepreneurship is the common focus of studies of private enterprise in China. However, the final chapter will examine the policy of corporatization or *gongsihua* which has created a corporate sector dominated by companies defined by shares in China, including private ones by the 2000s. This chapter will focus on the legal and institutional factors

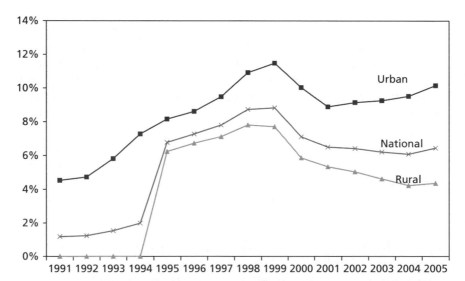

Figure 6.1. Self-employment as a share of total employment
Source: China Statistical Yearbook Tables 4–14, 4–1, 4–2.

which have shaped the development of the entrepreneurs in China that are the source of private enterprise formation.

Specifically, the lacuna of laws for private firms and the reluctance to recognize private property has posed obstacles, which the entrepreneurial have overcome through the use of social networks. The reliance on relational contracting in the face of an incomplete legal system, coupled with the long-standing use of *guanxi* or interpersonal relationships to transact business, are important reasons why private enterprises have rapidly developed in spite of legal and institutional impediments, or at least neglect. The continued growth of the needed private sector may well require reforms to the legal system as such trust-based forms of transactions will run into limits as firms become larger in scale and personal relations become unfeasible. This is not to suggest that relationships will not continue to be important; but, rather, as firms reach a certain scale, it is not possible to maintain the type of interactions required for informal relational contracting to take the place of a more developed contracting and enforcement system for contracts and disputes. Both are often seen in other economies and this will probably be the case in China.

6.2 **The laws and policies governing an evolving private sector**

In numerous respects, the laws which governed the private sector often lagged behind the development of the market. For instance, the 13th Congress of the Chinese Communist Party in 1987 recognized the 'private economic sector' as a necessary supplement to the state sector, whilst in 1988 the Constitution was amended to acknowledge the private sector as a 'complement' to the socialist public economy that is allowed to develop 'within the limits prescribed by law', indicating a somewhat grudging acceptance of the role of the private sector. However, *getihu* or sole proprietorships had already been operating in the midst of market-oriented reforms. Their development prompted a belated and limited recognition of their *de facto* status even as the non-state sector was powering China's 'dual track' transition whereby a market track was permitted to develop within the administered economy to help generate revenues for the gradual reform of the state-owned sector.

In June 1988, the Provisional Regulations on Private Enterprises were passed, which legitimized sole proprietorships, partnerships, and limited liability companies with eight or more employees. However, the regulations allow only a limited class of persons to form such enterprises: farmers, the urban unemployed, retired persons, etc. The regulations in a sense view private business formation as a supplementary activity undertaken by those outside of the primary socialist economy.

The absence of a basis in law hindered the development of the non-state economy during the first decade of reform. Clarke et al. (2006) note that legal obstacles were evident even in places like Wenzhou, where the private economy enjoyed strong local political support and extensive social networks. Furthermore, private enterprise owners felt they had no recourse when they encountered contract disputes, since courts were unwilling to recognize their claims (Lubman 2002).

By 1997, the Communist Party's 15th Congress recognized the private sector as an 'important' (not just supplemental) component of the economy. Amendments to the Constitution in 1999 went further and began to legitimize private ownership. Significantly, the Economic Contract Law of 1993, together with the Foreign Economic Contract Law and the Technology Contract Law, were replaced in that year by a unified Contract Law, designed to cover contracts formed by individuals and enterprises alike, regardless of ownership or nationality. Importantly, under the unified Contract Law of 1999, natural individuals—not just legal persons—can enter into legally enforceable contracts, paving the way for entrepreneurship to develop.

In 2001, President Jiang Zemin announced that private entrepreneurs could become Party members. Further constitutional amendments in 2004 provided that the 'non-publicly-owned' sector was not only permitted but encouraged, which gave more rhetorical protection to private property. Finally, the Constitution was amended in March 2004 to include guarantees regarding private property ('legally obtained private property of the citizens shall not be violated'). This was the first time that the legal status of private property was officially endorsed by the Party, leading eventually to the Property Law of 2007, which gave equal protection to public and private property. In other words, the legal reforms reflected the reality that private firms powered the transition and such belated measures in response to an evolving market with such firms that were in need of governance.

However, despite the constitutional amendment in 2004 protecting private property rights, private firms have not acquired equal status with other types of firms, such as state-owned enterprises and foreign-funded firms. Private firms in China not only experience political and social discrimination, but must also deal with the lack of a level playing field. State-owned enterprises continue to enjoy preferential status in obtaining bank loans and other key inputs (Brandt and Li 2003), while foreign firms face other forms of discrimination, but also preferential treatment in some respects.

Despite these obstacles, entrepreneurs and *de novo* private firms are rapidly growing, especially in the 2000s, motivated by the various legal reforms and greater opening of the market. Private as well as state-owned firms have increased exponentially and some are moving overseas. Firms such as handset maker, Ningbo Bird, have taken market share from the likes of Nokia and Motorola in the 2000s. The first global commercial M&A deal was when TCL purchased the manufacturing rights of all of RCA and Thomson television products from France's Thomson SA in 2004. Others soon followed, including Lenovo's acquisition of IBM's personal computer business, as well as failed attempts such as Haier's bid for Maytag. Chinese SOEs had invested overseas in energy and commodities to secure supplies for the several of decades, but the start of commercial outward investments marked a maturation of these and increasingly of private firms in the 2000s, known as the 'going out' policy. This policy is designed to encourage the development of companies able to operate as multinationals in global markets, such that China can achieve the industrial upgrading that it requires to sustain its economic growth. Private car maker Geely's aquisition of Volvo is another notable example.

However, private firms in China have been sometimes difficult to define, as some started out with state-finance or implicit backing, although a growing number are *de novo* firms. The 'going global' case study of the genesis and expansion of one of the first and few Chinese private multinational corporations, Lenovo, illustrates the complexities in operating and growing a business in a system of unclear property rights and legal protection of the non-state-owned sector.

6.3 **Constrained entrepreneurship**

6.3.1 SOCIAL NETWORKS

Self-employment should require many of the same personal traits as employed persons working for a wage, such as education, in a transition labour market. However, the self-employed must also contend with the need to obtain credit to start a business and buy inventory, gain access to suppliers and distributors, as well as the knowledge to navigate the uncertain regulatory and legal environment in China where licenses are often required for starting a business. Social networks are unsurprisingly useful in all of these respects.

In China, self-employed persons often encounter severe credit constraints due to the credit allocation system which is skewed toward state-owned enterprises (Fan 1994; Lin 2007). Small and medium enterprises find it difficult to obtain credit and often rely on family and friends, including remittances from migrated family members, to start a business (Oi 1999). Alternatively, self-employed persons use their social networks to arrange for inventory to be issued without advance payment. Anything which is sold is then split between the vendor and the supplier of the inventory, such as pedlars receiving their goods in advance of payment. The author encountered this type of trust-based relationship in conducting a household survey in China, notably in Liaoning which has a substantial proportion of heavy industry that was hard hit by the large-scale downsizing of the SOEs in the mid 1990s. Access to suppliers and distributors is a significant challenge in a partially marketized economy, and having a social network would facilitate self-employment by helping to overcome such obstacles (see e.g. Wu 2002). With the stagnation of the state-owned sector during this period, and the beginning of market liberalization measures facilitating the growth of the non-state sector, it is also likely that urban workers began to seek other sources of income and thus became self-employed.

For instance, in that 1999 survey, when asked the main reason why the respondent started his or her own business, 37 per cent of the survey respondents said that it was because he or she had the requisite skills and experience, 7 per cent had funds, 11 per cent had real estate, and 17 per cent started a business by joining in with relatives. The remainder chose 'other'. As this was during the period of the *xiagang* policy where there were large-scale layoffs in the SOE sector, it is likely that some became self-employed or more likely small goods pedlars out of necessity. Given the small proportion of the self-employed who started with their own funds, credit is likely to be a constraint that social networks can help with by improving information flows to attain credit or indeed access credit from personal networks. This figure may be understated since having funds may have been a subsidiary reason because respondents were limited to one response. Having real estate in China suggests a social network because all urban land is state-owned and land/buildings were only beginning to become privatized at the time. Those who had the resource of real estate would probably have had the connections to attain such an asset. This finding supports the argument that one of the motivations for entering self-employment is having overcome credit constraints.

Also, China has an imperfect legal system with a great deal of regulatory complexity (Chen 2003; Clarke 2003a). In such an environment, having the contacts and knowing how to obtain a licence would be important (see e.g. Oi 1999). Indeed, licences and permissions are needed not only for starting the business, but also for the transport of goods at the city and provincial levels. A social network would help in this instance. Interpersonal relationships would also reduce the costs of enforcement in such a system, where trusted individuals are preferred in the absence of an effective legal system (see e.g. Yang 1994; Yan 1996; Kipnis 1997). Networking would increase information flows and reduce the transaction costs of starting a business.

6.3.2 INSTITUTIONAL IMPEDIMENTS

China is a country known for its incomplete legal system, including the lack of an independent judiciary, and adjudication is not free from interference from the executive branch (see e.g. Allen, Qian, and Qian 2005). In addition, there is evidence of financial repression whereby legal and institutional constraints impede the development of financial intermediaries, thereby retarding the development of the financial sector. In China, this is manifested insofar as state-owned commercial banks favour state-owned enterprises despite three decades of reform. SOEs still dominate credit allocation, such that the majority of private small and medium- sized enterprises obtained no bank financing even in 2006 (Lin 2007).

For entrepreneurs in China, legal constraints—directly through the legal and regulatory system and indirectly via credit rationing due to financial repression—are factors influencing the start-up of a business. Entrepreneurship in China, therefore, is a product not only of the usual socio-economic factors such as motivation and overcoming wealth constraints, but is also affected by the legal and institutional environment (see e.g. Banerjee and Newman 1993; Blanchflower and Oswald 1998).

Moreover, there is imperfect protection of private property and commercial contracting, which adds to uncertainty for private firms (see e.g. Pei 2001). For instance, private property was not granted equal protection in a formal sense as public property until the Property Law was passed in 2007. On the regulatory front, governmental permissions, rather than a transparent regulatory structure, govern the commercial sector. For example, starting a business requires obtaining numerous licences, and operating a firm requires permission to transport and distribute goods and services. With respect to another important facet of the influence of law on entrepreneurship, the enforcement of contracts in China is fraught with difficulty due to the underdeveloped legal system. This will tend to lead to relational contracting, which refers to the self-enforcing nature of contracts where the parties adhere to the terms of the contract because of their own future self-interest (Bull 1987; Baker, Gibbons, and Murphy 2002). This can minimize the costs of contract enforcement if business is contracted with known associates and on a trust basis which is not enforced through courts, and fits with a long-standing cultural preference in China for reliance on interpersonal relationships or social networks (Bian 1994).

The economics of starting a firm are also influenced by the extent of financial repression. The banking system in China is considered to suffer from financial repression instigated by policies and rules that divert formal credit to state-owned enterprises via the state-owned banking system and which negatively affects non-state firms. Credit constraints restrict options for entrepreneurs. Reliance on savings, remittances from migrated family members, and the savings of relatives tend to provide an alternative source of capital when the formal banking system is difficult to access. The commonly observed wealth constraints among entrepreneurs also bind, because assets were not common in urban China until the advent of equity investments and the privatization of housing, both in the 1990s. The lack of financial intermediaries due to financial repression further compromises the augmentation of assets through avenues such as venture capital funding, and means that entrepreneurs rely upon their own assets. Those who start their own businesses, therefore, confront numerous legal and financial impediments to entrepreneurship in such an environment.

6.4 Entrepreneurial determinants

The determinants of entrepreneurship in the midst of China's challenging legal and institutional context are not well understood. The few studies of self-employment emphasize education and other observable personal traits such as membership of the Chinese Communist Party (Wu 2002; Zhang et al. 2006; Mohapatra, Rozelle, and Goodhue 2007) while a cross-country survey of entrepreneurs by Djankov et al. (2006) also delves into interpersonal relationships and concludes that the most robust determinant of entrepreneurship was knowing people who had tried entrepreneurship. This is consistent with the work on the importance of social networks in other facets of Chinese society (see e.g. Oi 1999). A study of rural China by Mohapatra, Rozelle, and Goodhue (2007) finds education to be the key factor in rural farmers leaving the agricultural sector to enter into both self-employment and wage employment, while Wu (2002) finds that education and Communist Party membership are a deterrent in urban areas. Education is found to be a factor that inhibits entrepreneurship in urban areas, which suggests that the preferred sector remains the more secure formal sector. As with most issues in China, there are significant urban–rural differences, as rural residents never had a privileged SOE sector. The findings for education are that the rural residents able to move into higher value-added work are the educated ones, while more educated workers in urban areas tend to remain in the institutionally favoured wage employment.

These studies focus on either rural residents or urban residents in the cities, that is, those with a rural or urban *hukou* (household registration system) in the appropriate areas. What are omitted are rural–urban migrants, who face an additional set of institutional obstructions on account of not having permission to settle in urban areas (see Solinger 1999). Migrants working in the urban economy are particularly important in the development of the private sector, as they constitute the surplus labour from rural areas which was shifted to the urban non-state sector to fuel growth (Fan 1994). These workers manned the factories in China's Special Economic Zones which produce goods for export in places such as the Pearl River Delta that supported China's growth while the inefficient state-owned sector which employed urban residents was gradually reformed and dismantled. In other words, they provided a ready workforce for the nascent private sector. In spite of the key role played by migrants in China's economy, they continue to face discrimination in the urban labour market, and have been prevented from competing for jobs that were reserved for urban residents (Knight and Yueh 2004). In many ways, the legal constraints and economic characteristics of these workers are more ferocious than those faced by urban residents starting their own firms.

Entrepreneurship thus is driven by not only the usual set of personal and socio-economic characteristics, such as being motivated by economic gain or facing credit constraints, but also by the incomplete legal and institutional environment. This is a factor also found in other countries, such as the United States, but relatively unexamined in marketizing economies like China's which are in the process of legal as well as economic reforms (see e.g. Holtz-Eakin, Joulfaian, and Rosen 1994; Djankov et al. 2006). The evolution of entrepreneurship in China could thus shed light on the path for other emerging economies which often have incomplete legal systems. This is particularly the case for migrants. Different factors are likely to determine the entrepreneurial decision of urban residents and rural–urban migrants, the latter group in particular has not been well studied despite their notable importance in forming China's non-state sector. Indeed, there are few studies of migrant entrepreneurs in urban China, so this chapter will also focus on the traits of those migrants who have been able to set up businesses and settle to some extent in the urban economy, and constitute a significant segment of entrepreneurial activity.

6.5 **The traits of entrepreneurs**

The national urban household data set used in this chapter is an original, representative survey administered across China in 2000, enumerated by China's National Bureau for Statistics (NBS), and designed by a team of international researchers from the Chinese Academy of Social Sciences, Japan, Australia and the UK, including the author. The selected households were randomly drawn from the NBS sample households, and the questionnaire was administered by trained enumerators working for the NBS, who would often make repeated visits to ensure accuracy. Details of the data set can be found in Li and Sato (2006). The sample size of the 1999 survey is 4,500 urban households and another 800 migrant households settled in urban areas, with around 14,000 working-age individuals, defined as those over the age of 16. Both household and individual-level responses are recorded. The survey covered thirteen cities in six provinces, including provincial level cities: Beijing, Liaoning, Jiangsu, Henan, Sichuan, and Gansu. Given the breadth of the survey, there is no need to attempt to normalize the sample as with smaller scale data typically used in studies of entrepreneurship.

There are 1,263 individuals in the sample who report that they started their own business. Eliminating the six respondents under the age of 16 (whose ages ranged from 12 to 15), the 1,257 individuals constitute around 8.7 per cent of all urban workers. Three are over the age of 65, but left in the sample as they report positive earnings for the sample year. Self-employed business people need not retire at a certain age, so allowing the inclusion of these three entrepreneurs seems appropriate. In this sample, seven entrepreneurs had a previous business venture, while fourteen entrepreneurs reported having started a business in their prior job but are no longer self-employed. In terms of the proportion of migrants and urban residents, some 955 (80 per cent) of all entrepreneurs are migrants, while 308 (20 per cent) are urban residents. Therefore, the picture of entrepreneurship in the urban economy quickly shifts towards considering the significant role played by migrants in developing the private sector, as they constitute four-fifths of all urban entrepreneurs. An estimated 120 migrant entrepreneurs left their previous job specifically to start their own business within this sample.

There is no measure of the size of these firms, but there is some limited information on profitability for those owned by urban residents but not for migrant-owned firms. Most respondents did not answer this question in the survey, perhaps because it is phrased as reporting on the profitability of an 'enterprise' and the common conception of an enterprise is a state-owned enterprise. Of those who did (30 per cent of the sample), only 5.6 per cent reported themselves as having made 'high profit' that year. This may, however, be due to a reluctance to report profits due to concerns about taxation. The majority (62.9 per cent) reported 'marginal profit', while the remaining 25.2 per cent declared that they were making a loss or at the edge of bankruptcy. These are the three general categories of answers allowed in the survey, so the precise quantification of such profits/losses is not available, though this gives at least a partial picture.

The average age of these firms is 5.3 years, which is higher for urban resident owned ones (8.1 years) than migrant owned businesses (4.4 years). This reflects two factors. In the mid 1990s, the promulgation of the Company Law in 1994 for the first time offered some legal guidance for businesses and fuelled the rapid increase in the number of small and medium-sized private enterprises. Also, the liberalization of the wholesale and retail sector by the early 1990s opened the market for private firms to serve the fast developing consumer market, which was still largely protected from foreign competition.

In terms of the sector in which these firms operate, the largest category for urban resident owned firms (43 per cent) is the wholesale, retail, and food services industry. This is followed by social services (19 per cent) and the transportation, storage, postal, and communications sector which comprises 13 per cent. Manufacturing firms account for only 8 per cent, while the

Table 6.1. Employed versus wage employed

	Wage employed (urban residents)	Entrepreneurs (urban residents)	Entrepreneurs (migrants)	Significance of mean difference	Significance of mean difference
	(1)	(2)	(3)	(1)–(2)	(2)–(3)
Personal characteristics					
Age	35.8	36.5	33.3	***	***
Gender	49.7% male	58.4% male	55.6% male		
	51.3% female	41.6% female	44.4% female	***	Insignificant
Marital status	84.2% married	78.5% married	92.5% married	***	***
Education, in years	9.4	10.1	8.0	***	***
Employment experience, in years	22.8	12.7	9.2	***	***
Experienced layoff	19.2%	28.9%	12.9%	***	***
Communist Party member	17.7%	5.8%	2.4%	***	***
Social network (size)	6.4	7.6	7.8	Insignificant	Insignificant
Income and Wealth (RMB)					
Annual income	5,986	8,425	11,227	***	***
Total household net wealth (assets minus debts)	20,250	11,778	13,511	***	Insignificant
Saved funds for family business	2,060	8,687	5,798	***	Insignificant
Debts incurred for family business	2,159	4,027	2,218	***	Insignificant

Source: China Household and Income Project, urban survey.
Notes: *** indicates significance at the 1% level, ** at the 5% level, and * at the 10% level in a two-tailed t-test for equality of means. For migrants, years of employment experience in the urban economy is reported.

remaining firms are spread out amongst construction (2 per cent), finance and insurance (1per cent), and others. There is a more detailed breakdown of the sectors for migrant firms, but the largest sectors are the same as privately-owned urban firms: 52 per cent are in the wholesale, retail, and food services industry, while 20 per cent are in the social services sector. Similarly, the next largest sector is manufacturing, but for migrants, it is the garment sector that accounts for 8 per cent of their firms, while another 3 per cent of firms operate in the production of consumer goods. Construction accounts for 2 per cent, as with the urban firms, as does transportation, storage, postal, and communications which constitute another 2 per cent. The latter category differs from the breakdown for urban-owned firms which seem to be more heavily in the transportation and communications business.

Table 6.1 presents the traits of entrepreneurs, divided into urban residents and migrants, and the wage employed, with conditional means to assess significant differences amongst these groups. The reported figures are conditional means with the difference tested first by Levine's test to establish equality in variances. The Levine's test does not require the same sample sizes and works even if the normality assumption does not hold. In other words, the Levine's test uses the test statistic constructed for an analysis of variance. By rejecting the null hypothesis, there is evidence of a difference in the population variances. If the Levine's test for the equality of variances did not result in a significant F value, then an equality of variances can be assumed. This is followed by a two-tailed Welch t-test to compare conditional means between both types of entrepreneurs and non-entrepreneurs. The difference in conditional means reflects whether there is significant difference between urban resident and migrant entrepreneurs as well as the wage employed conditional on the other observable characteristics identified in the table.

All personal characteristics except for the gender balance between migrant and non-migrant entrepreneurs and the size of their respective social networks are significant. Whereas the wage employed have a nearly 50–50 gender mix, some 58 per cent of urban firm owners and 56 per cent of migrant entrepreneurs are men, reflecting a significant male share of business start-ups in China. The size of their social networks is also not significantly different. Social networks are determined by measuring the reported number of close contacts of an individual in any context, social or economic. The survey question asked: 'In the past year, how many relatives, friends, colleagues or acquaintances did you exchange gifts with or often maintain contact with?' The mean size of social network is 6.4 persons and has a reasonable dispersion for non-entrepreneurs. The non-entrepreneurs have around 6.4 persons as compared with 7.6 for urban entrepreneurs and 6.5 for migrant entrepreneurs. Perhaps whilst all groups value interpersonal relationships, entrepreneurs may utilize them to start a business, while the wage employed may rely on networks for social utility. The social networks of migrant entrepreneurs are much larger by an alternative measure which didn't specifically ask about maintaining contact, but is based on the number of relatives, fellow villagers (*lao xian*) which is a very important relation in China, and friends or acquaintances that he or she has in the city. The mean size of that network is 14.4 persons, which is inflated by the assessment of the fellow villager category. Omitting that group, the mean size is virtually identical to the urban entrepreneurs at 7.8 persons. There is no statistically significant difference between the two measures. The latter will be used, as the first measure was only asked of migrants who had obtained urban *hukou*, while the latter was asked of all migrant households.

All the other characteristics of entrepreneurs and non-entrepreneurs are significantly different. Migrant entrepreneurs are around three years younger on average than urban resident entrepreneurs and non-entrepreneurs. The mean age difference between all three groups is significant. The differences indicate an age hierarchy of urban firm owners, urban wage employed, and then migrant entrepreneurs. Over 90 per cent of migrants are married, while this percentage falls for the wage employed to 84 per cent, and for urban firm owners, it declines to 79 per cent. There are also significant differences in average years of education. The most educated are the urban entrepreneurs who have completed around ten years, followed by the urban wage-employed with nine years and migrants who have eight years.

Entrepreneurs have on average a decade less experience than non-entrepreneurs. The likely interpretation of this question in the context of China is experience in paid employment, as the lifetime employment system or 'iron rice bowl' was only gradually dismantled starting in the mid 1990s, and working in a SOE is what urban residents would consider to be employment experience when answering the question. This would suggest that entrepreneurs have on average around ten years of experience starting their own businesses. This is consistent with the liberalization of consumer markets in particular during the late 1980s/early 1990s which created the opportunity for starting a business in consumer goods. The liberalization phase would also explain the average of nine years of work experience of migrants in urban areas. As the urban economy was reformed, opportunities for migrants to find work would explain their migration from rural to urban areas to seek opportunities that had previously eluded them under the allocated job system that was geared towards urban residents and excluded migrants. Finally, urban entrepreneurs are also more likely to have experienced being laid-off during the large-scale restructuring of the SOEs in the mid 1990s, thus prompting them to start their own business. A smaller proportion of migrant entrepreneurs had experienced lay-off, but that could reflect their exclusion from SOE and permanent jobs, which meant more short-term contracts that would terminate rather than result in redundancy.

There are notable significant differences distinguishing the entrepreneurs from the non-entrepreneurs in terms of Communist Party membership. Whereas around 18 per cent of all employed persons are Party members, only 6 per cent of urban entrepreneurs and just 2 per cent of migrants are members. If Party members are more likely to be allocated desirable jobs and less likely to be laid-off, then that could contribute to them being less likely to leave the more secure lifetime employment for self-employment, which is more risky.

The final set of comparisons is of income and wealth. There are significant differences in mean incomes across the three groups, but insignificant differences in wealth as between urban and migrant entrepreneurs. Urban entrepreneurs make around 30 per cent more than non-entrepreneurs, which is a significant difference in their conditional mean income after controlling for age, gender, education, employment experience, occupation, employment sector, and locale (cities). This is despite more entrepreneurs having experienced being laid-off, which typically reduces income upon re-employment. Impressively, migrant entrepreneurs make nearly twice the income of the wage employed, and 25 per cent more than urban business owners, despite having fewer years of education and facing tougher institutional constraints such as prohibitions on settling in cities. This is all the more so when their annual income prior to coming to urban areas was just 1,500 RMB as compared with 11,227 RMB in the city, reflecting a substantial increase in earnings through migration. It is possible that because they are less able to claim the social security support in urban areas which is granted to urban residents, such as a pension, they are more likely to work hard and earn more income. However, as the conditional mean controls for differences in net assets, which includes measures of in-kind support such as social securities for urban residents, it remains a significant difference even when net wealth is taken into account though pensions would not be included.

In terms of wealth, there are significant differences between the wage employed and the entrepreneurs, but no significant differences between the two types of entrepreneurs. Total household net wealth, calculated as assets minus debts, is 20,250 RMB for the wage employed, while it is 11,778 RMB for urban entrepreneurs and is slightly higher at 13,511 RMB for migrants. Unsurprisingly, the entrepreneurs have much more savings geared at their businesses (8,687 RMB for urban residents and 5,798 RMB for migrants) as compared to around 2,000 RMB that the wage employed have saved for family businesses. These savings might be geared at a future family business or may reflect savings to lend to relatives starting a business. Urban entrepreneurs have the largest share of debt (4,027 RMB or 50 per cent of annual income) as compared with migrant entrepreneurs who owe half of that amount (2,218 RMB, which is only 20 per cent of their annual income). Non-entrepreneurs also report debt incurred for family business around

2,000 RMB, which again may reflect family pooling of resources for a business. It appears that although entrepreneurs are richer than the wage employed in terms of income, they have less wealth, presumably because their assets are tied up in their businesses in a credit-constrained environment where businesses are largely funded through their own or familial savings.

Finally, there are measures of legal development and financial repression to utilize to try and understand the entrepreneurial decision. The variable of financial repression attempts to proxy for the extent of credit constraints in the economy. It is constructed as the inverse of financial repression or, a typical measure of financial development; for example, the share of credit allocated to the private sector as a ratio of the total amount of bank credit in a province (see e.g. Lu and Yao 2009). The more credit that is allocated to the private sector, the less financial repression exists. The second variable is the utilization of the legal system, which proxies for the extent that the formal legal system is invoked in solving commercial or civil disputes. Although an imperfect measure of the effectiveness of the legal system, an untrustworthy or incompetent legal system would get very few filings (see e.g. Lu and Yao 2009 who use a similar measure). The variable is constructed as the number of annual filings of civil or commercial cases per capita in a province. Computing this variable on a per capita basis addresses the bias of measuring legal system utilization which would increase with population size.

The empirical approach that follows investigates the impact of the uncertain legal and economic environment on entrepreneurship. Second, the estimations will attempt to distinguish whether these factors influence the entrepreneurs who are urban residents differently from rural–urban migrants.

A simple probabilistic (probit) model of becoming an entrepreneur is as follows:

$$ENTREPRENEUR_{i,j} = \alpha + \beta X_i + \gamma V_i + \phi F_j + \phi U_j + \eta_{i,j},$$

where entrepreneur equals one if person i in province j is an entrepreneur and zero if not. Entrepreneurship is determined by a vector of observable personal characteristics, X_i, associated with occupational choice, including education, age, gender, and other related factors, and those arising in response to the particular institutional setting, V_i, which could include characteristics such as having social networks or strong motivation. The specific measures of the legal and institutional context in the locale (province j) will also be included—financial repression (measuring the extent of credit constraint) and utilization of the legal system (measuring development of the legal system)—to determine if they influence the entrepreneurship decision. Financial repression (F_j) is measured as the extent of financial development in province j, which is the ratio of bank credit allocated to the private sector as a proportion of total credit for the province. Utilization of the legal system (U_j) is measured as the ratio of cases filed on a per capita basis, which could be viewed as an indication of the extent of the development of the courts as an avenue for resolving disputes.

There is the possibility of heteroskedasticity induced by the selection bias into labour force participation, and a clustering effect of using a household data set to estimate the individual outcomes, so robust standard errors adjusted for clustering at the household level are computed for $\eta_{i,j}$.

It is not possible to rule out omitted variable bias or reverse causality. Thus, the essential relationships between legal constraints and entrepreneurship will be re-estimated using instrumental variable (IV) techniques. Since the average age of these firms unsurprisingly coincides with the corporatization drive in China whereby enterprises were converted into shareholding companies and private firms began to form, the legal system for civil and commercial matters would have developed at the same time. Therefore, a province with a more developed legal system could lead to greater entrepreneurship, and more private firm activity increases the utilization of the legal system. There is thus a strong systemic element to these relationships. To address this endogeneity issue, two simultaneous equations will be estimated. One will be for entrepreneurship and the other for legal development.

In an attempt to disentangle the potential endogeneity and feedback among the legal variable and entrepreneurship, the 3SLS technique will be used. The three-stage least squares approach estimates a system which yields more efficient results than 2SLS. The 2SLS estimation produces consistent estimators, but neglects cross-equation correlations in the error terms (Greene 2003). The 3SLS achieves consistency through instrumentation, and efficiency through cross-equation error covariance terms. In 3SLS, all dependent variables are explicitly taken to be endogenous to the system and are treated as correlated with the disturbances in the system's equations. The first stage of the 3SLS estimator is identical to the first stage of 2SLS, whilst the second and third stages compute the covariance matrix of the error terms and then perform a generalized least squares (GLS) estimation to assess the full system. Both a 3SLS full system and a 'seemingly unrelated regression estimation' (SURE) are estimated. The SURE estimator treats all variables as exogenous within the system and is a form of 2SLS. It can provide further statistical evidence, but the full system estimates are preferred for the reasons stated above, and thus will be relied upon.

In terms of identification, the variable of the number of lawyers per capita pre-dating the take off of *de novo* firms has a direct impact on legal development and only an indirect one on entrepreneurship (via legal constraints), since lawyers will influence case development but not directly foster entrepreneurship except through the legal system. Second, the measure of wealth for urban residents is likely to be related to the success of being an entrepreneur in the survey year, so any interpretation concerning a significant influence of wealth constraints should be mindful of the relationship. By contrast, the measure of wealth for migrant entrepreneurs is that of assets brought from the countryside before starting a business in urban areas. This is more likely to be an exogenous measure and thus a more proximate indicator of wealth constraints on entrepreneurship. Thus, the instrumentation will use wealth brought from the countryside by migrants as directly affecting entrepreneurship, but only indirectly influencing legal development (via entrepreneurship), because the monies will fund entrepreneurship but not directly influence the existant of legal development in a city to which the migrant is a new entrant.

Finally, the first stage will include a further IV that is exogenous to the simultaneous equations system, appearing in the first stage, and chosen to have an effect on legal development but not on entrepreneurship, which is borne out in the estimations as being significant for the law and not the entrepreneurship variables. The measure is of legal system development between 1985 and before the mid 1990s (where data is unavailable for the 1980s), which marked the start of urban reforms and before private firms were permitted. Recall from the survey that these firms started in the mid 1990s. This indicator—'number of units with legal advisors'—measured on a per capita basis in a province before the mid 1990s will be associated with later legal development in the four provinces in which there is data. The difficulty of finding appropriate instruments for a system of equations will mean a focus on the direct rather than indirect relationships (such as financial repression which is a manifestation of legal impediments on the credit system, and social networks which work within the institutional framework) between law and entrepreneurship. Financial repression and social networks are both factors that work via, or in reaction to, the legal system on entrepreneurship, as well as potentially in reverse. They will be estimated in the probit models, but the 3SLS estimation will focus on testing the effect of the legal system on entrepreneurship decisions.

6.5.1 SOCIO-ECONOMIC FACTORS INFLUENCING URBAN RESIDENTS

Table 6.2 gives the marginal effects of the likelihood of becoming an entrepreneur and the influence of socio-economic factors, including the extent of social networks which can serve to ease the constraints of an imperfect institutional context, and household wealth as a factor influencing the decision to start a business, as well as motivation or drive to be entrepreneurial. First, column (1) provides the baseline model which only considers observable personal traits before turning to the institutional variables.

Table 6.2. Socio-economic factors influencing entrepreneurship, urban residents sample, probit regression, marginal effects (z-statistics in parentheses)

Dependent variable: 1 if entrepreneur 0 if non-entrepreneur	(1)	(2)	(3)	(4)	(5)	(6)	(7)
Personal characteristics							
Gender	−0.0113	−0.0104	−0.0045	−0.0046	−0.0047	−0.0048	−0.0046
	(−6.33)***	(−5.41)***	(−2.11)**	(−2.13)**	(−2.18)**	(−2.23)**	(−2.16)**
Age	0.0003	0.0003	0.0003	0.0003	0.0003	0.0003	0.0003
	(2.51)***	(2.31)**	(2.32)**	(2.29)**	(2.18)**	(2.28)**	(2.20)**
Marital status	0.0034	0.0042	0.0024	0.0026	0.0023	0.0022	0.0021
	(1.23)	(1.43)	(0.56)	(0.62)	(0.54)	(0.52)	(0.50)
Education, in years	−0.0014	−0.0014	−0.0013	−0.0013	−0.0013	−0.0013	−0.0014
	(−3.58)***	(−3.27)***	(−3.00)***	(−3.03)***	(−3.07)***	(−3.24)***	(−3.23)***
Employment experience, in years	−0.0018	−0.0018	−0.0012	−0.0012	−0.0012	−0.0012	−0.0012
	(−10.43)***	(−9.59)***	(−7.40)***	(−7.46)***	(−7.31)***	(−7.43)***	(−7.29)***
Experienced lay-off	0.0084	0.0094	0.0031	0.0033	0.0035	0.0035	0.0034
	(2.96)***	(3.05)***	(1.31)	(1.37)	(1.41)	(1.44)	(1.41)
Communist Party member	−0.0122	−0.0111	−0.0061	−0.0060	−0.0060	−0.0058	−0.0059
	(−4.22)***	(−3.65)***	(−2.10)**	(−2.07)**	(−2.06)**	(−2.01)**	(−2.05)**
Social network (size)	—	0.0002	—	—	—	—	—
		(2.67)***					
Attitudinal indicators: Has the importance of the following factors that influence household income changed compared with before? *1) decreased, 2) unchanged, 3) increased*							
Educational level	—	—	−0.0031	—	—	—	—

	(1)	(2)	(3)	(4)	(5)	(6)	(7)
Political status	—	— (−1.69)*	—	−0.0024 (−1.19)	—	—	—
Rank of work unit	—	—	—	—	−0.0019 (−1.22)	—	—
Social connections	—	—	—	—	—	−0.0016 (−0.82)	—
Urban *hukou*	—	—	—	—	—	—	0.0038 (1.56)
Cities	Yes	Yes	Yes	Yes	Yes	Yes	Yes
Wald χ^2 (19)	275.49***	—	—	—	—	—	—
Wald χ^2 (20)	—	254.10***	122.51***	121.01***	121.92***	117.46***	115.11***
Pseudo R^2	0.1675	0.1639	0.2009	0.1992	0.1974	0.2012	0.2033
Number of observations	9729	8390	4319	4314	4313	4308	4300

Source: China Household and Income Project, urban survey.

Notes: 1. Omitted dummy variables are: male, never experienced lay-off, not a Communist Party member, and Pingliang.

2. Robust standard errors adjusted for clustering at the household level are computed.

3. *** indicates significance at the 1% level, ** a: the 5% level, and * at the 10% level.

For urban residents who start their own businesses, personal characteristics differ significantly from those who are wage employed except for being married which is not a determinant. Gender, education, employment experience, and being a member of the Chinese Communist Party all reduce the likelihood of becoming an entrepreneur. By contrast, being older and having experienced unemployment increase the probability. Those in the latter category are likely to have been forced into the evolving labour market due to the large-scale downsizing and lay-offs associated with the *xiagang* policy of the late 1990s. At the same time, liberalization made self-employment a more viable option than before, which could explain why having experienced unemployment is a positive determinant of entrepreneurship. Interestingly, typically those who have experienced unemployment will suffer from 'scarring' whereby they earn less than before, but Chinese urban entrepreneurs make significantly more than the wage employed. Being a woman, more educated and experienced all reduce the likelihood of leaving the stability of wage employment, as well as Party membership. Party members have been on the rise in the reform period despite the economy being more marketized, though the proportion of Party members amongst entrepreneurs is lower than the wage employed. The findings are that Party membership reduces entrepreneurship, and fewer Party members wish to leave their positions to seek opportunities in the market-driven sector.

With the baseline model established, column (2) introduces social networks, which do not notably affect the coefficients of the baseline explanatory variables. Even controlling for observable personal traits, often tested in the entrepreneurship literature, social networks significantly increase the probability of entrepreneurship. This suggests that social networks aid entrepreneurial activity, probably through sharing information about how to start and operate a business in the imperfect legal environment. As marginal effects are reported, the coefficient on the continuous variable of social networks suggests that a unit increase in the average size of the network will increase the probability of entrepreneurship taking on the value of one by 0.01 per cent. It is a very small, but significant increase in the probability of entrepreneurship, though larger social networks would have a non-negligible impact.

The next six columns explore a multitude of attitudinal measures and find that most are insignificant. The one significant measure at the 10 per cent level asked respondents about whether educational attainment has increased in importance in affecting household income. The negative coefficient suggests that those who believe that education is associated with more earnings are not entrepreneurs, which reinforces the finding that more years of education deter entrepreneurship. Both are significant in column (3), which suggests that attitudinal effects exist beyond the measured impact of years of education attained in the entrepreneurship equation.

Therefore, social networks and attitudinal positions have some effect on the decision to become an entrepreneur even when observable personal traits are controlled for. Wealth turns out not to be a significant factor, suggesting that Chinese entrepreneurs are not as wealth constrained as those in other countries (see e.g. Evans and Leighton 1989). However, social networks do, which suggests that informal relationships play a role in enabling starting a business and this is consistent with the observed declarations of entrepreneurs across countries that knowing others who are entrepreneurial is important (see e.g. Djankov et al. 2005).

6.5.2 SOCIO-ECONOMIC FACTORS INFLUENCING MIGRANT ENTREPRENEURS

Migrant entrepreneurs in urban areas have not been much studied in China, and Table 6.3 presents the findings for this group who dominate the self-employed sector. Column (1) shows the baseline model. Unlike for urban residents, observable personal traits do not predict entrepreneurship for migrants. Gender, age, years of education, employment experience in urban areas, and Party membership are all irrelevant. Experience of unemployment was not estimated for this group because only urban residents who were on lifetime employment could be laid off. Migrants worked on contracts which terminated after a period of time and were not entitled to unemployment or *xiagang* benefits. Being married positively increases the probability of entrepreneurship, suggesting that those who are married and have families are more likely to start their own businesses in urban areas. Indeed, a higher proportion of migrants are married as compared with urban residents, as seen in Table 6.1. Migrant entrepreneurs earned ten times their annual income after moving to the city, and remitted 20 per cent of their income (2,195 RMB) on average to their home village where their families reside.

Social networks are significant for migrant entrepreneurs as with other urban entrepreneurs. The predicted probability of becoming an entrepreneur is 34.3 per cent at the sample mean (as compared with the observed probability of 35.1 per cent). Adding one contact (with a marginal effect of 0.4 per cent) would increase the probability to nearly 35 per cent and ten contacts would increase the probability to 38 per cent. The effect of networks is larger for migrant entrepreneurs than urban ones, though still fairly small.

Attitudinal measures are also important for migrants and underscore the relevance of social networks. A question which asked whether social connections had become more important for household income indicated that migrant entrepreneurs believed so. The variable retained its significance when social networks is also included in column (8). The coefficient on social networks was virtually unchanged, but the magnitude of the attitudinal

Table 6.3. Socio-economic factors influencing entrepreneurship, migrant sample, probit regression, marginal effects (z-statistics in parentheses)

Dependent variable: 1 if entrepreneur 0 if non-entrepreneur	(1)	(2)	(3)	(4)	(5)	(6)	(7)	(8)
Personal characteristics								
Gender	0.0150	0.0293	0.0151	0.0170	0.0157	0.0174	0.0329	0.0175
	(0.73)	(1.12)	(0.73)	(0.82)	(0.76)	(0.84)	(1.24)	(0.84)
Age	−0.0006	0.0003	−0.0007	−0.0005	−0.0007	−0.0001	0.0002	−0.0001
	(−0.27)	(0.09)	(−0.31)	(−0.22)	(−0.33)	(−0.05)	(0.06)	(0.03)
Marital status	0.1428	−0.0366	0.1420	0.1396	0.1479	0.1317	−0.0675	0.1422
	(1.84)*	(−0.34)	(1.84)*	(1.80)*	(1.91)*	(1.65)*	(0.61)	(1.79)*
Education, in years	−0.0017	0.0057	−0.0018	−0.0024	−0.0020	−0.0022	0.0053	−0.0024
	(−0.26)	(0.68)	(0.28)	(0.36)	(0.31)	(0.34)	(0.62)	(0.37)
Employment experience in urban areas, in years	−0.0014	−0.0034	−0.0010	−0.0009	−0.0007	−0.0011	−0.0033	−0.0002
	(−0.40)	(0.86)	(0.29)	(−0.26)	(0.20)	(0.30)	(0.86)	(0.06)
Communist Party member	0.0151	0.1139	0.0217	0.0175	0.0293	0.0048	0.1026	0.0148
	(0.15)	(0.67)	(0.22)	(0.18)	(0.30)	(0.05)	(0.59)	(0.15)
Social network (size)	—	0.0049	—	—	—	—	0.0048	—
		(1.82)*					(1.79)*	
Attitudinal indicators: Has the importance of the following factors that influence household income changed compared with before? 1) decreased, 2) unchanged, 3) increased								
Educational level	—	—	−0.0185	—	—	—	—	—
			(0.51)					

Political status	—	—	—	0.0236 (0.52)	—	—	—	—
Rank of work unit	—	—	—	—	−0.0867 (1.96)**	—	—	—
Social connections	—	—	—	—	—	0.0892 (2.24)**	0.1285 (2.40)**	—
Urban *hukou*	—	—	—	—	—	—	—	−0.1025 (2.26)**
Cities	Yes	Yes	Yes	Yes	Yes	Yes	Yes	Yes
Wald χ^2 (18)	40.81***	—	—	—	—	—	—	—
Wald χ^2 (19)	—	34.36**	38.72***	39.41***	43.66***	44.25***	—	44.57***
Wald χ^2 (20)	—	—	—	—	—	—	40.01***	—
Pseudo R^2	0.0391	0.0543	0.0370	0.0376	0.0399	0.0427	0.0622	0.0426
Number of observations	2302	1374	2288	2280	2280	2274	1358	2272

Source: China Household and Income Project, urban survey.

Notes: 1. Omitted dummy variables are: male, not a Communist Party member, and Pingliang.

2. Robust standard errors adjusted for clustering at the household level are computed.

3. *** indicates significance at the 1% level, ** at the 5% level, and * at the 10% level.

variable increased, suggesting that social networks reinforced the importance of the motivational indicator, and both significantly increase the likelihood of entrepreneurship among migrants. An unexpected result is that marital status ceases to be significant when social networks are included, which could be interpreted in a number of ways, including that spouses are likely to be included in the social network of migrants so that the two are collinear. Finally, migrants who thought that the *danwei* or work unit status mattered were less likely to be entrepreneurs. This reflects an attitude that values the paid employment sector and the status bequeathed by the government which is one that makes a migrant less likely to strike out on his or her own.

Therefore, migrant entrepreneurs in urban areas have vastly different profiles from urban resident entrepreneurs, though they share social networks and attitudes as drivers of the entrepreneur decision. However, all observable personal traits do not matter, including education and Party membership, which stands at odds with the findings in rural areas as the rural self-employed are significantly influenced by more education and membership in the Communist Party than those who start businesses in urban areas.

6.5.3 LEGAL DEVELOPMENT INFLUENCING BOTH SETS OF ENTREPRENEURS

Table 6.4 sets out two measures of the legal environment to determine whether the wider institutional environment plays a role in entrepreneurship in China. The utilization of the legal system is a significantly positive factor in entrepreneurship for both urban residents and migrants. Increasing the effectiveness of the legal system appears to be significantly associated with more entrepreneurship. By contrast, there is little evidence that financial repression influences entrepreneurs. There is no effect on urban residents, while there is a positive effect on migrants, as seen in column (2). However, when the variable that measures the extent of the development of the legal system is included, then the variable ceases to be significant, which suggests that the legal impediments to financial sector development are subsumed when a measure of the effectiveness of laws is included. By contrast, the legal system retains its significance and increases in magnitude when financial repression is included. Interestingly, when the social network variable is also included, it retains its significance though the size of the coefficient is reduced somewhat for urban residents, though not for migrants. This finding for urban entrepreneurs suggests that social networks continue to perform a function in facilitating relational contracting and business formation alongside the legal system even though its importance is reduced. For migrant entrepreneurs, an actively used legal system eliminates the effect of social networks, which had been small but significant. What is evident is that the extent of legal development is a significant and positive determinant for both urban residents and migrants.

Table 6.4. Legal factors influencing entrepreneurship, full sample, probit regression, marginal effects (z-statistics in parentheses)

Dependent variable: 1 if entrepreneur 0 if non-entrepreneur	Urban residents	Migrants	Urban residents	Migrants	Urban residents	Migrants	Urban residents	Migrants
	(1)	(2)	(3)	(4)	(5)	(6)	(5)	(6)
Legal environment								
Financial development (extent of financial repression)	0.0026	0.0476	—	—	−0.0009	−0.0076	−0.0006	−0.0274
	(1.62)	(1.82)*			(−0.85)	(−0.74)	(−0.49)	(−1.46)
Utilization of the legal system	—	—	0.0158	0.1818	0.0189	0.2070	0.0171	0.3244
			(2.70)***	(3.04)***	(2.75)***	(3.00)***	(2.24)***	(3.26)***
Social network (size)	—	—	—	—	—	—	0.0001	0.0022
							(1.74)*	(1.24)
LR χ^2 (7)	—	—	—	29.73***	—	—	—	—
LR χ^2 (8)	—	—	304.64***	—	—	30.27***	—	—
LR χ^2 (9)	—	—	—	—	305.35***	—	—	19.41**
LR χ^2 (10)	—	—	—	—	—	—	254.04***	—
Wald χ^2 (18)	—	40.81***	—	—	—	—	—	—
Wald χ^2 (19)	275.49***	—	—	—	—	—	—	—
Pseudo R^2	0.1675	0.0391	0.1432	0.0114	0.1435	0.0116	0.1409	0.0132
Number of observations	9729	2302	8355	2010	8355	2010	7264	1154

Sources: China Household and Income Project, urban survey, China Statistical Yearbook, China Provincial Yearbooks.

Notes: 1. All other variables are the same as column (1) in Tables 6.2 and 6.3. Only the variables of interest are reported for brevity.

2. Robust standard errors adjusted for clustering at the household level are computed.

3. *** indicates significance at the 1% level, ** at the 5% level, and * at the 10% level.

4. Financial development is measured as the ratio of bank credit allocated to the private sector as a proportion of total credit. It is measured for the cities of Shenyang and Chengdu, while all others are reported at the provincial level for 1999.

5. Use of legal system is measured as the ratio of cases filed on a per capita basis. For Beijing, the measure is of commercial cases, while it is civil cases excluding domestic cases for the other provinces for 1998. For Henan, the figures refer to 2000, while those for Sichuan are from 2004. Gansu is not included in the estimation due to lack of information regarding the legal system.

As discussed earlier, there is the potential issue of endogeneity. The estimators could suffer from reverse causality if legal development, for instance, did not increase the probability of entrepreneurship, but more self-employment in an area induces greater legal development. The interpretation of the results in this section should be an associational one. That is, in a probabilistic estimation of whether a person becomes an entrepreneur, the probability is higher in an area where there is a more developed legal system (measured through greater use of such a system). The system estimation now will attempt to address these issues of endogeneity. The same can be said for the measure of financial repression. However, the extent of financial development is not significant in the probit models, suggesting no association between financial sector development and entrepreneurship. Any effect that may be found could be via the legal development variable. Thus, in the next section, the 3SLS estimator will focus on the effect of the legal system on entrepreneurship as the test of the main hypothesis that the legal/institutions affect entrepreneurship and not just socio-economic characteristics.

6.5.4 ROBUSTNESS OF LEGAL DEVELOPMENT AND THE ENTREPRENEURSHIP DECISION

Table 6.5 sets out the first stage and the results of the 3SLS estimation, along with the SURE estimations as a further robustness test. In the first stage regressions, the instruments all indicate statistically significant relationships with the potentially endogenous variables. Wealth from the countryside predicts entrepreneurship for migrants but does not affect legal development, while the pre-1995 number of lawyers affects legal development but not migrant entrepreneurship. Both lawyers per capita and also the additional instrument of legal advisors in enterprises (also pre-1995) have significantly negative relationships with later legal development. This suggests that the provinces with larger numbers of lawyers and legal advisors experienced slower subsequent development of the legal system, indicating some degree of convergence whereby the earlier provinces which had less legal development progressed faster as compared with those which had more lawyers and legal advisors. This would fit with studies showing the harmonization of Chinese law across the country accompanying economic growth, such that the backward regions develop faster in order to catch up with the more advanced legal regions, propelled by a national legal system to which provinces reform to meet those standards (see e.g. Yueh 2009b for findings that provinces have similar rates of utilization of patent laws despite starting from different levels of legal and economic development).

Table 6.5. The results of the 3SLS estimates (t-statistics in parentheses)

	First stage		3SLS		SURE	
	Migrant entrepreneurship	Legal development	Migrant entrepreneurship	Legal development	Migrant entrepreneurship	Legal development
Dependent variable:	(1)	(2)	(3)	(4)	(5)	(6)
Legal development	—	—	0.4816***	—	0.3520***	—
			(0.0105)		(0.0578)	
Migrant entrepreneurship	—	—		2.0764***		0.0521***
				(0.0805)		(0.0085)
Personal characteristics						
Gender	-0.0117	-0.0013	-0.0118	0.0245	-0.0129	-0.0055
	(0.0252)	(0.0011)	(0.0252)	(0.0520)	(0.0219)	(0.0084)
Age	-0.0003	0.0002	-0.0008	0.0016	-0.0011	-0.0001
	(0.0016)	(0.0001)**	(0.0016)	(0.0032)	(0.0014)	(0.0005)
Marital status	0.2033	0.0053	0.1990	-0.4133	0.1375	0.0040
	(0.0632)***	(0.0026)**	(0.0631)***	(0.1313)***	(0.0548)**	(0.0211)
Education, in years	0.0010	-0.0004	0.0037	-0.0076	-0.0126	-0.0028
	(0.0052)	(0.0002)	(0.0052)	(0.0107)	(0.0042)***	(0.0016)*
Employment experience in urban areas, in years	-0.0054	-0.0007	-0.0031	0.0065	-0.0023	-0.0016
	(0.0033)	(0.0001)***	(0.0032)	(0.0067)	(0.0022)	(0.0008)*
Communist Party member	-0.0487	0.0036	-0.0360	0.0747	0.0232	0.0426
	(0.0917)	(0.0038)	(0.0915)	(0.1889)	(0.0692)	(0.0266)
Instrumental variables						
Wealth brought from countryside	5.30e-06	9.10e-08	—	—	—	—
	(1.96e-06)***	(8.17e-08)				

(Continued)

Table 6.5. Continued

Dependent variable:	First stage		3SLS		SURE	
	Migrant entrepreneurship	Legal development	Migrant entrepreneurship	Legal development	Migrant entrepreneurship	Legal development
	(1)	(2)	(3)	(4)	(5)	(6)
Lawyers per capita (pre-1995)	−0.0178	−0.1402	—	—	—	—
	(0.0445)	(0.0019)***				
Legal advisors per capita (pre-1995)	−0.0115	−0.0619	—	—	—	—
	(0.0407)	(0.0017)***				
Constant	−0.1036	−7.7890	3.0074	−6.2451	2.4322	−5.8282
	(0.1851)	(0.0077)***	(0.1193)***	(0.2106)***	(0.3471)***	(0.0344)***
Adjusted R-squared	0.0119	0.9838	0.004	−39.402	0.010	0.006
F-test	3.01	10127.88	303.27	95.28	8.16	6.94
p value	0.0015	0.0000	0.0000	0.0000	0.0000	0.0000
Observations	1498	1498	1498	1498	2006	2006

Sources: China Household and Income Project, urban survey, China Statistical Yearbook, China Provincial Statistical Yearbooks.

Notes: 1. To support the multivariate regression, small-sample t-statistics and F-tests are computed instead of z-statistics and χ^2.

2. Robust standard errors adjusted for clustering at the household level are computed.

3. *** indicates significance at the 1% level, ** at the 5% level, and * at the 10% level. R-squared can be negative in 3SLS because the estimation is not nested within a constant-only model of the dependent variable, so the residual sum of squares is not restricted to be smaller than the total sum of squares. As such, the F-test would provide the overall model significance.

4. Use of legal system is measured as the ratio of cases filed on a per capita basis. For Beijing, the measure is of commercial cases, while it is civil cases excluding domestic cases for the other provinces for 1998. For Henan, the figures refer to 2000, while those for Sichuan are from 2004. Gansu is not included in the estimation due to lack of information regarding the legal system.

5. The number of lawyers per capita is measured for Liaoning and Henan provinces in 1985, in Jiangsu (1990) and in Beijing (1995). Measures before the mid-1990s were not available for Sichuan and Gansu, so they were omitted from the estimation. The number of legal advisors working for an enterprise is measured on a per capita basis for the same years and provinces as in note 4.

The 3SLS estimations confirm the results of the earlier probabilistic models that were unable to address endogeneity. Once instrumentation is undertaken and a system of equations is estimated using the instrumented values, the key relationships can be disentangled and the hypothesis that there is a significant effect of legal development on entrepreneurship can be tested with greater confidence. In column (3), legal development is found to continue to have a significant and positive effect on migrant entrepreneurship. The SURE estimation offers further support. In turn, as can be seen in column (4), migrant entrepreneurship positively influences the development of the legal system, which is again echoed in column (6) of the SURE results. The other independent variables are largely unaffected (compare Table 6.4). Although this estimation was conducted solely on the sample of migrant entrepreneurs due to the lack of a comparable exogenous instrument for 'wealth brought from the countryside' for urban residents, migrants comprise 80 per cent of all entrepreneurs in urban China, so the findings would pertain to the vast majority of those starting their own businesses. In conclusion, the 3SLS findings confirm the probabilistic models and suggest that a better developed legal system would foster entrepreneurship.

6.5.5 PROVINCIAL RATES OF SELF-EMPLOYMENT

Another robustness test would be to estimate a panel over time of the incidence of provincial self-employment and legal development. Through a panel estimator, time-varying effects such as differential economic growth and levels of income, as well as time-invariant effects such as province-specific traits can be controlled so that the incidence of self-employment in a province can be determined. A panel data set of Chinese provinces from 1991–2006 is used in the estimates which generate evidence from the 2000s as well.

From virtually no self-employed (around 1 to 2 per cent), those who have started their own businesses reached around one in twelve in market-oriented provinces such as Zhejiang by the 2000s, while in Henan one in eight were entrepreneurs. The proportion is not as high for most provinces, but the upward trend since the early 1990s is evident in Figure 6.2 for places such as Beijing. For most provinces, the proportion peaked in the late 1990s at the height of the restructuring of the state-owned sector that opened up the labour market. The north-east province of Liaoning, which had been hard hit by the downsizing of SOEs, is an example. By the 2000s, the rate had declined somewhat, probably in response to the growth of private-sector employment that offered avenues other than self-employment, as seen in the steady proportion of self-employment in Shanghai.

Table 6.6 shows those results from both fixed-effect and random-effects panel estimators. The former controls for provincial fixed effects beyond that

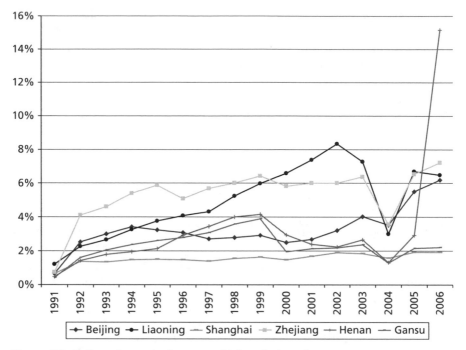

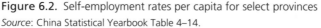

Figure 6.2. Self-employment rates per capita for select provinces
Source: China Statistical Yearbook Table 4–14.

which is measured by the control variables of GDP per capita, foreign direct investment (FDI), exports as a share of GDP, and educational enrolment rates. In other words, there are still provincial-specific influences on self-employment that exist but are not measured by the standard observed variables. The random effects estimator assumes that the provincial effects are orthogonal to the other co-variates. If the assumptions are satisfied, then the random effects model is preferred over the fixed effects model as it is more efficient. Using the Breusch–Pagan Lagrangian multiplier test, the null hypothesis is rejected which implies that the assumptions of the random effects model are not satisfied. Those and other test statistics, including an F-test of the joint significance of the fixed effects regressors, are reported in the table. Year dummies control for macroeconomic trends over time.

Relying therefore on the fixed effects model where individual provincial effects are controlled for (though the result is unchanged in the random effects model), legal development proxied by the number of civil cases filed per capita is significant and positive in determining self-employment, supporting the earlier findings. Also, the number of lawyers per capita continued to have no direct effect on the incidence of self-employment, again corresponding to the 3SLS

Table 6.6. The determinants of provincial self-employment, panel estimation, 1991–2006 (z-statistics in parentheses)

Dependent variable = log of self-employment rate per capita	Fixed-effects model (1)	Random-effects model (2)
GDP per capita	0.212	−0.296*
	(0.277)	(0.158)
FDI	0.117**	0.103***
	(0.046)	(0.037)
Provincial exports-to-GDP ratio	−0.138	−0.181
	(0.192)	(0.185)
Educational enrolment (primary and secondary schooling)	−0.965***	−0.902***
	(0.158)	(0.157)
Lawyers per capita	0.071	0.072
	(0.097)	(0.091)
Civil cases filed per capita	0.283***	0.242***
	(0.084)	(0.080)
Year	−0.062**	−0.012
	(0.024)	(0.013)
Constant	120.329**	25.881
	(46.503)	(24.349)
Adjusted R-squared	0.149	
R-squared		0.025
$F_{(7, 190)}$	9.43***	
Wald χ^2 (7)		57.67***
Breusch–Pagan Lagrangian multiplier test χ^2 (1)		290.41***
Number of provinces	22	22
Observations	219	219

Source: China Statistical Yearbook, Census Yearbook.

Notes: *** indicates significance at the 1% level, ** at the 5% level, and * at the 10% level. Independent variable are: log of deflated per capita GDP, log of foreign direct investment, export-to-GDP ratio, educational enrolment rate of school-aged children, log of lawyers per capita, log of civil cases filed per capita, dummies for 29 provinces (except for Tibet and Chongqing is included in Sichuan), and year.

whereby lawyers influence the development of the legal system which increases self-employment, but do not have a direct effect on entrepreneurship. These measures of self-employment at the province level include all urban and rural residents and migrants, which further supports the findings using the household survey that had focused on migrant entrepreneurs.

The conclusion that there is a significant impact of legal development on increasing the probability of entrepreneurship is therefore borne out through various estimation techniques. The provincial level estimates update the findings through the 2000s and confirm the importance of legal reform on promoting self-employment.

6.6. **Conclusion**

This chapter investigated the legal and economic constraints that could affect entrepreneurship in China due to its underdeveloped legal system and financial sector after much institutional reform. Nevertheless, the protections afforded to private firms are still scant, and an effective legal system is not yet in operation for those which truly operate as entrepreneurs.

Improving the legal system is found an increase entrepreneurship in urban China. The findings imply that entrepreneurship would be bolstered with improvements in the formal legal system, while entrepreneurs of both types are canny enough to start their businesses without being unduly influenced by China's imperfect credit markets and lack of financial depth, even if the latter is caused by legal impediments. Informal institutions like networks become less significant once the extent of legal development is taken into account, suggesting that relational contracting is largely used by migrants as a substitute for a developed legal system, though there is some evidence of their continuing use by urban residents.

Entrepreneurship is explained not only by the usual set of personal characteristics, but is also affected by the particular legal and institutional environment. Specifically, a more developed legal system is found to increase entrepreneurship. Further, there is evidence of feedback from entrepreneurship to further legal development. However, becoming an entrepreneur was not affected by the extent of financial repression. It may affect the further development of the business, but did not play a role in the decision to start up, probably reflecting the small scale of self-employment in its initial stages. Both migrants and urban residents were affected by the external legal environment when the personal traits which determine entrepreneurship otherwise differed for the two groups.

Notably, entrepreneurship in urban China is largely driven by migrants to cities who start their own businesses, and a handful of urban residents. Both groups earn substantially more than the wage employed, though they share a number of similarities in personal traits, such as educational attainment. However, they differ in what drives them to become entrepreneurs.

For those starting a business in China, having the right attitude and using one's social network are important as well as the legal environment, which has largely lagged behind the development of the private sector. As the effectiveness of the legal system improves, it should ease entrepreneurship. The significant rise in entrepreneurs in recent years could plausibly be traced to the corresponding improvements in China's laws and regulations, particularly with the increased attention paid to protecting private businesses after joining the World Trade Organization in 2001, such as the passage of the Property Law in 2007. For those willing to start their own businesses, an entrepreneurial attitude will be needed in the meanwhile at the least.

Case study 6

GOING GLOBAL—LENOVO AND THE PC INDUSTRY

The era of economic reform and opening up in China was marked by a dramatic increase in the inflow of foreign direct investment (FDI) into the country since the 'open door' policy took off in the early 1990s. More recently, there has been a rise in the outflow of FDI from China to other countries. This is a result of the 'going out' policy adopted by the government in 2000 to promote internationally competitive companies. Although commercially driven outward investment did not occur until 2004 with the acquisition by TCL (a Chinese electronics and mobile communications firm originated from Huizhou, Guangdong) of Thomson (a French-based and internationally renowned electronics manufacturer), state-owned companies (particularly those in the commodities and energy sectors) have made investments, and more recently pursued merger and acquisition activities overseas to secure supplies for China's rapidly growing economy.

From the late 1970s to the 2000s, the Chinese government's approach towards outward FDI has changed from one of restrictive control to gradual liberalization, followed by the active pursuit of the 'going out' strategy. Over the decades since the late 1970s, China has gradually emerged to be one of the largest sources of outward direct investment among developing countries. By 2007, the magnitude of China's FDI outflows (excluding Hong Kong and Taiwan) amounted to $22.5 billion, ranking above other more developed regional economies such as the Republic of Korea and Singapore (UNCTAD 2008). The amount doubled in 2008, and China was poised to become a net capital exporter by 2009, though the global financial crisis dampened other countries' outward FDI. Nevertheless, China's 'going out' policy had seemed to reach maturity in the mid 2000s and its firms—commercial ones and not just state-owned enterprises—were poised to 'go global'.

While China is rapidly becoming a leading investor in many developing countries, the reform period also saw Chinese firms investing heavily in developed countries, pursuing a range of 'internationalization strategies': joint ventures with multinational companies, transnational mergers and acquisitions, listing in foreign stock exchanges, etc. (Hong and Sun 2006). As a result, a few Chinese brands have achieved some success in the global market. These include Haier (home appliances), TCL (electronics), Tsingdao (beer), and Lenovo (computers).

Changes in the landscape of China's outward FDI have been shaped by policies at the governmental level as well as strategies at the firm level. The evolution in government policies, however, has been regarded as the most significant explanatory factor for the internationalization of Chinese corporations in general and the shifts in their overseas investment strategies in particular (Hong and Sun 2006). The story of the Lenovo Group, which by 2005 had become the third-largest personal computer (PC) company in the world (falling to fourth in the 2008 global financial crisis), serves as an illustrative case of how the combination of government policies and firm-level strategies has made 'going out' a success in some respects for private firms.

Lenovo's predecessor, the Legend Group, had its origins as a 'spin-off' from a government-funded research institute—the Institute of Computing Technology (Institute of Computing Technology) under the Chinese Academy of Sciences (CAS) (White and Xie 2004). In 1984, Liu Chuanzhi (subsequently President and CEO of Lenovo) and 10 other researchers from Institute of Computing Technology set up the Legend Group, an information technology firm, in a gatekeeper's room in Beijing (Liu 2007). Liu recounted afterwards how they left Institute of Computing Technology to found their own company because they were frustrated that the results of their work there could not be commercialized (Liu 2007). In its infant years, Legend focused on the distribution and installation of PCs from foreign brands, including IBM and Hewlett Packard (Hennock 2004).

The same period marked the early years of China's economic reform. The government's approach towards outward FDI has been described as 'eclectic, ad hoc or even half-hearted' (Hong and Sun 2006). This was based on pragmatic considerations about the need to control capital outflows and to maintain the country's exchange rate. It also had to do with ideological disputes within the Chinese policy-making circles, where there were concerns about the potential diversionary impact of outward FDI on domestic investments and economic development (Voss, Buckley, and Cross 2008). Also, given the predominance of state-owned enterprises and the inexperience of Chinese managers with the international investment environment, the nature of the economic system as a whole did not favour a liberal approach to outward FDI (Voss, Buckley and Cross 2008). Government circulars and regulations promulgated around this time showed the restrictive and experimental nature of China's outward FDI. In a 1979 State Council document, the setting up of overseas operations by Chinese enterprises was identified as one of the thirteen official policies for opening the economy. This was nevertheless followed by measures such as the 'provisional regulations governing the control and the approval procedure for opening non-trade enterprises overseas' in 1985 and the 'regulations governing the approval of setting up of trade-related enterprises overseas' in 1988, which imposed ceilings and other restrictions on outward FDI.

In relation to the computer industry, the government since 1984 had sought to nurture domestic PC production and set high import tariffs for the sector. Although Legend was not one of the firms designed by the government to spearhead China's PC manufacturing, the company did benefit from government policies in both direct and indirect ways. As the start, CAS invested 200,000 RMB into Legend and became the company's sole shareholder. It allowed the company to use the facilities of Institute of Computing Technology free of charge. Being affiliated with CAS, China's leading government research institute in the sciences, also conferred substantial advantage and legitimacy to the company in the initial phase of its business. As a matter of fact, CAS was the first major client of Legend, awarding the company with a contract worth 700,000 RMB to install and test imported computers. This provided capital for the subsequent growth and expansion of the company's business. Over the course of the late 1980s, Legend built up a nationwide distribution network. It did not start launching its own brand until 1991, when it received the licence to manufacture PCs. In retrospect, that Legend was not one of the government's chosen firms for domestic PC production might well have been a blessing in disguise. Compared with state-owned distributors, Legend was much more responsive to market conditions and customer demands.

The decade of the 1990s witnessed the gradual liberalization of China's outward FDI policies. Deng Xiaoping's southern tour and the 14th Chinese Communist Party Congress in 1992 gave new momentum to outward FDI. The Congress explicitly affirmed an official policy of encouraging Chinese firms to invest abroad as part of China's overall strategy of joining global markets (Hong and Sun 2006). Restrictions were relaxed and approval ceilings raised for overseas investment activities. The government's policy orientation towards the computer industry changed from one of 'nationalism to pragmatism' (White and Xie 2004). It started to encourage domestic firms to acquire foreign technologies and become part of the international production network of PCs. It is at this time when Legend's previous experience with its distribution and marketing strategies began to pay off. Compared with its state-owned counterparts, the company was more competitive with its lower cost structure, better management practices, customer-oriented services and stronger R&D development. Legend began to export its products to overseas markets, such as countries in the Asia Pacific. Benefiting from the loosening of China's capital controls regime, the company was listed on the Hong Kong Stock Exchange in 1994. Legend was able three years later to wrap Beijing Legend's assets into the Hong Kong listed-subsidiary to tap international investors. By 1996, the company became the largest PC manufacturer in China, with a market share of over 30 per cent. In 2003, the Hong Kong-listed subsidiary changed its name from Legend to 'Lenovo'. This change in brand name was claimed to signify the company's spirit of innovation (with 'novo' meaning 'new' in Latin) (Liu 2007). But Lenovo was also picked as to resolve trademark registration issues when the Legend name turned out to be too widespread (Hennock 2004).

In the 2000s, China's outward FDI policies were further liberalized to reflect the government's active encouragement for overseas direct investments. Under the state's 10th Five-Year Plan, announced in 2001, the strategy of enterprises "going out" to invest beyond Chinese borders was described as one of the four key thrusts to enable China to "adjust itself to the trend of economic globalisation" (Hong and Sun 2006). With the country's accession to the World Trade Organization (WTO) in December 2001, the government had further incentives to deepen its role in the international economy and to produce 'global champions' to compete in world markets. This period saw a proliferation in the number of Chinese companies investing in highly developed and competitive markets (such as the United States and the European Union) in the strategic pursuit of foreign technologies, managerial know-how, and global distribution networks, as well as internationally renowned brand names (Hong and Sun 2006). Examples of Chinese companies taking advantage of this favourable policy environment to 'go global' include the Haier Group, TCL Corporation, and the Shanghai Automotive Industry Corporation. However, to date, Lenovo is in the vanguard as most Chinese firms have not achieved global brand recognition and Lenovo's efforts to do so hinged on purchasing IBM's PC business, as well as using IBM's brand for five years as part of the deal.

China's entry into the WTO also brought about greater pressures for the country to liberalize its domestic industries to be more open foreign investment. With respect to the PC manufacturing sector, this meant more multinational firms were starting enter into the domestic market. This greatly intensified the level of competition faced by domestic manufacturers such as Lenovo. It also implied that domestic firms would need to adjust their development strategies since their cost advantage vis-à-vis multinational companies was likely to fall over time, with the latter setting up their own production bases within China. It was therefore not surprising that the early 2000s coincided with a period of key changes within the company. The company's shares moved onto Hong Kong's main Hang Seng index in 2000, signifying its increasingly important market position in Hong Kong. Facing stiff competition and an increasingly saturated market at home, the top management of Lenovo saw potential in the global PC market and, by the end of 2003, decided to set globalization as the company's target.

In spite of this lofty target, the company lacked a strong presence on the global stage, and a brand name with worldwide recognition, as well as sufficient human resources to run a multinational firm. It was also confronted with the dilemma between growing organically or expanding through mergers and acquisitions. According to Liu Chuanzhi, then President and CEO of the company, the quicker, albeit riskier second approach was ultimately chosen. Coincidentally, the company was approached by IBM at the end of 2003 to buy the latter's PC business (Liu 2007). The primary reason behind

IBM's proposal was for it to dispose of its PC division and focus on its other more lucrative business services market. The challenge for Lenovo, however, was whether it could eventually turn the PC division from a money-losing venture to a profitable business.

Near the time of the proposed deal, the annual revenue of IBM was $13 billion (with a 5.5 per cent share of the global PC market) while that of Lenovo was $3 billion (with a 2.2 per cent share). The deal was viewed by some as being typified by the Chinese idiom of 'a snake swallowing an elephant' (Liu 2007). Negotiations for it went ahead nevertheless, and they culminated in Lenovo's acquisition of IBM's PC division in May 2005, with a total transaction consideration of approximately $1.75 billion. IBM took an 18.9 per cent equity stake in Lenovo. The parties also concluded a five-year brand licensing agreement whereby Lenovo could use the well-established IBM brand on the PCs that it produced—the idea being that Lenovo would become synonymous with the quality associated with IBM. It was then observed that 'Lenovo [was] not the first Chinese firm to move beyond its home market by buying up struggling operations from an international brand, but its deal [was] the biggest and boldest so far' (Hennock 2004). Although the deal was successfully completed and looked promising to onlookers, it was by no means devoid of risks. For example, Lenovo had to ensure the smooth integration of the two companies and the retention of employees by fostering a global culture and a stimulating working environment within the firm.

A major challenge faced by Lenovo, and other Chinese firms that 'go global', is the need to build up and maintain an internationally recognized brand name. This actually reflects a mature segment in corporate development: generic firms relying on the pricing of their products can be easily out-competed by the next cheapest producer, whilst firms with established brand names can better able to retain customer loyalty. In Lenovo's case, the acquisition of IBM's PC business certainly helped the company to leverage IBM's brand name recognition. This was achieved through the brand licensing agreement as well as Lenovo's ownership of IBM's 'Think' family of trademarks. On top of these, Lenovo pursued a variety of strategies to raise its international profile. In 2004, for instance, the company joined the Olympic Partner Programme of the International Olympic Committee (IOC) as the first Chinese company to become the computer technology equipment partner of the IOC. It also engaged in active promotion of the 2008 Olympics, and its design for the Olympics torch was selected by the Beijing Organizing Committee.

By 2010, Lenovo was the fourth largest PC maker in the world and the largest in Asia (outside Japan). It has its headquarters in New York, branches in 66 countries, businesses in 166 countries and R&D centres in Beijing, Tokyo, and Raleigh. But it is uncertain whether the company could compete with its international rivals and fare well amidst the volatile global economic environment. One obvious fact is that Lenovo's business has been hit hard by the 2008 global financial crisis. The company reported a $97 million net loss in the fourth quarter of 2008 and a drop in its global market share to 7.3 per cent from 7.9 per cent (Hille 2009a; Hille 2009b). After the IBM acquisition, Lenovo was disproportionately exposed to corporate customers (such as large companies that turned out to be severely affected by the financial crisis), with the sale of high-end computers making up the bulk of its revenues (Hille 2009d). The company is said to be slow in catching new trends, launching new products and, generally, developing its consumer business outside China (Hille, Betts and Hill 2009; Hille 2009d).

These are unlikely to be what Lenovo expected before the acquisition, but its top management is now more concerned with seeking ways to retain its market share. They are adjusting the company's strategy from a focus on premium brands that it adopted following the acquisition of IBM's PC unit, and returning to cheaper computers and the lower-end segment of the industry in order to tap into emerging markets such as India and Poland (Hille 2009b). There also appears to be a renewed focus on the company's traditional home market, which is now a rare bright spot for the company, with strong growth in sales. Yet this growth was partly due to the company's recent participation in a government-funded subsidy programme to equip rural residents with cheap PCs (Hille 2009e). The company is also seeking a credit line from Chinese banks to support potential acquisitions. These moves suggest that the company is able to count on the support of the Chinese government as it struggles with losses in the global market (Hille 2009c). This is by no means astounding given that Lenovo is after all one of the most important forerunners in the government's 'go global' strategy. In 2009 in the midst of the global financial crisis, the Chinese government announced that it would use its foreign exchange reserves to help Chinese firms enter global markets by funding international expansions and M&A. In a very tangible sense, China's 'going out' strategy has come to fruition and Lenovo is a good case of the aspirations and the challenges.

It is worth noting that the CAS still holds 65 per cent of Legend Holdings, the parent company of Lenovo which holds 42.3 per cent of Lenovo's shares. Yet CAS has recently offered to sell a 29 per cent stake of $405 million. The government research institute has indicated before that it wanted to transform its subsidiaries into more market-driven entities by introducing a larger number private share-holders. After the divestment plan, it would still be Legend Holding's largest shareholder, with a 36 per cent stake (Hille and Lau 2009). Despite the uncertainties in Lenovo's future, the company's story serves as a case of how a domestic Chinese firm skilfully took advantage of favourable government policies and corporate opportunities and eventually emerged as a global player. No matter how the company performs in the future, the successes that it has achieved have already made it a harbinger of the future which will include Chinese multinational corporations.

7 Foreign Firms: Law Leading the Market

7.1 Introduction

At the second session of the Fifth National People's Congress in July 1979, the Chinese–Foreign Equity Joint Venture Law was adopted, granting foreign investors legal status to operate in the Chinese economy as a joint venture (JV) partnered with a Chinese firm. The Chinese partners were always state-owned enterprises (SOEs) at the start, as there were few other types of firms in China. This remained so throughout most of the 1990s, particularly as foreign investment was desired as a way of improving the performance of inefficient SOEs by attracting more advanced technology and introducing better management practices through working with a foreign partner.

The JV law was the first piece of corporate law in China. It reflected the importance of attracting foreign direct investment (FDI) at the very start of the reform period through formulating corporate laws that did not otherwise exist. In other words, it created legal economic entities in a system consisting only of SOEs and non-legally defined organizations like urban collectives. The laws governing foreign-invested enterprises (FIEs) (in addition to the first JV law, a law governing wholly foreign-owned enterprises (WFOEs) was passed in 1986 and a law governing cooperative joint ventures was passed in 1988) and the laws pertaining to economic contracts passed in the 1980s all pre-dated the passage of China's primary corporate statute. The Company Law of 1993, effective from 1994, is the centrepiece of Chinese law governing corporations. Quite unusually, the FIE laws existed in the absence of an overall corporate law framework. FIEs were afforded earlier legal recognition and better property rights protection via such commercial legislation than Chinese firms.

Although the Chinese government was keen to attract FDI with its resultant benefits such as superior technology and managerial know-how including how to operate on global markets, FIEs were closely monitored until WTO accession in 2001 loosened those restrictions. In other words, the Chinese government understood that to manage globalization successfully and prevent multinational corporations from dominating the domestic economy while maximizing the benefits of opening to the world economy, it was important to regulate their entry. The creation of Special Economic Zones (SEZs) where FIEs were allowed to operate seemingly achieved that goal.

However, even though China had the advantage of a large, low-cost labour force that should be attractive to foreign direct investment seeking to reduce costs by locating production in developing countries, it had a strong disadvantage in terms of its legal system. Although most developing countries have underdeveloped legal systems, China's system was virtually non-existent, since it was a communal property state with no private enterprises that would have required governance by corporate law in 1979. Therefore, it didn't have such a system. Other transition economies in Eastern Europe and the former Soviet Union would have faced a similar challenge; however, when they undertook transition in the late 1980s/early 1990s, the creation of private property rights via privatization of state-owned firms was one of the pillars of reform (see Stiglitz 2003 for some of the downsides of this policy). By contrast, China's much more gradual transition process did not include mass privatization at the start of market-oriented reforms in 1979; instead, China's reform of its enterprises has been described as 'reform without ownership change', that is, from state to private hands, as efficiency gains have instead been wrought through incentives and not through privatizing SOEs (see e.g. Fan 1994).

Therefore, to attract FDI, China created a set of corporate laws that proffered legal form and protection to foreign investors which existed on their own and did not reside within a larger framework of basic company or contract (or even civil) laws. Not surprisingly, there were immediate difficulties, as evidenced by the passage of the Economic Contract Law in 1981 two years after the first JV law, with a version that governed foreign parties in 1985. Moreover, in such an underdeveloped legal system with a judiciary not accustomed to adjudicating economic matters, China also quickly joined the Convention on the Recognition and Enforcement of Foreign Arbitral Awards in 1986. This again pre-dated the passage of the generally applicable Arbitration Law of 1994 that introduced alternative dispute resolution into China.

This distinct regime led to an uneven playing field in many respects, particularly for non-state firms which were beginning to operate in the 1980s and 1990s within the transitioning economy (see e.g. Huang 2003). However, in the absence of such FIE laws, the lack of legal vehicles for FDI may well have deterred foreign investment, particularly the large, multinational corporations operating in technology sectors of interest to Chinese policymakers. Indeed, another law which pre-dated the Company Law was the Patent Law, passed in 1985 and subsequently revised considerably in the 1990s and 2000s. By creating a system to protect intellectual property rights, however imperfect, China attempted to establish legal parameters around proprietary information that is usually expected by multinational corporations used to such protections and guidance.

Therefore, in a very unusual sense, although laws in China and elsewhere largely do not establish markets, FIE laws in China sometimes appear to lead and develop the market. Laws governing FIEs establish markets in which foreign firms could operate, which then lead to the creation of further laws and regulation to govern new developments in those markets. But, because there was not an established corporate legal system in China, the FIE laws created marketized segments of the economy, which in the earlier period were the only corporate laws outlining the areas in which market activities could take place for foreign firms. In the latter part of the reform period, it was particularly evident in terms of capital market regulations. For instance, without the WFOE law, foreign investors would not have had a vehicle to enter the Chinese wholesale and retail markets that were opening in the 1980s and 1990s to establish retail stores selling consumer goods. In the 2000s, the promulgation of the Qualified Foreign Institutional Investors (QFII) scheme of 2002 permitted foreign investors to operate in China's stock market and trade RMB-denominated shares.

By contrast, as seen in the earlier chapters, Chinese firms largely operated without explicit legal permissions or protections. Permitting 'experimentation' by allowing, sometimes banning but then relenting, the Chinese government's 'no encouragement, no ban' policy (Naughton 1995) meant that SOEs, TVEs, and private firms frequently acted without ex ante laws governing their actions. Undoubtedly, foreign firms also 'experimented' in this sense once they were within China, and are often active stakeholders in pushing for further reform. However, in the early stages, the FIE laws carved out the market for foreign firms that defined their activities and offered protection that was fairly unique.

7.1.1 LAW LEADING THE MARKET

This chapter sets out the argument that the FIE laws led the development of segments of the market and also the corporate law framework in China in many respects. Unlike Chinese firms which were accustomed to, and more accepting, of vague legal protection and property rights, foreign firms required the certainty of formal laws governing their investments in China. Multinational corporations from more developed countries were used to operating according to laws and regulations. Without such laws, the investments of billions of dollars into China were unlikely to have been as feasible, since such transfers would need to be documented and governed by contract especially for large, multinational companies. The lack of legal vehicles for FDI specifying rights and obligations, as well as formal governing rules contracts and transactions would probably have been a deterrent to invest-ment. For instance, whereas the legal system of a developed economy could under certain circumstances recognize the rights of a contract even if it were not in written form and formally signed (e.g. under common law in the US, a contract is considered to be legally binding if there was a 'meeting of the minds'), the lack of an independent judiciary and case law to set that precedent would have meant no recourse if a contract was reneged upon in China.

Again, this is in stark contrast to the effect of laws on domestic enterprises in China. SOEs and TVEs were largely ungoverned by law and depended on government policy, while private firms often developed in spite of the laws. FIEs were, unusually, governed by laws and regulations, tighter in some areas where licensing is required and looser in others since they often received preferential treatment as compared with private Chinese firms, but were nevertheless governed by rules. This regime remained quite separate from the domestic legal system until the late 1990s when the disparate contract laws were unified into one law governing all contracts in China, irrespective of the entity (domestic or foreign), for instance.

7.1.2 STRUCTURE OF THE CHAPTER

This chapter will first outline the notable growth of FDI and the major policies towards foreign firms in terms of creating Special Economic Zones that generated such inward investments which supported China's global integra-tion and opening. The chapter will then analyse the ways in which the legal regime and other policies guided the development of FIEs in China. Next, the unification of the disparate legal regimes governing foreign and domestic firms in 1999 will be explored in the post-2001 WTO accession environment. The chapter will analyse the subtle ways in which regulations governing FIEs have changed after China signed up to the strictures of international economic laws as opening progresses under its WTO obligations. Yet, it remains both an 'open' economy and imposes controls on foreign investment. The chapter concludes with an assessment of the role of FIE law on China's corporate sector developments and the likely trajectory of further corporate law developments, which will increasingly no longer lead or create markets, but respond to the needs of stakeholders and constituents such as multinational corporations operating in China which seek further legal and regulatory reforms. Therefore, legal developments are likely to evolve in response to changing market conditions, including those pertaining to foreign firms.

Four case studies analysing China's opening to world markets and the role of foreign firms will be featured in the chapter. Two illustrate how China developed its successful low-technology, labour-intensive export sector of textiles and clothing through its 'open door' policy, but also its mixed record in fostering medium-technology goods that require global supply chains such as the automobile industry. The other two cases focus on the two main types of FDI vehicles and the experience of FIEs constituted in such forms in China: JVs in the mobile phone industry (Nokia) and WFOEs in the retail industry (Carrefour).

7.2 **Foreign direct investment and Special Economic Zones**

7.2.1 FDI IN CHINA

FDI was an important part of total investment funds in China in the first decade and a half of the transition. In the early 1990s, FDI accounted for around half of all investment in China (Figure 7.1). Up until the mid-1990s, FDI contributed over 20 per cent of total investment; largely in the form of Chinese–foreign joint ventures (see Figure 7.2). Although WFOEs were permitted as of 1986, the preference of the Chinese authorities for joint ventures that were thought to facilitate more learning and positive spillovers meant that wholly foreign-owned enterprises did not become numerous until 1992 when the 'open door' policy took off, permitting more FDI. It coincided with the liberalization of the wholesale and retail markets in China, which appealed to WFOEs such as food stores like the US's McDonald's and France's Carrefour. Opening such consumer markets gave a new impetus to FDI since the domestic market was still largely characterized by undersupply of goods and services, and the urban population alone exceeded 321 million at that time. In other words, China was attractive for its large population, both as a low-cost source of labour for production and as a potential market for sales, fulfilling two of the main drivers of inward FDI (the third being resource-seeking investments, such as in oil and commodities).

However, the phenomenon of 'round-tripping', whereby Chinese capital exited and re-entered the country as FDI in order to benefit from the superior treatment granted to foreign capital, may inflate the figures (see e.g. Xiao 2004). But, Figure 7.3 shows the constancy in terms of volume of FDI throughout the 1990s and 2000s, and the share of FIEs in Chinese exports seen in Figure 2.4 attests to the importance of foreign firms. Figure 7.1 suggests that this was particularly so during a period when China was much poorer and FDI was therefore relatively more important in bringing in funds for investment, particularly in terms of producing the exports that gave China access to world markets. Indeed, the inflow of FDI is closely correlated with China's 'opening' and the growth in exports seen in Figure 2.7.

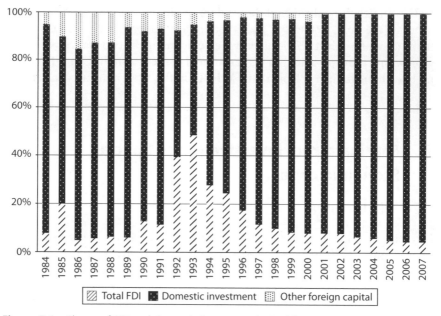

Figure 7.1. Shares of FDI and domestic investment in total investment
Source: China Statistical Yearbook Table 17–14.

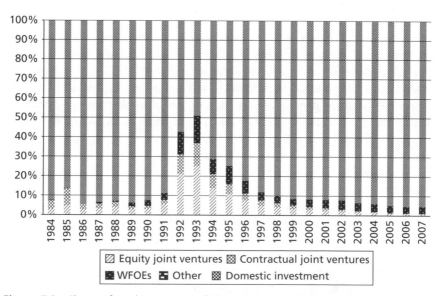

Figure 7.2. Shares of total investment of FIEs and domestic investment
Source: China Statistical Yearbook Table 4–2.

Table 7.1. FDI inflows to select countries (US billions, current dollars)

	1991–6 (cumulative)	1997	1998	1999	2000	2001	2002	2003	2004	2005	2006	2007
World	1675	468	696	1094	1518	794	737	641	751	1116	1457	2139
United States	333	105	179	289	321	157	84	63	145	112	241	237
Brazil	25	19	31	28	32	22	16	10	18	15	18	138
China	156	44	43	38	38	44	49	47	54	79	78	54
India	7	3	2	2	3	5	5	4	5	6	17	8
Malaysia	30	5	2	3	3	0.6	3	2	4	3	6	24
Mexico	46	12	12	13	17	29	21	15	22	20	19	22
Poland	13	4	6	7	9	5	4	4	12	10	19	55
South Africa	3	4	2	3	2	2	3	8	15	12	29	5
Russia	5	3.8	0.6	1.5	0.9	7.0	0.7	0.8	0.7	6.0	-0.2	197

Source: World Bank World Development Indicators.
Notes: The figure for Russia covers 1994–6.

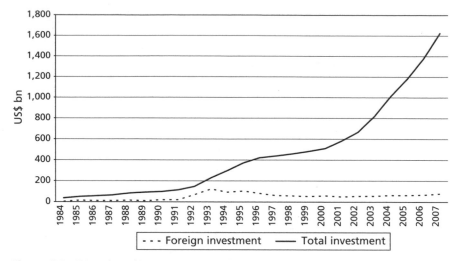

Figure 7.3. FDI and total investment, 1984–2007

Source: China Statistical Yearbook Tables 17–14, 17–16, 18–16.

Nevertheless, Figure 7.3 also shows that the importance of FDI diminished rapidly through the 1990s and 2000s in terms of being a source of investment funds, though perhaps not in terms of technology and 'know-how'. Since 1978, foreign investment accounted for about 13 per cent of total investment, but the share has changed dramatically from 8 per cent in the 1980s when opening slowly began in a few SEZs to peaking in the early 1990s as the 'open door policy' was avidly implemented, and then falling to 6 per cent in the 2000s. Even though FDI began to decline in relative terms, Table 7.1 shows the steady increase in inward capital flows in China during the 2000s to an impressive average of some $60 billion per year from around $45 billion the decade before. The growth of domestic investment simply outpaced what has been an impressive and constant inflow of FDI for the past two decades, particularly as compared with other emerging economies. Table 7.1 shows inward FDI into select economies. China compares significantly favourably with other large developing countries (Brazil, Mexico), transition economies (Russia, Poland), and populous nations (India). All the while, it lacked a complete legal system but did utilize a rich array of policies to attract FDI, namely focused in Special Economic Zones.

7.2.2 SPECIAL ECONOMIC ZONES

The primary purpose of SEZs was to attract foreign investment and promote international trade by creating what were essentially export-processing zones with an aim of developing China's own productive capacity. For instance, to gain approval to invest in China, foreign firms had to demonstrate that they possessed advance technology that was demanded in export markets. By situating FDI within SEZs, the state could control the foreign firms to prevent them from entering the domestic market, but still offer terms within these zones that would make them attractive places to locate and produce for export.

In its initial phase, the Chinese government established Special Economic Zones in the southern provinces of Guangdong and Fujian that are close in proximity to Hong Kong and Taiwan. Special incentives were offered to FDI in these SEZs, such as preferential tax policies. The State Council awarded rights of autonomy in foreign trade to these provinces and, in 1980, set up four SEZs in Shenzhen, Zhuhai, and Shantou in the Pearl River Delta of Guangdong, and Xiamen in Fujian.

Given China's comparative advantage in possessing abundant labour, it is unsurprising that it is dominant in exports of textiles and clothing— labour-intensive, low-technology goods. The initial beneficiary of China's opening was the textiles and clothing industry. Case study 7 illustrates how this straightforward comparative advantage was nevertheless shaped by a complex mix of strategies related to opening and industrial policies.

Despite success in the low-technology end of exports, the Chinese author- ities however felt that there was insufficient technological content embodied in the FDI in the SEZs and wished to upgrade their industrial structure by attracting more advanced industries. Thus, Open Port Cities were established in 1984 which became Economic and Trade Development Zones (ETDZs) in 1985. These were more successful in attracting foreign investment embodying higher technological content, particularly in the areas of consumer electronics and computing. A telecommunications industry is presented as case study 9 which illustrates the entry of firms such as Nokia and Motorola at that time.

Hainan island separated from Guangdong and became a province in 1988 and the fifth and largest SEZ in the same year. After the central government granted preferential treatment to these first coastal cities, twenty-four inland cities lobbied for the same privileges. Also in that year, the State Council announced that the number of 'open' cities and counties nearly doubled from 148 to 284 (covering nearly half of the total number of cities) and would embrace a population totalling 160 million.

Around that time in 1985, the first 'development triangles' were created in the Yangtze River Delta near Shanghai; the Pearl River Delta in Guangdong, the Min Nan region in Fujian, Liaodong and Shandong peninsulas, and the Bohai sea coastal region bordering Tianjin were also opened to foreign investors. These eventually became the best established areas for FDI as they linked together SEZs and the internal market, notably the Pearl River Delta. This policy continued with the Pudong District of Shanghai being designated as a new development zone in 1990 to attract investment and lead development along the Yangtze River. This opening-up process led to a scramble for further development, particularly following Deng Xiaoping's Southern Tour in 1992 that marked the take-off of FDI in China.

Free Trade Zones (FTZs), of which China has around fifteen, started in the same year. FTZs removed tariffs on numerous exports and imports. These were previously the only places where foreign investors could establish WFOEs, though this restriction was lifted after WTO accession.

In 1992 and 1993, eighteen more ETDZs were set up by the State Council and a third group was authorized in 2000–2. In April 2000, the State Council additionally approved fifteen cities such as Guangzhou, Beijing, and Dalian to have Export Processing Zones (EPZs). The EPZ is a special area supervised by Customs and established within the confines of an existing development zone, usually an ETDZ. EPZs provide a less bureaucratic method of carrying out export-processing activities. At that time, the State Council also ratified Suzhou Industrial Park, Hainan Yangpu ETDZ, Shanghai Jinqiao Export Processing Zone, Ningbo Daxie ETDZ, and Xiamen Haicang Investment Zone, to enjoy the same preferential policies as these national ETDZs.

Finally, High-Technology Development Zones (HTDZs) were developed in 1995 which, unlike the earlier zones, are widespread and located in nearly every province except for the western province of Qinghai and the Tibet and Ningxia Autonomous Regions. The HDTZs are focused on attracting technology in production as well as research centres, including industrial and science parks. The rapid growth of coastal regions which received FDI much earlier than the slower growing interior provinces prompted the government in the Ninth Five Year Plan (1996–2000) to try and move FDI westward into the interior.

There are others as well as different nomenclature for what are essentially SEZs. For instance, in the north-east of China, there are National Border and Economic Cooperation Zones (NBECZs). Fourteen NBECZs have been approved by the State Council since 1992 in provinces such as Liaoning and Heilongjiang. Some of the established SEZs are listed in Appendix 7.1.

Despite the proliferation of SEZs, including those focused on attracting more advanced FDI, technological upgrading is a challenge, as evidenced in the case study on the automobile industry. Although more technologically advanced investment may be entering China, the translation of such knowledge into developing a domestic industry is fraught with challenges. In the automobile industry, joint ventures were developed between Chinese and foreign companies in order to learn from established car makers. Moreover, to sustain a medium-technology industry like automobiles, supply chains with skilled upstream and downstream producers/distributors are also required. Thus, the car industry presented in case study 8 can be viewed as an indicator of technological upgrading in an economy, since a successful sector would reflect more widespread technological development. Designated as a 'priority industry' in 1986, the automobile industry is thus a good case of the success and set-backs in China's FDI policy, which has been geared at attracting technology to help develop its own industrial capacity as well as to have a competitive export sector.

7.3 **FDI policies and laws**

SEZs enjoyed both privileged political and fiscal status, which granted them exceptional authority and resources in implementing market-driven economic policies denied to other segments of the economy. For instance, the SEZs were normally placed under the direct control of the mayor or vice mayor. This not only guarantees the zone a favourable allocation of government resources, but also facilitates faster decision-making at the municipal level. Special Economic Zones were also granted independent fiscal authority (*yiji caizeng*), which enabled them to collect tax revenues and otherwise assume fiscal responsibility.

Due to these institutional arrangements, foreign firms located in the SEZs enjoyed tax benefits and access to well-developed infrastructure and facilities at very low cost. Red tape associated with applications for and licensing of investment, plant establishment, imports and exports was reduced so that foreign investors could start and run their projects with minimal bureaucracy. These benefits, together with an abundant low-cost labour supply drawn from permitted migration from rural areas, created an attractive investment environment for foreign firms.

This more flexible regime was expanded by a large increase in activity in 1986, which saw a raft of more favourable regulations and provisions used to encourage FDI inflow. In 1986, the Law on Wholly Foreign-Owned Enterprises was passed. This statute allowed for the first time an enterprise organized under Chinese law to be wholly owned by one or more foreign investors, with no Chinese equity participation. However, numerous restrictions applied that limited the approval of WFOEs, since Chinese–Foreign joint ventures which held the greater capacity for positive spillovers of knowledge were still preferred.

Also in that year, the State Council promulgated the Provisions of the State Council for the Encouragement of Foreign Investment. These so-called 'Article Provisions' provided Chinese–Foreign joint ventures with preferential tax treatment, the freedom to import inputs such as materials and equipment, the right to retain and swap foreign exchange with each other, and simpler licensing procedures. Additional tax benefits were offered to export-oriented joint ventures and those employing advanced technology. The government also attempted to guarantee further the autonomy of joint ventures from external bureaucratic interference, to eliminate many 'unfair' local costs, and to provide alternative ways for joint ventures to balance foreign exchange. Privileged access was provided to supplies of water, electricity, and transportation (paying the same price as state-owned enterprises) and to interest-free RMB loans.

Then in 1988, the Law on Chinese–Foreign Cooperative Joint Ventures was passed, which allowed for a joint venture with more flexible features than the Law on Chinese–Foreign Equity Joint Ventures. Finally, the Corporate Income Tax of Foreign-Invested Enterprises in 1991 formalized some of the tax breaks.

With this backdrop, FDI took off in the spring of 1992 when Deng Xiaoping circulated the southern coastal areas and SEZs. His tour renewed fervour among local governments for the creation of SEZs. In order to rein in the rampant expansion of local special zones, the State Council promulgated a circular stating that only those special zones designated by the central and provincial governments could legally operate. A two-level approval system was established. The central government granted more privileged status to the newly established Pudong district in Shanghai and approved eighteen national ETDZs, including in Beijing, Shenyang, Hangzhou, and Chongqing. Meanwhile, it shut down as many as 1,000 zones set up without the proper approval by the central and provincial governments.

The results were remarkable and quick. This was also due to the early 1990s coinciding with the liberalization of the wholesale and retail markets in China, for example food vouchers were ended in 1992. China thus became attractive due to its cheap and large labour force, but also because its internal market was opening.

But by the mid 1980s in the early stages of opening, well-known multinational companies such as Nokia, Motorola, and Ericsson in the telecommunications industry had entered China and started large-scale JV operations. Case study 9 shows their progress in the context of a rapidly evolving market and shifting policies. These JVs originally geared at exports also eyed the emerging domestic market, but had to navigate the changing parameters of Chinese policies which were intent on developing both a competitive export sector and utilizing FDI as a source of know-how to help its own industries develop. The dominance of FIEs in the mobile phone industry in the 1990s and eventual loss of market share to Chinese firms in the 2000s illustrate the complexities of operating in China.

Another interesting case is the largest retailer in China, which is France's Carrefour, and not US's Wal-Mart, the biggest retailer in the world. Entering China in 1995, Carrefour was part of the influx of FDI following the take-off of the 'open door' policy and the opening of consumer markets by the early 1990s. WFOEs had control over their enterprise so did not have a Chinese partner with its attendant benefits and disadvantages. In the retail sector, moreover, when a multinational store replicates itself in a foreign country it is less likely to be in need of a local partner since it is focused on sales and not production. Case study 10 illustrates the challenges and advantages of a WFOE operating within China's fast-paced market and coping with the less than transparent business environment.

In any case, FIEs entered China en masse and produced more than half of Chinese exports by the 2000s, and an even higher proportion of high-tech goods. However large their presence may be in export-oriented SEZs, their penetration into China's domestic market remains limited. Although China has committed to opening large swathes of its domestic market—particularly services—as part of its WTO commitments, FIEs face numerous non-tariff barriers that limit their presence in China.

In sum, the early contributions of FIEs were to provide foreign exchange earnings and employment for surplus rural migrant workers, and they continue to do so. The collapse in exports during the 2008 global recession resulted in an estimated 20 million migrant workers losing their jobs (out of an estimated 200 million rural–urban migrants) in a sector where FIEs account for half of the output (see Orlik and Rozelle 2009). Moreover, FIEs are a source of know-how and learning for Chinese firms, either formally through technology transfers or informally through working with foreign managers. They are also a source of growth in China's 'dual track' transition as part of the non-state sector that enabled the gradual reform of the state-owned enterprises and provided competition during the transition. SOEs could then be gradually reformed whilst the non-state sector generated economic growth and jobs (see e.g. Lau, Qian, and Roland 2001). For its part, China offers to foreign firms the fastest growing economy in the world, with a rapidly expanding middle class, particularly in urban areas. The Carrefour case study illustrates that point well.

The next section turns to examining the ways in which the legal regime, in addition to the policies outlined above, guided the development of FIEs in China. By doing so, FIE laws in some ways led the development of the market for foreign investment but also became the precursor for similar laws to govern domestic, non-state-owned firms and they prompted the development of a system of company law in China.

7.4 **Laws leading market development**

Although it is hard to generalize, the start of reforms in 1979 and the laws of the 1980s marked an era in which most corporate laws were geared at FIEs. The 1990s, by contrast, were characterized by the creation of two centrepiece laws, the Company Law of 1993 and the Securities Law of 1998, and others which eventually extended the legal recognition of corporate laws to all Chinese firms, as well as unifying what had become a separate legal system for foreign and domestic enterprises. By the 2000s, and particularly after WTO accession in 2001, when greater market opening was expected, key laws like the M&A and anti-trust laws were passed. Though facially neutral, market access for foreign firms was still closely circumscribed: this was especially evident in capital markets. In a number of ways, FIE laws led the development of the subsequent laws that formed part of China's corporatization drive of the 1990s when it sought to transform its enterprises into shareholding companies as a way of privatizing some SOEs (Garnaut et al. 2003). By 1999, though, corporate laws covered all firms, even private Chinese ones.

The laws governing FIEs preceded the development of corporate laws in a manner that resonates with the experimental process of reform evident in China's overall transition. Such laws also circumscribed the market for foreign firms, dictating their form as JVs in the initial stages and also opening specific segments for them to operate in, clearly seen in the 2002 Qualified Foreign Institutional Investors (QFII) scheme that permitted transactions in the Chinese stock market under certain parameters.

As with all such processes of markets and laws, there is an iterative process. In many respects, the FIE laws provided the lead on market development for foreign investors and even the development of corporate laws in China. Until China completes its marketization process, foreign firms are strongly affected and constrained by the parameters proffered by the authorities for their operations in China, ranging from approvals to set up shop to obtaining permission to trade stocks. The laws and regulations governing foreign firms, therefore, have a unique place in Chinese law and in understanding the evolution of the market environment for business during the reform period.

The 1979 Chinese–Foreign Equity Joint Venture Law was the first piece of corporate law in China and was promulgated in spite of the absence of a larger legal framework governing firms and contracts. In 1986, the Law on Wholly Foreign-Owned Enterprises was passed and was followed two years later by the 1988 Law on Chinese–Foreign Cooperative Joint Ventures. WFOEs were a small proportion of all FIEs until much later, since the authorities favoured joint ventures which had the greater scope for positive spillovers of knowledge and technology that could benefit failing Chinese SOEs. Cooperative JVs were similar to equity JVs except that their shareholding structure was defined by contract and they were a more flexible form which had been experimented with by FIEs before the passage of the law.

The difficulties of firms operating essentially in a legal void in terms of other corporate laws were apparent fairly quickly. China lacked laws governing not just corporations, but also contracts, torts, property, etc. In an attempt to provide an overall legal framework, the General Principles of Civil Law was promulgated in April 1986, which was followed by the Civil Procedure Law in 1991. The General Principles of Civil Law attempted to produce the basic legal principles for an increasingly decentralized system, but failed to cover crucial areas such as property and tort.

After the July 1979 passage of the first FIE law, the Economic Contract Law was passed in December 1981 covering contracts between domestic entities other than individuals. It was intended largely to regularize transactions taking place between SOEs as liberalization in the domestic economy began to take shape and there were a growing number of Chinese–Foreign JVs beginning to transact as well. Shortly thereafter, in March 1985, the Foreign Economic Contract Law was passed which covered contracts between Chinese and foreign entities. It reinforced the emerging separate legal regimes covering foreign firms and foreign-related transactions. In 1987, a third contract law, the Technology Contract Law, was passed. This law gave legal recognition and protection to technology transfers and licensing, granting additional protection to the technology diffusion hoped for from FDI. With the Patent Law passed in 1985, these statutes were heavily geared towards protecting technology contracts and therefore encouraging 'positive' FDI spillovers of transferring proprietary knowledge from foreign to Chinese firms. A 1993 amendment to the Economic Contract Law extended the coverage to individual industrial and commercial households (*getihu*), which had previously only been loosely covered by the General Principles of Civil Law. In other words, by 1993 at the time of the passage of the Company Law, all economic entities were in principle covered by some form of contract law, albeit separate ones. The three contract laws were repealed in October 1999 when the unified contract law took shape, but until then, China operated a preferential and disparate legal regime favouring FIEs and their technology over private firms for the first two decades of the reform period. It was also evidently a regime that largely existed in the absence of an overall legal framework.

Unsurprisingly, there were numerous gaps in the legal regime which became evident. With a legal system unaccustomed to resolving commercial disputes, enforcement of these newly created contracts meant resorting to arbitration or alternative dispute resolution. China joined the Convention on the Recognition and Enforcement of Foreign Arbitral Awards in 1986, and eventually adopted an Arbitration Law in 1994. The China International Economic and Trade Arbitration Commission (CIETAC) was set up in 1988;

a previous entity was set up in 1980 as the Foreign Economic and Trade Arbitration Commission, so right from the start such a forum for resolving contractual disputes was necessary. CIETAC has since become a preferred forum to the underdeveloped Chinese courts to resolve disputes. International arbitration is also used, but not necessarily when the party involved is a SOE, thereby limiting the ability to contract for dispute settlement in a foreign country.

In a sense, the need to attract FDI propelled the move to create a legal regime that would eventually establish a system of corporate law for all firms, including private enterprises. However, importantly, the JVs were established between a foreign firm and an SOE, with the Chinese partner holding a majority stake (e.g. 51 per cent of the shares) such that control rested with the state-owned entity so that JVs were not private firms per se. The approval process for JVs typically entailed the foreign partner demonstrating that it had superior technology that could be used to produce goods for export, as imports into the domestic market were heavily discouraged and subject to 100 per cent tariffs. The usual arrangement would be for the Chinese partner to provide the land, factory, and employees, and for the foreign partner to supply the capital. The Chinese partner would take the lead in obtaining licences needed to operate and contract with suppliers and distributors. The foreign firm would introduce management skills and open the way to global markets.

This structure and set of laws suited the Chinese state as it undertook a gradual transition toward becoming a market-based economy and not a radical path involving wholesale adoption of a new economic/political/legal system. Thus, the laws themselves became the pre-cursors to the corporate laws adopted throughout the 1990s and 2000s that have created a legal structure for firms in China. The centrepiece of China's corporate laws is the Company Law of 1993, effective as of 1994. Although originally designed for the restructuring of SOEs, the subsequent revisions in 1999 and 2005 meant that for the first time, domestic firms, albeit restricted to SOEs at the outset, were granted the legal recognition and governance by statute that had been provided to foreign firms under the JV and WFOE laws.

As mentioned earlier, a 1993 amendment to the Economic Contract Law extended the coverage of the contract laws to all economic entities in the economy, moving the system some way towards having a rudimentary set of laws that governed how corporations are formed and the rules of their contracts. In March 1999, the Contract Law was passed and repealed the prior three laws governing contracts (the 1981 Economic Contract Law, the 1985 Economic Contract Law for Foreign Parties, and the 1987 Technology Contract Law). The separate legal regime for foreign firms was coming to an end as China moved ahead with adopting unified laws that governed all firms, foreign and domestic, state and non-state.

By the 2000s, therefore, the earlier corporate and contract laws of the 1980s that were created to grant legal form to foreign-invested firms were incarnated into general company and contract laws that governed widely in China. The forerunners of these later laws were the FIE laws that were driven by the need to afford legal recognition to foreign firms.

Therefore, by the end of the 1990s, following on from the early laws governing FIEs in the 1980s, the 1990s witnessed the passage of laws that offered legal recognition to Chinese firms. In the 2000s, the laws continued to develop but in a unified manner, joining together the disparate legal regimes that had sprung up as a result of the historical anomaly of creating laws first to attract FDI. The Law on Mergers and Acquisitions of 2003, the 2006 significant amendments to the 1986 Bankruptcy Law, the Anti-Monopoly Law of 2007, and the Employment Law of 2008 were all largely facially neutral in their applications to domestic and foreign firms in China. Since even sole proprietorships were recognized in the third decade of reform, it was necessary for a unified legal regime to govern the corporatized enterprises in China.

However, the playing field was not necessarily level. SOEs remained privileged in many respects, including exemptions from aspects of the Anti-Monopoly Law, although foreign and private firms were increasingly on an equal legal if not substantive footing, since many foreign firms were valued for their technology and expertise. When it came to fleshing out the other aspects of corporate laws and making such 'laws-on-the-books' effective, such as the securities laws, the 2000s showed that laws still led market development for foreign firms, governing where they could act, and barriers remained despite the efforts to create a unified legal regime. For foreign firms, although laws were offering a largely level playing field insofar that one set of corporate laws applied to companies in China, the disparate legal regime remained particularly evident in capital markets. Laws still led the development of the market for FIEs, though WTO accession implies that within the next couple of decades, restrictions may well begin to lift.

For instance, the Qualified Foreign Institutional Investor (QFII) scheme promulgated by the China Securities Regulatory Commission (CSRC) in December 2002 permitted foreign investors to trade on China's stock markets but only up to a quota. The WTO-agreed Securities Companies Regulations and Fund Management Companies Regulations, passed in the same year, similarly offered limited opening to foreign firms to transact in equities and bonds, with numerous restrictions in place.

The widely anticipated Regulations on the Administration of Foreign-Funded Banks issued by the China Banking Regulatory Commission (CBRC), which was promulgated precisely five years after WTO accession in December 2006, serves as perhaps the best example. These regulations marked the entry of foreign banks into China's large and potentially lucrative banking system characterized by an extraordinarily high savings rate in the country, of some 45–50 per cent of GDP. Deposits in China increased from just under $1.5 trillion in 1999 to $6.2 trillion by 2008, according to the People's Bank of China. As with other reforms, the WTO-mandated opening was preceded by numerous measures to strengthen and prepare the banking system for competition from foreign banks. For instance, the recapitalization of the four big state-owned banks in the 1990s and the sales of minority equity stakes in Chinese banks, as well as IPOs, were all geared at improving the competitiveness and efficiency of the domestic banking sector in advance of opening to foreign banks.

The opening of the banking sector, though, was circumscribed, and the parameters of the type of market access available to foreign banks were set out by regulation. To operate in the RMB retail banking business, the conditions imply that most banks will have to incorporate as local subsidiaries or operate as joint ventures. As most banks prefer to operate through branches, the regulations would prevent them from offering services such as bank cards to the high-saving population. Branches of foreign banks, for instance, were banned from engaging in RMB services except for those individuals with deposits of one million Yuan (over $120,000) and the approval of the CBRC, severely limiting the expansion of retail banking, as average incomes in China were only around $3,000 in the 2000s.

Previous to the 2006 regulations, branches of foreign banks and subsidiaries or joint ventures were governed under identical rules. But, although geographical restrictions have been lifted for foreign banks in accordance with China's WTO commitments, the new regime implies that foreign banks have to restructure to become Chinese-incorporated firms or joint ventures to operate in the lucrative RMB retail business.

The Chinese government sought to encourage locally incorporated firms in order to minimize the risks for depositors and Chinese customers, since they would be subject to Chinese rather than foreign laws. The deterrent of operating as Chinese firms in an incomplete legal system and the higher capital requirements under the new regulations have meant that three years later, the entry of foreign banks into the RMB retail business remains limited. The big four state-owned banks continue to dominate the market, accounting for over half of all credit in the economy (Shen et al. 2009). The 2008 global financial market further marked a retreat in the sector when foreign banks pulled out of China, but the overall pattern is still one in which market opening is determined by laws and regulations for foreign firms who were the early beneficiary of legal protection but have latterly increasingly complained about restrictive market access.

7.5 **Post-WTO accession and international economic laws**

7.5.1 FDI LAWS AND POLICIES CONTINUING TO CIRCUMSCRIBE THE MARKET

Entry into the World Trade Organization in December 2001 was the culmination of fifteen years of negotiations with each existing member state, and marked the start of significant global integration for China in terms of trade links and, increasingly, capital markets. China committed to reduce tariffs across the board and, importantly for foreign firms, it agreed a number of measures to liberalize the services sector that should increase market access and increase China's global integration by becoming a market as well as a destination for offshoring low-cost production. The opening of its hitherto fairly closed services sector elicited the most anticipation among foreign firms. China agreed to open its markets for banking, financial services, and professional services, such as law and accountancy and education. Although China retains the 'Catalogue Guiding Foreign Investment in Industry and the Related Regulations on Foreign Investment Guidelines', these were substantially revised after WTO accession in 2001 (see e.g. Lardy 2002). Sectors that were not expressly prohibited were open to investment, subject to other restrictions and usually to permission. There were also dates set out for the opening of sectors, such as banking in 2006, discussed in the previous chapter. However, even where sectors are opened, there are often non-tariff barriers which remain.

The agreement to open the relatively underdeveloped and thus less competitive services sector may appear surprising, but the approach follows an overall pattern of actively managing FDI that was established for manufacturing in the first stages of opening. When China needed to increase the productivity of its industrial firms, it attracted foreign investors with their know-how and technology to become joint venture partners with Chinese firms to help them become more efficient and market-oriented. When it wished to develop a retail sector, it selectively allowed WFOEs to enter whilst promoting domestic firms to learn from the 'demonstration effect' of having well-honed multinational retailers operating in the consumer market.

China followed a similar strategy for developing the services sector. Under the planned economy, the services sector was small, as the state allocated or ran the activities usually associated with services such as health insurance and banking through its state-owned enterprises and banks. There was thus a need to make the state-owned banks run on a commercial basis as with the other inefficient SOEs, but there were also notable gaps in the sector, such as not having had the need for a corporate bond market.

Therefore, China aimed to attract FDI into the services sector to help develop it. As with the earlier FDI policies with respect to manufacturing, the process was to selectively open and control the foreign investment. For instance, total foreign investment is limited to a ceiling of 25 per cent in a Chinese bank, with a single investor limited to holding less than 20 per cent. These minority equity shares would therefore not challenge the control of a state-owned commercial bank which is similar to the control associated with a majority 51 per cent shareholding by the Chinese partner commonly imposed on Chinese–foreign joint ventures.

Again, laws paved the way for FDI into the banking system. China anticipated the competition in its banking sector after WTO accession, so began to prepare the large state-owned commercial banks by attracting foreign investment before opening and restructuring them to become publicly listed companies with international as well as domestic IPOs. Thus, the 1995 Commercial Bank Law enabled minority equity stakes to be purchased by foreign banks starting in 1996, which accelerated by the time of WTO opening in 2001. The 2001 Regulations on the Administration of Foreign-Invested Financial Institutions (which superseded the 1994 regulations by offering more market access) and the 2002 Implementing Rules for the Administration of Foreign-Invested Financial Institutions hastened the investments which had previously been limited to small banks. But, this changed after WTO accession. In 2003, the China Construction Bank (CCB) was selected from the 'Big Four', which also include Bank of China, Industrial and Commercial Bank of China (ICBC), and the (ABC), to be the first, and it sold a minority share of nearly 17 per cent to Bank of America prior to its initial public offering in 2005. By 2011, all but one of the big four state-owned commercial banks had become listed companies, with foreign banks and other institutions as minority shareholders. Similarly, dozens of the lower-tier banks also sold shares to foreign investors, such as the fifth largest state-owned commercial bank, the Bank of Communications, in which the global bank HSBC purchased a 19.9 per cent stake in 2004. Although some foreign banks have exited China in the midst of the 2008 global financial crisis, such as the Royal Bank of Scotland which had a 4.3 per cent stake in the Bank of China and sold it for $2.34 billion to shore up its balance sheets when it became part-nationalized by the British government, the select management of inward FDI into the financial system provided the expertise that the Chinese government wanted for its banks as they restructured in a process that echoed the earlier policies governing the manufacturing and retail sectors.

7.5.2 THE INFLUENCE OF INTERNATIONAL ECONOMIC LAW

WTO-related changes to the business environment are broader than the agreed opening of certain sectors and extend to institutional reforms related to international economic law. For one, the longstanding geographical restrictions will be lifted. Law firms can have offices in both Beijing and Shanghai as an example. However, approvals must still be obtained.

WTO principles, such as transparency and non-discrimination, will also play a role. Laws and regulations will need to be published and transparent which increases the accountability of the decision-making process. Non-discrimination as between foreign and domestic firms is a fundamental precept of WTO membership. Though restrictions will remain, laws will be facially neutral or sufficiently so, and this is evident in the 2000s' M&A legislation, Anti-Monopoly Law, and other statutes.

Quite unusually, the trade-related aspects of intellectual property rights (TRIPs) of the WTO have directly shaped China's intellectual property rights (IPRs) regime. Now stalled, the debates in the Doha Round of the WTO negotiations may portend other direct effects of international laws and rules on domestic statutes and regulations. For this reason, TRIPs offers a glimpse of the possible evolution of the influence of WTO law on China's legal system, particularly with respect to foreign firms in the years to come.

For foreign firms, protection of proprietary knowledge and IPRs are of paramount importance. Nowhere is China's underdeveloped legal regime more often criticized than with respect to piracy and ineffectual protection of patents and other IPRs. The focus of FDI policy on technology diffusion made foreign firms wary that the aim is to imitate cheaply to help China 'catch up'. By the same token, poor IPR protection can deter innovative activity by both foreign and domestic firms, making the policy counterproductive. In any case, TRIPs has changed the system considerably. Even though TRIPs had come into effect from the time of WTO accession without the deferral period granted to other developing countries, the IPR system is likely to remain underdeveloped so long as the overall legal system is incomplete in China.

The TRIPS agreement harmonized IPR laws for all WTO member countries and introduced a much more stringent set of requirements than that which most developing countries had implemented in their own legal systems. It radically altered the previous global IPR regime governed by the Paris and Berne Conventions. The Paris and Berne Conventions of 1867 and 1871, respectively, provided a legal framework for IPRs in the international arena that had lasted for more than a century. China had signed both the Conventions prior to WTO accession, making it a part of the then global IPR regime. These embodied the two major doctrines relating to IPRs under public international law. The first is territoriality, stating that property rights are to be honoured under each state's own laws. The second is the doctrine of independence, which states that the grant of property rights within one country does not have force in another. However, after World War II, an increasing concern of the balance between the innovator and the benefits of diffusing knowledge, particularly to developing countries, challenged the existing legal norms. The needs of developing countries, particularly the least developed ones, for technology and industrialization seemed to justify a reduction of benefits to innovators by those governments. Two typical actions dictated by national policies were: (1) a patent could only be granted if the intellectual property was worked and exploited within the boundary of a country (a working requirement) and (2) the terms and royalties for licences of intellectual property could be determined by the government in the absence of agreement by the innovator (compulsory licensing).

TRIPs replaced the prior regime with a uniform global IPR standard modelled after the most stringent system in the world, that of the United States. Across all nations that had signed up to the WTO which encompasses some 150 countries, patent protection would last for twenty years, copyright protection for fifty years, and trademark protection for seven years and could be renewed indefinitely. This framework reinforces the view that the justification for granting IPRs is to present to the innovator some monopolistic return from an investment that will benefit society and which would otherwise not occur, with some provisions allowing for the issues of concern to developing countries such as those related to pharmaceuticals, and least developed countries (LDCs) were granted more time to adjust their legal systems before the adoption of TRIPs.

However, numerous problems remain, particularly in terms of implementation for developing countries, including China despite its early adoption. Common features of LDCs' legal systems are that IPRs are subject to inconsistent coverage, uncertain terms of protection, arbitrary transferability, and inadequate enforcement.

There is recourse in terms of using the dispute settlement mechanism of the WTO. Countries which believe that the TRIPS agreement has not been satisfactorily implemented can bring action before the WTO to force a change in the IPR regime of the allegedly offending country, as in the 2007 action by the US against China. Indeed, developed nations use the dispute settlement mechanism more often than developing countries, and always against developing countries (Geuze and Wager 1999). This is likely to be the result of developed countries having more inventions to protect and also the difficulties faced by developing countries in rapidly formulating an IPR system when their legal systems generally are underdeveloped, as in China.

There are, however, several limitations with respect to expecting TRIPs or other aspects of international economic laws to transform the system in China and indeed in other developing countries. The restricted scope of international economic law means that enforcement before the WTO is of limited scope. Unless the WTO Doha Round expands into areas of competition policy, government procurement policy, etc., the influence of the international legal system on domestic institutional arrangements will be narrow. Also, most jurisdictions such as the US and the EU will not give direct effect to WTO law in its courts, so the process is that of most international treaties which require adoption by legislative bodies and action is taken on the basis of domestic legislation. The use of the dispute settlement mechanism is further limited to states, so that individual actors are unable to seek enforcement or redress directly before the WTO. The clear contrast is with the EU, whereby citizens of the member states can bring cases concerning European laws directly before European courts. Therefore, legal and institutional reform is less a matter of compulsion under international economic laws than at first appears.

The present scope of international economic law will not, for instance, necessarily protect an investor against expropriation by a government through nationalization or improve contracting security, since the functioning of a particular legal system is outside its purview law so long as the relevant laws are transparent with respect to the WTO principles.

The scope of things to come in China in terms of IPRs or other issues, therefore, is not predicated on the strictures of international economic laws, but depends on China's development priorities, though it is increasingly improving its rule of law to support a burgeoning market economy. Hence, whilst it does so with increasing global integration, international norms will affect its legal and institutional reforms. Indeed, Chinese enterprises such as China Life list in New York as well and voluntarily meet the higher disclosure requirements of the NYSE when ample funds are available on the domestic stock exchanges. This could be an attempt to demonstrate their quality by meeting more stringent standards than if they were to offer shares solely on domestic bourses (see Sun and Tobin 2009). By so doing, these and multinational firms can help China 'leapfrog' legal development by pushing for adoption of legal best practices in the same way that China has been 'catching up' in economic aspects. China's policies towards attracting foreign investment in the services sector so that financial firms and others can bring their expertise into China underscore the positive spillovers still being sought from more developed foreign sources and markets.

With more global integration, other aspects of international economic law, such as the emerging principle-based global regulatory framework for capital markets in the aftermath of the 2008 global financial crisis, will further shape the environment for foreign firms. It is no longer a question of multinational corporations seeking transparent and harmonized governance measures in some instances, but the need for uniform norms to guide globalized banks and capital markets that has become glaringly apparent in the aftermath of the worst financial crisis in nearly a century. As the world's second largest economy, China is increasingly in the midst of the negotiations over what such rules should be in the G20 group of major economies that has become the global forum for international economic matters. What it shapes on the world stage will also influence the contours of domestic regulation for foreign as well as domestic firms.

7.6 Conclusion

Throughout the reform period, FDI has flooded into China in spite of the restrictions and an underdeveloped legal system. Preferential policies and a large labour force, plus a sizeable potential market, have seemingly overridden those concerns and made China one of the foremost destinations for multinational corporations.

Foreign firms entered China in the early 1980s pursuant to the sole pieces of corporate law designed for them and which existed in isolation in many respects. The early 1980s FIE laws led the development of the later corporate law framework of the 1990s and such regulations continue to circumscribe the market for foreign investors. It wasn't until the end of the 1990s that the separate and distinct legal system was unified, and still in the 2000s, foreign firms are increasingly, but not entirely, treated on an equal footing with Chinese state-owned enterprises. But, the regime of the 2000s increasingly looks to be one characterized by facially neutral statutes and also exhibits harmonization with international rules since China's accession to the World Trade Organization.

The post-WTO regime has fundamentally altered some aspects for foreign firms, though many other areas are similar to the pre-accession regime. Licensing requirements and ceilings on shareholdings remain, but China has also moved significantly towards market liberalization and a unified, and more complete legal regime.

And, as its population has become wealthier and its domestic markets have opened, firms ranging from Tesco to Goldman Sachs increasingly view China as a key growth market. Firms like Nokia which had entered China initially to utilize its cheap and large labour force moved to sell to its consumers, as China has become the largest mobile phone market in the world. China certainly has the potential, with its population of 1.3 billion, to outpace the hitherto largest consumer market in the world, the United States, with a population of about 300 million that is only one-fourth the size of China. However, despite much improvement to its corporate laws and the positive influence of many aspects of international economic law, foreign firms seeking to sell and operate in China will find that it remains a challenging, though much improved, market.

For their part, foreign firms have been a source of knowledge and technology for China, while benefiting in return from the cost advantages offered by its large labour force and the growth potential of its consumer market. Among the many noted potentially positive attributes, this chapter posits that the regime created for foreign firms influenced the subsequent development of corporate law in China. Those laws in turn supported market development that has led to a system of laws governing corporations—whether state-owned or controlled, private, or foreign—by the 2000s.

Case study 7

SPECIALIZING IN LOW-TECH EXPORTS: TEXTILES AND CLOTHING

In 1970, China accounted for less than 5 per cent of global clothing exports. Yet, at the beginning of 2005, the world prepared itself for a flood of Chinese textile and clothing (T&C) exports as worldwide quota restrictions were finally lifted. In the first two months of 2005 alone, many Chinese textile and clothing manufacturers did more business than they did in the whole of 2004. Outraged American and European manufacturers sought, and obtained, governmental protection.

This case study traces the development of the Chinese textile and clothing industry into an exporting powerhouse via the 'open door' policy which heralded the opening and eventual global integration of China. It shows the extent of state direction through a deliberate regime of quotas and permissions that developed the important export sector. It illustrates the controlled opening of China, and certainly demonstrates the role of regulation and policy in directing the marketization of a sector which China has a natural comparative advantage.

History

In 1950, China was a significant textile exporter. However, inward-looking policies under central planning led to gradual erosion of China's market share, and thus it was unable to exploit its vast labour resources by specializing in labour-intensive exports such as textiles and clothing. When China adopted market-oriented reforms in 1979, the choice of textile and clothing as a priority industry, which as a labour-intensive sector should be a natural source of Chinese comparative advantage. It utilizes China's vast labour force and does not require advanced technology. Accordingly, the government launched a policy called 'Six Priorities' to promote the textile and clothing industry. Under this policy, the industry enjoyed favourable treatment in six areas: supply of raw materials, fuel and power, innovation and infrastructure construction, bank loans, foreign exchange, imported foreign advanced technology, and transportation. As a result, the industry's output rose rapidly. From 1979 to 1982, the average annual growth rate of the total value of textile and clothing output was 13.2 per cent.

Textiles and clothing also reaped the benefits of an expansion of internal trade in the domestic market. In 1983, China abandoned its coupon allocation system, which resulted in an expansion of both demand and supply of domestic textile and clothing products. With the implementation of the managerial responsibility system (Contract Responsibility System) in industry and the *kaifang* ('reform and opening') programme formally promulgated, the State Council took a number of steps to liberalize internal trade within China. The 3rd Plenum of the 12th Party Congress permitted exchanges within industrial sectors in order to allow enterprises greater scope for marketing their own products, and encouraged the collective sector to expand (Solinger 1991).

The 'Horizontal Economic Alliances' policy was also established. Advanced areas would invest in the development of resource production, transportation and infrastructure, and basic industry in less advanced areas. This, theoretically, would allow wealthier areas access to greater amounts of raw resources, and stimulate industrialization in less developed areas, closing regional economic gaps. In 1984, cloth rationing was also abolished. These policies allowed considerable scope for expansion in domestic demand.

The other major factor in the booming growth of the Chinese textile market was the prioritization of export-oriented development, and the institution of various export promotion policies. In 1987, the Five Year Plan aimed to increase total import and export volumes by 35 per cent within five years, while expanding the scale of foreign investment and advanced technology.

The textiles industry was an overt priority industry under this policy and entered a considerable boom period. In 1980, the textile and garment industry

Table 1. Textile and garment exports, 1980–2002

Year	Global exports ($ billion)	China's exports ($ billion)	China's share of global exports (%)	China's global rank
1980	95.5	4.41	4.6	9
1985	103.2	5.29	5.1	6
1990	218.9	13.85	6.3	4
1995	307.7	37.97	12.3	1
2000	356.4	52.08	14.6	1
2001	342.0	53.48	15.6	1
2002	353.0	63.54	18.0	1

Source: Qiu (2005).

exported $4.41 billion, accounting for 4.6 per cent of global exports and ranking at the ninth position in the world. By 1995, China's export of textiles and garments was the largest in the world and has remained so ever since (Table 1). In 2002, its textile and garments exports accounted for an impressive 18 per cent of global market share.

With the phase out of the Multi Fibre Agreement (MFA, also known as the Agreement on Textiles on Clothing or ATC) in January 2005 that had imposed a worldwide quota system since 1974, the projected global market share of China in these goods was as high as a potential 50 per cent. Much of this export growth came at the expense of traditional textile and clothing powers such as the New Industrializing Economies (NIEs) of East Asia such as South Korea. Since the early 1990s, trade that formerly was directed at the traditional NIEs has been captured by China, ASEAN, and South Asia. As real wages increase and labour skills upgrade, the NIEs lost much of their comparative advantage in clothing while maintaining it in textiles. The dramatic decline in the importance of the NIEs in the world clothing market reflects the fact that clothing is more labour-intensive than textiles.

Government quota allocation and preferential treatment for SOEs

This early expansion of the market through external trade was dominated by State-owned enterprises (SOEs). Much of this was because the early foreign textile and clothing trade quota allocation regime heavily favoured large SOEs in the coastal regions. Only companies allocated by the government as 'exporters' were eligible to receive export quotas. In contrast to most other countries, quotas were allocated to the China Textile Import and Export Corporation and its provincial counterparts via government-controlled regional commissions of economic and trade affairs (local arms of the Ministry of Commerce). Foreign trade corporations (FTCs) then purchased export products from these enterprises according to the export task and quotas assigned to them.

Hence, until 2005 when the global regime was altered, the Ministry of Commerce controlled 100 per cent of quotas. Quotas were allocated to each export enterprise on the basis of that exporter's total export volume to four key export destinations: Japan, South Korea, the EU, and the United States. Foreign enterprises and joint ventures were not eligible for quotas until 1996. Even that eligibility was limited to a very small number of quotas. Township and village enterprises (TVEs) were allocated quotas only if they were included in state export plans.

Despite the abolition of the export plan at the beginning of 1994, most quotas continued to be allocated to the formerly designated exporters. The higher the total export a company had, the more quotas that company could get from the government. If, at the end of the year, there were extra quotas left, the company was not allowed to trade them freely on market demand. China's quota allocation was essentially based on past performance, with some incentives for product upgrading and diversification and the use of domestic inputs. Clearly, administrative discretion played an important role in China's quota allocation regime, favouring large enterprises and SOEs which had greater access to the government departments in charge of quota allocation. Following the 2005 change of the global MFA, a new system was introduced in 2006. The Ministry of Commerce still controls 100 per cent of the quotas; however, they only allocate 30 per cent and the other 70 per cent are sold through competitive bidding.

China's comparative advantage in labour

Thus, only during the reform period did China's trade pattern begin to conform with its comparative advantage, leading to a rapid growth of labour-intensive exports. Textiles and clothing was a major beneficiary. The liberalization of China's internal market since the mid 1980s allowed non-state enterprises, especially TVEs, to become increasingly dynamic players in the domestic T&C sector. These small firms grew outside the planned economy and thus had the ability to respond to market signals. One of their sources of advantage is their link with labour-intensive industries, particularly in rural areas.

Moreover, a large market for labour-intensive consumer goods was left un-addressed prior to the 1980s as a result of the heavy industry-oriented development strategy pursued by China. This gave small enterprises a perfect opportunity to fill the gap. In the 1980s, small firms produced 80–90 per cent of the output in textile, garment, leather, furniture, and plastic products. These non-state industries led the growth in the country in that period while the SOEs were gradually reformed.

As the result of the strong growth of the non-state sector, the rural sector's share in national textile and clothing output grew dramatically. In 1986, rural township and village enterprises accounted for less than 20 per cent of total textile output and 30 per cent of clothing output. By 1992, the respective shares had climbed to 35 and 50 per cent. It should be noted that these percentages do not fully take into account output by other private rural enterprises. In terms of incremental output, the contribution of the rural sector is even greater. Between 1986 and 1992, township and village enterprises accounted for 61–75 per cent of the total incremental output. During the period 1986–94, rural textile output grew at 19 per cent per annum and rural clothing output at 27 per cent, while the output of the urban sector (to which the state sector belongs and dominates) grew at an annual rate of 3 per cent for textiles and 11 per cent for clothing (Yang and Zhong 1998).

Despite the quota system, this was reflected in exports. In 1988, township and village enterprises alone accounted for about half of China's total clothing exports, and 16 per cent of textile exports. By 1991, clothing exports had climbed to 78 per cent and textile exports to 25 per cent. Clothing exports further increased to 90 per cent in 1992, fuelling the rapid growth of T&C exports (Yang and Zhong 1998).

Reform of the industry

In spite of this dramatic export growth led by small firms, the development of the industry was constrained by its unique ownership and industrial struc-ture, largely the legacy of the planned economy. Most of China's textile and clothing exports during this golden period were produced in the coastal regions, with Guangdong, Jiangsu, Shanghai, Fujian, and Shandong in the lead. Yet after the early 1990s' take-off of the 'open door' policy, shortages in unskilled labour began to emerge in some of these provinces. Simultaneously, rental costs for land rose exponentially, exerting pressure for production facilities to move west. The soaring costs led to diversification of production activities. In the period 1995–8, the shares of textiles and clothing in total rural industrial output showed a declining trend (Yang and Zhong 1998).

This, in the textile industry, was concomitant with a large-scale rationalization programme. In 1999, 41 per cent of 4,247 state-owned textile firms suffered from losses. The total industry output share of state-owned textile firms declined dramatically to less than 25 per cent by the end of the 1990s. Aside from the downturn in the production of the moribund SOEs, it was felt that valuable financial resources were being drained away through the existence of tens of thousands of small and medium-sized enterprises (SMEs) proliferating all over the country.

Yeung and Mok (2004) argued that these SMEs supported a significant proportion of the budgets of local governments. Yet, bank reform in 1994 fundamentally changed the relationship between banks and local authorities. Before 1994, local branches made 70 per cent of the loans in China. Banking sector reform centralized the lending authorities to upper-level banks, which reduced the local government's influence on the bank's lending decisions. By the end of 1997, Brandt and Li (2003) concluded that 66 per cent of the township branches could not make lending decisions at all, 30 per cent had limited lending authority, and only 4 per cent could lend with full authority to local firms. This greatly affected SOEs' access to capital. The government also shifted some of its purchasing practices, and private enterprises began to become an important influence on sub-contracting.

Table 2 shows the total after-tax profits of the SOEs in various categories of the textile and clothing industry from 1996 to 1998. The performance of SOEs in this industry was very poor over this period. Much of this was due to a considerable number of new entrants into the market.

To strengthen this important pillar industry, the government instituted new reforms. It permitted surplus workers to be laid off to lower excess production capacity, and eliminated outdated equipment. Hundreds of

Table 2. Profits for state-owned enterprises, 1993–2001 (RMB billion)

Year	Total	Garments	Other fibre products	Fibres	Machinery
1993	6.83	−4.73	28.94	32.93	11.12
1994	100.44	33.97	32.55	37.85	4.07
1995	32.76	−41.3	24.39	46.03	3.65
1996	−16.97	−71.3	33.13	20.26	0.81
1997	36.54	−26.52	38.14	23.64	1.16
1998	8.63	−32.33	41.75	1.69	−2.48
1999	43.24	−10.16	31.99	21.93	1.07
2000	14.46	−13.3	37.5	−13.56	1.42
2001	65.72	22.61	41.56	−11.28	3.92

Source: Qiu (2005).

Table 3. Number of SOEs in the textile and clothing industry

Year	1995	1996	1997	1998	1999	2000	2001	2002
Number of SOEs	53,600	51,200	45,600	19,300	18,900	18,862	21,412	23,600

Source: Qiu (2005).

money-losing companies were shut down and profitable firms were permitted to acquire unprofitable ones. The reforms led the industry to return to profitability by the 2000s.

Impact of a more competitive market

This reduction in the number of SOEs was matched by a reduction in the number of firms in the market in general. Much of this was a result of increased competition, due, in part, to progress by TVEs in the clothing industry. The high labour intensity and simple technology of the clothing industry was well suited to small and medium-sized enterprises. Textile production and garment production, by contrast, became more advanced. Garment production remained very labour-intensive. But, some textile production became more technology and capital-intensive, for example chemical fibre, while some others remain quite resource-intensive, for example cotton yarn. Thus, there was growing competition in clothing, while textiles remained dominated by SOEs.

Moreover, competition from developed countries was not diminishing. Firms in developed countries such as Japan continue to innovate and produce new technologies for textile production, which offset the low labour cost advantage enjoyed by Chinese firms. Furthermore, there exists excess capacity for textile production in China due to local governments' policies to encourage local production, and keen competition among existing manufacturers to expand their production scale.

Despite the quota system and constraints on the market, Chinese–foreign joint ventures (JVs) made inroads as of the mid 1990s. Most of these companies were originally state-owned enterprises. Upon change of ownership to a JV, the foreign investor's capital was given to the government to settle existing obligations, such as the support to their retired and laid-off employees. Thus, JVs could have a fresh start without any long-term financial burden inherited from their former state-owned enterprises. These more deep-pocketed, largely foreign-financed firms alone accounted for 34 per cent of the total export value of the Chinese textile and clothing industry in 1999, eight times more than the far more prevalent SMEs (Qiu 2005).

Structure of the Chinese industry

External economies of scale are strong in China's textile and apparel industry. Firms are concentrated in Guangdong, Shanghai, Jiangsu, Zhejiang, Shandong, and Fuijian. The industrial value produced by these regions made up 67 per cent of the total industrial value of the industry in 2001 (Qiu 2005).

In these clusters, the textile and apparel industry accounts for a very large percentage of the local economy, and is often the only industry. The first tier of the clusters existed in the late 1970s and early 1980s, when China first opened to the outside world. Taking advantage of proximity and low labour cost, many Hong Kong textile and apparel companies invested in the Pearl River Delta, and a few clusters of textile and apparel firms appeared. These clusters grew quickly, as new investments also came from Taiwan and elsewhere, and many local entrepreneurs emerged as well. These clusters include Shenzhen (though later much diluted as it is now one of the largest cities in China), Dongguan (similar to Shenzhen but to a lesser degree), Humen, Shaxi, and others.

One of the important features of this industry, especially clothing, is that firms need to be able to quickly adapt their production to changing market demand. Therefore it is very important for a firm to be located in an area where information can be obtained easily. Companies in the textile and clothing industry are advantaged by locating themselves near each other and forming production clusters. The structure of the textiles industry and the low entry barrier were undoubtedly major factors in the growth of these clusters. To start up, only one manually operated device to knit socks or just a

Table 4. Examples of well-known industrial clusters in China

Province	City	Featured products
Zhejiang	Pinghu	Apparels
	Shengzhou	Neckties
	Tiantai	Filter cloth
	Yuhang	Various fabrics
Jiangsu	Changshu	Casual wear
	Jintan	Apparels
Shandong	Changyi	Dying and printing
	Jimo	Knitting
Hebei	Qinghe	Cashmere
Fujian	Shishi	Casual wear

Source: Zhang, To, and Cao (2004).

few sewing machines were needed. Simultaneously, there was a large supply of cheap labour. As the enterprises expanded, some shrewd entrepreneurs lured technicians and skilled labourers who were retired from state-owned enterprises to work for them. As these firms were started by farmer-entrepreneurs in towns and even villages, they set examples and became models to others. Often, later entrants just followed the footprints of the pioneers, starting with the same methods, making the same products, and selling in the same market. As villagers often belong to the same family, they did not view each other as competitors, and helped each other in terms of capital, technique, and even customers, through a strong sense of kinship. These firms were the seeds of the industrial clusters for textiles and apparel.

These clusters were also highly efficient. Clusters create vertically integrated industries that produce almost all the inputs that could conceivably be used in apparel production (i.e. zippers, buckles for brassieres, handles and wheels for luggage, etc.). This allows areas to become efficient, low-cost producers of many types of products.

According to the China National Textile Industry Council (CNTIC), there are now 19 such township industrial clusters, which altogether have a total output of 238 billion RMB (nearly $30 billion), accounting for about one quarter of the total textile and apparel output of the country. About 1.81 million workers are employed in these clusters.

WTO accession

China was, without doubt, expected to be the biggest winner after 1 January 2005, with the phase-out of the MFA. In 2004, China's clothing exports totalled $41 billion, and textile exports at $20 billion. In the first month after the end of the MFA, imports to the United States from China grew by 75 per cent. In January 2005, the United States imported more than $1.2 billion in textiles and apparel from China, up from about $701 million a year earlier. Imports of major apparel products from China jumped 546 per cent. For example, China shipped 941,000 cotton knitted shirts in January 2004 as limited by the quota. After January 2005, it shipped 18.2 million shirts, a 1,836 per cent increase. Imports of cotton knitted trousers were up 1,332 per cent from a year before. Moreover, those figures may be understated because China ships a large part of its goods through Hong Kong.

This greatly inflamed tensions between Washington and Beijing, in particular with respect to American manufacturing plants closing and thousands of jobs lost in the T&C sector (see e.g. Barboza and Becker 2005). In January, the first month after global quotas were lifted, 12,200 jobs were lost in the United

States apparel and textile industries, according to the US Bureau of Labor Statistics.

Perhaps unsurprisingly, this rapid growth was very quickly quelled. A number of trade provisions were in place that allowed other WTO members to utilize two safeguard mechanisms against Chinese clothing and textile products if the importing country believes that the Chinese imports are causing or threatening to cause domestic 'market disruption'. The first safeguard mechanism is unique and it applies only to clothing and textile products. The second is a general safeguard mechanism applied to all Chinese exports. Any WTO member can invoke the clothing and textile specific safeguard mechanism by requesting consultation with China. The simple act of requesting consultation immediately imposes a quota on the product either equal to 6 per cent of the total imports for the year to date or 7.5 per cent more than the amount imported over the previous twelve months. Even if there is no agreement with China on the safeguard measure, the WTO member has the option to continue to enforce the import quota. There is no requirement for WTO notification; nor are there provisions for multilateral surveillance. These quotas can only be imposed for one year without China's agreement.

These trade provisions were used by a number of countries in order to stem the flow of Chinese textiles. The China–US textile agreement which took effect as of 1 January 2006 imposed quotas on a total of twenty-one categories of clothing and textiles from China until 2008. Some ten kinds of Chinese textile and apparel products exported to EU countries have also been put under quota restrictions, according to an agreement reached by the two sides in June 2005. This safeguard mechanism was also until the end of 2008. Brazil and Colombia have also made use of this provision. These were largely ineffective in one sense, as the EU quota was met within two months of the agreement because European retailers placed their orders to beat the quota.

Conclusion

The potential dominance of China in the textiles and clothing industry is undoubtedly linked to its comparative advantage in labour-intensive goods. In a sense, it should not be surprising that China can develop a large export sector. The history, though, shows that it was not simply market forces at play.

For instance, it is important to note the effects of the trading environment on this development. In particular, trade quotas and the privileged position of SOEs limited the initial development of the market, despite external and internal market opening.

Yet, this was only a small part of the textiles and clothing story. TVEs, the big early winners, combined the policy advantages of the SOEs with the ability to face competition. JVs, through partnering with SOEs, also experienced an advantage in manoeuvring the system that was not possible for foreign-invested firms.

The other part of the case study shows the need for constant reform. The reconsolidation process of reducing SOEs in the textile industry, and the development of small and nimble clusters of enterprise both allowed China to continue making the textile industry more competitive, a process aided by the steady domestic demand. Thus, when WTO accession took effect, China was amazingly successful, but the foundations of this were laid in the 1990s. In this sense, from both the early periods to the removal of the MFA, domestic and global market constraints heavily shaped the development of a natural source of specialization for China. Nevertheless, the end result is a strong export sector for China that has come to be viewed as synonymous with its successful opening and global integration.

Case study 8

DEVELOPING A MEDIUM-TECH SECTOR—AUTOMOBILE INDUSTRY

The automobile industry was designated by the Chinese government as one of the country's 'pillar' industries early on in the economic reforms. The automobile sector has much appeal to a developing economy, not only because of its contribution to national output and employment, but also for its potential as a 'medium-tech' industry in enhancing a country's technological capability and moving the country upward in value-added terms in the global production chain. Realizing this potential is by no means a straightforward task, however. In the early stages of manufacturing automobiles, a developing country will aim to draw on the knowledge, experience, and technical expertise of industrialized economies. Unsurprisingly, this was the route chosen by China in its reliance on foreign direct investment (FDI) to stimulate the development of its automobile sector. Further down the path of development, however, the challenge becomes one of trying to take advantage of, and yet not perpetually depend upon, foreign technological inputs. China's automobile sector will illustrate these dilemmas in the country's quest to utilize FDI to develop its technological capacity.

A 'pillar' industry

In the late 1970s at the start of the reform period, China was in a state of industrial and technological backwardness. Domestic automobile production was negligible and inefficient, with a primary focus on the manufacturing of trucks (Harwit 1995). The early period of the economic reform was marked by the central government's effort to transform traditional state-owned factories into 'pillars' of a modern economy (Thun 2006). The first turning point came in 1984, when then Premier Zhao Ziyang announced that the country would seek to manufacture automobiles up to world standards by 1990, double production volumes, and switch to an industrial system based on modern technology (Thun 2006).

The next few years continued the efforts of the Chinese government in promoting the automobile industry. In 1986, the automobile sector was formally designated as a 'pillar' industry, alongside several other important industries such as aircrafts, petrochemicals, telecommunications, machineries, and electronics (Thun 2006; Moore 2002). At that time, the five objectives of the government in relation to the automobile sector were: (1) consolidating production, with the official designation of 'three big and three small' players in the industry; (2) prioritizing passenger car development; (3) upgrading technological capabilities through linkages to international companies; (4) steadily increasing the local content of manufactured automobiles; and (5) setting production volumes to reach 600,000 units a year.

In relation to (1) above, the three major automobile manufacturers were First Auto Works in Shanghai, Second Auto Works in Hubei (commonly known as Dongfeng), and the Shanghai Automotive Industry Corporation (SAIC), while the three minor players were the Chinese–foreign joint venture (JV) companies of Beijing Jeep Corporation, Guangzhou Peugeot, and Tianjin Automotive Corporation (Harwit 1995).

Beijing Jeep, the first JV in the car industry, was forged between the state-owned Beijing Automotive Industry Corporation (BAIC) and the then American Motors Corporation (a company that was later bought by the Chrysler Corporation) in 1983. American Motors took a minority stake (31 per cent) in, and supplied the required technologies for the new JV company (Gallagher 2006; Thun 2006). The major players also set up JVs. SAIC and Germany's Volkswagen (VW) formed a JV, which proved to be more successful than Beijing Jeep. The SAIC-Volkswagen JV soon became the largest annual producer of passenger cars in China.

JVs and the localization policy

By 1994, the then State Planning Commission's formal policy on the automobile sector was to consolidate automobile firms, obtain technology transfer from foreign firms, and support market creation in terms of private ownership of passenger cars (Gallagher 2006). A notable initiative under the 1994 policy was that, from then on, Chinese–foreign automobile JVs would be required to use at least 40 per cent of Chinese-made component parts in their manufacturing processes (Gallagher 2006). This initiative probably stemmed from the government's reconsideration of its previous policy, which gave foreign partners in JVs the scope to select what and how technologies were to be transferred to the domestic sector, without necessarily enabling the development of local firms as part of the supply chain in the sector. These upstream and downstream linkages have been shown to be more effective in transmitting technological upgrading than when foreign firms import components instead of fostering domestic firms to provide them. The explicit imposition of 'localization' requirements would prompt foreign firms to work with their Chinese counterparts to improve the quality of locally manufactured components. In a 1996 report commissioned by the Development Research Centre of the State Council, it was observed that the domestic industry was still producing automobiles of an inferior quality but at a higher price compared to foreign manufacturers (Thun 2006). However, the 1994 policy had at least effectively obliged foreign firms to increase the local content of their products (Gallagher 2006).

The preference for establishing Chinese–foreign JVs in the automobile industry was reflective of China's efforts to offer access to foreign firms to the fast-growing market, in exchange for their superior technology and managerial skills. As shown in Table 1, Gallagher (2006) records that about sixteen Chinese–foreign JVs were formed between 1984 and 2005. In the earlier JVs, in particular, the Chinese government had the upper hand in setting the terms of the deals and taking advantage of the intense competition among firms that were seeking to tap into the Chinese market (Thun 2006). When each JV assembly project was created, the foreign partner initially imported 100 per cent of the components and the JV had zero local content. The objective of the Chinese partner was to gradually increase the percentage of parts that were sourced locally (Thun 2006). However, it was observed that foreign manufacturers might lack the incentives to teach their Chinese partners about technology and design—unless they were required to do so, as they were under the 1994 policy (Gallagher 2006). Even when some foreign partners play a key role in transferring technology to the JV and teaching their Chinese partners how to run a modern assembly plant, their role is necessarily focused on the operation of the JV itself (Thun 2006). The development of a broader supply network—critical to a successful domestic

Table 1. Major Chinese–foreign joint ventures in the Chinese automobile industry

Chinese partner	Joint venture (location)	Foreign partner (dates)	Ownership shares
Beijing Automotive Industry Corporation (BAIC)	Beijing Jeep (Beijing)	DaimlerChrysler, originally with American Motors Corporation (1983–)	42% DaimlerChrysler, 58% BAIC
Shanghai Automotive Industry Corp. (SAIC)	Shanghai Volkswagen (Shanghai)	Volkswagen (1984–)	50% VW, 25% SAIC, 25% Bank of China and others
Tianjin Automobile Xiali Company (TAIC)	Tianjin Automobile Xiali Company (TAIC)–First Auto Works (FAW) (Tianjin)	Licensing agreement with Daihatsu (1986–93), initial arrangement with Toyota in 2000 before FAW takeover in 2002 (see below)	
First Auto Works (FAW)	FAW–Volkswagen (Changchun, Jilin)	Volkswagen (1990–)	40% VW, 60% FAW
Dongfeng Motor Corp. (formerly Second Auto Works)	Dongfeng Citroën (Wuhan, Hubei)	Citroën (1992–)	30% Citroën, 70% Dongfeng
FAW Jinbei Automotive	Jinbei GM (Shenyang, Liaoning)	General Motors Corp. (1992–5, 1999–)	50% FAW Jinbei, 50% GM
Chang'An Automobile (Group) Corp.	Changan Suzuki (Chongqing)	Suzuki Motor Corp. (1993–)	51% Chang'An, 35% Suzuki, 14% Nissho Iwai
Shanghai Automotive Industry Corporation (SAIC)	Shanghai GM (Pudong, Shanghai)	General Motors (1997–)	50% SAIC, 50% GM
Guangzhou Automotive Group	Guangzhou Honda Automobile Co. Ltd (Guangzhou, Guangdong)	Honda Motor Co. (1998–)	50% Guangzhou, 50% Honda
Jiangsu Yueda Group (originally), later Dongfeng Motor Co.	Dongfeng Yueda-KIA (Jiangsu)	Kia Motor (1998–)	30% Jiangsu Yueda, 50% Kia, 20% Dongfeng
Yuekin Motor (Group) Corporation	Jiangsu Nanya Auto Co., Ltd (Nanjing, Jiangsu)	Fiat Auto S.p.A. (1999–)	50% Fiat, 50% Yuejin

Dongfeng Motor Corporation and Jing'An Yunbao Motor Corporation	Fengshen (Aeolus) Automotive Co. Ltd (also known as Guangzhou Nissan) (Guangzhou, Guangdong)	Yulon Motor Corporation (Taiwan, 25% owned by Nissan) (2000–)	45% DMC, 25% Yulon (Taiwan), 30% Yunbao
First Auto Works Car Corporation	FAW Hainan Motor Co. (Hainan)	Mazda (Ford owns 33.4% of Mazda) (2001–)	17.5% Mazda, 82.5% FAW
Chang'An Automobile (Group) Corp.	Changan Ford (Chongqing)	Ford Motor Co. (2001–)	50% Chang'An, 50% Ford
Beijing Automotive Industry Holding Corporation (BAIHC)	Beijing Hyundai Motor Corporation (Beijing)	Hyundai Motor Co. (2002–)	50% BAIHC, 50% Hyundai
First Auto Works (FAW) and Tianjin Auto Xiali Corporation	FAW–Tianjin–Toyota (Changan Ford and Tiankin)	Toyota Motor Corp. (2002–)	50% Toyota, 50% FAW
Dongfeng Motor Corporation	Dongfeng Nissan (Hubei)	Nissan (2002–)	50% Dongfeng, 50% Nissan

Source: Gallagher (2006).

automobile sector given its intensive backward linkages—would have to be a product of government policy.

Building supply networks

Another factor that affects the technological capacity of China's automobile industry is how local governments implement the industrial directives from the central government. Local authorities in China enjoyed much autonomy during the economic reform and sometimes acted outside the central government's purview. For instance, while the central government wanted to build a 'national team' of automobile enterprises through mergers and acquisitions, local authorities might pay less heed to economies of scale and protect inefficient firms within their jurisdictions. Moreover, localities in China have diverged in their developmental paths in relation to the automobile sector, which has given rise to different industrial outcomes (Thun 2006).

The Shanghai automobile industry, compared with Beijing and Guangzhou, has been much more successful. The Shanghai automobile sector has strong local supply networks, and even other localities rely on Shanghai suppliers. Also, cars manufactured in Shanghai have a higher local content. Approximately 90 per cent of the component parts for Shanghai Volkswagen Santana and over 60 per cent for Shanghai General Motors (GM) are manufactured within Shanghai, for example (Thun 2006). The government in Shanghai has actively taken on many roles of a developmental state to nurture firms within the locality, promoting foreign investment while retaining a sizeable ownership share (Thun 2006).

WTO provisions

Another important development is China's entry into the WTO in 2001, which had a profound impact on the automobile sector. Given the previously protected nature of the industry, it was expected to undergo more upheaval by virtue of liberalization than any other sector in the economy except agriculture (Gallagher 2006). The Permanent Normal Trading Relations agreements made between China and its trading partners such as the United States and the European Union contained specific concessions regarding the Chinese automobile sector, reversing many of the protectionist policies in 1994. For instance, tariffs on imported cars were to decrease from 100 per cent to 25 per cent by 2006. Import licenses would be phased out in 2005. Furthermore, on accession, China would no longer condition importation or investment approvals on whether any competing domestic suppliers existed, or on performance requirements of any kind, such as local content, technology transfer, etc. (Gallagher 2006). The government did try to get around some of these concessions with creative mechanisms that are consistent with WTO obligations, such as an automatic import licensing system introduced in 2005 which allowed the government to monitor the number of imports of vehicles and components (Gallagher 2006). Nevertheless, the challenge of upgrading faced by Chinese firms inevitably became more daunting in light of closer integration with the global market and more intense competition from multinational companies.

Subsequent to WTO accession, multinational automobile companies were eager to enter into the previously protected market, fuelling competition in the sector. Between 2001 and 2003, there was exponential growth in the sale of passenger cars in China, driven largely by the country's expanding middle-class consumers, and their easier access to credit with banking liberalization that also came about through WTO accession (Thun 2006). With increasing demand for new models, more JV agreements were made with global companies such as Ford Motor Company and Toyota Motor Corporation. The continual formation of Chinese–foreign JVs shows that the Chinese government was still trying to maximize the prospects for learning and technology transfer from more advanced foreign companies, even though it had to open the country's door to foreign vehicles under WTO requirements. In 2004, the National Development and Reform Commission (formerly the State Planning Commission) issued a policy statement on the automobile industry, specifically affirming the government's encouragement of the integration between imported technologies and the indigenous technologies of local firms, and continued to push for industrial restructuring, such that domestic automobile companies would eventually grow into large-sized conglomerates. It is also noteworthy that the government expressed its intention in the 2004 policy to conduct research on electric and hybrid-electric vehicles given the environmental impact of growing vehicle ownership in China, and to support R&D activities through preferential tax policies so as to stimulate technological innovation and capacity building (Gallagher 2006).

A growing industry

In 2004, there were 130 automobile companies in China (Thun 2004). The three largest companies remained those initially singled out for government support—SAIC, First Auto Works, and Dongfeng—which accounted for 67 per cent of the sedan market in 2002, and their combined production in 2003 was 1.38 million sedans (Thun 2006). It is notable that each of these dominant groups has formed JVs with foreign manufacturers. For example, SAIC has JVs with Volkswagen and GM; Dongfeng with Citroën and Yulon Motor Group from Taiwan (Yulon is 25 per cent owned by Nissan); First Auto Works with Volkswagen (Gallagher 2006; Thun 2006). By 2007, the total number of auto manufacturers has reportedly risen to 150, despite the government's effort to restructure and consolidate the industry. An example of China's efforts at consolidation were the investment control measures, announced in December 2006, that banned the building of new plants if the car-maker in question failed to sell at least 80 per cent of the previous year's output (*BusinessWeek* 2007).

However, in 2008, the top three automakers—which remained SAIC, First Auto Works, and Dongfeng—were still able to capture a total of 48.7 per cent of the domestic market and sell the largest number of cars through their respective JV companies (*Xinhua* 2009a). Although foreign manufacturers can now set up wholly foreign-owned companies in China, the market continues to be dominated by the government favoured Chinese–Foreign JVs, at least for the time being. For instance, Volkswagen set up its first wholly foreign-owned enterprise in China, the Volkswagen Automatic Transmission (Dalian) Co., Ltd, in Dalian in 2007. This is testament to the Chinese government's success in promoting JVs over the years. It also gave the early foreign JV partners a leading position in the Chinese market. GM, for example, has been the biggest foreign car maker in China, with sales of 876,000 cars in 2006, through its joint ventures with local partners (Schiefferes 2007). The Buick Excelle model, which was built and sold by GM and SAIC, was the best-selling car in China in the first half of 2009 (Erickson 2009). However, companies like GM and Volkswagen are facing competition, which is increasingly rife, with foreign rivals like Nissan and Toyota, introducing new brands to China and manufacturing cars locally (Schiefferes 2007). Challenges are also coming from their local JV partners, some of which have made sufficient technical progress to develop their own vehicles outside of the JVs (Rowley 2009a). SAIC, for instance, has launched its own brand called the Roewe 750 (based on the Rover 75) (Schiefferes 2007). The British MG Rover Group was in 2005 bought by Nanjing Automotive (Group) Corporation, a state-owned carmaker which merged with SAIC two years later. This trend is very likely to continue in light of China's ultimate goal to develop its own branded car models.

Another recent, and rather unexpected, development in China's auto industry is the rapid emergence of domestic carmakers without initial foreign linkages. In the first quarter of 2009, indigenous Chinese car brands enjoyed a market share of 30 per cent, while foreign manufacturers and their JV companies in China occupied the remaining 70 per cent (Rowley 2009b). Two notable examples of these domestic manufacturers are the Anhui-based Chery and the Zhejiang-based Geely. Another two examples are the Shenzhen-based BYD Auto and the Shenyang-based Brilliance China Auto. Chery was founded in 1997 by five of Anhui's local state-owned investment companies. After beginning to produce cars only in 1999, Chery had annual sales of over 80,000 cars only four years later (Thun 2006). Geely was incorporated in 1996 and has now emerged as China's biggest privately-owned car firm (*The Economist* 2009). According to Thun (2006), these companies are putting undeniable pressures on the JVs. He also points out that the rapid rise of these firms was possible because they could draw heavily on the already well-established local supply network in Shanghai, discussed earlier. Other analysts suggest that their successes were also driven by an aggressive low-cost strategy, that is, appealing to the lower segment of the market with extremely competitive prices (Schiefferes 2007). Apart from manufacturing in China, Geely assembles cars from kits in Russia, Ukraine, and Indonesia (*The Economist* 2009). This may be one factor that gives Geely certain cost advantages. Another possible, and more often cited, factor that enables these companies' low-cost strategy is that they have been closely following the designs of existing foreign models (Thun 2006). For example, GM has sued Chery over its QQ model, alleging that the little 'city car' was a thinly disguised clone of its Chevy Spark (Erickson 2009). QQ is now one of the most popular models in China. Priced at $4,000, it has outsold GM's car, which costs 25 per cent more, by four to one (Schiefferes 2007).

China had become the largest car market in the world, surpassing Japan in 2006 and the United States in early 2009 (Dyer 2007; Erickson 2009). Nevertheless, manufacturers are facing more and more intense competition. The industry is also vulnerable to fluctuations in the economy. For example, auto sales growth in China hit a ten-year low in 2008, with total sales of 9.38 million units (including exports) because of the global financial crisis but began to recover by the second half of 2009 (*Xinhua* 2009b). Against a competitive and fluctuating domestic environment, the Chinese government and car manufacturers have their sights on the international market, including exports and foreign acquisitions. While Beijing has long wanted to produce globally competitive models, automobile exports from China had been negligible in the past. But the situation has changed in recent years, with total auto exports reaching 340,000 units in 2006, nearly twice the 2005 figure of 173,000 (*BusinessWeek* 2007). The major destinations of exports are the developing markets of the Middle East, Eastern Europe, Latin America, Africa, and South East Asia (*BusinessWeek* 2007). The JV between Tianjin Auto Group and Toyota made the first-ever export shipment to the United States of its Xiali economy cars in 2002 (*People's Daily* 2002). Yet, the US is certainly not a major export destination of China's cars. Although Chinese exports of auto and auto parts made up just 0.7 per cent of global total in 2007, the government is seeking to push this to 10 per cent over the next decade (*BusinessWeek* 2007). It designated eight cities as auto export hubs, meaning that firms in these areas can get special loans and tax breaks (*BusinessWeek* 2007). While some manufacturers (like SAIC) are inclined to focus on the domestic market, other firms—especially Geely and Chery—have announced aggressive export plans (Schiefferes 2007). These companies have certainly gained some ground in developing overseas markets, with Chery (for instance) seeing its exports reach 50,000 units in 2006 (*Business-Week* 2007). But developed markets like the United States and Europe, where these companies are also looking for a foothold, remain more distant goals (*The Economist* 2009). Geely, for example, has exhibited its low-cost cars in motor shows in Frankfurt and Detroit, but there are lurking suspicions in these markets that the company's models are not developed to the same quality standards as Western ones (*The Economist* 2009). In an effort to raise export quality, the Ministry of Commerce announced in 2006 that automobile manufacturers would only be allowed to engage in exports with the state's authorization (*Xinhua* 2006c). Individual firms are also seeking to upgrade their products in different ways. Chery, for instance, has formed a JV with Italy's Fiat (*BBC News* 2007). It remains to be seen whether the control and support measures from the government, together with the initiatives of manufacturers, can eventually break new ground in terms of exports to Western markets.

A global business?

In the 2000s, there has been a spate of efforts on the part of Chinese auto firms to acquire the ownership of assets from global car makers that have gone bankrupt. In 2005, the state-owned Nanjing Automotive (Group) Corporation purchased the British MG Rover Group for a little more than £50 million (*Financial Times* 2005). Interestingly, Nanjing Automotive won the bid at that time against its stronger rival bidder, SAIC—although the two Chinese car-makers were eventually merged in 2007, as part of China's ongoing strategy to consolidate its national car companies (Automotive News Europe 2007; *Financial Times* 2007). Following the collapse and rescue of GM in the 2008 global economic crisis, Chinese firms have aimed to purchase the different brands of the American automotive giant.

In the aftermath of the large-scale losses at American carmakers, GM and Chrysler sought to shed overseas divisions. China's overseas efforts accelerated. Beijing Automotive Industry Corporation submitted a bid for GM's Opel business based in Germany. It offered GM a residual 49 per cent stake in Opel and planned to open a $2 billion factory in China (*Financial Times* 2009a). Its bid was ultimately rejected in favour of Canadian Magna, a parts supplier, in part due to GM's concerns about technology being transferred to the emerging competition from China. But, BAIC was not deterred, and sought to become a minority shareholder by offering financing as part of a bid for another GM division, Saab. More surprising was perhaps the quest by a Chinese construction equipment maker—Sichuan Tengzhong Heavy Industrial Machinery—to take over Hummer, another brand of GM. As soon as the proposed deal was announced, there was speculation that it would be blocked by the government on environmental grounds because Hummer—a gas-guzzling, military-inspired off-road vehicle—is at odds with China's attempts to decrease pollution from Chinese manufacturers (*BBC News* 2009; *Financial Times* 2009b). There are also doubts that Tengzhong, a privately-owned maker of special-use vehicles, structural components for highways, bridges, and construction machinery, has the necessary expertise to run the Hummer brand (*BBC News* 2009; Merx and Chan 2009). It was ultimately blocked. SAIC's losses from the purchase of a unit of SUVs from Korean Hyundai had made the officials wary of the potential success of such purchases which are against the tide of 'green' cars. In the end, the Tengzhong bid was blocked by the Chinese authorities.

Also, in 2009, Geely launched a bid for Volvo from troubled Ford, hoping again to reduce costs by producing it in China but acquiring the technology associated with a well-respected brand in order to make forays into developed markets as well as sell to an increasingly crowded domestic one. This bid succeeded in 2010 and it became the largest ever acquisition in the Chinese automobile industry.

An indicator of industrial capacity

On the whole, while the recent acquisition attempts hold out promises of a stronger Chinese automotive industry, they also raise concerns about the capability of these Chinese firms to turn the foreign brands into successes— in cases where their Western counterparts have failed (*Financial Times* 2009c). It also remains to be seen whether China is now viewing overseas acquisitions as a viable means (in addition to its traditional strategy of forming JVs) to further technological upgrading and enhanced competitiveness and, if so, whether this new strategy will eventually bear fruit. If so, then success in this 'medium technology' industry would suggest that China has achieved some industrial upgrading; a target yearned for from the start of the reform period and essential for the country's sustained economic growth.

Case study 9

EARLY FDI POLICY—JOINT VENTURES AND THE MOBILE PHONE INDUSTRY

It wasn't until 1987 that China deployed its first wireless phone system. When mobile phones appeared in the late 1980s, each cost 10,000–20,000 RMB (roughly double the average household income at the time), and was the size of a brick. Regarded as the ultimate status symbol, it was called the *da ge da*, meaning very influential person. At that time, sales of mobile phones were under state control, and stocks were limited. Purchasers were required to place an order and make an 80 per cent down payment. Moreover, this slow development continued through the mid 1990s. By the end of 1995, there were only about three and a half million users in China.

The picture rapidly changed. A decade later, China had become the largest mobile phone market in the world, one in which many mobile phone companies try out their newest designs before global release. There were over 616 million subscribers of mobile communication services in China as of the end of August 2008, growing by 1.26 per cent each month and 19.46 per cent every year, according to China's Ministry of Information Industry (MII). Mobile phones are becoming a major industry for China, with exports of $14.7 billion in the first half of 2008. In 2007, China's mobile phone exports accounted for around 51 per cent of the global total.

How China became a major player in the mobile phone industry highlights both the strengths and weaknesses of its foreign direct investment (FDI) policy geared at promoting industrial development. The ebbs and flows of the fortunes of Nokia, the world's biggest mobile phone manufacturer, illustrate the unique nature of how China utilized foreign investment while promoting its own domestic industries and show how its FDI policy fostered Chinese–foreign joint ventures (JVs).

China's development of a domestic mobile phone industry

The transition to a more market-oriented economy under Deng Xiaoping was reflected by seismic changes in Chinese telecommunications policy. The Chinese government mandated early infrastructure spending in order to later attract foreign investment. Under this encouraging regime, government targets for new fixed lines were rapidly met and exceeded by the late 1980s and early 1990s.

In the mid 1990s, further efforts were made to develop the telecom network, including forgiving local government loans and permitting provincial telecommunications offices to plough their profits into further expansion. Rates for international call completion were set high to generate income for the system's expansion, and foreign investment to build the system (though not to operate it) was encouraged. High connection fees of 2,000 to 3,000 RMB (about $240 to $360) per line in the mid 1990s also provided an important revenue source to support the development of the system, extending beyond fixed lines into mobile telecommunications. Since then, the industry has entered into a period of explosive growth particularly in the 2000s, as Table 1 shows.

Another area of government intervention came through the creation of home-grown mobile phone service providers. In March 1998, the government passed a telecommunications law that changed the regulatory structure and allowed more competition in the industry, but only between state-owned companies. China wished to enter the World Trade Organization (WTO), and entry into the WTO required proof of a 'competitive atmosphere and a demonstrated customer-centred market environment' in the telecommunications industry (Kimura 2007). Up to this point, China Telecom, a massive

Table 1. Telecommunications sector development, 1995–2004

Indicator	1995	2000	2001	2002	2003	2004
Investment (billions RMB)	199.5	231.4	264.2	210.6	224.6	217.3
Local phone switches and gates	72.04	178.26	255.66	286.57	350.83	423.47
Long distance fibre laid (1000 km)	110	290	400	490	590	700
Users of fixed line phones (millions)	40.71	144.83	180.37	214.42	263.31	312.44
Fixed line phone penetration (sets per 100 people)	3.35	11.45	13.9	16.8	21.2	24.9
Users of mobile phones (millions)	3.62	85.27	144.81	206.62	268.69	334.82
Mobile phone penetration (sets per 100 people)	0.3	6.77	11.2	16.19	20.9	25.9

Sources: Kimura (2007), Ministry of Information Industry (2008).

state-owned enterprise responsible for all aspects of Chinese telecommunications, dominated the industry. However, a state-owned competitor, China United Telecommunications Corporation (China Unicom), was also trying to gain a foothold in the sector.

In early December 1998, the government announced it was considering breaking up the China Telecom monopoly by splitting up the company itself. The process began in 1999 and took more than two years to complete. China Telecom was offering essentially four services at this point: fixed-telephone lines, mobile communications, paging, and satellite transmissions. Each of these parts was broken into separate, state-owned companies.

In 2000, the mobile operations were spun into a separate company called China Mobile, and this soon became the second largest mobile network in the world. By the end of 2000, China Mobile served 78 per cent of China's mobile subscribers. China Unicom was still struggling to emerge, despite being the recipient of China Telecom's paging business. As the sole holder of operational licences in China, the company forged ahead and offered an initial public offering (IPO) of US$6.9 billion in June 2000. It was permitted to charge 10–20 per cent less in mobile fees than its only competitor, China Mobile.

Thus, China has two major service providers: China Mobile, a state-owned enterprise which has a 67.5 per cent share of the competitive mobile market as of 2008, and Unicom which has the rest of the market. To put these figures into perspective, China Mobile is the world's largest mobile phone operator ranked by number of subscribers, with 415 million customers (as of 30 June 2008) (MII 2008).

The massive size of these companies and their state ownership led to an occasionally tenuous and unpredictable policy environment for the industry. Much of this is traceable to the Ministry of Information Industry. In spite of WTO regulations mandating the separation of its regulatory and operational functions, the ministry still maintains extensive influence and control. A recent effort to promote its own unique standard (TD-SCDMA) for third generation (3G) wireless telephony serves an example. This was in contrast to a global push for more unified standards rather than less, and appeared to be an attempt to use industrial policy to benefit domestic companies against foreign-based firms. It was ultimately dropped, but is suggestive of the role of the state in China's marketizing economy.

Foreign handset providers in China

The Chinese government was instrumental in creating a mobile phone network, and in the regulation and management of the dominant mobile phone service providers. However, the handsets, themselves necessary for people to use these services, have been historically largely provided by foreign companies. The main equipment providers for the very early Chinese phone networks were Motorola and Ericsson, who thus unsurprisingly then dominated the mobile phone market for most of the 1990s.

Motorola entered China very early. In 1987, it set up an office in Beijing. In 1992, Motorola (China) Electronics Ltd, a wholly foreign-owned company was incorporated, and it opened a manufacturing facility at Tianjin. Initially, Motorola manufactured pagers, semiconductors, two-way radios, and automobile electronics in China. As the demand for pagers was expected to be low in China, Motorola planned to export the surplus production to other markets (Kimura 2007). However, since fixed-line telephone penetration was low in China in the early 1990s, pagers became an instant hit, and the company was soon selling its weekly output of 10,000 units in the Chinese market itself. The annual demand for pagers grew from one million in 1991 to 14 million in just five years. Later, when mobile phones began gaining popularity in the mid 1990s, Motorola started concentrating on the production of handsets. Until 2000, it had invested some 28.5 billion RMB—the largest investment in the Chinese IT industry at the time. At around the same time, Ericsson opened its first office in Beijing which was in 1985. In 1992, a joint venture with China Putien was set up. Up until 2000, Ericsson had invested about 3 billion RMB in China, covering a wide range of products from telecom systems to end products such as handsets.

However, it was neither of these two multinational companies, but rather the Finnish firm Nokia, the world's biggest mobile handset manufacturer, which was probably the biggest beneficiary of the liberalization of the mobile telephone sector in China. Like Motorola and Ericsson, Nokia opened its first office in Beijing in the mid 1980s, indeed in 1985, the same year as Ericsson. However, it was not until the introduction of the newer mobile phone networks in the 1990s that Nokia became a force in the Chinese market. This coincided with a period of rapid global growth for Nokia. In the matter of only a couple of years during the growth phase of the mobile phone boom from 1995 to 2001, Nokia had taken a leading edge in the development, production, and marketing of mobile phones worldwide.

Nokia then poured some of these resources into the Chinese market. It invested in two plants in Special Economic Zones (SEZs) in Beijing and Dongguan producing mobile phone handsets. By 2001, it had invested around 13 billion RMB in 8 Chinese–foreign joint ventures employing 5,000 workers. It also built the largest mobile phone production base in Beijing, the Xingwang (International) Industrial Park, with a Chinese partner. The 10 billion RMB ($1.2 billion) park manufactures Nokia handsets and other products by attracting part suppliers and other companies from around the world.

Table 2. Market shares of mobile phone handsets in China (%), 1999–2006

	1999	2000	2001	2002	2003	2004	2005	2006
Foreign-invested firms								
Motorola	39.4	35.4	29.3	28.5	9.3	8.9	13.3	24.1
Nokia	32.3	25.1	22.3	18.2	11.1	15.0	23.8	33.6
Siemens	6.0	8.1	9.7	4.7	2.5	1.4	n.a.	n.a.
Sony	6.4	9.2	6.5	2.1	1.1	2.9	4.1	7.4
Samsung	n.a.	n.a.	n.a.	n.a.	n.a.	8.3	9.6˙	9.0
Philips	n.a.	n.a.	n.a.	n.a.	n.a.	2.8	n.a.	n.a.
Local firms								
Ningbo Bird	n.a.	3.2	6.4	9.9	14.2	10.2	6.1	4.1
TCL	n.a.	1.0	3.0	8.7	11.2	6.5	3.7	1.9
Konka	n.a.	n.a.	n.a.	n.a.	6.2	5.8	2.8	2.5
Lenovo	n.a.	n.a.	n.a.	n.a.	n.a.	n.a.	n.a.	4.7
Amoi	n.a.	n.a.	n.a.	n.a.	n.a.	n.a.	n.a.	4.1

Source: Kimura (2007).

By the end of 2001, Nokia had invested a total of 11 billion RMB (compared to 28 billion RMB by Motorola and 3 billion RMB by Ericsson) and established itself as the largest player in the mobile phone market in the 2000s. They were not the only company to follow this path: Philips, Siemens, and Samsung all also announced that they would transfer all or part of their handset production to China. Many mobile phone manufacturers in Japan and South Korea also moved their mobile phone production lines to China.

As Table 2 also shows, by the end of 2001 before WTO entry, foreign phone manufacturers had the lion's share of the domestic mobile phone market. However, this situation was about to change rapidly.

Competition from Chinese firms

Prior to 1998, the Chinese handset market was dominated by foreign firms. In 1999, only 130,000 mobile phones or 5 per cent of all handsets were produced by domestic enterprises. With fast-growing demand for mobile phones and saturation in the market for other consumer appliances, Chinese consumer appliance companies began to enter the mobile handset business; thus becoming competition for multinational companies such as Nokia. Also, government policy shifted in that year to promote domestic industrial development in this sector.

As a result, the market share of domestic firms about doubled every year from 1999 until nearly one-third of the market had been captured by Chinese firms, such as Ningbo Bird and TCL, which rapidly joined the ranks of the top firms in the sector. Domestic handset enterprises suddenly challenged the dominant position of foreign-funded enterprises.

Indeed, in 1999, the Chinese government, concerned lest Chinese firms might fail to seize the opportunities of rapid demand expansion, introduced an industrial policy that fostered the growth of the local handset industry. The policy included a licence system, the provision of a subsidy to local firms for research and development, and local content legislation aimed at the foreign-invested firms. The licence system, in particular, helped local firms to enter the market. As a result, the scale of production of the Chinese firms rapidly expanded to 50 million handsets in 2003.

Part of this growth was aided by Chinese legislation governing high-tech companies which mandated a certain level of technological ability in order to attract tax breaks and investment help. In China, a firm is to register and to be certified as high tech only if it meets the following requirements: at least 30 per cent of its employees have college or higher level education, more than 5 per cent of its sales is spent on R&D, and more than 60 per cent of its sales is related to technology services and high-tech products. These companies designated as 'high tech' then receive considerable tax breaks and other advantages from the central government as part of the focus on technology which emerged in economic policy during the mid to late 1990s.

The central government also helps Chinese domestic phone companies through other means. The MII is thought to prefer local manufacturers in the awarding of contracts and to support them in other less obvious ways. There have been some widely reported cases: when the government issued licences for the manufacture of CDMA handsets in 2000, for example, eighteen of nineteen contracts went to domestic companies (Bekkers, Duysters, and Verspagen 2002).

Moreover, although local Chinese firms suffered from inadequate techno-logical capability, they grew quickly by employing a sales and marketing-oriented strategy. Many of them were unable to develop and manufacture handsets independently. Consequently, their basic strategy was to buy hand-sets from existing suppliers and sell the products under their own brand name. They mainly bought simple models which, being equipped with only a narrow range of functions, differed from those produced by the foreign-invested firms that dominated the market.

'A' share listed on the Chinese stock exchange, Ningbo Bird provides one of the best examples of this form of development. This former pager maker emerged from obscurity to become China's leading handset manufacturer and the only local manufacturer to specialize in mobile handsets. While other local producers were either government-owned or already established players in the consumer goods market before moving into handsets, Ningbo Bird took advantage of the JV policy to set its own course. Teaming up with French electronics group Sagem in 1999 in a joint venture, Ningbo Bird imported machinery and later integrated handset modules that allowed it to churn out a self-branded product almost immediately with minimal start-up costs. Ningbo Bird first hit upon the formula that led to explosive growth in the local handset industry, that is, importing nearly finished mobile phones and customizing them with its own brand. Focusing on distinctive and low-cost handsets that are tailored to quickly changing local tastes, domestic firms had an advantage in understanding that fashionable designs and price were what was important to the Chinese consumer.

Ningbo Bird also pioneered the use of grassroots distribution channels to reach customers directly. This strategy has revolutionized the local industry and been slavishly imitated by its competitors. These distribution networks comprise thousands of employees and dedicated shops throughout China that can push handset sales at the retail level.

The emergence of grassroots retailing was particularly fruitful because Chinese mobile operators do not bundle services and handsets together in a single package. This is a process whereby one buys the usage of the mobile network's services and receives a cheap or free handset (e.g. a 24-month mobile contract with a free phone). This makes point-of-sale marketing more important in China than in Western markets, where handsets are often sold along with services. Chinese handset manufacturers such as TCL, Haier, and Legend were also significant producers of other consumer goods. Hence, they were also able to leverage pre-existing distribution and retail networks used by their consumer goods businesses to drive up sales.

Chinese companies made medium-sized and small cities their major target markets, where they could avoid direct competition with multinational brands while still addressing substantial demand. Foreign brands, by contrast, relied largely on wholesale agents to distribute their wares. The number of tiers of agents used by foreign companies is large and has never been efficient, which means limited market penetration and increased costs.

However, Chinese domestic firms still lagged behind multinational firms such as Nokia. They often lacked critical technology such as chipset development programmes (a chipset is the device which allows the SIM card inside the phone to work with the rest of the electronics of the phone); thus, they are not considered in the same league as the world's big players in size, technology, quality, or performance of the equipment, because most of the manufacturers are technology followers rather than innovators. By the time they develop the manufacturing capability to imitate them, their international competitors will have introduced a successive generation. This is evident in the very low levels of sales for Chinese companies' phones in overseas markets. It is telling that no Chinese branded mobile phone is among the top five phone manufacturers in any of the other major Asian, or indeed global markets.

Nevertheless, because of their presence and the growing competition induced by the considerable number of entries encouraged by the central government's licensing schemes, foreign firms have had to bow out of the low-end product market or reduce prices for similar products sold in China. Thus the Chinese-owned manufacturers have been quite successful within China itself.

Downturn in the market and the upgrading of Chinese capabilities

At the start of 2003, the Chinese handset market entered an intensely competitive phase, increasing pressure on domestic firms and multinationals alike. Handset sales rose quickly, and with entry barriers set so low, the market had become overcrowded.

By the end of 2002, the MII had licensed some thirty-seven handset manufacturers, and there was a worrying level of overcapacity: Chinese handset production capacity stood at 200 million units. This was double the level of China's total annual sales, including exports. Moreover, the MII calculation of domestic firms' market share tallies sales into distribution channels and not to end-users. Therefore, there were also a substantial number of unsold handsets (as many as 30 million units) in stores and warehouses (Cao 2004).

With inventories and capacity rising far faster than sales, handset prices and profit margins began to decline. In 2003, the mobile phone market price showed a hefty 13.2 per cent year-on-year decline. TCL disclosed that gross margins on handsets had slid almost six percentage points. Even greater declines were anecdotally reported by other Chinese companies (Moon and Yu 2004). As a result, the growth of domestic firms began to level off and foreign firms like Nokia re-emerged in the frame.

What caused this market shift? Most Chinese domestic enterprises sought only to expand their production scale and paid little attention to upgrading their products such as through R&D. Most, following the Ningbo Bird example, did not own the intellectual property rights to the core technology, so development potential was limited. Moreover, new local firms have continuously entered the market. The entry of new firms following the same strategy as existing ones greatly intensified price competition.

Consumers' preferences also shifted. Replacement demand increased, and they also began to prefer advanced, multi-functional handsets to ones with a narrow range of functions. The highly competitive Chinese market had produced an enormous array of options. By the end of 2003, there were some 760 models on the market with a new model introduced every four days, and only five of these had a market share over 2 per cent. Moreover, replacement times became quicker and quicker—from eight months for low-end users to six months for high end users.

This shift in consumer preferences benefited brands more able to produce its own goods. Core technology and product upgrading constituted the largest disparities between Chinese and foreign brand names. Hence, since the mid 2000s, the focus of competition in the industry has shifted from sales and marketing to development and design. It began to be important for local firms to build up a development and design capability equal to that possessed by their foreign-affiliated counterparts. Nokia's particular strength in this area gave it an advantage.

For instance, it had a greater technological ability to customize its phones to Chinese idiosyncrasies, such as language input mechanisms. Also aiding this process was the diversification in sales channels. Large electronics stores and telecommunications carriers began to sell handsets through their retail outlets, reducing the advantage hitherto enjoyed by local firms in respect of sales networks and marketing.

Indeed, Nokia's Chinese Head of Operations (cited in Chang 2006: 189) stated: 'In this business, manufacturing activities alone will not take you there. We had distribution in place in China, starting in the big cities, and then we moved to the second-tier cities. Now we cover all of China. That is very important, because there are a lot of remote places which are very important from the business point of view. Our distribution network in China is second to none.'

Changing nature of policy and conclusion

Simultaneously, the very advantages enjoyed by Chinese firms became disadvantages. The second-generation mobile communications system, Global System for Mobile Communications (GSM) that broadly prevailed in China had already been commercialized in the middle of the 1990s in Europe. As such, some key components such as IC chips and basic software could be modularized as platforms, as used to such good effect by firms like Ningbo Bird.

Chinese handset manufacturers, therefore, did not need to independently develop the key components for new product development, as they had already been developed by other manufacturers. Thus before the early 2000s, Chinese firms used this advantage and their better sales and distribution forces, to gain considerable market share. Yet, although the use of platforms simplified the product structure to some extent, the technology of handsets is nevertheless complex in comparison with that of other electronic products. Firms in the handset industry, therefore, need experience in development and design. Furthermore, local firms depended on a sales and marketing-oriented strategy, and accumulated little in the way of development and design experience. Consequently, price competition after 2003 resulted in many local firms leaving the industry altogether.

While it is clear that local firms need to build up their own development and design capability, this is by no means an easy task. Moreover, the government still remains a pervasive influence on the mobile phone market. For example, the two mobile phone service providers, China Mobile and China Unicom, have collectively purchased more mobile phones for rural locations since the first half of 2007. They have purchased mainly low-end and mid-range handsets, in which local brands enjoy a comparative advantage. This purchasing behaviour has helped domestic handset manufacturers, but considerable debate remains as to how much this actually means that the Chinese industry can 'stand on its own two feet' (see Kimura 2007).

From the start of the liberalization of the telecom sector, China's FDI policy attracted multinational firms like Nokia to invest as joint venture partners. Their help in developing the market laid the foundation for the later entry of domestic firms, which were also helped by an active industrial policy by the government. The competition and demonstration effects of the foreign firms in their sales and product development served as an impetus to develop the telecommunications industry. The subsequent rise and fall and rise again of Nokia exemplify the trajectory of foreign investors aiming to produce and sell in China from the start of the reform period to the present. Throughout, the complex interaction of FDI and industrial policies permeate their experience. So far, the technology advantage that they enjoy remains; the future looks less certain as Chinese firms learn the lessons of the past.

Case study 10

WHOLLY FOREIGN-OWNED ENTERPRISES—CARREFOUR AND THE RETAIL SECTOR

Jonathan Story, INSEAD

'Everyone is dreaming about China,' Jean-Luc Chéreau told McKinsey Quarterly in 2006, reviewing his years as president of Carrefour China. 'It's the new El Dorado. But it's a difficult market and will remain a difficult market.'[1]

Leaping lightly from hyperbole to understatement in the same breath, Chéreau could scarcely have better reflected the agile corporate spirit that has made the French chain the world's second biggest retailer after the American giant Wal-Mart. In recent years, that spirit has brought Carrefour remarkable results in its triangular struggle with Wal-Mart and the UK's Tesco for supremacy in the enormous but frustratingly diverse and complex market of mainland China. Over the past decade and a half, the French company has consistently out-smarted, out-run, and out-gambled its more slow-footed rivals. The same Gallic flair that underlay Carrefour's pioneering of the hypermarket concept—in France from 1963 onwards, then around Europe and into North Africa, the Middle East, Latin America, and Asia—doubtless explains its success in China, but that success came at the price of some rapid reappraisal of established corporate wisdom. It was Taiwan that provided the learning experience. Reasoning that similar people with similar customs and similar needs could provide a template for future clients on the mainland, Carrefour came to the island in 1989, signed up to a joint venture with a local retailer and set to work. Its management team was confident in its expertise— but, crucially, they were also ready to abandon doctrine and adapt to reality.

'We had a very clear picture of what we wanted to do,' Chéreau remembered. 'Open a 10,000-square-meter store on the ground floor with a big parking lot in front, just as in France.'

But Taiwanese clients, they discovered, were not inclined—or even able, for the most part—to drive miles and load up in bulk, as in France. Lesson number one: many more Chinese shoppers came by bus, bike, taxi, or foot than by car: they bought frequently, in small quantities. Carrefour revised its thinking and opened its Asia operation more modestly, with a 3,500-meter basement store in a high-density urban area in Taiwan's second city, Kaohsiung. The 250 parking spaces it provided were for motorcycles alone. A surprised Chéreau also discovered that the Chinese view of a contract was different from a European's: an agreement, certainly, but one that was always open to revision and negotiation, rather than immutably graven into stone. You had to talk to people, learn their conditions, habits and needs, understand why they were they way they were. Go to them, talk, adapt, and negotiate. In short: localize.

'If you come to China with preconceived ideas after having been successful in Europe or the United States,' Chéreau warned, 'you make mistake after mistake.'

Carrefour didn't make many when, in 1995, it made the step from Taiwan to the mainland—or, rather, it invented as it went along and gambled on 'mistakes' that proved to be strokes of genius. China was then in the curious economic no-man's-land that lay between the ironclad, 100 per cent state control over commerce of Maoist Marxism, and the entrepreneurial freedom that was soon to transform the country into today's powerhouse. In this vaguely defined period—half open, half closed, protean regulations changing almost daily in detail and application—Carrefour's French flair served extra-ordinarily well. Rather than wasting time with the bureaucracy in Beijing, Chéreau and his lieutenants raced around the country talking to the locals. In provincial and major city administrations they discovered a fascination with Carrefour's modern, hygienic, one-stop, all-in, help-yourself layout, and a unanimous craving for the development and innovation the foreigners could offer, for the jobs they could provide, and for the taxes they would pay. Ignoring the central authorities in the capital was a wildly cavalier approach to attacking business in a communist country, but it allowed Carrefour to snap up prime locations in Beijing, Shanghai, Chongqing, Qingdao, Shenyang, Wuhan, and elsewhere. Employing the legalistic slight of hand of a 'consultancy', and setting up separate holding companies for each outlet, Carrefour managed by 2001 to erect twenty-seven stores in twelve different cities, several of them wholly owned and unencumbered by Chinese partners. Strictly speaking they had been implanted illegally, but they were faits accomplis. Meanwhile, Wal-Mart continued to dither in molasses by seeking central government licences, and Tesco had not yet even opened a single store. A Chinese retail analyst admiringly compared Carrefour's Napoleonic *fuite en avant* to 'playing on the white rim of the ping pong table'.[2]

It worked, but even so it was clear that this end-run around national regulations could not go unchallenged—after all, the company's dance on the white rim was common knowledge, and a hypermarket is not exactly a clandestine object. It was all too glaringly apparent; Beijing would eventually have to assert its authority. But how far would it go, and what price would it exact? The showdown came early in 2001. Faced with a chorus of complaints from competitors, the State Economic and Trade Commission (SETC) ruled that Carrefour had flouted government rules, ordered the company to halt expansion and to open all of its stores to 35 per cent Chinese ownership.

Oof!—it was hardly more than a slap on the wrist. Those jobs and those taxes spoke with a loud voice in Carrefour's favour. The miscreant happily complied with the ruling, and CEO Daniel Barnard flew in from Paris to demonstrate seemly contrition with a public apology. What counted, though, was the end result: Carrefour retained its twenty-seven stores, those great locations, and the support of the local administrations. For its part, the central government had saved face by obliging Bernard to kowtow. Fortuitously enough, 2001 was also the year when China entered the World Trade Organization, with all its rules about liberalizing trade. By November, the SETC had given Carrefour the green light to resume expansion: it was a winning scenario all around.

Four years later, China officially threw the gates open to unrestricted foreign investment in retail, and Carrefour was free to plunge ahead again, now faster than ever in its company history. Chéreau spread his operations—both the hypermarkets and the smaller, more Spartan Dia deep-discount stores—into the second- and third-rank cities of the vast hinterland. What would have been considered breakneck folly in Europe became run of the mill for China: Carrefour's total in China grew to 60 hypermarkets by 2005, 76 by 2006, 100 by 2007. When, in July 2007, Carrefour opened its thousandth hypermarket worldwide, that store was inevitably one of its Chinese constellations. The number rose to 112 by 2008 and to 138 by July of 2009, with more to come.

The Chinese experience is unique. At more than 1.3 billion, the population is so huge and consumer demand so pressing that even a small slice of the market means big money: fractions of fractions are worth billions. The Institute of Chartered Financial Analysts of India (ICFAI) points out[3] that by the mid 2000s, in this land still dominated by small mom and pop grocery stores, the top hundred chains (Chinese and foreign combined) claimed only about 10 per cent of total retail sales—and that the share of foreign firms was only 23 per cent of this 10 per cent. Naturally, it was Carrefour that was leading the foreign pack, and the potential for profit in the fractions of fractions was enough to make any grocer suck in his breath at the prospect: total retail spending in China stood at $756 billion in 2005, and it is projected to grow to $2.4 trillion by 2020. By then, it will be the world's second market, surpassed only by the US.

A Carrefour executive famously likened the Chinese market, not to chess, but to a game of Go, 'where you have to continuously develop a new strategy to expand on the map'.[4] Chéreau's operatives found how apt that simile was as they swarmed around the country on their scouting missions. On the one hand, every corner of China was different from the others in its habits, demands, and even language, but on the other hand, the buying public displayed a remarkable similarity nationwide: always careful, discerning, thrifty, and demanding. Tough customers: the average purchase was less than $14. Carrefour's response was to decentralize its structure, giving store managers wide autonomy and powers of decision, stocking shelves with local foodstuffs—live fish and seafood right up front by the entrance, as in the small, traditional 'wet' markets—and familiar manufactured goods, always keeping the accent on their Chinese character. In any Carrefour in China in the 2000s, the products on display will be 95 per cent Chinese and the staff local. Of the company's 40,000-plus employees, 98 per cent are Chinese— managers included, trained in company ways by the Carrefour Institute of China. When a failure of standards occurs, or a hint of corruption or hanky-panky—a fake Louis Vuitton bag here, an imitation Adidas football there, a bribe demanded by a manager for favourable treatment anywhere else— Carrefour moves swiftly to correct the fault with its own in-house investigation and policing unit. Keenly aware of the power of good public relations (and potential savings), the company is now studying a new, 'greener' design to equip stores with better insulation and energy-sipping, low-polluting refrigeration and air-conditioning systems, and like most other major companies operating in China, Carrefour donated generously to the relief fund for victims of the 2008 Sichuan earthquake.

Withal, not everything has gone Carrefour's way. In early 2007, Wal-Mart, which at the time was lagging behind with a mere seventy-three stores, struck a strong blow by out-bidding Carrefour in a $1 billion deal for a 35 per cent share of the Taiwan-based Trust Mart. The clear intention was to gain control of all 101 of Trust-Mart's mainland hypermarkets, putting it ahead of its French rival. A year later, Carrefour suffered a potential calamity, not of its own doing, when a French supporter of the Dalai Lama and Tibetan independence wrenched the torch of the 2008 Beijing Olympics from the hands of a handicapped Chinese athlete carrying it through the streets of Paris in her wheelchair. At once a cruel discourtesy to a young handicapped woman and an affront to Chinese dignity, the incident became dangerously magnified on the internet in China. Suddenly the country was seized with a need to strike back at a French scapegoat, and the biggest, most visible target was Carrefour.

The inevitable boycott movement grew to alarming proportions, and a Carrefour spokeswoman's blubbering that the company did not wish to be involved in politics, soon followed by an apologetic interview with the company CEO in Paris, which did nothing to quell the chauvinist passions. It was only after French President Nicolas Sarkozy sent Senate President Christian Poncelet to Beijing to kowtow in his place, while inviting the ill-treated athlete to come visit him in Paris, that the Chinese government spread the word to its netizens to cool down. Once again, Carrefour had skipped free of peril.

The future looks bright for the company in China. With Wal-Mart still in the process of digesting the Trust Mart it swallowed in 2007, and 2009 sales projected to grow at more than 15 per cent, Carrefour's adopted Chinese name, *Jia Le Fu*, seems more fitting than ever. Its translation: Happy and Lucky Family.

■ APPENDIX 7.1 SPECIAL ECONOMIC ZONES

Special Economic Zones (SEZs): Shenzhen, Zhuhai, and Shantou in Guangdong; Xiamen in Fujian; Hainan.

Open Coastal Cities (OCCs): Dalian in Liaoning; Qinhuangdao in Hebei; Tianjin; Yantai and Quingdao in Shandong; Lianyungang and Nantong in Jiangsu; Shanghai; Ningbo and Wenzhou in Zhejiang; Fuzhou in Fujian; Guangzhou and Zhanjiang in Guangdong; Beihai in Guangxi.

Economic and Technological Development Zones (ETDZs): Dalian, Yingkou, and Shenyang in Liaoning; Qinhuangdao in Hebei; Tianjin; Yantai, Quingdao, and Weihai in Shandong; Lianyunggang, Kunshan, and Nantong in Jiangsu; Guangzhou and Zhanjiang in Guangdong; Ningbo in Zhejiang; Fuzhou, Rongqiao, and Dongshan in Fujian; Minhang, Hongqiao, and Caohejin in Shanghai; Wenzhou in Zhejiang; Harbin in Heilongjiang; Changchun in Jilin; Wuhu in Anhui; Wuhan in Hubei; Chongqing in Sichuan; Dayawan and Nansha in Guangdong; Xiaoshan and Hangzhou in Zhejiang; Beijing; Urumqi in Xinjiang.

■ **NOTES**

1. Peter Child, Interview in *McKinsey Quarterly*, 26 July 2006.

2. Analyst Liu Lin, quoted in *South China Morning Post*, 2 September 2004.

3. ICFAI Center of Management Research, Multinational Retail Chains and the China Opportunity, Case Study no. 208-102-1.

4. Ibid.

8 Conclusions: Business in China—The Evolution of Laws and the Market

8.1 Introduction

The business environment in China has loosened a great deal in the 2000s, particularly with China's accession to the World Trade Organization (WTO) in December 2001 when it agreed to a number of market-opening measures. At the same time, China completed the large-scale restructuring of its state-owned sector in the 9th Five Year Plan that concluded in 2000. This meant the downsizing of state-owned enterprises (SOEs), significant reform of the labour market with the shattering of the 'iron rice bowl' of lifetime employment, and granting legal status to private firms, which all point to a significant degree of marketization. With the restructuring of the state-owned sector and the increasing recognition granted to the non-state sector that took place during the 1990s, China had a corporate sector with diverse forms of ownership which needed governance, that is, by laws and regulation.

The 2000s witnessed a slew of both, for example the first ever M&A and Anti-Monopoly laws and numerous regulations improving corporate governance. These facially neutral laws superseded the previous separate legal regime for domestic and foreign firms, notably seen in the 1999 unification of the Contract Law. This type of non-discriminatory and transparent law is the fundamental premise of the WTO principles, but the remaining state-owned enterprises still appeared to receive preferential treatment. For instance, Article VII of the Anti-Monopoly Law states that: 'in industries that implicate national economic vitality and national security, which are controlled by state-owned enterprises, and in industries in which there are legal monopolies, the state shall protect the lawful business activities of those enterprises, supervise and control their conducts and prices for the products and services pursuant to law, protect the interests of consumers, and promote technological progress.' However, the statute also provides that state-owned enterprises shall not abuse their dominant position or engage in anti-competitive behaviour to the detriment of consumers, so it remains to be seen whether SOEs are fully subject to the law.

More generally, China has actively pursued an industrial policy aimed at promoting national (and global) champions and is highly sensitive to foreign dominance in its still developing domestic market. Thus, a lingering concern is over whether or not these laws will create a level playing field, particularly vis-à-vis foreign firms. For instance, in one of the first cases involving a foreign firm to come before the Anti-Monopoly Law, the proposed merger between a domestic juice company, Huiyuan, and America's Coca-Cola was rejected in March 2009. As a piece of legislation which appears consistent with competition policy in Europe and elsewhere, legally the issue would be whether a proposed merger between Huiyuan, which controls nearly half of the pure juice sectors but less of other segments, with Coke, will be anti-competitive. In which case, a divestment of parts of the company or a refusal of permission would follow. That largely seemed to be the logic of the decision, but there were also suggestions that the Chinese authorities were worried about losing a famous domestic brand and reportedly were encouraging domestic firms to counter-bid for Huiyuan. In fact, the Anti-Monopoly Law has the stated purpose of 'promoting the healthy development of the socialist market economy' (Article I) that this proposed merger seems to have fallen afoul of. The failure of that merger cast some doubt on the application of what appears to be a facially neutral law, with provisions that appear to be objective but with certain 'Chinese characteristics'.

Of course, 'law on the books' does not equate to effective rule of law, particularly when the judiciary is not independent of the ruling Communist Party. Policy in China remains unwaveringly geared at economic growth. China may be a major economy (second largest in the world and the largest trader), but its per capita GDP is about $4,000, one-tenth of that of the US, and ranking it in the bottom half of countries in the world. Having such motivation, however, raises further doubts over the willingness of China to develop an effective legal system if it might run counter to the goal of growth. For instance, protecting land rights could increase the cost of development. China, moreover, recognizes the possibility that foreign multinationals could overwhelm indigenous firms in the domestic market based on their economies of scale garnered from decades of operating on world markets, while Chinese firms are at a less developed stage. This is most acute in terms of the technological advantage of most foreign firms, but exists elsewhere too. Finally, tensions are also evident in the commodities and energy sectors, as China feels the insecurity of being a net importer of the inputs that it needs to continue to industrialize and grow.

These tensions have always existed but will be made worse in the 2000s when the better developed legal system is expected to deliver. The strictures placed on foreign firms in China are unlikely to ease completely in the near term, but the otherwise seemingly objective laws in place will make many who take them at face value bridle against the constraints. For instance, firms like

Google may or may not entirely withdraw from China, but it could be a harbinger of things to come. More significantly, the 2010 trial and fairly harsh sentences imposed on four executives of the Australian mining firm, Rio Tinto, in a largely closed legal process has generated a sense of disquiet among foreign firms. Although China has had an underdeveloped legal system without an independent judiciary, its track record with regard to business, particularly foreign firms that it wishes to attract, had been fairly good, that is, there is no widespread risk of expropriation or capricious prosecution. Foreign investors may well become more wary about operating in China, but that will depend on whether it is an isolated case stemming from long-standing tensions with Rio Tinto that date back to tensions over iron ore pricing, a botched investment by the SOE Chinalco due to a political backlash in Australia, among others. The Rio Tinto case, though, does highlight how far the legal system still lags behind economic reforms. It may also point to the limits of the rule of law to provide an institutional foundation for the market if it bends to the will of the Party. In other words, China has pushed through legal reforms in lieu of political reform to support its marketizing economy. There could be a limit to this strategy. If so, then China's position as an attractive place to do business could be dented. Multinational corporations may need the fast-growing Chinese market, but China also needs to be integrated in the global economy to help it develop as it seeks to grow from being a lower middle-income country to one that achieves the standard of living of developed countries.

Correspondingly, the robustness or effectiveness of the legal system to underpin the commercial market will be an issue, not only for foreign but also private domestic businesses. By the 2000s, corporate laws were largely complete in China with the revised Company and Securities Laws providing the overall framework, which applied not only to SOEs but also the non-state sector, including private and foreign firms. The Contract Law further provided a unified contracting regime for domestic and foreign firms, covering individuals also for the first time instead of only legal persons (firms), that could herald a period of greater contracting security which is fundamental to supporting market development. The improvements to property rights were also evident through numerous revisions to the Constitution and the eventual adoption of a Property Law in 2007, though still arguably incomplete as the state retains ownership of land that prevents the use of such assets as collateral. The misgivings, though, about the effectiveness of laws remain, even as China looks to have a set of laws to support its markets. Thus, it becomes an empirical question as to whether the legal reforms are indeed market-supporting or if they are largely inconsequential. It is also a crucial question for assessing the future development of the business environment in China, the world's fastest growing economy and market.

Therefore, this final chapter is divided into two sections. The first examines whether the corporate laws that have transformed Chinese enterprises into shareholding corporations have mattered in generating improvements in firm performance. The corporatization policy, based on developing a set of corporate laws, covers not only state-owned enterprises but also private firms which have finally received formal legal recognition and protection in the 2000s. In other words, the first section will ask whether the corporate laws passed over the past three decades with full coverage extended by 2000 have been effective. The second section of the chapter reviews the business environment in China and how it is likely to evolve. The differing regimes for SOEs, Chinese private and foreign firms remain in some forms, but China is moving toward a unified rule of law system to govern its increasingly decentralized and marketized economy. The chapter and the book conclude with some reflections on the business environment in China after thirty years of reform and its likely trajectory in the twenty-first century.

8.2 **Do corporate laws matter in China?**

Ever since the passage of the Company Law in December 1993 established the corporate law framework that was completed with the adoption in 1998 of the Securities Law, China's corporate sector in the 2000s has for the first time been governed by laws and regulations which extend, not only protection, but importantly legal recognition to commercial firms, regardless of ownership. The 1999 unification of the Contract Law also removed the previous disparate regimes for domestic and foreign firms, and extended legal protection over contracts to individuals, thereby allowing sole proprietors (the previous *getihu*) to contract with greater security as well as legal status.

The implication of these reforms is that corporatization or incorporation, as has been found in other economies, should improve firm performance. By granting firms such legally protected corporate forms, they have greater contracting security to transact business, can more easily raise financing from capital markets and thus expand, and market discipline can be instilled, particularly into formerly state-owned enterprises, through creating shareholders with greater incentives to reform inefficient firms. However, given the weakness of the Chinese legal system, there is an open question as to how much legal recognition under such a system would matter. In light of the numerous criticisms of the incomplete legal system and the lingering uncertainty over the status of private property despite the constitutional and legal protections extended in the past few decades, the effects of China's corporate framework are less than obvious. This section will investigate the evidence as to whether corporate laws in China do support market development, measured on a number of metrics of firm performance, in the 2000s, at a time when the formal legal system is finally in place and applicable to private companies.

As discussed in Chapter 4, the corporatization process started in the 1990s. Corporatization involves the transformation of enterprises from public/state-owned or privately-held firms into ones defined by shareholding. Ownership can become dispersed and legal protections such as limited liability can be applied via the corporate laws within a commercial legal system responsible for regulation and dispute resolution. This process of establishing companies defined by shares has been seen over the past two centuries ranging from the advanced economies of Europe and the United States to the transition economies of the former Soviet Union, to developing countries in Africa, which have all promoted the development of a modern corporate sector through laws that govern such entities and define their rights and obligations to shareholders, whilst incorporation better allows companies to raise financing from capital markets. For instance, corporate laws were passed in the United States at the end of the nineteenth century during its industrial revolution that supported the legal rights and specified the obligations of its emerging industrial firms (see Chapter 3). Notably, restructuring public firms as corporations with private shareholders has been used as a method of privatization in both developed (Britain in the 1980s) and transition (Eastern Europe in the 1990s) economies.

For China, this was the strategy that was eventually the preferred avenue for reforming its state-owned enterprises and collectively-owned enterprises in the 1990s, after initial experiments with incentivizing output alone failed to stem the inefficiencies of communal ownership. As corporate laws and regulations were passed, the corporatization framework eventually encompassed private firms—a hitherto neglected category—as public ownership was favoured. In other words, China developed a modern corporate sector from the laws designed to also restructure its state-owned firms during the 1990s.

By the 2000s, China's enterprise sector consisted of a range of incorporated firms (some of which were listed on domestic and international stock markets), limited liability companies (LLCs), partnerships (granted limited liability in 2006), among many others, including foreign-invested firms (FIEs). Some were reformed (privatized) SOEs and collectively-owned enterprises, but a number were also of the *de novo* private sector which was finally granted legal recognition through the corporate law system during the third decade of reform. They received more secure property rights and were extended the legal protections previously granted only to public or state-owned as well as foreign firms.

The implication of these reforms is that corporatization, as has been found in other economies, should improve firm performance through granting formal legal forms that include limited liability protection and help with raising financing from capital markets. For state-owned enterprises, it can instil market discipline if shareholders other than the state are able to exert influence, though control rights would be a key factor. Particularly in China's case, poorly defined property rights could mean that a change in the law as had happened in 1999 to recognize the legality of sole proprietorships and grant private firms the right to utilize the new corporate laws and transform into corporations, would bolster their performance. However, given the weakness of the Chinese legal system (Allen, Qian, and Qian 2005), there is a question as to how much legal recognition under such a system would matter.

Moreover, corporatization differed from privatization in China. The government can remain as the controlling shareholder of an incorporated entity, but has little or no ownership rights in a privatized firm. The process was facilitated by the passage of the Company Law in 1993, the basic corporate statute. Starting in the 1990s, this shareholding transformation (*gufenhua*) changed SOEs and collectives into shareholding companies, some of which remained state-controlled (even if listed), while others were privatized following the issuance of shares. Share issue privatization (SIP) described the latter process, which sometimes but not always involved initial public offerings (IPOs) on the Shanghai and Shenzhen stock exchanges. As such, the Securities Law of 1998 completed the set of laws governing corporations, as publicly listed firms were subject to additional requirements concerning trading and disclosures.

This creation of a framework for corporate entities was initially limited to SOEs and collectives, though foreign firms had enjoyed like legal recognition through the late 1970 and 1980s laws governing Chinese–foreign joint ventures (JVs) and wholly foreign-owned enterprises (WFOEs). Private Chinese firms were granted limited formal protection and the self-employed or *getihu* were not officially counted in government statistics until the early 1990s. However, in 1999, the Law on Individual Wholly-Owned Enterprises was passed and granted private firms the same ability to utilize the corporate laws, including transforming into limited liability companies, partnerships, and incorporated firms. Sole proprietorships were also recognized with the 1999 revisions to the Contract Law offering individuals, and not just legal entities, the right to contract. Some of these so-called private firms were privatized state-owned and collectively-owned firms, but many were *de novo* firms started by entrepreneurs. Indeed, self-employment—a clear measure of new private firms—began to be measured, and grew rapidly from the 1990s onward (see Chapter 6).

By 2000, these private firms began to take on the various legal forms, and *getihu* ceased to exist, to be replaced by the recognized legal category of sole proprietorships (see Chapter 5). These firms could also register as limited liability companies or partnerships and even list on the bourses by the third decade of reform. Previously, explicit priority for the stock market listing had been given to SOEs, especially the larger ones. Consequently, the stock market was dominated by former SOEs throughout the 1990s, with private firms not permitted to list until 2001. Arguably, listed firms, subject to greater market discipline through trading of shares and potential takeovers, could perform better than non-listed ones, though the peculiar nature of the stock market, which includes a majority of non-tradable shares held by the state and SOEs also makes it an empirical question.

There are numerous types of firms, therefore, in China in the 2000s. Appendix 8.1 provides the formal definitions under the various statutes. The main categories of SOEs, collectively-owned enterprises, private firms, and foreign firms are further sub-divided into their legal forms. Focusing on the domestic firms, these can be registered as corporations (incorporated firms), LLCs, LLPs, or remain as SOEs, collectives, or private sole proprietorships—the latter being a category that was only recognized for private enterprises starting in the 2000s. They can also be publicly listed as a further sub-division. There are also other categories such as state and collective shareholding cooperatives, which would be a form of restructuring but not of corporatization, so these are reported for completeness only.

To assess the effect of corporatization, a set of estimations of firm performance is undertaken to compare those which have become incorporated versus those which are not restructured under China's corporate laws. The estimation in Table 8.1 is undertaken using the dynamic panel technique that can control for firm fixed and other contextual effects to isolate the impact of corporatization. Differential firm performance by ownership type is assessed by controlling or excluding other possible effects, such as time-varying macroeconomic conditions, the firm's own specific effects like industry, location, and technology. Some 1,200 firms are divided into different ownership categories, including whether they are listed on a stock exchange. A production function covering the period from 2000 to 2005, which includes the usual inputs of capital and labour as well as those control variables, is reported in Table 8.1. The performance differential (measured as value-added, return on assets, sales growth, etc.) of the various types of firms relative to the omitted category of SOEs are computed. It turns out that on measures such as sales growth, the ratio of sales to assets, and return on assets, the F-test that the coefficients on the different ownership types are equal cannot be rejected.

Table 8.1. Performance indicators for different types of firms

Dependent variables:	Log of value-added (1)	Return on assets (2)	Sales/assets ratio (3)	Sales growth (4)	Log of output (5)
Log of employment	0.565*** (0.033)	0.010 (0.037)	2.220*** (0.753)	0.020 (0.038)	0.069*** (0.011)
Log of capital	0.309*** (0.022)	−0.138** (0.061)	−5.079*** (1.377)	0.005 (0.033)	0.027*** (0.009)
Log of intermediary inputs					0.884*** (0.012)
SOEs *listed* after SIP	1.153*** (0.208)	−0.101 (0.363)	9.655* (5.088)	−1.008* (0.521)	0.230*** (0.038)
Corporatized SOEs (LLCs and incorporated) *non listed* firms	0.119 (0.123)	0.116 (0.197)	2.924 (2.621)	0.085 (0.213)	−0.062* (0.032)
Corporatized SOEs (LLCs and incorporated) *listed* firms	0.920*** (0.176)	0.246 (0.347)	10.398 (7.000)	−0.254 (0.227)	0.074* (0.038)
Privatized SOEs *non listed*	0.532*** (0.205)	0.060 (0.172)	6.324* (3.222)	−0.097 (0.189)	−0.009 (0.034)
Collectively-owned *non listed firms*	0.363** (0.184)	−0.079 (0.186)	−3.359 (2.795)	0.100 (0.213)	−0.026 (0.041)
Collectively-owned *listed* firms	0.000 (0.000)	0.000 (0.000)	0.000 (0.000)	0.000 (0.000)	0.000 (0.000)
Shareholding cooperative *non listed* firms	0.218 (0.168)	−0.172 (0.206)	−4.234 (3.415)	−0.203 (0.254)	−0.008 (0.047)
State-owned LLCs and incorporated *non listed* firms	0.313*** (0.121)	0.126 (0.125)	1.351 (1.416)	−0.190 (0.196)	−0.008 (0.033)
State-owned LLCs and incorporated *listed* firms	0.568*** (0.137)	0.324* (0.167)	2.619 (1.949)	−0.138 (0.197)	0.045 (0.035)
Private sole proprietorship *non listed* firms	0.158 (0.173)	0.203 (0.213)	4.898 (3.829)	−0.008 (0.208)	−0.072* (0.038)
Private partnership *non listed firms*	0.920*** (0.334)	0.129 (0.345)	−1.271 (2.981)	0.055 (0.182)	0.061 (0.065)
Private LLCs and incorporated *non listed* firms	−0.004 (0.128)	−0.116 (0.168)	1.019 (1.791)	−0.018 (0.165)	−0.074* (0.038)
Hong Kong, Macao, Taiwan-invested *non listed* firms	0.304** (0.127)	0.006 (0.147)	5.173* (3.020)	−0.215 (0.174)	0.001 (0.036)
Hong Kong, Macao, Taiwan-invested *listed* firms	0.218 (0.345)	0.406* (0.234)	10.443** (4.707)	0.091 (0.251)	0.053 (0.044)
Foreign invested *non listed* firms	0.470*** (0.138)	0.207 (0.162)	3.899* (2.350)	−0.173 (0.219)	0.008 (0.035)

Foreign invested *listed* firms	0.292	0.285	0.159	2.434	−0.028
	(0.237)	(0.185)	(3.902)	(1.800)	(0.055)
F-test	6.08	2.00	0.79	1.46	6.81
p-value	0.0000	0.0131	0.6909	0.1132	0.0000
Firms	714	714	714	702	714
Observations	3276	3325	3325	2624	3311
Industry dummies (36)	Yes	Yes	Yes	Yes	Yes
Year dummies (5)	Yes	Yes	Yes	Yes	Yes
Province dummies (11)	Yes	Yes	Yes	Yes	Yes

Source: Enterprise survey.
Notes: Panel of firms covering 2000–5 and includes dummies for firm fixed-effects, whether the firm has changed ownership type, firm age, year appeared in data set, whether it was an outlier, industrial sector, year, and provinces. Omitted dummy variables are SOEs, coal mining, and cleaning industry, year 2000, and Hubei province. The F-test is that the restriction coefficients on all of the various ownership types are equal.
*** indicates significance at the 1% level, ** at the 5% level, and * at the 10% level.

This suggests that sales alone are insufficient to discern performance differentials, so that the more precise measures of value-added, which is the preferred measure of productivity based on the sum of gross profit and the wage bill, is the relevant metric. Output, which controls for the input of intermediate products as well as the input factors, is also a robust, alternative gauge.

SOEs which have been privatized or transformed into corporations through share issue privatization (becoming listed former SOEs) produce higher value-added output than unreformed SOEs. Privatized SOEs, which are not listed, have higher value-added but do not produce significantly different amounts of output than unrestructured SOEs. By contrast, corporatized SOEs which are not listed, that is, simply transformed into shareholding companies that could still be under the control of the state, do not differ significantly from SOEs. Thus, for SOEs, the listed firms outperform the unreformed firms. Corporatization without listing does not produce a productivity differential; however, a closely held privatized SOE does, but a smaller one than listed firms. In other words, becoming publicly listed may signal the eventual privatization of the SOE, and since the better performing SOEs had been selected for listing, these corporatized former state-owned enterprises have a larger productivity differential than privatized SOEs which are not listed firms, though the latter still have a 50 per cent productivity premium over unreformed SOEs.

The picture differs for collectives in that they outperform SOEs in terms of value-added. And, all forms of shareholding transformation, including joint ventures with SOEs, are more productive than unreformed collectives. However, because of the conflation with state-ownership through SOEs, and the hybrid public–private nature of collectives, it is not possible to separate the effects of corporatization and listing. Nevertheless, collectively-owned enterprises have stronger productivity growth than SOEs in the 2000s, echoing their long-standing greater efficiency discussed in Chapter 5, though they may produce less output as they tend to be smaller in scale.

For private enterprises, listing was not permitted until the 2000s. Corporatization in the form of partnerships and LLCs was an option, though a number of private firms remained sole proprietorships. Of these three categories, only partnerships have higher productivity than SOEs. In terms of output, private firms produce less than SOEs. The implication is that corporatization does not uniformly generate the most productivity gains, probably due to the underdeveloped legal system and capital markets which do not offer the full benefits of legal protection and market discipline that can help improve the performance of firms which become corporations. But, partnerships which do benefit from legal protection but do not have dispersed shareholders may be a form that works best to manoeuvre such an evolving system. The incompleteness of law could deter the development of dispersed shareholdings, given the uncertainty of legal protection should a problem arise such that partnerships, which include the important elements of corporatization but typically among known parties, are the more efficient organizational form.

Turning briefly to foreign firms, listed firms do not have significant productivity differences from SOEs, but non-listed foreign-invested firms do. Only those foreign-invested firms with Chinese partners—which are often SOEs—can become listed, so this should not be surprising. The overall greater productivity is found regardless of whether the FIE is from Hong Kong, Macao, Taiwan (HMT) or further afield, with the non-HMT firms having the larger performance differential.

Therefore, there does seem to be higher productivity in the private firms, with some evidence of the same for reformed SOEs. However, public listing is not a uniform trait for increasing firm value-added for firms other than SOEs. The restrictive nature of the Shanghai and Shenzhen bourses which are characterized by less than 100 per cent tradable shares would diminish the market discipline normally associated with being listed companies. For SOEs, though, listed firms outperform non-listed ones transformed by corporatization. The process of being chosen to be listed does appear to support the studies that provincial authorities select the better-performing SOEs per the provincial quota system which could explain their stronger performance (Du and Xu 2009).

The overall impression is that firms which are listed (in the case of SOEs) or incorporated (for private firms) are more productive. However, the not entirely consistent evidence (not all corporatized firms have a significant productivity differential compared to unreformed SOEs) suggests it could be that better firms become incorporated. There appears to be a positive impact from better legal protection of corporations, but also that the stronger firms are the ones which take advantage of it.

Another way of asking whether the strengthening of the legal system has helped private sector development is to estimate another panel, but this time at the provincial level, to determine if legal development supports the creation of a non-state sector. Although this will be an imprecise exercise in that provincial statistics isolate the output of SOEs and collectives so that the residual is thought to be the non-state sector, the presence of state-controlled but restructured SOEs and collectives would be counted, which would tend to overstate the size of the private sector. Another measure that strips out those biases but introduces others is the rate of self-employment in a province that was analysed in Chapter 6. This would measure only *de novo* private firms started by entrepreneurs so would underestimate the development of the private sector. Both measures, though, provide another set of evidence on the relationship of the development of corporate/commercial laws to private sector development.

Tables 8.2 shows the results for the determinants of the non-state sector in a province estimated using a fixed-effect and random-effects panel estimator covering the period 1991–2006 for all of China's provinces. The fixed-effect regression takes into account provincial fixed effects beyond that which is measured by the control variables of GDP per capita, foreign direct investment (FDI), exports as a share of GDP and educational (primary and secondary) enrolment rates. In other words, there are still provincial-specific influences on self-employment that exist. Year dummies control for macroeconomic trends over time in both estimators. The random effects estimator assumes that the provincial effects are orthogonal to the other co-variates. If the assumptions are satisfied, then the random effects model is preferred over the fixed effects model as it is more efficient. Using the Breusch-Pagan Lagrangian multiplier test, the null hypothesis is rejected which implies that the assumptions of the random effects model are not satisfied. Those and other test statistics, including a F-test of the joint significance of the fixed effects regressors, are reported in the table. The Ordinary Least Squares (OLS) regression is also reported as a comparator, though it is biased for such a panel regression.

Relying therefore on the fixed-effects model where individual provincial effects are controlled for (though the result is unchanged in the random-effects model), neither legal system measure (lawyers per capita and legal commercial cases filed per capita) is significant in determining the size of the non-state

Table 8.2 The determinants of provincial share of non-state sector, panel estimation, 1991–2006 (z-statistics in parentheses)

Dependent variable: share of private sector output in province	1991–2006			1991–1999		2000–2006	
	(1) OLS	(2) FE	(3) RE	(4) FE	(5) RE	(6) FE	(7) RE
Log of GDP per capita	−0.011	0.476*	0.089	0.286	0.044	0.295	0.374***
	(0.104)	(0.268)	(0.143)	(0.541)	(0.182)	(0.259)	(0.141)
Log of FDI	0.224***	0.235***	0.222***	0.357	0.260***	0.028	0.097***
	(0.026)	(0.045)	(0.034)	(0.219)	(0.052)	(0.039)	(0.032)
Export-to-GDP ratio	0.348**	0.052	0.085	3.652	0.444	−0.489***	−0.378***
	(0.165)	(0.186)	(0.174)	(2.739)	(0.451)	(0.127)	(0.121)
Educational enrolment	0.168	0.142	0.182	3.177	−0.255	0.372***	0.323***
	(0.189)	(0.153)	(0.149)	(2.630)	(0.971)	(0.095)	(0.095)
Log of lawyers per capita	−0.084	0.069	0.020	−0.256	−0.190*	0.078	0.037
	(0.071)	(0.094)	(0.085)	(0.402)	(0.112)	(0.095)	(0.090)
Log of cases filed per capita	0.092	−0.073	−0.036	−0.070	0.086	−0.071	−0.057
	(0.065)	(0.081)	(0.076)	(0.319)	(0.119)	(0.063)	(0.063)
Year	0.034***	0.003	0.036***	−0.033	0.002	0.114***	0.091***
	(0.009)	(0.024)	(0.011)	(0.072)	(0.033)	(0.027)	(0.013)
Constant	−71.890***	−14.190	−76.820***	53.634	−9.874	−231.935***	−187.274***
	(18.432)	(45.026)	(21.896)	(143.264)	(64.573)	(52.426)	(24.312)
Adjusted R-squared	0.618	0.435	0.6092	−0.303	0.6157	0.748	0.5403
$F_{(8, 210)}$	45.14***						
$F_{(7, 190)}$		28.03***					
$F_{(7, 36)}$				1.87			
$F_{(7, 125)}$						68.71***	
Wald χ^2 (7)			232.34***		90.96***		459.47***
Breusch–Pagan Lagrangian multiplier test χ^2 (1)			133.09***		3.00*		188.39***
Number of provinces	22	22	22	22	22	22	22
Observations	219	219	219	65	65	154	154

Source: China Statistical Yearbook, Census Yearbook.
Notes: *** indicates significance at the 1% level, ** at the 5% level, and * at the 10% level. Independent variables are: log of deflated per capita GDP, log of foreign direct investment, export-to-GDP ratio, educational enrolment rate of school-aged children, log of lawyers per capita, log of civil cases filed per capita, dummies for 29 provinces (except for Tibet, and Chongqing is included in

sector. This is the case for the 1990s as well as the 2000s when the corporate law system was better established by being applicable to all firms and not primarily SOEs. By contrast, recall in Table 6.6, the number of civil cases filed per capita is significant and positive in increasing provincial self-employment, suggesting that a better utilized or functioning legal system is more important for starting a business than it is for determining the overall development of the private sector. Interestingly, in the 2000s, better human capital in a province and the growth rate (captured in the time trend) will tend to increase the relative proportion of the non-state sector, whilst being highly export-oriented may reduce it, which probably refers to the competitiveness impact of foreign firms that can squeeze domestic firms in the same market. For the entire period of 1991–2006, FDI increased the non-state sector of a province, so the competitiveness effect was a later development since early FDI—mostly in the form of Chinese–foreign joint ventures—appeared to foster rather than compete against domestic private sector development.

Consistently though, legal sector development does not seem to matter in the third decade of reform, echoing the earlier finding that there is not a straightforward relationship between China's better, but still incomplete, corporate law system and private sector development or firm performance. It is more likely that better performing firms utilize the legal system, though they may well find it easier to start up new businesses in the 2000s than before. However, as much of the benefits of a legal system relate to having better legal protection for contracting, or being able to use firm assets as collateral for loans and investment, the still lagging court system and the repressed financial system tilted toward SOEs could mean that the mechanisms for improving firm performance are still hampered, even as the legal system has improved. Indeed, the legal system has only just started developing in the early 2000s and it could be some years yet before the positive impact on firms are fully realized. Helping entrepreneurs could be an initial effect, while improving productivity will have to wait until the other aspects of the legal system catch up. However, the trend and direction of reform point to a more coherent legal framework for corporations, even for listed ones, which bodes well for the future. In the meanwhile, the corporate sector continues to reform.

8.3 Ongoing corporate sector reforms

8.3.1 TRANSFORMATION OF STATE-OWNED ENTERPRISES

After thirty years of marketization and reform, the business environment in China remains a mixed picture of state-led policies and a growing number of facially neutral laws. The major reform of the state-owned sector was largely completed prior to WTO accession in 2001. The Ninth Five Year Plan from 1996–2000 led to the large-scale restructuring of the state-owned enterprises, including the first significant lay-offs in China's history. The *xiagang* policy resulted in some 50 million urban workers being made redundant from SOEs, with millions more losing their previous 'iron rice bowl' of a job (and benefits) for life in various forms of *ligang* or being 'off the job'. This allowed the SOE sector to shed surplus labour and move away from one of their main tasks which had been to provide employment for urban residents to achieve the state's full employment policy. SOEs' share of urban employment fell from 56 per cent in 1996 to 38 per cent by 2000. SOEs in turn were restructured or underwent *gaizhi*. The 'save the large, let go of the small' policy resulted in a dramatic fall in the number of SOEs such that their numbers declined from 7.99 million in 1996 to 162,885 in 2000. But, this was not the end of SOEs. Their numbers increased by 100,000 by 2006, though their share of industrial output continued to fall from 38 per cent to 27 per cent, and their share of employment by a further 15 per cent to 23 per cent over the same period, having been squeezed by the rapid growth and higher productivity of the private sector. Nevertheless, the share of employment is less than the proportion of industrial output, in contrast to the pre-1996 period when SOEs accounted for 60–70 per cent of urban employment, which largely matched its share of industrial output, suggesting that the large SOEs after restructuring are more capital-intensive, such as the National Oil Companies (NOCs), utilities, commodity firms like Baosteel, etc. After the Tenth Five Year Plan in 2006, the move toward such industries was even more pronounced as the commodity boom of the mid 2000s hastened China's focus on energy and raw materials.

Despite becoming less important and largely restructured, SOEs still suffer from 'soft budget constraints' whereby they remain inefficient even when profitable because of the cheap inputs received from the state, including investment funds from the state-owned commercial banks and subsidized energy and other input prices. With a profit motive introduced through marketization and performance-related pay, the incentives are to increase output but without the significant constraint of costs ordinarily faced by private firms. The inability to rid the state-owned commercial banks of non-performing loans can be traced to the continuing flow of such debts traced to SOEs. The continued use of state-owned commercial banks to, for instance, finance the bulk of the government's fiscal stimulus package during the global recession of 2008/9 further illustrates the continuing presence of state-owned banks and the state-owned sector. However, the ongoing relationship between the state, state-owned commercial banks, and the retention of state-owned enterprises raises the spectre of a banking crisis.

In anticipation of competition five years after WTO accession in 2001 and the shareholding transformation of its state-owned banks in the share issue privatization process used for SOE reform, the non-performing loans of the banking system were largely addressed through capitalization and the creation of asset management companies in the late 1990s and 2000s. Between 2003 and 2005, around $60 billion was injected from China's foreign exchange reserves into three of the big four state-owned commercial banks (SCBs): Bank of China ($22.5 billion), China Construction Bank ($22.5 billion) and Industrial and Commercial Bank of China or ICBC ($15 billion)—all before their initial public offerings. Four AMCs had been previously set up in 1999, each attached to one of the big four state-owned commercial banks. These AMCs took non-performing loans (NPLs) out of the banking sector, eventually totalling some 2.4 trillion RMB (around $350 billion). In turn, these AMCs issued bonds, which paid 2.25 per cent interest to the banks for the (bad) assets. For the banks, a troubled asset thereby became fee-generating. The AMCs in turn attempted to sell the bad assets to private investors, including joint venture funds. Some of these were bought, initially because foreign investors believed that debt-for-equity swaps were possible, which would have allowed equity purchases into SOEs that had been difficult with China's restrictions on foreign investment. However, of the ones that were sold, the debt-for-equity swaps never materialized, so the appetite for these assets dwindled.

Accordingly, the better assets were sold, leaving the AMCs with the worst ones, and still burdened with paying interest on the bonds. This meant that as the demand dried up, so did their revenues, which made it increasingly difficult to pay the interest. As the AMCs are state-owned and run, as are the banks, these are effectively liabilities of the state. Counting these liabilities would increase China's national debt (counting the central government's liability but not the local governments' debts) by four percentage points to around a quarter of GDP.

With the removal of the NPLs and the recapitalizations, the Chinese banking system may look solid, but it has merely transferred the problems elsewhere. Ultimately all this accrues back to the state. The AMCs were to last for ten years, but still exist. Moves to commercialize the AMCs are an attempt to address this problem, but selling stakes in an undesirable set of companies is not easy. Thus, the state-owned banks have purchased stakes in the AMCs, which re-exposes them to the liabilities on the AMCs' books and completes the circle on the NPL problem.

With NPLs thought to have worsened during the 2008 global financial crisis as the SCBs were used to finance the government's fiscal stimulus measures, the issue rears its head again. For instance, the $11 billion rights issues by the SCBs in 2010 to recapitalize using the stock market and the government using its foreign exchange reserves to purchase a 50 per cent stake in the Agricultural Bank of China before its IPO are indicative of the lingering problems in the state-owned banks.

With the political economy of state ownership at play, SCBs as well as SOEs are managed by Party cadres and are unlikely to become completely privatized. The establishment of SASAC (State-owned Assets Supervision and Administration Commission) further suggests the retention of SOEs in the Chinese economy. However, the problems with doing so are evident, no less in the banking sector. State-owned/publicly-run companies can exist in a market economy without causing instability, but the legacy issues of the command economy means that for Chinese SOEs, the past and future problems of policy-directed operations must not overwhelm the commercial motive.

8.3.2 'GOING OUT' POLICY

The ambition for SOEs is not restricted to the domestic market. Chinese banks in 2009, albeit an unusual year in the midst of the global financial crisis, were four of the five largest banks in the world. The bankruptcy of two of America's 'Big Three' car makers also offered acquisition targets for Chinese car firms, including the privately-owned Geely which bought the long-established Volvo brand from Ford.

SOEs and, increasingly, private firms are being encouraged by the Chinese government to 'go out' and compete on global markets. Launched in 2000, 'going out' is intended to create Chinese multinational corporations that are internationally competitive. By doing so, China aims to become more than a generic producer of low-end manufacturing goods, branded under the moniker of Western firms. The ability to do so is an indicator of industrial upgrading, the very thing that China needs to ensure a sustained growth rate if its firms are innovative and productive as against leading global companies.

For instance, Haier is the largest white goods maker in China and is sold in Wal-Mart but does not command brand recognition and loyalty in world markets. The strategy of Lenovo, therefore, was to not only purchase IBM's PC business but also to license the use of the brand name for five years so that Lenovo can eventually assume the trusted name of IBM in world markets. These are all developments which took place starting in the mid 2000s, when the first commercial outward investment by a Chinese firm was permitted in 2004 with TCL's purchase of France's Thomson.

Most outward FDI remains state-led investments in energy and commodities, but the maturing of Chinese industry indicates that the trend is changing as China seeks to move up the value chain and develop multinational companies that can follow in the footsteps of other successful countries like Japan and South Korea. These countries, unlike most developing countries, managed to join the ranks of the rich economies through possessing innovative and technologically advanced firms that enabled them to move beyond what is sometimes termed the 'middle income country trap'. Nations start to slow down in growth when they reach a per capita income level of $14,000. The process of growth through adding labour or capital (factor accumulation) slows or reaches its limit, and they are unable to sustain the double digit growth rates experienced at an earlier period of development. By increasing productivity instead through developing industrial capacity and upgrading that is stimulated by international competition, it is more likely that a country can maintain a strong growth rate. The need for energy as well as upgrading industrial capability is the motivating force for China to invest overseas. Nevertheless, by the end of the 2000s, the share of commercial outward investment remains small, whilst state-owned firms continue to constitute the bulk of outgoing FDI. The shape of things to come, though, points to China becoming a net capital exporter and the 'going global' of its firms heralding an era of Chinese multinational corporations.

Figure 8.1 shows the explosive growth of outward FDI since the mid 2000s, which points not only to SOE investment in commodity sectors, but also the commercial M&As private companies like Lenovo, which purchased the IBM PC business for the then-record of $1.75 billion in 2005, later exceeded by Geely's acquisition of Volvo for $1.8 billion in 2010. Becoming a net capital exporter is also viewed as a marker of a country reaching a level of industrial development as its firms are able to operate and compete on world markets. With outward FDI accelerating and close to overtaking inward FDI by the end of the 2000s, China could be on track to demonstrate that its industrial capacity is not only a function of FIEs producing its exports, but indicative of a more widespread upgrading of its industry. 'Going out' or 'going global' points to the policy aim that looks to be realized by the end of the first thirty years of reform.

8.3.3 PRIVATE FIRMS

Having gained legal recognition in the 2000s, private firms are on a better footing than before. But, challenges remain. A notable one is the continued existence of financial repression that could ultimately restrict their development.

The ongoing preference for SOEs by the SCBs highlights the difficulty of private firms have in accessing credit. In an economy which has undergone significant marketization, there are still several areas where reforms are needed. The financial system is a key one and a significant problem is the unliberalized interest rate. Interest rates remain controlled, hampering the development of a financial sector that inefficiently allocates risk and returns to investment. Private firms have trouble obtaining credit—whether from banks or the underdeveloped domestic capital markets—so they rely

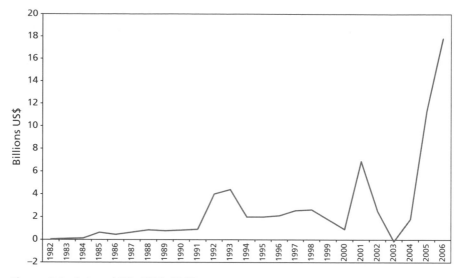

Figure 8.1. Outward FDI, 1982–2006

Source: IMF Balance of Payments Statistics Yearbook 2007.

heavily on retained earnings to finance growth. Capital controls prevent them from accessing global capital markets as an alternative. As a result, to finance themselves in a fast-growing market, corporate savings have increased even more than household savings during the 2000s, contributing to high savings within the Chinese economy, which is ultimately detrimental to growth, as domestic consumption (the counterpart to savings) plummets to a historic low of 35 per cent of GDP in 2009 when it had been a more usual 50 per cent during the early 1990s. For private firms largely confined to the domestic market, this is a troubling combination.

Complete liberalization of interest rates would both improve credit allocation to private firms and reduce the savings incentive. Although interest rates were partially liberalized in 2004 when the ceiling on interbank lending rates was lifted, there are still limits on the 'floor' of such rates, as well as a ceiling on deposit rates, distorting investment decisions but maintaining margins for banks. If interest rates were liberalized, it would reduce financing costs for firms and thus the need to save.

Gradual capital account liberalization, in particular the 'going out' policy, will also help if more private firms are permitted to operate in global markets and allowed to access funding from better-developed overseas credit markets. In other words, firms can raise money on capital markets and not just rely on China's banking system with its controls on credit.

For private firms, the ability to operate in overseas markets can help them grow and gain economies of scale. In the three decades of the reform period, these firms have grown from a very low base to being the largest driver of output and GDP growth in China. Private firms were the source of growth that allowed China to gradually transition away from central planning. Yet, it was not until the 2000s that they were granted legal protection, such as the *getihu* or sole-proprietors, and began to have access to credit. Continuing this reform process is still needed.

The domestic market in China is highly competitive in numerous respects, with monopolies largely in the capital-intensive industries dominated by SOEs. But, private firms still face a difficult environment in China. For China to sustain its remarkable growth rate, promoting efficient private firms and allowing them to gain scale and financing on world markets is a necessary policy move.

8.4. **The Chinese business environment in the twenty-first century**

8.4.1 THE SECOND THIRTY YEARS OF REFORM

The Twelfth Five Year Plan is viewed as marking the start of the second phase of China's market-oriented reforms. Covering 2011–15, it was launched in 2009/10 during the global recession and the start of the global recovery that has made China significantly aware of the likelihood that exports and world demand will be weak for some time. With a global market share of some 10 per cent in manufactured goods, China became the largest trader in the world in 2009. Even though world trade was weak during the global downturn, China overtook Germany. By doing so in the late 2000s, China's global market share rivalled that of the largest traders in the world at their peak, for example United States, Japan, and Germany have never accounted for more than 10 per cent of world markets. It indicates that China may well face slower export growth, especially as its wages are likely to rise with the end of the reallocation of cheap, agricultural/migrant labour. Coupled with the volatility from being export-oriented (exports accounted for 37 per cent of GDP in 2007), the global recession caused massive unemployment in China, estimated to be around 20 million in export-oriented factories, primarily of rural–urban migrant workers. Exports caused a three percentage point drop in GDP, and China's GDP growth declined in the last quarter of 2008 and first quarter of 2009 to just over 6 per cent. Although perhaps admirable in the midst of the worst global recession since World War II, the instability wrought through export-dependence and the likely limit on export growth has caused the government to seriously contemplate a re-orientation toward domestic demand. It also points to significant macroeconomic reforms that are needed for China to rebalance its economy and continue to support its marketization process.

First, although China's current account is fairly open in terms of exports (though less so with respect to imports due to limits on market access), its capital account remains largely closed and restricted. China controls the inflow of FDI as well as the outflow. Inflow is controlled through licensing requirements for foreign investors, though more sectors have opened since WTO accession. Outflow is being gradually increased through the slow implementation of the 'going out' policy. Portfolio or short-term capital flows remain restricted, though capital controls have not prevented billions of 'hot money' speculating on the currency and in assets, since all such controls are imperfect.

In the 2000s, with liquidity building up and monetary aggregate (M2) growth racing ahead of the long-term target of 17 per cent, reaching nearly 30 per cent at the end of 2009 in the midst of a large stimulus package, China began to gradually increase by small amounts the quantity of money that can be moved overseas. For instance, households could move $4,000 each year into Hong Kong, the Special Administrative Region (SAR) that had become the place where China experiments with financial liberalization.

However, much more reform is needed. China had built up $2.8 trillion in reserves by the end of 2010. With M2 growth exceeding the target and concerns over the value of the reserves which are largely invested in the US dollar that was under pressure from mounting American debt, the liquidity build-up and structural concerns over further reserve accumulation call for capital account liberalization.

Indeed, capital account liberalization can support the 'going out' policy, that is, allowing state-owned and non-state-owned firms to invest and compete on global markets will serve the dual purposes of improving productivity as well as reaching new sources of demand directly in new markets instead of through trade. It would reduce corporate savings by allowing firms to expand and operate in global credit markets. It further reduces the need for government purchases of dollar-denominated assets, since capital outflows can balance the current account surplus in lieu of reserve accumulation. This reform is also integral to the reforms of the two major market tools that determine the macroeconomy: the interest rate and the exchange rate.

The major market tool that is incompletely reformed is the interest rate. Even though interest rates will be limited in their use so long as China operates a fixed exchange rate, reform would still have significant effects in a number of areas. Liberalizing interest rates would improve the efficiency of credit allocation that would reduce savings and allow for better risk assessment. For instance, the 'ceiling' on deposit rates reduces interest payments on savings to households which depresses their income and therefore consumption. Raising incomes and reducing the motives for precautionary savings, such as through improved social security provision, would significantly help rebalance the economy toward domestic demand.

Reforming interest rates would also facilitate the development of capital markets which also reduces the savings motive if there are more sources of finance available to firms. As the determinant of the internal rate of return (IRR) to capital, without reform, the restricted interest rate prevents efficient allocation of resources and had seriously underpriced risk until the 'ceiling' on the lending rate was removed in 2004. It is also one of the reasons why China has an underdeveloped financial market where lending is predominantly via bank lending, and by state-owned banks. Capital market development has been hampered and China's considerable levels of savings were inefficiently allocated.

Unreformed and low deposit rates also contributed to a search for yields that raises the spectre of macroeconomic instability. With deposit rates lower than inflation, negative real interest rates prevailed. Capital account restrictions preventing the outward flow of investments also trapped China's high savings within the economy itself. Investors, therefore, sought to gain positive returns through investing in assets, such as housing and the stock market. With little financial sector development, investment vehicles were also few. Therefore, housing and the stock market became the favoured destinations for investors. In the face of an inadequate pension system, housing also became a vehicle for retirement. Finally, not reforming interest rates also has macroeconomic implications, particularly when viewed in conjunction with the exchange rate which is also in need of reform.

The RMB was pegged to the US dollar from 1994 until July 2005 when it was instead fixed to a trade-weighted basket of currencies. In 2008, in the midst of the global recession, the exchange rate was re-pegged to the US dollar until June 2010. The RMB is a restricted currency, though China began to loosen the limitations on its use in the late 2000s. By agreeing to bilateral currency swaps with trading partners such as Russia and Asian countries, China began to increase the convertibility of the RMB, perhaps with an ultimate aim of it becoming a reserve currency.

The Chinese authorities have indicated that they will increase the flexibility of the exchange rate, which is a necessary outcome with greater capital account liberalization to support the 'going out' policy. If this is coupled with interest rate reforms, there should be a better balance between the internal (savings/investment) and external (current account) positions. The exchange rate determines the cost of imports which affects consumption and the cost of production and the value of outward investments, while the interest rate determines the returns to, and costs of, investment. Taken together, the macroeconomy achieved internal and external balance for consumption, investment, government spending, and the current account. With both of these tools restricted, it is not surprising that China's economy had become so unbalanced by the mid 2000s that consumption had declined to a record 35 per cent, not seen in any other country during the course of their economic development.

Reforming these market tools of the exchange rate and interest rate as well as capital account liberalization must be taken in conjunction with institutional reforms. But, institutional reforms at the domestic and international levels to deepen financial markets would be needed too. For instance, active engagement in the global regulatory body, the Financial Stability Board (FSB), can increase stability if markets are increasingly governed by transparent rules and laws generating more certainty and depth, with positive implications for household and firm behaviour.

China is likely to favour the stability of the fixed exchange rate for some time over the less predictable flexible exchange rate, as with most developing countries. It can, nevertheless, undertake reforms that would rebalance the Chinese economy and put it on a less volatile path. Due to China's size, it is a large, open economy that can affect the global terms of trade, that is, the prices of worldwide exports and imports. As such, it can be one of the largest traders in the world and still have its economy be primarily driven by domestic demand, much like the United States. Moving ahead on reforming these essential market tools will further the marketization process that will ultimately allow China to develop a more efficient and stable market economy structure. This is not to say that there are not other areas which will remain state-owned or distorted, such as energy prices and land ownership. But, developing a financial sector, opening the capital account, and reforming interest rates and the exchange rate will improve China's ability to sustain its development and provide a more conducive environment for firms as the engines of growth to flourish.

8.4.2 THE EVOLVING MARKET

It is always hard to predict where the Chinese market is headed since China itself has seemingly defied expectations by transforming itself in the space of thirty years into a major economy. The state-owned structure remains after these three decades of economic transition, setting China apart from other centrally planned and administered economies in the former Soviet Union which have embraced the market system. Retrenchment in Russia and backtracking in parts of Eastern Europe attest to the difficulties of shedding the old system. Nevertheless, much of Eastern Europe has re-integrated with Europe and ten countries have acceded to the European Union's single market. China, for its part, has become a formidable force on the world stage and its actions carry repercussions from Africa to the United States.

Yet, China retains the single Party state and a strong state-led development path. This is not to deny that regional experimentation and marketization happens to a large extent outside of, and sometimes in conflict with, the dictates of the central government, but rather that China's markets are still influenced by the aims of the state's industrial strategy. For instance, capital account liberalization may well be undertaken to relieve the build-up of excess liquidity (money growth over real GDP gains) in the economy, but it can also serve to support the 'going out' policy. Of course, too much capital outflow would not be permitted, because the partially reformed system still carries a large degree of bad debts in its banking system, so keeping savings in the country will be a competing priority.

Furthermore, China is not developing in a vacuum. Instead, it is integrated into a world system increasingly characterized by global rules and norms. Even before the 2008 global financial crisis, there was a growing harmonization of governance of markets. Intellectual property rights were governed by the WTO TRIPs agreement and corporate governance systems were converging (see Hansmann and Kraakman 2001). In addition, WTO accession introduced a number of institutional measures in China that will call for transparency alongside market opening. Case study 11 on financial sector development after WTO membership illustrates the impact of such agreed rules on the development of China's nascent financial system.

After the global financial crisis, the pace of global reform accelerated, since the crisis exposed the inadequate governance of linked international capital markets. Funds can move instantaneously across borders and yet were hardly tracked, much less regulated. This became glaringly apparent when the American investment bank, Lehman Brothers, failed in September 2007. Its broker-dealer model meant that creditors around the world lost billions whilst its unmonitored, extensive linkages in world markets raised the spectre of the prospect of systemic banking failure for the first time since the Great Depression. Lehman Brothers was allowed to fail, but the subsequent rescues of other banks and the historic attempts to shore up markets attests to the calamitous consequences of its collapse.

It propelled a new push for better global regulations of financial markets. The G20 group of major economies, including China, entrusted a reconstituted Financial Stability Board based in the Bank for International Settlements or BIS (the central banks' central bank) in Basel with the task of fashioning regulations for global capital markets, including greater capital and liquidity requirements. This will reflect back onto China and other economies to harmonize their domestic regulations with global guidelines.

For China, it feeds into the trend of growing laws and regulations to govern its markets. Although imperfect in many respects, the rule of law is being pursued in China to instil confidence and in some ways substitute for the lack of political reform that has not progressed significantly in the thirty years of the reform period. Courts and regulators serve as avenues for redress and consultation in a way that the government does not. Laws provide the veneer of certainty to reassure investors and shareholders. Although imperfect, and hampered by the lack of an effective court system, laws in China have been effective in a number of respects. Case study 12 analysing the heavily criticized patent law in China provides an illustration.

For most issues, though, the rule of law is unlikely to be effective in the manner expected in the United States or Europe. The dominance of the state further casts doubt on the objectivity of the judiciary which is not independent and is manned by a generation of judges with minimal legal training. It has not deterred foreign investors thus far, and Chinese firms are accustomed to the system. Nevertheless, the further development of the market will require more robust laws and regulations. China is headed down that path, but it will take some years yet before the legal system is better developed. Even then, with a one-Party state, the extent of effectiveness of the law may be stymied by the dictates of policy.

China will pursue continued marketization and will increase the degree of institutional foundations such as laws and regulators to support and govern the market. In some respects, it will proceed quickly, whilst in others it will proceed cautiously, with an eye toward its overall development goals. China, though, has not had a track record as a capricious state. Instead, policies have been adopted gradually and often been subject to improvement as the needs of the market and investors became more evident. The power of localities and provinces can be a hindrance but in terms of reforms can be a great strength, since the decentralized state often means that markets can develop more rapidly and fruitfully in areas far from the direct control of the central government. The state-owned sector will probably continue to receive preferential treatment, and the playing field is unlikely to be completely level. However, it is evident that the driving force of Chinese growth is the nonstate sector, including the expertise and know-how introduced by foreign firms. China's own development is the paramount aim of its government. With a per capita GDP of only $3,000 (or $8,000 at purchasing power parity), China ranked 105th in the world in 2009, belying its status as the world's second largest economy. Being a lower middle-income country means that one-third of its populace still lives on less than $2 per day. Yet, at the same time, being less developed offers numerous possibilities for rapid growth and its 1.3 billion population is undoubtedly attractive to global businesses.

Developing a market system to achieve that goal will depend on getting its laws and policies right and providing a suitable environment for business. As the vehicles for job and wealth creation, reforms to establish a marketized economy remain paramount. Despite being a Communist state, the pro-market stance of the government has served it well in the first three decades of reform. The next thirty years are unlikely to be different. They might even be better.

8.5 **Assessing the future contour of China's market**

China has one of the most difficult markets to assess. One principle appears clear. China is intent on increasing marketization to sustain economic growth. Even though it is the world's second largest economy, its low level of income and consumption suggest that it has the capacity for continued growth in its markets. Urban incomes have largely kept pace with economic growth and yet remain still at a low level. Household disposable income averaged 17,175 RMB ($2,642) in 2009. Even with only the 500 million urban residents consuming, China is already one of the largest markets in the world in terms of automobiles, Internet users, mobile phones, etc. But, with 800 million rural residents yet to emerge as consumers, the potential is immense. Their disposable household incomes, though, lag considerably behind at 5,153 RMB ($793) per annum in 2009.

The sector that China wished to develop the most in the first thirty years of reform was industry and manufacturing. The next phase is moving to services and increased urbanization to bring rural residents into cities to create new sources of consumption and reasons for continued investment and industrialization. In other words, China is looking to create domestic sources of consumption as export growth is expected to slow. Urbanization will require new roads, transport, infrastructure, housing, schools, and a range of services for these new urban residents. In turn, this will create employment and sources of domestically driven growth. Developing the services sector is key to this process. As a partly non-tradable sector, the service sector can create low-skill and high-skill jobs ranging from barbers to professionals like accountants that are not dependent on global markets and therefore less subject to volatility.

The services sector is very underdeveloped in China. Accounting for only around 40 per cent of GDP in 2010, it is a smaller sector than in other countries at a comparable level of development, that is, lower middle-income countries. Unlike industry, there was virtually no service sector in the planned period. Industrialization was achieved in China through Soviet-style planning so that by the time market-oriented reforms started in 1978, industry accounted for half of GDP, and China was industrialized despite being a very poor country. The reform period witnessed the reform and upgrade of manufacturing, moving away from the dominance of heavy industry and instead diversifying into consumer goods and light industry.

By contrast, the services sector was small, as the state provided all of the essential services, and there was little development in the pre-reform period as workers were allocated vouchers for food and essentials, and household incomes were very low (10 per cent of GDP in 1978) since the state retained any surplus to invest in industrialization. Services like banking and medical care were organized and run by the state, leaving no scope for the sector to develop.

As such, starting from a low point with minimal government impetus behind its development, services accounted for less than one-quarter of GDP in 1978 and slowly increased to only around 40 per cent of the economy three decades later. When China agreed to open its services sector upon accession to the WTO, it was one of the most questioned decisions due to the extent of underdevelopment of the sector. Competition from foreign service firms is a driver for reform, even as the Chinese government has forestalled the complete opening of the sector. Services, nevertheless, is increasingly seen as a policy priority as export-oriented growth has run its course, and China's large population can constitute a sizeable market to sustain its economic development.

This will make China an ever-more attractive market. And there will be a new policy of 'bringing in, going out' that seeks to attract know-how and expertise from foreign firms. The next phase of reform will see service firms serving the role that manufacturing firms served during China's re-industrialization phase as it sought to re-orient its inefficient industry from the days of the administered economy to one run by market practices and geared at innovation and technology. Like those earlier firms, foreign services sector firms will need to balance market access with preserving their competitive advantage.

In conclusion, China's growth has been aided by a favourable business environment in spite of an underdeveloped legal system. Yet, adopting legal and, importantly, institutional reforms alongside marketization measures has been beneficial for growth. In the next thirty years of China's reform period, though, more effective legal reforms will be needed to support an increasingly marketized and decentralized economy. The speeding up of legal and regulatory changes in particular in the 2000s bodes well for a shift in priority toward creating more market-supporting institutions and mechanisms that are also compatible with international standards and therefore business expectations. Whether China can do so will be an important factor in whether it can sustain what has been a remarkable growth story.

Business has been an integral part of China's development. Supporting enterprise through a favourable business environment characterized by laws will be needed in the future. To remain enterprising, China's market reforms will need further institutional changes, namely relating to a plethora of laws and rules to govern the market. Although imperfect, the track record of the first thirty years is promising. Continuing in this way will be key for China to achieve its considerable potential, which can power not only its own prosperity but that of the rest of the world into another golden era of growth.

Case study 11

POST-WTO FINANCIAL MARKET DEVELOPMENT

Sanzhu Zhu, School of Oriental and African Studies (SOAS), University of London

One of the central themes running through the development of financial markets in post-WTO (World Trade Organization) China since December 2001 has been the implementation of China's WTO commitments relating to financial services. This implementing process has brought about positive legal and regulatory reforms in Chinese financial services law, which in turn serve to underpin an opening up and transformation of China's financial markets in the 2000s and beyond. This case study aims to give an assessment of China's WTO-related legal and regulatory reforms in Chinese financial services law and the development of financial markets in post-WTO China. The study examines briefly the legal and regulatory reforms and developments in some of the areas in banking, insurance, and securities sectors. The development of the financial markets in post-WTO China is a result of the comprehensive commitments China made to grant broad market access to China's financial markets, as well as a corresponding progress that it has made to implement these commitments and to reform its financial services law and regulations; however, various regulatory restrictions are still in place limiting the presence of foreign financial institutions and their investments in Chinese financial markets. This may well change with further liberalization.

In December 2001 upon accession to the WTO, China made a comprehensive list of commitments to further open up its banking, insurance, and securities markets. The commitments and schedules were stated in detail in section 7 of the *Schedule of Specific Commitments on Services*,[1] supplementary to China's general commitments stated in the Protocol on the Accession of the People's Republic of China[2] and the Report of the Working Party on the Accession of China.[3]

China's commitments on banking and other financial services (excluding insurance and securities) covered, among other things, deposit services, lending of all types, financial leasing, all payment and money transmission services, guarantees and commitments, and foreign exchange trading on its own account or for customers, provision and transfer of financial information, financial data processing, and credit reference and analysis. In summary, China committed that upon accession, foreign financial institutions would be permitted to provide foreign currency services without client or geographical restrictions; that within two years after accession foreign financial institutions could provide local currency services to Chinese enterprises, and within five years to all Chinese clients; that geographical restrictions on local currency business would be be phased out within five years; and that any existing non-prudential measures restricting ownership, operation, branching, and licences would be eliminated within five years after accession.[4]

China's commitments on insurance and insurance-related services covered life insurance, health, pension and annuities insurance, non-life insurance, reinsurance, and services auxiliary to insurance. A distinction was made between non-life insurers and life insurers. In summary, non-life insurers were permitted to establish as a branch or as a joint venture with 51 per cent foreign ownership and within two years after accession as a wholly-owned subsidiary; life insurers were permitted upon accession 50 per cent foreign ownership in a joint venture with the partners of their choice; non-life insurers were permitted to provide a full range of non-life insurance services to both foreign and domestic clients within two years after accession, and within three years health insurance, group insurance, and persons annuities insurance to foreigners and Chinese were allowed.[5]

China's commitments on securities covered A-share, B-share, and H-share businesses, membership of Chinese stock exchanges, and the establishment of joint ventures to conduct domestic securities investment fund management businesses. In summary, foreign services suppliers, upon China's accession, were permitted to establish joint ventures with foreign investment up to 33 per cent to conduct domestic securities investment fund management businesses, and within three years after China's accession, foreign investment could be increased to 49 per cent. Within three years after China's accession, foreign securities institutions were permitted to establish joint ventures with a foreign minority ownership not exceeding one-third of the equity to engage directly in underwriting A-shares and underwriting and trading B- and H-shares as well as government and corporate debts, and launching investment funds.[6]

The implementation of these commitments led to a corresponding reform of Chinese financial services law and regulations. Over the past decade, China has promulgated and amended a range of regulations and rules in banking, insurance, and securities,[7] which provide an improved regulatory environment suitable for the development of financial markets in post-WTO China. The establishment of the China Banking Regulatory Commission (CBRC) in April 2003, and the adoption in December 2003 of the Law of the People's Republic of China (PRC) on Banking Regulation and Supervision[8] moved China's financial regulatory system into a new and strengthened tripartite system, consisting of the CBRC, CIRC (China Insurance Regulatory Commission), and CSRC (China Securities Regulatory Commission). Between 2002 and 2009, amendments were made to the Law of the PRC on the People's Bank of China,[9] the Commercial Bank Law of the PRC,[10] the Insurance Law of the PRC,[11] and the Securities Law of the PRC[12] to codify policy changes for the post-WTO development of Chinese financial markets.

At the heart of China's implementation of its commitments relating to financial services is a question of whether China has indeed fulfilled its commitments in letter as well as in spirit. At the time of China's accession, a transitional review mechanism (TRM) was established, under which reviews of the implementation by China of its WTO commitments were to be held in each year for eight years, and a final review in year 10 or at an earlier date decided by the General Council.[13] With regard to financial services, the Committee on Trade in Financial Services was mandated as a body for the TRM reviews. Since the first such review in December 2002, the Committee had carried out eight annual TRM reviews by the end of 2009, in which WTO Member States had opportunities to voice their concerns and assess the progress made by China in complying with its WTO commitments. On the one hand, it was clear that China had indeed seriously implemented its commitments, but on the other hand, concerns were raised at the annual TRM reviews by Member States, questioning China's existing restrictive regulatory measures and practice in banking, insurance, and securities services, some of which are discussed below.

Banking

Since 1979 when the first representative offices of foreign banks were set up in China, China's banking market had been gradually opening up to foreign financial institutions. The opening-up process has moved from the cities within Special Economic Zones and coastal regions to cities in other parts of China, and from foreign currency business to local currency business. In complying with China's WTO commitments, China had phased out client and geographical restrictions to local currency business at the end of 2006, five years after China's accession to the WTO, by amending and promulgating the 2006 Foreign-funded Banks Regulations and the 2006 Foreign-funded Banks Implementing Rules. Foreign-funded banks could engage in local currency business without client and geographical restrictions, which is in contrast to the restrictions they were faced with prior to China's accession to the WTO. However, the foreign-funded banks, particularly those direct foreign bank branches, nevertheless face some other regulatory restrictions and limitations in various areas, such as the scope of business of foreign bank branches, the minimum working capital required for foreign bank branches, and the foreign equity ownership in Chinese banks.

Among the banking regulations and rules promulgated or amended since 2001, the Regulations of the PRC on the Administration of Foreign-funded Banks (2006 Foreign-funded Banks Regulations)[14] and the Rules for

Implementing the Regulations of the PRC on the Administration of Foreign-funded Banks (2006 Foreign-funded Banks Implementing Rules)[15] are two of the key regulations and rules in the implementation of China's WTO commitments in the banking industry. The 2006 Foreign-funded Banks Regulations was originally promulgated in 1994 under a different name,[16] and the amendments made in 2001 and 2006 were aimed at implementing the commitments China made for opening up the banking market; the 2006 Foreign-funded Banks Implementing Rules, on the other hand, were first issued by the People's Bank of China in 1994, and since then amendments have been made once before 2001, and three times after 2001 following the changes of the 2006 Foreign-funded Banks Regulations.[17]

In accordance with the 2006 Foreign-funded Banks Regulations, a 'foreign-funded bank' (*waizi yinhang*) can take one of the following three forms, namely, a wholly foreign-funded bank established by a single foreign bank or jointly by one foreign bank and other foreign financial institutions; a Chinese-foreign equity joint venture bank established jointly by foreign financial institutions and Chinese companies or enterprises; and a branch of a foreign bank. Besides these three forms, foreign banks can also establish a representative office in China.

By the end of 2008, foreign banks from twelve countries and regions had established 28 wholly foreign-funded banks (with 157 branches), two joint venture banks (with five branches and one subsidiary), and two wholly foreign-funded finance companies, and 116 branches had been set up by 75 foreign banks from 25 countries and regions (Table 1). The total assets of foreign banks in China amounted to over 1.3 trillion RMB and their share of the total banking assets was 2.16 per cent (Table 2). In addition, 237 representative offices had been established by 196 banks from 46 countries and regions.

The 2006 Foreign-funded Banks Regulations and the 2006 Foreign-funded Banks Implementing Rules restrict foreign bank branches from conducting retail RMB business to Chinese domestic depositors by setting out a one

Table 1. Status of foreign banks in China (as of end 2008)

	Foreign banks	Wholly foreign-funded banks	Joint venture banks	Wholly foreign-funded finance company	Total
Head offices of locally incorporated banks		28	2	2	32
Branches and subsidiaries of locally incorporated banks		157	6	0	163
Foreign bank branches	116	0	0		116
Total	116	185	8	2	311

Source: 2008 Annual Report of CBRC (English version), p. 47.

Table 2. Business outlets and assets of foreign banks in China (2004–2008)

Item/Year	2004	2005	2006	2007	2008
Operational banking entities*	188	207	224	274	311
Assets (100 million RMB)	5,823	7,155	9,279	12,525	13,448
Share of the total banking assets in China (%)	1.84	1.91	2.11	2.38	2.16

Source: 2008 Annual Report of CBRC (English version), p. 47.
Note: * Including head offices of locally incorporated banks, branches and subsidiaries of locally incorporated banks, and foreign bank branches.

million RMB threshold for time deposits.[18] In answering the questions and comments from WTO Member States concerning this restriction on foreign bank branches and its conflict with China's accession commitments, China's argument focused on the risks associated with direct branches and the need for the protection of interests of depositors in China. China argued that because branches were not legal entities, it was difficult for China, as a host country, to control the overall risk and to separate the risks arising from the parent foreign banks from those arising from their branches in China; it was therefore important for China to take prudential measures to protect Chinese depositors. China insisted that if a foreign bank wished to engage in more RMB local currency business, it could transform its branches in China into subsidiaries.

Applying the same prudential arguments, China keeps a high requirement of up to 300 million RMB for the minimum operating capital for foreign bank branches, as stipulated by the 2006 Foreign-funded Banks Regulations and the 2006 Foreign-funded Banks Implementing Rules.[19] WTO Member States were concerned with this requirement, commenting that such a requirement is much higher than minimum capital requirements in most other countries and effectively limits market access for foreign banks. China's explanation and argument were based on a prudential consideration which, it argued, takes into account the special organizational structure, the risks associated with the business scope of branches, and China's existing regulatory capacity.[20] Apart from this requirement, foreign bank branches are required to deposit 30 per cent of their operating capital in no more than three Chinese commercial banks within the territory of China in the form of interest-generating assets as designated by the banking regulators. Again, similar prudential arguments are applied to justify this deposit requirement.

The limitation on foreign equity ownership in Chinese banks is another area where concerns were raised among the WTO Member States. As of 2010, the percentage of equity investment in a non-listed or listed Chinese financial institution by an individual overseas financial institution is limited to 20 per cent, while the aggregate percentage of foreign investment of multiple overseas financial institutions could reach 25 per cent;[21] where the aggregate percentage of foreign investment of multiple overseas financial institutions exceeds 25 per cent, such a non-listed Chinese financial institution shall be regarded as a foreign-funded financial institution in supervision and administration, and a listed Chinese financial institution shall still be regarded as a Chinese financial institution. The WTO Member States regard this as a limitation on equity shareholdings in Chinese banks related to China's WTO commitments,[22] but China argued that it was a voluntary opening measure to allow foreign equity below 25 per cent to enter into Chinese financial sectors, insisting that foreign investment in Chinese-funded financial institutions did not relate to China's specific commitments.

The above examples show that the question really is, first, where to draw a line between prudential and non-prudential regulatory measures and practice, and second, whether a given regulatory measure, such as the 20 per cent cap on foreign equity ownership from a single foreign financial institution in Chinese banks, is or is not related to China's WTO commitments. At the time of the WTO accession, China committed that any existing non-prudential measures restricting ownership, operation, branching, and licences were to be eliminated within five years after accession. Apparently, the answer to the question whether China has fulfilled this commitment depends on an analysis of the line between prudential and non-prudential regulatory measures and practice under particular circumstances. In the aftermath of the 2007/8 global financial crisis, it is not difficult to appreciate China's intention to stick to the policy goal of financial security and the principle of sound and prudential market supervision, but an overly undue emphasis on the prudential principle would affect China's future legal and regulatory reforms in further opening up its banking services, ranging from e-card, provision and transfer of financial information, and financial data processing, to credit reference and analysis.

Insurance

Upon accession to the WTO, China promulgated the Regulations of the PRC on the Administration of Foreign-funded Insurance Companies (2001 Foreign-funded Insurance Companies Regulations)[23] to implement China's commitments in insurance services. In 2004, the Rules for Implementing Regulations of the PRC on the Administration of Foreign-funded Insurance Companies (2004 Foreign-funded Insurance Companies Implementing Rules) was issued,[24] which provided interpretations and further detailed rules for the implementation of the 2001 Foreign-funded Insurance Companies Regulations. This set of regulatory promulgation became a primary source of regulations for the implementation of China's commitments in insurance services. In addition, the Regulations on Administration of Insurance Companies, amended most recently in September 2009,[25] which apply primarily to domestic insurance companies, also apply to foreign-funded insurance companies.

At the statutory level, China's insurance law, the Insurance Law of the PRC, was first enacted in 1995 and has since been amended twice, in 2002 and 2009 respectively. The amendment in 2009, a long-awaited amendment, brought about a range of important and positive changes to the legal framework of China's insurance services, some of which were made in the light of the development of the post-WTO insurance services market. For example, the 2009 amendments removed the previous Article 103 of the 2002 Insurance Law of the PRC which gave priority to Chinese insurance companies for the re-insurance business. The removal of this restrictive requirement is consistent with the commitments China made for opening up its insurance services market and the implementation of the principle of national treatment.

In accordance with the 2001 Foreign-funded Insurance Companies Regulations, foreign-funded insurance companies (*waizi baoxian gongsi*) can take one of the following three forms: a joint venture insurance company established by foreign insurance companies and Chinese companies or enterprises, a wholly foreign-funded insurance company established by a foreign insurance company, and a branch insurance company established by foreign insurance companies.[26] Besides these three business forms, foreign insurance companies can establish representative offices. By the end of May 2007, 200 representative offices had been set up by 135 foreign insurance institutions.[27] By the end of October 2009, 52 foreign insurance companies from 15 countries and regions had established 277 foreign-funded insurance companies and branches in China;[28] by the end of May 2007, the insurance premium income of foreign-funded insurance companies was 14.21 billion RMB, which was 4.24 times higher than at the time of China's accession.[29]

One of the ongoing complaints from the WTO Member States has been about China's relatively high capital requirements for foreign insurers. China requires foreign-funded insurance companies to have an initial minimum paid-up capital of 200 million RMB for the establishment of the company, and an additional 50 million RMB for each branch of the company to be established. In response to the concerns of the WTO Member States, the 2004 Foreign-funded Insurance Companies Implementing Rules lowered the 50 million RMB to 20 million RMB and allowed no further capital requirement for new branches if the registered capital of joint venture foreign-funded or wholly foreign-funded insurance companies reached 500 million RMB. The move was regarded by the WTO Member States as an important and highly welcome step. Yet, since then no further reduction has been made, and the WTO Member States regard the current level of capital requirement as still 'indeed high in light of international standards'.[30] China's arguments have been threefold: first, there was no uniform international standard on this issue; second, the requirement applied equally to domestic and foreign insurers; and third, the requirement is for prudential reasons. This last prudential argument echoes that which was made in respect of its banking regulations.

Foreign insurers' branch or sub-branch licensing and geographic expansion is another area where the WTO Member States have expressed concern. China presented at the 2007 and 2008 annual TRM meetings that the review and approval of internal branch applications from foreign insurance companies had been done in accordance with China's accession commitments and was consistent with the national treatment requirement; the applications of Chinese and foreign companies were subject to the same regulation, which was fully in line with WTO rules; and the national treatment did not simply mean equal in quantity. The WTO Member States observed that Chinese domestic insurers could apply for several branch licences simultaneously, while foreign insurers were constrained to apply for one branch licence at a time; the approval process for foreign insurer branches was lengthier than for domestic insurers; foreign insurers experienced much greater difficulties than Chinese insurers; and foreign insurers did not enjoy the same rights in practice as Chinese domestic insurers regarding their ability to increase their number of branches. These concerns suggest that there may be a gap between what was prescribed in the regulatory procedures[31] and what was happening in practice.

In the early 1980s, foreign insurers began to establish representative offices in China, and in September 1992 the first foreign insurance company, AIA Shanghai Branch, was granted an insurance licence and established in Shanghai. The pace of the growth of China's insurance services industry, one of the fast-growing industries in the Chinese economy, accelerated in post-WTO period. The annual insurance premium income in 2006 in China had reached 564.1 billion RMB, which was 1.8 times the annual income in 2002, and was equivalent to the total income of the 19 years from 1980 to 1998.[32] In accordance with its WTO commitments, China had phased out various restrictions within two and three years of post-WTO accession, covering areas from the forms of foreign-funded insurance companies to client bases in different areas of insurance services. The legal and regulatory reforms since 2001, particularly the recent 2009 amendments made to the Insurance Law of the PRC created a legal and regulatory environment for developing China's insurance services market in the post-WTO era. But, on the other hand, as has been shown by the above two examples, foreign insurers still face restrictions of various kinds, which they argue should have been eliminated in accordance with China's commitments. One of the tasks of the regulatory reform for the foreign investment and participation in China's insurance services is to implement the amendments of the 2009 Insurance Law of the PRC, and in the long-term, the future development of China's insurance services market depends also on the further opening up of this sector beyond China's WTO commitments.

Securities

In implementing its WTO commitments in securities services, China promulgated in June 2002 the Rules on the Establishment of Fund Management Companies with Foreign Equity Participation (2002 JV Fund Company Rules) and the Rules on the Establishment of Securities Companies with Foreign Equity Participation (2002 JV Securities Companies Rules). The 2002 JV Fund Company Rules were later replaced by the Measures on Administration of Fund Management Companies for Securities Investment (2004 Measures on Fund Companies)[33] following the enactment in 2003 of the Securities Investment Fund Law of the PRC.[34] The 2002 JV Securities Companies Rules were amended in November 2007 and effective from January 2008.[35] As of 2010, the 2004 Measures on Fund Companies and the 2007 JV Securities Companies Rules, under the overall legal framework established by the 2005 Securities Law of the PRC, are a key set of regulations for the implementation of China's WTO commitments in opening up its securities market.

Starting from the early 1990s, China gradually opened up its securities market. A B-share pilot programme was launched at the end of 1991; joint venture securities companies and fund management companies were formed following the promulgation of the 2002 JV Securities Companies Rules and the 2002 JV Fund Company Rules; in November 2002, the so-called QFII (Qualified Foreign Institutional Investors) scheme was introduced on a trial basis, which allowed select QFIIs to invest in China's securities market.[36] By the end of 2008, China had approved eight joint venture securities companies and 33 joint venture fund management companies, and the foreign equity stake in 16 joint venture fund management companies had reached 49 per cent;[37] the Shanghai Stock Exchange and the Shenzhen Stock Exchange had each accepted three special members and 39 and 19 overseas securities brokers had been trading B-shares directly on the Shanghai and Shenzhen stock exchanges respectively; 160 representative offices had been established by foreign securities institutions and eight overseas stock exchanges opened their representative offices in Beijing; 109 companies had issued a total of 10.7 billion B-shares, raising 38.1 billion RMB; 76 overseas financial institutions had been granted QFII status and 13 banks, including five branches of foreign banks in China, had been licensed to provide QFII custody services.

As the above figures show, joint venture fund management companies, joint venture securities companies, and the QFII scheme are areas which have been undergoing positive growth and development since 2001, thanks to the implementation of China's WTO commitments in the securities services sector. On 9 July 2003, UBS, through its QFII agent Shenyin & Wanguo Securities Co. Ltd, completed the first purchase of A-shares, which marked the official entry of QFII funds into China's A-share market. In January 2004, the State Council issued a so-called '9-point blueprint' for the future development of China's capital market, which states: '[We must] strictly fulfil China's WTO commitments on opening up the securities services sector, to encourage qualified foreign securities institutions to invest in securities companies and fund management companies, and to continue trials of the QFII scheme.'[38]

These policies stated in the '9-point blueprint' in respect of opening up China's securities services in accordance with China's WTO commitments have been carried out since 2004. In 2006, the provisional regulations on the trial programme of the QFII scheme were amended, which updated the status of those regulations from provisional to a formal set of regulations. However, the degree of the opening up and the foreign participation in Chinese securities market are still limited, and restrictive rules and requirements are found in a range of areas, including, among others, the rules of the 2007 JV Securities Companies Rules that cap the holdings directly or indirectly by a single foreign investor of shares of a publicly traded Chinese securities company at 20 per cent, and the holdings by all foreign investors at 25 per cent, and the rules of the 2004 Measures on Fund Companies that require a fairly high level of capital contribution from foreign shareholders in a joint venture fund management company. The WTO Member States again expressed their concerns about these and other limitations and requirements in the regulation of foreign participation in Chinese securities market.

China's securities market, a young and emerging market, was dominated by individual investors and speculative investments in the 1990s at its early stage of development. The establishment of Chinese–foreign joint venture securities companies and fund management companies and the introduction of the QFII scheme helped improve standards of services and increase the competitiveness of Chinese companies, limited short-term speculation, and promoted medium- and long-term investments in the securities market. Both before and after China's WTO accession, a paramount concern about the securities market in China has been its potentially negative impact on the national economy and social stability, which contributed to the adoption of a cautious and restrictive approach in the regulation of the securities market, including the rather restrictive regulation of foreign participation in the Chinese securities market. The future development of the regulation of the Chinese securities market in the post-financial crisis era will undoubtedly still be shaped to a large degree by such a paramount concern from the Chinese government and securities regulators, but on the other hand, in order to develop the Chinese securities market into an efficient, open, and competitive global market compatible with the pace and scale of China's overall economic growth, it is necessary for China to consider reform of current regulations beyond its WTO commitments and open up further its securities market for foreign financial and securities institutions in their equity participation in Chinese securities companies and fund management companies as well as in their engagement in a broader range of securities and securities-related businesses, such as the trading of A shares, securities' credit rating services, and financial futures business.

Conclusion

China's WTO accession in 2001 and the subsequent implementation of China's commitments in banking, insurance, and securities services marked a new stage in the process of China's gradual and continuous opening up of its financial services markets over the past decades. Since then, China has promulgated and amended a range of laws, regulations, and rules in banking, insurance, and securities, with an aim of bringing China's financial services law and regulations into conformity with its WTO accession commitments. The reform of the banking, insurance, and securities laws and regulations provided an improved legal and regulatory framework for the post-WTO opening up and development of China's financial markets.

The financial markets in post-WTO China have undergone substantial liberalization as a result of the comprehensive commitments China made to grant broad market access to its financial markets as well as a corresponding progress to implement these commitments and to reform its domestic financial services law and regulations. On the other hand, foreign financial institutions are still subject to regulatory restrictions and limitations in various areas including, among others, requirements for a minimum level of operating capital, restrictions on the scope of business, and limitations on foreign equity ownership in Chinese financial institutions. Where to draw a line between prudential and non-prudential regulatory measures and practice, and whether a given regulatory measure is or is not related to China's specific WTO commitments, were two of the perennial issues presented in the assessment by the TRM annual reviews about whether China has fulfilled its WTO commitments relating to financial services liberalization.

A paramount concern of Chinese government and financial regulators, both before and after WTO accession, has been focused on financial security, which contributed to a cautious, risk control-oriented and restrictive regulatory approach. This is evident in the regulation of banking, insurance, and securities sectors, including the regulation of foreign investment and participation in these industries. In the aftermath of the worst financial crisis in nearly a century, China will undoubtedly continue to stick to the policy goal of financial security and the principle of prudential market supervision, which will in turn contribute to the shape of China's future legal and regulatory reforms in financial services law and regulations. However, it is necessary for China to balance the application of such prudential principles against the need to become an open, efficient, and competitive global market compatible with the pace and scale of China's overall economic growth in the 2000s and beyond.

Case study 12

EFFECTIVENESS OF LAWS—EVALUATING THE PATENT LAWS

Even with 'laws on the books', poor enforcement can diminish the effectiveness of laws. More than the letter of the formal laws themselves, how effective a legal regime is, is considerably more important in governing markets and indeed society as a whole. This is nowhere more apparent than patent laws in China.

Patent laws create intellectual property rights (IPRs) which would not otherwise exist, rendering these laws to be more important than most others in providing the legal protection that develops a particular market, in this case, the market for innovation that can drive economic growth which relies on technological progress. In China, patent laws exemplify the distinction between having laws on the books and effectiveness. Formally, China's patent laws fit the demands of a stringent set of international economic laws governing IPRs to the American standard. Yet, one of the most commonly heard complaints about China's legal system can be found in the area of IPRs where foreign firms fear the rampancy of piracy and theft of intellectual property despite the 'laws on the books'. With its incomplete legal system, characterized by weak enforcement, the effectiveness of patent laws in China is a particularly interesting question, especially as the number of patents has grown steadily during the 1990s and 2000s in spite of the often mentioned enforcement problems. It is thus a good case study of the effectiveness of laws, an important dimension in assessing China's legal and economic reforms as they pertain to business development and the growth of markets.

China's first patent law was passed at the same time as the start of urban reforms in the mid 1980s, making it one of the first economic statues on the books as China started down the path toward marketization. The Patent Law was enacted in 1984 and promulgated in 1985. In 2001, China adopted TRIPs (trade-related aspects of intellectual property rights) as part of its WTO obligations whereby its IPR standards (including copyright and trademarks) were harmonized with international rules.

Patent laws are promulgated through an IPR system that centres on a set of regulators which examine patent applications. Thus, as elsewhere, innovation is determined by the formal laws that establish IPRs as well as the regulatory system that effectuates those laws. Imperfection in the legal and regulatory system can refer to both the formal written laws or the regulations and regulators entrusted with their enforcement. The IPR system in China is centralized around the State Intellectual Property Office (SIPO) founded in 1980 as the Patent Office and renamed in 1998, the Trademark Office which started in 1982, and the 1985 agency, National Copyright Administration. The Ministry of Commerce has a department that deals with trade-related intellectual property issues and the Chinese People's Court system addresses enforcement in this national IPR system.

China's set of patent laws appears to largely meet the standards of international law, as do the processes of its IPR system. However, the adoption of laws does not necessarily imply effective enforcement, which has come under increasing scrutiny with the implementation of TRIPs. TRIPs should strengthen the IPR regime in China, particularly in terms of its enforcement provisions within the WTO. Approximately 10 per cent of cases brought before the Dispute Settlement Mechanism of the WTO relate to the TRIPs provisions, and the United States brought China before the WTO over the imperfect implementation of its IPR system.

Thus, China is challenged to adhere to strict standards that will permit less imitation and require more innovation by its own firms, both sources of technological progress necessary for economic growth. Imitation had been the main process which China and other developing countries have used to 'catch up' in growth. For instance, TRIPs removed the use of compulsory licensing which developing countries had imposed to license proprietary technology at low cost, since IPRs before TRIPs were not respected across national borders. In China's case, the reliance on technology transfer agreements in its joint ventures with foreign partners made innovation available to them, rather than licensed at monopoly prices under patents.

With an ineffective domestic legal system, patents should be stymied in spite of TRIPs which can only govern enforcement to a limited extent as it cannot revamp a country's entire legal system. Actions can only be brought before the WTO by countries, often urged by companies, but nevertheless, it is not an avenue that can be pursued by most firms aggrieved by the IPR regime. Nevertheless, there has been a rapid growth of patents in China starting in the 1990s when the system was reformed, and this sped up after WTO accession when the IPR system was further strengthened.

In 1985, there were just 138 patents, which rose exponentially to over 20,000 two decades later. It has grown strongly in line with China's overall impressive rate of growth, as seen in Figure 1. Curiously, the success rate of patent applications was roughly uniform across provinces despite vast disparities in wealth between the interior and the 'gold coast' which accounts for no less than three-quarters of GDP.

There is indeed evidence of wide variation among provinces both in terms of GDP and of patents, as seen in Table 1. When comparing patents granted per capita, the variation remains, so it is not a result of population differences. For instance, Shanghai is about 40 per cent richer than Beijing per capita, but Beijing has twice as many patents granted per capita. Comparing two of the poorest provinces, Anhui and Ningxia, with per capita incomes that are virtually identical, Ningxia has twice as many patents per capita. Although patents have grown alongside national income, provincial variations cannot be explained simply by reference to per capita GDP. Again, in terms of total patents granted in 2002, Guangdong holds 168,363. It is also one of the richest provinces, with a GDP per capita of 7,482 RMB. By contrast, Guizhou, the poorest province, has a per capita GDP of 1,574 RMB and just 10,038 patents. However, the rates of patent application to granted patents do not differ a great deal across provinces, suggesting that the reasons for the smaller number

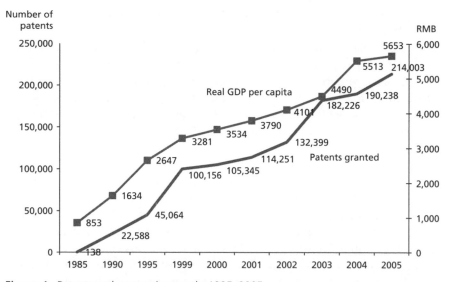

Figure 1. Patents and economic growth, 1985–2005

Source: China Statistical Yearbook, China Statistical Yearbook of Science and Technology.
Note: Patents granted are on the left axis while real GDP per capita (in 1990 RMB) is on the right axis.

of patents in Guizhou is not necessarily the result of fewer successful applications.

Table 2 gives the patent grant rate for selected years and the average success rate. The average rate of patents granted to patents filed is similar across provinces despite vastly different amounts of patents granted and levels of economic development. The lowest average success rate is 53 per cent in Hubei, while the highest is Yunnan with 68 per cent. Hubei is not the poorest province, while Yunnan is not the most innovative. Zhejiang is typically

Table 1. Patents and GDP per capita by province, 2002

Province	Patents filed	Patents granted	Success rate (granted/filed)	GDP per capita (RMB)	Patents granted per capita
Beijing	111,065	60,826	54.77%	14,205	0.004398
Tianjin	30,758	16,951	55.11%	11,174	0.001688
Hebei	44,434	26,750	60.20%	4,551	0.000399
Shanxi	16,012	9,308	58.13%	3,069	0.000284
Inner Mongolia	11,031	6,152	55.77%	3,661	0.000259
Liaoning	80,134	45,965	57.36%	6,484	0.001096
Jilin	27,594	14,672	53.17%	4,161	0.000545
Heilongjiang	39,194	20,986	53.54%	5,085	0.000551
Shanghai	76,986	36,474	47.38%	20,295	0.002260
Jiangsu	84,880	51,960	61.22%	7,185	0.000706
Zhejiang	91,119	56,119	61.59%	8,407	0.001217
Anhui	18,599	11,229	60.37%	2,891	0.000177
Fujian	36,523	22,150	60.65%	6,739	0.000644
Jiangxi	17,645	9,382	53.17%	2,910	0.000224
Shandong	93,836	54,088	57.64%	5,814	0.000598
Henan	39,953	22,367	55.98%	3,214	0.000234
Hubei	37,148	19,221	51.74%	4,154	0.000322
Hunan	49,366	26,336	53.35%	3,278	0.000399
Guangdong	168,363	111,874	66.45%	7,482	0.001437
Guangxi	19,183	10,581	55.16%	2,546	0.000221
Hainan	3,860	2,037	52.77%	4,030	0.000256
Sichuan	62,911	36,918	58.68%	3,586	0.000315
Guizhou	10,038	5,239	52.19%	1,574	0.000138
Yunnan	16,035	10,275	64.08%	2,586	0.000281
Shaanxi	27,775	16,397	59.04%	2,847	0.000637
Gansu	8,612	4,724	54.85%	2,243	0.000903
Qinghai	1,988	1,067	53.67%	3,208	0.000204
Ningxia	3,344	1,879	56.19%	2,898	0.000334
Xinjiang	10,459	5,917	56.57%	4,185	0.000315

Source: China Statistical Yearbook, China Statistical Yearbook for Science and Technology.
Note: GDP per capita has been deflated where 1990 is the base year.

Table 2. Patent grant rate by province, selected years

Province	1995	1998	2001	Average grant rate, 1995–2003
Beijing	63.27%	60.12%	51.31%	*57.02%*
Tianjin	62.74%	70.17%	59.36%	*58.82%*
Hebei	58.37%	63.43%	59.45%	*63.08%*
Shanxi	62.05%	60.19%	71.08%	*63.07%*
Inner Mongolia	64.14%	66.62%	68.35%	*59.29%*
Liaoning	61.70%	56.03%	59.20%	*58.06%*
Jilin	59.32%	53.62%	54.93%	*53.62%*
Heilongjiang	54.61%	56.29%	50.95%	*57.31%*
Shanghai	58.47%	68.27%	42.04%	*57.50%*
Jiangsu	59.17%	64.97%	59.49%	*63.39%*
Zhejiang	52.72%	63.19%	64.80%	*62.87%*
Anhui	55.95%	62.87%	62.49%	*61.49%*
Fujian	47.15%	68.32%	66.30%	*63.50%*
Jiangxi	50.50%	60.76%	56.19%	*55.69%*
Shandong	61.87%	54.32%	60.21%	*58.28%*
Henan	47.99%	57.00%	63.08%	*57.78%*
Hubei	50.75%	48.12%	50.99%	*52.70%*
Hunan	57.65%	50.33%	55.94%	*54.63%*
Guangdong	59.66%	79.47%	66.17%	*67.59%*
Guangxi	54.02%	64.77%	59.79%	*59.49%*
Hainan	59.02%	51.07%	77.69%	*59.67%*
Sichuan	63.37%	58.15%	86.86%	*63.81%*
Guizhou	48.75%	52.25%	67.58%	*56.22%*
Yunnan	59.33%	73.24%	75.13%	*67.65%*
Shaanxi	63.04%	65.53%	58.21%	*62.16%*
Gansu	47.07%	58.36%	69.75%	*59.00%*
Qinghai	65.00%	45.26%	62.35%	*56.45%*
Ningxia	65.68%	53.63%	56.07%	*59.45%*
Xinjiang	51.23%	47.24%	69.52%	*59.00%*

Source: China Statistical Yearbook, China Statistical Yearbook for Science and Technology.

viewed as the most driven by market forces and its rate of patent success lags behind that of Yunnan. When considering regions, the interior has the highest success rate of patent applications on average (61.04 per cent) followed by the coast (60.51 per cent) and the central region (57.28 per cent) despite incomes in the coastal region being more than double that of the central and interior regions over this period (5,447 RMB as compared with 2,426 RMB and 2,024 RMB, respectively). However, these figures are very close and, given the small number of patents in the interior, they probably reflect insignificant differences in success rates.

Success rate is one measure of the economic effect of IPR rules. Applications are considered nationally, and the patent grant rate is fairly uniform across provinces despite their very different levels of development. Although not conclusive, the substantial differences in patent outcomes must be viewed within the context of underlying economic differences across provinces, and not only as a result of institutional differences within the national patent system. Therefore, what produces patents should be considered within the context of relevant policies and factors that affect innovation, such as R&D spending, as well as the provincial environment including its level of education and extent of openness and market development. In other words, the effectiveness of patent laws is not simply a matter of the IPR system, legal system, or implementation process, which is insufficient to explain why some provinces have considerably more intellectual property than others when the grant or success rate is fairly uniform in a national framework.

Innovation as captured by patents has been increasing in China. The expectation of the implementation of TRIPs probably increases this incentive to patent, though interestingly the rate of successfully innovating is roughly the same as before WTO accession. Nevertheless, the amount of formally captured innovation in the form of patents is indeed growing in China despite a much criticized imperfect legal system. Moreover, in spite of vastly different levels of regional economic development, the patent laws in China have produced a steady rate of growth of patents across the country.

Despite similar grant rates, there are still vast differences among provinces in terms of their levels of innovation. Contextual factors and industrial and R&D policies probably play a role in explaining innovation. Yueh (2009b) finds that innovation in China is thus determined not only by the legal system but also by factors that affect the production of patents, such as R&D personnel, and provincial traits that could influence the propensity to innovate.

The determinants of innovation are difficult to assess for any country, and patents are an undermeasurement. China's patent laws have created these formal measures of innovation despite an imperfect IPR system. Moreover, it has a growing stock of patents which has accompanied its economic growth.

Therefore, China's patent laws have produced innovation despite their imperfections. Both domestic and foreign firms have patented rapidly during the 1990s and 2000s in spite of concerns about the IPR system and the protections afforded therein. The evidence suggests that R&D spending is a more important driver of patenting in China than it is in other countries (Yueh 2009b), which will ultimately influence long-run economic growth, even within a less than perfect legal system.

■ APPENDIX 8.1 COMPANY REGISTRATION IN CHINA

1. State-owned enterprises

State-owned enterprises refer to industrial enterprises where the means of production or income are owned by the state, including: (1) state-owned enterprises; (2) state-owned joint ventures; (3) state sole proprietorships.

2. Collectively-owned enterprises

Collectively-owned enterprises refer to industrial enterprises where the means of production are owned collectively, including urban and rural enterprises invested by collectives, and some enterprises which were formerly owned privately but have been registered in the industrial and commercial administration agency as collective units through raising funds from the public.

3. Joint stock cooperative enterprises

Joint stock cooperative enterprises refer to economic units set up on a cooperative basis with funding partly from members of the enterprise and partly from outside investment, where the operation and management is decided by the members who also participate in the production, and the distribution of income is based both on work (labour input) and on shares (capital input).

4. Joint operation enterprises

Joint operation enterprises refer to economic units that are established by joint investment by two or more corporate enterprises or institutions of the same or different types of ownership on a voluntary, equal, and mutual-beneficial basis. They include: (1) state-owned joint operation enterprises; (2) collective joint ventures; (3) state-owned and collective joint ventures.

5. Limited liability corporations

Limited liability corporations (LLCs) refer to economic units with capital from two to forty-nine investors and each investor bears limited liability to the corporation depending on his/her holding of shares, while the corporation bears liability to its debt to the maximum of its total assets.

The registered capital of a limited liability company shall be the amount of the paid-up capital contributions of all its shareholders as registered with the company registration authority. The amount of the initial investment contributed by all shareholders shall not be lower than 20 per cent of the registered capital or the minimum amount prescribed by the law. The minimum amount of the registered capital of a limited liability company shall be 30,000 RMB.

6. **Incorporated company**

An incorporated company refers to an economic unit with total registered capital divided into equal shares and raised through issuing stocks. Each investor bears limited liability to the corporation depending on the holding of shares, and the corporation bears liability to its debt to the maximum of its total assets.

Any of the following enterprises which are qualified as legal persons can register as such in accordance with the relevant provisions of the regulations:

(1) enterprises owned by the whole people;
(2) enterprises under collective ownership;
(3) jointly operated enterprises;
(4) Chinese–foreign equity joint ventures, Chinese–foreign contractual joint ventures and foreign-capital enterprises established within the territory of the People's Republic of China;
(5) privately operated enterprises;
(6) other enterprises required by the law to register as legal persons.

An incorporated company may be established either by sponsorship or public share offering. Establishment by sponsorship means the establishment of the company through subscription by the sponsors for all the shares to be issued by the company. Establishment by public share offer means establishment of the company through subscription by sponsors for part of the shares to be issued by the company, and public or targeted placement of the remaining shares. In order to establish an incorporated company, there shall not be fewer than 2 but no more than 200 sponsors, half of whom shall be domiciled in China. The registered capital of an incorporated company established by public share offer shall be the total amount of share capital subscribed for by all the sponsors and registered with the company registration authority. The initial capital contribution of all the sponsors shall not be less than 20 per cent of the registered capital.

7. **Private enterprises**

Private enterprises refer to economic units invested or controlled by holding the majority of the shares by natural persons who hire labourers for profit-making activities. Included in this category are private limited liability corporations, private shareholding corporations, private partnership enterprises, and private sole proprietorships.

(1) PRIVATE LIMITED LIABILITY CORPORATIONS

To constitute a private limited liability corporation means the investors shall bear the liabilities of the company according to their contributions and the company shall bear liability to its debt to the maximum of its total assets. The number of investors shall range from 2 to 30. The public issue of stocks shall not be permitted.

(2) PRIVATE PARTNERSHIP ENTERPRISES

A private partnership enterprise means the enterprise is funded according to an agreement, managed by partners, and whose profits and losses are born jointly by more than two persons. The partners shall assume unlimited joint liability for the debts of the enterprise unless registered as a limited liability partnership.

(3) PRIVATE SOLE PROPRIETORSHIPS

A private sole proprietorship refers to an enterprise which is invested in and managed by one person. The investor of the personally funded enterprise shall assume unlimited liability for the debts of the enterprise.

(4) PRIVATE INCORPORATED COMPANY

A private incorporated company is governed by the same parameters as non-private incorporated companies.

8. Enterprises with funds from Hong Kong, Macao, and Taiwan (HMT)

These are the firms from Hong Kong, Macao, and Taiwan which can take the forms of Chinese–foreign joint ventures or wholly foreign-owned companies and be constituted in any of the forms under the Company Law in permitted sectors.

9. Foreign-funded enterprises

These firms are from areas other than Hong Kong, Macao, and Taiwan; otherwise, the above definitions for HMT firms pertain.

▓ NOTES

1. See for details Section 7 of the Schedule of Specific Commitments on Services, WT/ACC/ CHN/49/Add.2. This and all the following WTO official documents are available at http:// www.wto.org.

2. WTO official document WT/L/432.

3. WTO official document WT/ACC/CHN/49.

4. See Section 7 of the Schedule of Specific Commitments on Services, supra note 1 at B: Banking and Other Financial Services (excluding insurance and securities).

5. See Section 7 of the Schedule of Specific Commitments on Services, supra note 1 at A: All Insurance and Insurance-Related Services.

6. See Section 7 of the Schedule of Specific Commitments on Services, supra note 1 at B: Securities.

7. For example, between late 2006 and early 2007 alone, a number of rules and regulations were adopted or amended covering banking, insurance, and securities including among others: Regulations of the PRC on the Administration of Foreign-funded Banks, Rules for Implementing the Regulations of the PRC on the Administration of Foreign-funded Banks, Administrative Measures for Insurance Licences Administrative Measures for Trust Companies Rules on Information Disclosure of Commercial Banks, Administrative Measures for Representative Offices of Foreign Stock Exchanges in China, Administrative Measures for Financial Leasing Companies.

8. Adopted at the 6th meeting of the State Council (SC) of the 10th National People's Congress (NPC) on 27 December 2003; amended at the 24th meeting of the SC of the 10th NPC on 31 October 2006 and effective as of 1 January 2007.

9. Adopted at the 3rd meeting of the 8th NPC on 18 March 1995; amended at the 6th meeting of the SC of the 10th NPC on 27 December 2003, effective as of 1 February 2004.

10. Adopted at the 13th meeting of the SC of the 8th NPC on 10 May 1995, amended at the 6th meeting of the SC of the 10th NPC on 27 December 2003, effective as of 1 February 2004.

11. Adopted at the 14th meeting of the SC of the 8th NPC on 30 June 1995; amended at the 30th meeting of the SC of the 9th NPC on 28 October 2002; and amended at the 7th meeting of the SC of the 11th NPC on 28 February 2009.

12. Adopted at the 6th meeting of the SC of the 9th NPC on 29 December 1998; amended at the 8th meeting of the SC of the 10th NPC on 27 October 2005 and effective as of 1 January 2006.

13. See paragraph 4 of section 18 of the Protocol on the Accession of the People's Republic of China, WTO official document WT/L/432.

14. The 2006 Regulations of the PRC on the Administration of Foreign-funded Banks was adopted by the State Council on 8 November 2006 and effective as of 11 December 2006. It replaced the Regulations of the PRC on the Administration of Foreign-funded Financial Institutions which was promulgated on 20 December 2001, upon China's accession to the WTO in December 2001.

15. The 2006 Rules for Implementing the Regulations of the PRC on the Administration of Foreign-funded Banks was adopted by the CBRC on 17 November 2006 and effective as of 11 December 2006. It replaced the Rules for Implementing Regulations on Administration

of Foreign-invested Financial Institutions which was promulgated by the CBRC on 26 July 2004.

16. The Regulations of the PRC on the Administration of Foreign-funded Financial Institutions, promulgated by the State Council on 25 February 1994 and effective as of 1 April 1994.

17. The Detailed Rules Implementing the Regulations of the PRC on the Administration of Foreign-funded Financial Institution (Trials), issued by the People's Bank of China on 29 March 1994; amendments were adopted respectively on 30 April 1996, 25 January 2002, 26 July 2004, and 24 November 2006.

18. Article 31 of the 2006 Foreign-funded Banks Regulations states that 'A branch of a foreign bank may take in time deposits from residents within China, each of which shall not be less than 1 million Yuan'; Article 50 of the 2006 Foreign-funded Banks Implementing Rules requires that the operating capital of a branch of a foreign bank 'shall not be less than 300 million Yuan or the equivalent value in a freely convertible currency, of which the RMB operating capital shall not be less than 100 million Yuan' if such a branch intends to engage in the foreign exchange business and RMB business.

19. See Article 8 of the 2006 Foreign-funded Banks Regulations, and Articles 49 and 50 of the 2006 Foreign-funded Banks Implementing Rules.

20. See the presentation made by the representative of China at the annual TRM meeting held on 1 December 2008, WTO official documents S/FIN/M/57 para. 33; see also the arguments made by the representative of China at the annual TRM meeting held on 12 November 2007, S/FIN/M/55 paras. 45, 46, and 47 (stating that '... countries were independent to set their own requirements for regulation based on different conditions in different periods. China was different from other Members in terms of its banking sector's structure, risk, market condition and regulatory framework, so it was improper to judge China with the criteria of other Members').

21. Article 8 of the 2003 Measures for the Administration of the Investment and Shareholding in Chinese-funded Financial Institutions by Foreign Financial Institutions (issued by CBRC on 8 December 2003 and effective as of 31 December 2003) states that 'The proportion of the investment or shareholding in a Chinese-funded financial institution by a single foreign financial institution may not exceed 20 per cent.'

22. See the comments made by the delegations of the European Communities and the United States at the annual TRM meeting held on 12 November 2007, WTO official documents S/FIN/M/55 para. 82 (European Communities) and para. 91 (United States).

23. The Regulations of the PRC on the Administration of Foreign-funded Insurance Companies was adopted by the State Council on 5 December 2001 and effective as of 1 February 2002.

24. The Rules for Implementing Regulations of the PRC on the Administration of Foreign-funded Insurance Companies was adopted by the CIRC on 15 March 2004 and effective as of 15 June 2004.

25. The Regulations on Administration of Insurance Companies was adopted by the CIRC and came into effect on 1 March 2000; amended on 15 March 2004 and effective as of 15 June 2004; amended on September 18 and effective as of 1 October 2009.

26. Article 2 of the 2001 Foreign-funded Insurance Companies Regulations.

27. Ibid.

28. See an interview with CIRC, 'CIRC Responsible Person was Interviewed by Journalist on Issues Concerning the Development of Foreign-funded Insurance Companies in China', 16 December 2009.

29. See the information provided by the representative of China at the annual TRM meeting held on 12 November 2007, WTO official document S/FIN/M/55 para. 34.

30. See the communication from Japan prior to the annual TRM meeting held on 1 December 2008, WTO official document S/FIN/W/64 para. 5.

31. For example, Articles 31 and 33 of the 2004 Foreign-funded Insurance Companies Implementing Rules prescribe a 20 day period for the CIRC to make a decision on the foreign insurers' application to set up a branch; and then the applicant, if approved, has six months to prepare for the establishment of the branch, which is followed by another 20 day period for the CIRC to make a final decision whether the branch would be licensed to commence the business.

32. See a speech by Wu Dingfu, Chairman of the CIRC, at the 2007 Annual International China Insurance Development Forum on 28 April 2007. The speech (in Chinese) is available at www.circ.gov.cn, last accessed on 22 February 2010.

33. The Measures on Administration of Fund Management Companies for Securities Investment was promulgated by the CSRC on 16 September 2004 and effective as of 1 October 2004.

34. Adopted at the 5th meeting of the SC of the 10th NPC on 28 October 2003 and effective as of 1 June 2004.

35. The amendments were adopted by the CSRC on 29 November 2007 and effective as of 1 January 2008.

36. The Provisional Measures on Administration of Securities Investment in China by Qualified Foreign Institutional Investors was promulgated by the CSRC and the People's Bank of China on 5 November 2002 and effective as of 1 December 2002; amended and changed from a set of provisional regulations to a formal set of regulations on 24 August 2006 and effective as of 1 September 2006.

37. See 2008 Annual Report of CSRC (English version) at pp. 39–40, and Tables 1 and 2 in the case study.

38. See Point 9, the Opinions of the State Council on Promoting Reform, Opening up, and Stable Development of the Capital Market, issued by the State Council on 31 January 2004.

■ BIBLIOGRAPHY

Acemoglu, D. and Johnson, S. (2005). 'Unbundling Institutions'. *Journal of Political Economy*, 113/5: 949–95.

——and Robinson, J. (2005). 'Institutions as the Fundamental Cause of Long-run Economic Growth', in P. Aghion and S. Durlauf (eds.), *Handbook of Economic Growth*. Amsterdam: Elsevier, 385–472.

Agarwal, A. (2006). 'FDI in Retail Hiked China's Textile Exports 700%: Study'. *Associated Chambers of Commerce and Industry of India Trade Report*, issued 18 January, pp. 1–6.

Ahlstrom, D., Bruton, G. D., and Yeh, K. S. (2008). 'Private Firms in China: Building Legitimacy in an Emerging Economy'. *Journal of World Business*, 43: 385–99.

ALB Legal News (2007). 'ICBC Eyes Foreign Targets and Foreign Advice?' 1 March, p. 5.

Alford, W. (2000). 'The More Law, the More...? Measuring Legal Reform in the People's Republic of China'. Stanford University, Stanford Center for International Development Working Paper No. 59.

Allen, F., Qian, J., and Qian, M. (2005). 'Law, Finance and Economic Growth in China'. *Journal of Financial Economics*, 77/1: 57–116.

American Textile Manufacturers Institute (2003). 'The China Threat to World Textile and Apparel Trade'. American Textile Manufacturers Institute Working Paper No. 1, pp. 1–23.

Appleton, S., Song, L., and Xia, Q. (2005). 'Has China Crossed the River? The Evolution of Wage Structure in Urban China During Reform and Retrenchment'. *Journal of Comparative Economics, Symposium: Poverty and Labour Markets in China*, 33/4: 644–63.

Asian Times (2006). 'Pricing the "Biggest IPO in History,"' 29 September, p. B1.

Automotive News Europe (2007). 'China's SAIC Motor, Nanjing Auto to Merge' (online), available from: <http://www.autonews.com/apps/pbcs.dll/article?AID=/20071227/COPY/497909481/1131/ANE> (created 27 December 2007, accessed 11 July 2009).

Bai, C.-E., Li, D. D., Qian, Y., and Wang, Y. (1999). 'Anonymous Banking and Financial Repression: How does China's Reform Limit Government Predation Without Reducing its Revenue?' Stanford University Department of Economics Discussion Paper No. 99014.

—— ——, and Wang, Y. (2000). 'A Multitask Theory of State Enterprise Reform'. *Journal of Comparative Economics*, 28/4: 716–38.

Baker, G., Gibbons, R., and Murphy, K. J. (2002). 'Relational Contracts and the Theory of the Firm'. *Quarterly Journal of Economics*, 117/1: 39–84.

Banerjee, A. and Duflo, E. (2007). 'What is Middle Class about the Middle Classes Around the World?' CEPR Discussion Paper No. 6613.

——and Newman, A. (1993). 'Occupational Choice and the Process of Development'. *Journal of Political Economy*, 101/2: 274–98.

Banner, S. (1997). 'What Causes New Securities Regulations?: 300 Years of Evidence'. *Washington University Law Review*, 75: 849–55.

Barboza, D. and Becker, E. (2005). 'Free of Quota, China Textiles Flood the U.S.' *New York Times*, 10 March, pp. C1–2.

BBC News (2004). 'Chinese Firm Buys IBM PC Business', available at: <http://news.bbc.co.uk/1/hi/business/4077579.stm> (created on 8 December 2004, accessed 18 February 2009).

——(2007). 'Fiat Teams up with Chery in China', available at: <http://news.bbc.co.uk/2/hi/business/6935107.stm> (created 7 August 2007, accessed 8 August 2009).

BBC News (2009a). 'China "to Block" Hummer Takeover', available at: <http://news.bbc.co.uk/1/hi/business/8120231.stm> (created 26 June 2009, accessed 11 July 2009).

—— (2009b). 'Lenovo Makes Third Yearly Straight Loss', available at: <http://news.bbc.co.uk/2/hi/business/8186822.stm> (created 6 August 2009, accessed 18 August 2009).

Beck, T., Demirguc-Kunt, A., and Levine, R. (2003). 'Law and Finance: Why does Legal Origin Matter?' *Journal of Comparative Economics*, 31/4: 653–75.

—— Levine, R., and Loayza, N. (2000). 'Finance and the Sources of Growth'. *Journal of Financial Economics*, 58/1–2: 261–300.

Bekkers, R., Duysters, G., and Verspagen, B. (2002). 'Intellectual Property Rights, Strategic Technology Agreements and Market Structure: The Case of GSM'. *Research Policy*, 31: 1141–61.

Bellabona, P. and Spigarelli, F. (2007). 'Moving from Open Door to Go Global: China Goes on the World Stage'. *International Journal of Chinese Culture and Management*, 1/1: 93–108.

Berger, A. N., Hasan, I., and Zhou, M. (2007). 'Bank Ownership and Efficiency in China: What Will Happen in the World's Largest Nation?' *Journal of Banking and Finance*, 18/1: 22–40.

Berkowitz, D., Pistor, K., and Richard, J. (2003). 'Economic Development, Legality, and the Transplant Effect'. *European Economic Review*, 47/1: 165–95.

Bernanke, B. (2004). *Essays on the Great Depression*. Princeton: Princeton University Press.

Bian, Y. (1994). '*Guanxi* and the Allocation of Urban Jobs in China'. *China Quarterly*, 140/December: 971–99.

Björkell, S. (2006). 'China's Airlines and the Development of the Nation's Aviation Industry'. Radio86 All About China (online), available from <http://www.radio86.co.uk/explore-learn/business-china/1060/chinas-airlines-and-the-development-of-the-nations-aviation-industry> (created on 10 November 2006, accessed on 2 July 2009).

Blanchflower, D. G. and Oswald, A. J. (1998). 'What Makes an Entrepreneur?' *Journal of Labor Economics*, 16/1: 26–60.

Borensztein, E. and Ostry, J. D. (1996). 'Accounting for China's Growth Performance'. *American Economic Review*, 86/2: 225–8.

Bosworth, D. and Yang, D. (2000). 'Intellectual Property Law, Technology Flow and Licensing Opportunities in the People's Republic of China'. *International Business Review*, 9/4: 453–77.

Boycko, M., Schleifer, A., and Vishny, R. (1996). *Privatizing Russia*. Cambridge, Massachusetts: MIT Press.

Brandt, L., Giles, J., and Park, A. (2003). 'Competition under Credit Rationing: Theory and Evidence from Rural China'. *Journal of Development Economics*, 71/2 463–95.

—— and Li, H. (2003). 'Bank Discrimination in Transition Economies: Ideology, Information, or Incentives?' *Journal of Comparative Economics*, 31/3: 387–413.

—— and Zhu, X. (2000). 'Redistribution in a Decentralized Economy: Growth and Inflation in China under Reform'. *Journal of Political Economy*, 108/2: 422–51.

Brock, G. J. (1998). 'Foreign Direct Investment in Russia's Regions 1993–95. Why so Little and Where has it Gone?' *Economics of Transition*, 6/2: 349–60.

Brooks, R. and Tao, R. (2004). 'China's Labour Market Performance and Challenges'. *China & World Economy*, 12/1: 21–35.

Bull, C. (1987). 'The Existence of Self-enforcing Implicit Contracts'. *Quarterly Journal of Economics*, 102/1: 147–59.

BusinessWeek (2007). 'China Car Industry's Export Ambitions', available at: <http://www.businessweek.com/globalbiz/content/may2007/gb20070503_461214.htm> (created 3 May 2007, accessed 18 June 2009).

Cai, H. and Treisman, C. (2005), 'Does Competition for Capital Discipline Governments? Decentralization, Globalization, and Public Policy'. *American Economic Review*, 95/3: 817–30.

Cao, C. (2004). 'Challenges for Technological Development in China's Industry: Foreign Investors are the Main Providers of Technology'. *China Perspectives*, 54/July–August: 80–105.

Chan, C. (2006). 'Goldman's Bet on ICBC May Pay Off Handsomely'. *International Herald Tribune*, 10 October, p. 8.

Chan, K., Wei, J. K. C., and Wang, J. (2004). 'Under-pricing and Long-term Performance of IPOs in China'. *Journal of Corporate Finance*, 10/3: 109–30.

Chandler, C. (2005). 'Rolling the Dice on China's Banks'. *Fortune Magazine*, 14 December, p. 18.

——(2006). 'Wall Street's War for China'. *Fortune Magazine*, 29 May, p. 21.

Chang, C. and Wang, Y. (1994). 'The Nature of the Township-Village Enterprise'. *Journal of Comparative Economics*, 19/3: 434–52.

Chang, T. S. (2006). 'Entry and Marketing Strategies of FDI Firms in China', in W. H. Yeung (ed.), *Handbook of Research on Asian Business*. Cheltenham: Edward Elgar, 162–81.

Che, J. and Qian, Y. (1998). 'Institutional Environment, Community Government, and Corporate Governance: Understanding China's Township-Village Enterprises'. *Journal of Law, Economics, and Organization*, 14/1: 1–23.

Chen, H. (2000). *The Institutional Transition of China's Township and Village Enterprises: Market Liberalization, Contractual Form Innovation and Privatization*. Aldershot: Ashgate.

Chen, Z. (2003). 'Capital Markets and Legal Development: The China Case'. *China Economic Review*, 14/4: 451–72.

Chery Automobile Co. Ltd's website: <http://www.cheryinternational.com/node/15> (accessed on 15 August 2009).

Chi, R. (2006). 'Structures and Functions of Small Enterprise Innovation Cluster: A Case Study in Zhejiang Province of China'. *18th WAITRO Biennial Congress Conference Proceedings*, Beijing, China, 1: 24–40.

China Briefing (2008). 'China's Textile Industry Slumps Amid Slowing Global Economy', 10 July, pp. 1–6, available at: http://www.china-briefing.com/news/2008/07/10/chinas-textile-industry-slumps-amid-slowing-global-economy.html (accessed 8 August 2008).

China Daily (2004). 'Policy Support Needed in ICBC Reform'. 13 August, p. 13.

—— (2005). 'Haier Remains the Most Favored Boss for Students' (20 July), http://www.chinadaily.com.cn/english/doc/2005-7/20/content_461755.htm (accessed 24 April 2008).

——(2006). 'Haier: Patent Pioneer', 16 October, p. 24.

——(2008a). 'China's Textile Exports Grow Faster, Clothing Exports Slower in First Five Months', 14 June, available at: http://www.chinadaily.com.cn/bizchina/2008-06/14/content_6760851.htm (accessed 24/8/2008).

——(2008b). 'China's Textile Export Growth Slows', 3 September, available at: http://www.chinadaily.com.cn/bizchina/2008-09/03/content_6994473.htm (accessed 24 November 2008).

——(2009). 'Geely's Volvo bid not "Worth it"', available at: <http://english.peopledaily.com.cn/90001/90778/90857/90860/6718762.html> (created 5 August 2009, accessed 9 August 2009).

China Toy Association (2009). 'Briefing of China Import & Export Toys in 2006 (Part I)', available at: <http://www.toy-cta.org/mail/en/9/> (accessed 23 August 2009).

Choo, C. and Yin, X. (2000). 'Contract Management Responsibility System and Profit Incentives in China's State-owned Enterprises'. *China Economic Review*, 11/1: 98–112.

Chow, G. C. (1994). *Understanding China's Economy*. London: World Scientific Publishing Co. Pte. Ltd.

Chun, C., McCall, B. P., and Wang, Y. (2003). 'Incentive Contracting Versus Ownership Reforms: Evidence from China's Township and Village Enterprises'. *Journal of Comparative Economics*, 31/3: 414–28.

Chung, O. (2008). 'China's Banks Churn out Profits'. *Asian Times*, 27 August, p. 16.

——(2009). 'China's Shoppers Learn "Made in China" Hazard'. *Asian Times Online*, 11 June 2009, available at: <http://www.atimes.com/atimes/China_Business/KF11Cb01.html> (accessed 18 August 2009).

Civil Aviation Administration of China (CAAC) (2009). Website, available at: <http://www.avbuyer.com.cn/en/> (accessed 12 May 2009).

Clarke, D. C. (2003a). 'Economic Development and the Rights Hypothesis: The China Problem'. *American Journal of Comparative Law*, 51/1: 89–111.

——(2003b). 'China's Legal System and the WTO: Prospects for Compliance'. *Washington University Global Studies Law Review*, 2/1: 97–118.

——(2003c). 'Corporate Governance in China: An Overview'. *China Economic Review*, 14/4: 494–507.

——(2007). 'China: Creating a Legal System for a Market Economy'. The George Washington University Law School Legal Studies Research Paper No. 396, pp. 1–32.

——Murrell, P., and Whiting, S. H. (2006). 'The Role of Law in China's Economic Development'. GWU Law School Public Law Research Paper No. 187.

Coase, R. (1937). 'The Nature of the Firm'. *Economica*, 4/16: 386–405.

Coffee, Jr., J. C. (2001). 'The Rise of Dispersed Ownership: The Roles of Law and the States in the Separation of Ownership and Control'. *Yale Law Journal*, 111/1: 1–82.

Cull, R. and Xu, L. C. (2005). 'Institutions, Ownership, and Finance: The Determinants of Profit Reinvestment among Chinese Firms'. *Journal of Financial Economics*, 77/1: 117–46.

Dam, K. W. (2006). *The Law–Growth Nexus—The Rule of Law and Economic Development*. Washington DC: The Brookings Institution.

Davies, H. (2006). 'Financial Reform in China: What Next?' Speech at the London School of Economics and Political Science, 17 October, pp. 1–20.

Denizer, C., Desai, R. M., and Gueorguiev, N. (1998). 'The Political Economy of Financial Repression in Transition Economies'. World Bank Policy Research Working Paper No. 2030.

Dewatripont, M. and Roland, G. (1995). 'The Design of Reform Packages under Uncertainty'. *American Economic Review*, 85/5: 1207–23.

Ding, F. (2004). 'Haier Group'. Department of Management Studies, University of Waterloo Working Paper 22(1), pp. 1–12.

——and Ning, L. (2007). 'China's Capital Market Reform: Problems and Prospects', in J. Wong and W. Liu (eds.), *China's Surging Economy: Adjusting for More Balanced Growth*. London: Routledge, 201–64.

Djankov, S., Miguel, E., Qion, Y., Roland, G., and Zhuravskaya, E. (2005). 'Who are Russia's Entrepreneurs?' *Journal of the European Economic Association*, 3/2–3: 587–97.

——, Qian, Y., Roland, G., and Zhuravskaya, E. (2006). 'Who are China's Entrepreneurs?' *American Economic Review Paper and Proceedings*, 96/2: 348–52.

Dong, Y. and Li, M. (2004). 'Mobile Communications in China'. *International Journal of Mobile Communications*, 2/4: 395–404.

Dong X.-Y. and Xu, L. C. (2008). 'The Impact of China's Millennium Labour Restructuring Program on Firm Performance and Employee Earnings'. *Economics of Transition*, 16/2: 223–45.

Dougan, M. (2002). *A Political Economy Analysis of China's Civil Aviation Industry*. New York and London: Routledge.

Dougherty, S., Herd, R. and He, P. (2007). 'Has a Private Sector Emerged in China's Industry? Evidence from a Quarter of a Million Chinese Firms'. *China Economic Review*, 18: 309–34.

Du, J. and Xu, C. (2006). 'Regional Competition and Regulatory Decentralization: Case of China'. Chinese University of Hong Kong, London School of Economics and Hong Kong University of Science and Technology Working Paper.

——(2009). 'Which Firms went Public in China? A Study of Financial Market Regulation'. *World Development*, 37/4: 812–24.

Du, Y. (2003). 'Haier's Survival Strategy to Compete with World Giants'. *Journal of Chinese Economic and Business Studies*, 14/1: 1–8.

Dyer, G. (2007) 'China: Tricky Path to Success in the World's Second-biggest Market'. *Financial Times*, available at: <http://www.ft.com/cms/s/1/21071dec-c8f0-11db-9f7b-000b5df10621.html> (created 6 March 2007, accessed 14 August 2009).

Economic Survey of China 2005: Reforming the Financial System to Support the Market Economy. Paris: OECD.

The Economist (2004). 'China's Global Brand? Haier's Purpose', 370(8367), p. 72.

——(2008). 'Western Banks Adrift in China I Needed: A Strategy', 30 December, p. 44.

Eichengreen, B., Rhee, Y., and Tong, H. (2007). 'China and the Exports of Other Asian Countries'. *Review of World Economics*, 143/2: 201–27.

Erickson, J. (2009). 'Mass Transit: The Best-Selling Cars in China'. *Time*, available at: <http://www.time.com/time/photogallery/0,29307,1909818,00.html> (created 2009, accessed 16 August 2009).

Evans, D. and Leighton, L. (1989). 'Some Empirical Aspects of Entrepreneurship'. *American Economic Review*, 79/3: 519–35.

Fan, G. (1994). 'Incremental Change and Dual-track Transition: Understanding the Case of China'. *Economic Policy*, 19/Supp: 99–122.

——(2003). 'China's Nonperforming Loans and National Comprehensive Liability'. *Asian Economic Papers*, 2/1: 145–52.

Fan, J. P. H., Monk, R., Xu, L. C., and Yeung, B. (2009). 'Institutions and Foreign Direct Investment: China versus the Rest of the World'. *World Development*, 37/4: 852–65.

Financial Times (2005). 'Nanjing wins Rover for £50m' (online), available at: <http://www.ft.com/cms/s/0/89f18166-fb16-11d9-a0f6-00000e2511c8.html> (created 23 July 2005, accessed 13 July 2009).

——(2007). 'Chinese Carmakers Moot Merger', (online) available at: <http://www.ft.com/cms/s/0/f1c7c594-3df8-11dc-8f6a-0000779fd2ac.html> (created 29 July 2007, accessed 13 July 2009).

——(2009a). 'Opel/Beijing Automotive' (online), available at: <http://www.ft.com/cms/s/1/eddfa8c6-6ad2-11de-861d-00144feabdc0.html> (created 7 July 2009, accessed 11 July 2009).

——(2009b). 'Chinese Company to buy Hummer', (online) available at: <http://www.ft.com/cms/s/0/345a9a70-4f69-11de-a692-00144feabdc0.html?nclick_check–1> (created 3 June 2009, accessed 11 July 2009).

——(2009c). 'Chinese Hummer Takeover in Doubt' (online), available at: <http://www.ft.com/cms/s/0/3da2da8e-53c4-11de-be08-00144feabdc0.html> (created 8 June 2009, accessed 11 July 2009).

——(2009d). 'China Car Sales', (online) available at: <http://www.ft.com/cms/s/1/fc31cdb6-6c60-11de-a6e6-00144feabdc0.html> (created 9 July 2009, accessed 18 July 2009).

Flannery, R. (2001). 'China Goes Global'. *Forbes*, 8 June, p. 43.

Franks, J. R., Mayer, C., and Rossi, S. (2009). 'Ownership: Evolution and Control'. *Review of Financial Studies*, 22/10: 4009–56.

Frye, T. and Zhuravskaya, E. (2000). 'Rackets, Regulation and the Rule of Law'. *Journal of Law, Economics and Organization*, 16/2: 478–502.

Fu, X. and Balasubramanyam, V. N. (2003). 'Township and Village Enterprises in China'. *Journal of Development Studies,* 39/4, 29–46.

Gallagher, K. (2006). *China Shifts Gears: Automakers, Oil, Pollution, and Development.* Cambridge, Massachusetts: MIT Press.

Garnaut, R., Song , L., Yao, Y., and Wang, X. (2001). *The Emerging Private Enterprise in China.* Canberra: National University of Australia Press.

—— —— —— ——(2003). *Study on Restructured SOEs (Gaizhi) in China.* Washington, DC: World Bank.

Geely Holding Group's website: <http://www.geely.com/general/memorabilia.html?year=1986–2003&keyword=> (accessed 15 August 2009).

Geuze, M. and Wager, H. (1999). 'WTO Dispute Settlement Practice Relating to the TRIPS Agreement'. *Journal of International Economic Law,* 2: 347–84.

Glaeser, E., La Porta, R., Lopez-de-Silanes, F., and Shleifer, A. (2004). 'Do Institutions Cause Growth?' *Journal of Economic Growth,* 9/3: 271–303.

Gompers, P, Lerner, J., and Scharfstein, D. (2005). 'Entrepreneurial Spawning: Public Corporations and the Genesis of New Ventures, 1986–1999'. *Journal of Finance,* 60/2: 577–614.

Goswani, R. (2006). 'Socialist China Creates Capitalist History through ICBC,' *Blogger News Network,* http://www.bloggernews.net/11011 (accessed 23 April 2008).

Granger, C. (1969). 'Investigating Causal Relationships by Econometric Models and Cross-spectral Methods'. *Econometrica,* 37: 424–38.

Greene, W. H. (2003). *Econometric Analysis.* New Jersey: Pearson.

Greif, A. (1993). 'Contract Enforceability and Economic Institutions in Early Trade: The Maghribi Traders' Coalition'. *American Economic Review,* 83/3: 525–48.

Groves, T., Hong, Y., McMillan, J., and Naughton, B. (1995). 'China's Evolving Managerial Market'. *Journal of Political Economy,* 103/4: 873–92.

Guangdong Huawei Toys Craft Co. Ltd (2008). Guanghai Huawei's website: <http://www.huaweitoys.com/en/about.asp> (accessed 18 August 2009).

Guo, G. (2008a). 'Clothing and Textiles: Benefits Down Evidently While Export and Import Grew Slowly'. China National Textile and Apparel Council Press Release, 18 August, pp. 1–2.

——(2008b). 'Clothing and Textiles: Key Strengths Behind Zhongwang's Success'. China National Textile and Apparel Council Press Release, 16 September, pp. 1–2.

Haier (2006a). '2005 Haier Annual Report'. www.haier.com/reports, accessed 24 March 2008, pp. 1–88.

——(2006b). '2006 Financial Statement'. www.haier.com/reports, accessed 24 March 2008, pp. 1–15.

——(2006c). 'Background Information'. www.haier.com/reports, accessed 24 March 2008, pp. 1–2.

——(2006d). 'Company Facts'. www.haier.com/reports, accessed 24 March 2008, pp. 1–2.

Hamermesh, L. A. (2006). 'The Policy Foundations of Delaware Corporate Law'. *Columbia Law Review,* 106/7: 1749–92.

Hansmann, H. and Kraakman, R. (2001). 'The End of History for Corporate Law?' *Georgetown Law Journal,* 89: 439–68.

Hart, O., Shleifer, A., and Vishny, R. W. (1997). 'The Proper Scope of Government: Theory and an Application to Prisons'. *Quarterly Journal of Economics,* 112/4: 1127–61.

Harwit, E. (1995). *China's Automobile Industry: Policies, Problems, and Prospects.* Armonk, N.Y. and London: Sharpe.

Hennock, M. (2004). 'Lenovo: The Making of a Legend?' *BBC News*, available at: <http://news.bbc.co.uk/1/hi/business/4078301.stm> (created 8 December 2004, accessed 18 February 2009).

Hille, K. (2009a). 'Lenovo Chief Replaced in Reshuffle'. *Financial Times*, available at: <http://www.ft.com/cms/s/0/380f96ea-f3f0-11dd-9c4b-0000779fd2ac.html> (created 6 February 2009, accessed 1 August 2009).

——(2009b). 'Back to the Future for Lenovo'. *Financial Times*, available at: <http://www.ft.com/cms/s/0/461f3822-f859-11dd-aae8-000077b07658.html> (created 12 February 2009, accessed 1 August 2009).

——(2009c). 'Lenovo Seeks Expansion Loans'. *Financial Times*, available at: <http://www.ft.com/cms/s/0/881b770c-09ef-11de-add8-0000779fd2ac.html> (created 6 March 2009, accessed 1 August 2009).

——(2009d). 'Lenovo Predicts further Gloom and Loss'. *Financial Times*, available at: <http://www.ft.com/cms/s/0/0c930dc4-45fa-11de-803f-00144feabdc0.html> (created 21 May 2009, accessed 1 August 2009).

——(2009e). 'Lenovo Beats Expectations on China's Strength'. *Financial Times*, available at: <http://www.ft.com/cms/s/0/530f9822-822b-11de-9c5e-00144feabdc0.html> (created 6 August 2009, accessed 7 August 2009).

——Betts, P., and Hill, A. (2009). 'Lenovo Faces Battle to Recover Market Share'. *Financial Times*, available at: <http://www.ft.com/cms/s/0/fd455810-f868-11dd-aae8-000077b07658.html>(created 11 February 2009, accessed 1 August 2009).

——and Lau, J. (2009). 'Chinese Group Offers Stake in Lenovo Parent'. *Financial Times*, available at: <http://www.ft.com/cms/s/0/234e4b24-8573-11de-98de-00144feabdc0.html> (created 10 August 2009, accessed 11 August 2009).

Ho, P. (2006). *Institutions in Transition: Land Ownership, Property Rights and Social Conflict in China*. Oxford: Oxford University Press.

Holtz-Eakin, D., Joulfaian, D., and Rosen, H. S. (1994). 'Entrepreneurial Decisions and Liquidity Constraints'. *Rand Journal of Economics*, 25/2: 334–47.

Holz, C. (2003). *China's Industrial State-Owned Enterprises: Between Profitability and Bankrupcy*. Singapore: World Scientific Publishing Co. Pte. Ltd.

Hong, E. and Sun, L. (2006). 'Dynamics of Internationalization and Outward Investment: Chinese Corporations' Strategies'. *China Quarterly*, 187: 610–34.

Hong Kong Commercial Newspapers Co. Ltd (2009). 'Legendary Person in the Toy Industry,' March 5th, available at: <http://www.hkcd.com.hk/content/2009-03/05/content_2259997.htm> (accessed 18 August 2009).

Horwitz, M. J. (1992). *The Transformation of American Law, 1870–1960: The Crisis of Legal Orthodoxy*. Oxford: Oxford University Press.

Hu, A. G. Z., Jefferson, G. H., and Qian, J. (2005). 'R&D and Technology Transfer: Firm Level Evidence from Chinese Industry'. *Review of Economics and Statistics*, 87/4: 780–6.

Huang, J. and Rozelle, S. (1996). 'Technological Change: The Re-discovery of the Engine of Productivity Growth in China's Rural Economy'. *Journal of Development Economics*, 49: 337–69.

Huang, Y. (2003). 'One Country, Two Systems: Foreign-invested Enterprises and Domestic Firms in China'. *China Economic Review*, 14/4: 404–16.

——(2006). *Selling China*. Cambridge: Cambridge University Press.

——and Woo, W. T. (2004), 'Free to Lose: Autonomy and Incentives in Chinese State Enterprises'. Australian National University mimeo.

Hutchens, W. (2003). 'Private Securities Litigation in the People's Republic of China: Material Disclosure about China's Legal System?' *University of Pennsylvania Journal of International Economic Law*, 24/3: 599–689.

Ianchovichina, E. and Walmsley, T. (2005). 'Impact of China's WTO Accession on East Asia'. *Contemporary Economic Policy*, 23/2: 261–77.

ICBC Hong Kong (2006a). 'ICBC and Goldman Sachs Start Their Strategic Cooperation'. *ICBC Press Release*, 22 March, http://www.icbc.com/releases (accessed 23 April 2008).

——(2006b). 'ICBC IPO Documentation Appendix VII: Summary of Principal Legal and Regulatory Provisions'. *ICBC Press Release*, 22 March, http://www.icbc.com/releases (accessed 23 April 2008), pp. 1–29.

——(2006c). 'ICBC IPO Documentation Appendix: Risk Factors'. *ICBC Press Release*, p. 16.

Ikenson, D., Hufbaue, G. C., and Tang, Y. (2004). 'How Should China and America Respond to the Age without Textile Quotas?' Cato Institute Center for Trade Policy Studies Working Paper, 27 September, pp. 1–18.

Imam, M. (2004). 'The Chinese Interbank Markets: Cornerstone of Financial Liberalization'. *China & World Economy*, 12/5: 17–33.

Information Center of Chenghai Shantou (2009a). Chenghai Government's website: <http://www.gdchenghai.gov.cn/english/brief_introduct.html> (accessed 18 August 2009).

——(2009b). 'Historical Developments' (in Chinese), available at: <http://www.gdchenghai.gov.cn/chgk/lsyg.htm> (accessed 23 August 2009).

InterChina Investment Consulting Company (1997). *The Automotive Sector of China: Vision and Reality*. London: Economist Intelligence Unit.

Jane's Information Group (1997). *China's Aerospace Industry: The Industry and its Products Assessed*. Coulsdon: Jane's Information Group.

Jefferson, G. H. (1993). 'Are China's Rural Enterprises Outperforming State-owned Enterprises?' Research Paper No. CH-RPS#24. Washington DC: The World Bank.

——and Rawski, T. (2002). 'China's Emerging Market for Property Rights'. *Economics of Transition*, 10/2: 586–617.

————and Zheng, Y. (1992). 'Growth, Efficiency, and Convergence in China's State and Collective Industry', *Economic Development and Cultural Change*, 40/2: 239–66.

——and Su, J. (2006). 'Privatization and Restructuring in China: Evidence from Shareholding Ownership, 1995–2001'. *Journal of Comparative Economics*, 34/1: 146–66.

Jia, C. (2007). 'The Effect of Ownership on the Prudential Behavior of Banks—the Case of China'. *Journal of Banking and Finance*, 18/1: 41–52.

Jian, S. (2005). 'A Flowchart Approach to the Haier Household Electrical Appliances Industrial Cluster'. Institute of Developing Economies Working Paper Series No. 139, Tokyo, pp. 50–119.

Jin, H., Qian, Y., and Weingast, B. R. (2005). 'Regional Decentralization and Fiscal Incentives: Federalism, Chinese Style'. *Journal of Public Economics*, 89/9–10: 1719–42.

Jing, Z. (2005). 'An Analysis of the Barriers in Free Trade and Countermeasures'. *Problems in International Trade*, 1/1: 8–16 (in Chinese).

Jones, W. C. (2003). 'Trying to Understand the Current Chinese Legal System', in C. S. Hsu (ed.), *Understanding China's Legal System: Essays in Honor of Jerome A. Cohen*. New York and London: New York University Press, 7–45.

Kaufmann, D., Kraay, A., and Mastruzzi, M. (2007). 'Governance Matters, VI: Governance Indicators for 1996–2006'. World Bank Policy Research Working Paper No. 4280.

Keck, E. (2001). 'Commercial Aviation Takes Off'. *China Business Review*, 28: 14–17.

Kimura, K. (2007). Growth of the Firm and Economic Backwardness: A Case Study and Analysis of China's Mobile Handset Industry'. Institute of Developing Economies Discussion Paper No. 130, pp. 1–28.

King, A. G. (1974). 'Occupational Choice, Risk Aversion, and Wealth'. *Industrial and Labor Relations Review*, 27/4: 586–96.

King, J. K. and Lin, Y. (2007). 'The Decline of Township-and-Village Enterprises in China's Economic Transition'. *World Development*, 35/4, 569–84.

Kingsbury, K. (2007). 'Eyes on the Skies'. *Time*, 11 October 2007.

Kipnis, A. (1997). *Producing Guanxi: Sentiment, Self, and Subculture in a North Chinese Village*. Durham and London: Duke University Press.

Knappe, M. (2003). 'Textiles and Clothing: What Happens after 2005?' International Trade Forum White Paper No. 1, pp. 1–28.

Knibb, Gormezano, & Partners (1997). *The Chinese Automotive Industry: Pitfalls and Opportunities to 2010*. London: FT Automotive, Pearson Professional.

Knight, J. and Yueh, L. (2004). 'Job Mobility of Residents and Migrants in Urban China'. *Journal of Comparative Economics*, 32/4: 637–60.

——(2008). 'The Role of Social Capital in China's Urban Labour Market'. *Economics of Transition*, 16/3: 389–414.

Komter, A. (2005). *Social Solidarity and the Gift*. Cambridge: Cambridge University Press.

Koo, A. Y. C. (1990). 'The Contract Responsibility System: Transition from a Planned to a Market Economy'. *Economic Development and Cultural Change*, 38/4: 797–820.

Kornai, J. (1992), *The Socialist System*. Oxford: Clarendon Press.

Kraakman, R., Armour, J., Davies, P., Enriques, L., Hansmann, H. B., Hertig, G., Hopt, K. J., Kanda, H., and Rock, E. B. (2004). *The Anatomy of Corporate Law*. Oxford: Oxford University Press.

Kraemer, K. and Dedrick, J. (2001). 'Creating a Computer Industry Giant: China's Industrial Policies and Outcomes in the 1990s'. Center for Research on Information Technology and Organization, University of California at Irvine Working Paper 235.

Krugman, P. (ed.) (2000). *Currency Crises*. Chicago: University of Chicago Press.

Kudrna, Z. (2007). 'Banking Reform in China: Driven by International Standards and Chinese Specifics'. *RePEc Munich*, Munich Personal RePEc Archive Paper No. 7320, pp. 1–46.

La Porta, R., Lopez-de-Silanes, F., Shleifer, A., Vishney, R. W. (1997). 'Legal Determinants of External Finance'. *Journal of Finance*, 54/20: 1131–50.

—— —— —— ——(1998). 'Law and Finance'. *Journal of Political Economy*, 106/6: 1113–55.

Lardy, N. R. (1998). *China's Unfinished Economic Revolution*. Washington DC: Brookings Institution Press.

——(2002). *Integrating China into the Global Economy*. Washington DC: Brookings Institution Press.

Lau, L. J., Qian, Y., and Roland, G. (2001). 'Reform Without Losers: An Interpretation of China's Dual-track Approach to Transition'. *Journal of Political Economy*, 108/1: 120–43.

Lenovo Group (2004). 'Lenovo to Acquire IBM Personal Computing Division', press release (online), available at: <http://www.lenovo.com/news/us/en/2005/04/ibm_lenovo.html> (created on 7 December 2004, accessed on 18 February 2009).

——China website: <http://www.lenovo.com.cn/> (accessed on 18 February 2009).

——Hong Kong website: <http://www.lenovo.com/hk/en/> (accessed on 18 February 2009).

Levine, R. (1997). 'Financial Development and Economic Growth: Views and Agenda'. *Journal of Economic Literature*, 35/June: 688–726.

——(1998). 'The Legal Environment, Banks, and Long-run Economic Growth'. *Journal of Money, Credit, and Banking*, 30/3 (Part 2): 596–613.

Li, D. (2001). 'Beating the Trap of Financial Repression in China'. *Cato Journal*, 21/1: 77–90.

Li, H. and Zhou, L. (2005). 'Political Turnover and Economic Performance: The Incentive Role of Personnel Control in China'. *Journal of Public Economics*, 89/9–10: 1743–62.

Li, S. and Sato, H. (2006). 'Introduction', in S. Li and H. Sato (eds.), *Unemployment, Inequality and Poverty in Urban China*. London and New York: Routledge, 1–16.

Li, W. and Putterman, L. (2008). 'Reforming China's SOEs: An Overview'. *Comparative Economic Studies*, 50: 353–80.

Li, Y. (2009). 'The Competitive Advantage of Chenghai's Toy Industry'. *Alibaba News Online*, 2 April, available at: <http://info.china.alibaba.com/news/detail/v5000180-d1004738293.html> (accessed 18 August 2009).

License Union (2008). 'Information on Brands', available at: <http://www.sqlm.com.cn/Band/ShowBand.asp?ID=505> (accessed 23 August 2009).

Lin, J. Y. (1992). 'Rural Reforms and Agricultural Growth in China'. *American Economic Review*, 82/1: 34–51.

——(2007). 'Developing Small and Medium Banks to Improve Financial Structure'. Peking University, China Center for Economic Research Working Paper (in Chinese).

——Cai, F., and Zhou, L. (2003). *The China Miracle: Development Strategy and Economic Reform*. Hong Kong: Chinese University Press.

Lin, T. (2007). 'Lessons from China: Haier Group Has Achieved Extreme Success through Unique Performance-Management Systems'. *Strategic Finance*, 13: 1–8.

Lin, X. and Zhang, Y. (2007). 'Bank Ownership Reform and Bank Performance in China'. *Journal of Banking and Finance*, 12/1: 1–10.

Linton, K. (2006). 'Access to Capital in China: Competitive Conditions for Foreign and Domestic Firms'. US International Trade Commission Occasional Paper, pp. 1–17.

Liu, C. (2007). 'An Executive's Note. Lenovo: An Example of Globalization of Chinese Enterprises'. *International Business Studies*, 38: 573–7.

Liu, H. and Li, K. (2002). 'Strategic Implications of Emerging Chinese Multinationals: The Haier Case Study'. *European Management Journal*, 20/6: 699–706.

Liu, M. (2004). 'Improving Corporate Governance in Chinese Banks'. *The China Conference: Capital Markets and Corporate Governance*, 1 December, conference proceedings available online: http://www.cbrc.gov.cn/english/home/jsp/docView.jsp?docID=1026, pp. 1–19.

Liu, M and Yu, J. (2008). 'Financial Structure, Development of Small and Medium Enterprises, and Income Distribution in the People's Republic of China'. *Asian Development Review*, 25/1–2: 137–55.

Liu, X. L. (2006). 'Path-Following or Leapfrogging in Catching-Up: The Case of Chinese Telecommunication Equipment'. Chinese Academy of Science Working Paper WP(1), pp. 1–46.

Lo, W. C. (2001). *A Retrospect on China's Banking Reform*. London: Routledge.

Lu, F. S. and Yao, Y. (2009). 'The Effectiveness of Law, Financial Development, and Economic Growth in an Economy of Financial Repression: Evidence from China'. *World Development*, 37/4: 736–77.

Lu, X. (2007). 'Financial Development, Capital Accumulation and Productivity Improvement: Evidence from China'. *Journal of Chinese Economic and Business Studies*, 5/3: 227–42.

Lu, Z. (2008). 'Capital Growth'. *Dalian News*, 13 May, p. 9.

Lubman, S. (2000). *Bird in a Cage: Legal Reform in China after Mao*. Stanford: Stanford University Press.

MacDonald, S., Pan, S., Somwaru, A., and Tuan, F. (2004). 'China's Role in World Cotton and Textile Markets'. *American Agricultural Economics Association Annual Meeting Conference Proceedings*, 1/1: 101–29.

McKinnon, R. (1973). *Money and Capital in Economic Development.* Washington, DC: Brookings Institution.

——(1993). *The Order of Economic Liberalization: Financial Control in the Transition to a Market Economy.* Baltimore: Johns Hopkins University Press

Maddison, A. (2001). *The World Economy: A Millennial Perspective.* Paris: OECD.

Martin, M. (2007). 'U.S. Clothing and Textile Trade with China and the World: Trends since the End of Quotas'. *Congressional Reporting Service Report,* Report No. RL34108, pp. 1–32.

Merx, K. and Chan, C. (2009). 'GM to Sell Hummer to China's Tengzhong, Helping Shed Brands'. *Bloomberg,* available at: <http://www.bloomberg.com/apps/news?pid=20601087&sid=aaHNTf_69dGY#> (created 3 June 2009, accessed 13 July 2009).

Miller, M. (1977). 'Debt and Taxes'. *Journal of Finance,* 32/2, 261–75.

Ministry of Information Industry (China) (2008). *Chinese Telecommunications Industry Statistics,* available at: http://mii.gov.cn (accessed 25 September 2008), pp. 1–4.

Mohapatra, S., Rozelle, S., and Goodhue, R. (2007). 'The Rise of Self-employment in Rural China: Development or Distress?' *World Development,* 35/1: 163–81.

Montinola, G., Qian, Y., and Weingast, B. R. (1995). 'Federalism, Chinese Style: The Political Basis for Economic Success in China'. *World Politics,* 48/1: 50–81.

Moon, H. C. and Yu, Y. L. (2004). 'The Competitiveness of China's Telecommunications Industry before and after China's Accession to the WTO'. *Global Economic Review,* 33/2: 79–98.

Moore, T. (2002). *China in the World Market: Chinese Industry and International Sources of Reform in the Post-Mao Era.* Cambridge: Cambridge University Press.

Moran, T. H. (2000). 'The Product Cycle Model of Foreign Direct Investment and Developing Country Welfare'. *Journal of International Management,* 6: 297–311.

Mu, Q. and Lee, K. (2005). 'Knowledge Diffusion, Market Segmentation and Technological Catch-Up: The Case of the Telecommunication Industry in China'. *Research Policy,* 34: 759–83.

Mu, Y. (2007). 'Chinese Bank's Credit Risk Assessment'. Doctoral dissertation, University of Stirling, pp. 1–420.

Muroi, H. (2005). 'The Haier Electronics Group of China: Price Competition Cuts into Profitability'. Japan Center of Economic Research Researcher Report No. 62, http://www.jcer.or.jp/eng/pdf/kenrep050624e.pdf (accessed 23 April 2008), pp. 1–41.

Murphy, K. M., Shleifer, A., and Vishny, R. W. (1992). 'The Transition to a Market Economy: Pitfalls of Partial Reform'. *Quarterly Journal of Economics,* 107/3: 889–906.

Murphy, P. (2008). 'Made in China: What Does $200bn Get You?' *Financial Times,* 28 February, p. 28.

Myers, S. C. (1997). 'Determinants of Corporate Borrowing'. *Journal of Financial Economics,* 5/2: 147–75.

Nanfang Journal (2008). 'ICBC Becomes World's Most Lucrative Bank', 25 August, p. 16.

National Bureau of Statistics (NBS) of China (various years). *China Statistical Yearbook.* Beijing: China Statistics Press.

Naughton, B. (1992). 'Implications of the State Monopoly over Industry and its Relaxation'. *Modern China,* 18/1: 14–41.

——(1995). *Growing out of the Plan: Chinese Economic Reform, 1978–1993.* Cambridge: Cambridge University Press.

——(2007). *The Economy of China.* Cambridge, Massachusetts: MIT Press.

Nee, V. (1996). 'The Emergence of a Market Society: Changing Mechanisms of Stratification in China'. *American Journal of Sociology,* 100/4, 908–49.

Ni, Y. and Wu, X. (2004). 'Secondary Innovation and Strategies for China's Manufacturing Industry in the Global Competition'. Zhejiang University Working Paper 1(1) at: scholar.ilib. cn/A-QCodekxjsygc200202005.html (accessed 22 April 2008), pp. 82–8.

Nolan, P. and Zhang, J. (2003). 'Globalization Challenge for Large Firms From Developing Countries: China's Oil and Aerospace Industries'. *European Management Journal*, 21: 285–99.

North, D. C. (1991). 'Institutions'. *Journal of Economic Perspectives*, 5/1: 97–112.

Oi, J. C. (1999). *Rural China Takes Off: Institutional Foundations of Economic Reform*. Berkeley: University of California Press.

Olson, P. (2007). 'China Grabs a Slice of Africa,' *Forbes*, 25 October, p. 13.

Orlik, T. and Rozelle, S. (2009), 'How Many Unemployed Migrant Workers are There?' *Far Eastern Economic Review*.

Pei, M. X. (1998). 'The Political Economy of Banking Reforms in China, 1993–1997'. *Journal of Contemporary China*, 7/18: 321–50.

——(2001). 'Does Legal Reform Protect Economic Transactions? Commercial Disputes in China', in P. Murrell (ed.), *Assessing the Value of Law in Transition Countries*. Ann Arbor: University of Michigan Press, 180–210.

People's Daily (South China) (2001a). 'Chenghai Produced Toys Worth RMB 6 billion and Exported over 70% of its Toy Products in a Year', 18 April.

——(2001b). 'A Brief Introduction to the Guangdong Auldey Toy Industry Company Limited', 19 April.

——(2002). 'China Exports First Shipment of Compact Cars to U.S.', available at: <http://english.peopledaily.com.cn/200206/11/eng20020611_97576.shtml> (created 11 June 2002, accessed 10 July 2009).

—— (2005). 'ICBC Receives Funds of US$15 Bn', 28 April, p. 8.

—— (2006). 'Shanghai's Exports to EU, U.S. Drop Drastically', 13 September, available at: http://english.peopledaily.com.cn/200609/10/eng20060910_301377.html (accessed 24 August 2008).

—— (2008). 'Chinese Textile Firms Moving to Reform amid Falling Orders', 5 April, available at: http://english.people.com.cn/90001/90776/6386913.html (accessed 24 August 2008).

Pistor, K. (2002). 'The Standardization of Law and its Effect on Developing Economies'. *American Journal of Comparative Law*, 1/Winter: 97–130.

——Keinan, Y., Kleinheisterkamp , J., and West, M. (2003). 'The Evolution of Corporate Law: A Cross-country Comparison'. *University of Pennsylvania Journal of International Economic Law*, 23/4: 791–871.

——K., Martin R., and Gelfer, S. (2000). 'Law and Finance in Transition Economies'. *Economics of Transition*, 8/2: 325–68.

——and Xu, C. (2005). 'Governing Stock Markets in Transition Economies: Lessons from China'. *American Law and Economics Review*, 7/1: 1–27.

Podpiera, R. (2006). 'Progress in China's Banking Sector Reform: Has Bank Behavior Changed?' IMF Working Paper No. 71, pp. 1–25.

Portes, A. (1998). 'Social Capital: Its Origins and Applications in Modern Sociology'. *Annual Review of Sociology*, 24; 1–24.

Press, A. (2008). 'China's ICBC Is Banking World's Top Earner'. *Sydney Morning Herald*, 22 August, p. 22.

Qian, Y. and Roland, G. (1998). 'Federalism and the Soft Budget Constraint'. *American Economic Review*, 88/5: 1143–62.

——and Xu, C. (1993). 'The M-form Hierarchy and China's Economic Reform'. *European Economic Review*, 37/2–3: 541–8.

Qiu, L. (2005). 'China's Textile and Clothing Industry'. Hong Kong University of Science and Technology Working Paper No. 1, pp. 1–35.

Ravallion, M. and Chen, S. (2007). 'China's (Uneven) Progress Against Poverty'. *Journal of Development Economics*, 82/1: 1–42.

Rees, H. and Shah, A. (1986). 'An Empirical Analysis of Self-employment in the U.K.'. *Journal of Applied Econometrics*, 1/1: 95–108.

Reuters (2008). 'Qingdao Haier Co Ltd (600690.Ss)'. *Thomson Reuters Stock Analysis*, www.thomsonreuters.com/stocks, (accessed 22 April 2008), pp. 1–2.

Reuters Commercial Analysis Reports (2008). 'Haier'. 22 May, p. 12.

Riedel, J., Jin, J., and Gao, J. (2007). *How China Grows: Investment, Finance, and Reform.* Princeton and Oxford: Princeton University Press.

Riskin, C. (1987). *China's Political Economy: The Quest for Development since 1949.* Oxford: Oxford University Press.

Roberts, D., Arndt, M., and Zammert, A. (2002). 'Haier's Tough Trip from China'. *BusinessWeek Online*, April 1, http://www.businessweek.com/magazine/content/02_13/b3776139.htm, (accessed 22 April 2008).

Rodrik, D., Subramanian, A., and Trebbi, F. (2004). 'Institutions Rule: The Primacy of Institutions over Geography and Integration in Economic Development'. *Journal of Economic Growth*, 9/2: 139–65.

Rowley, I. (2009a). 'China's Carmakers Are Gaining on Foreign Rivals'. *BusinessWeek*, available at: <http://www.businessweek.com/magazine/content/09_23/b4134000377117.htm?chan=top+news_special+report+–+general+motors+new+landscape_special+report+–+general+motors+new+landscape> (created 27 May 2009, accessed 16 August 2009).

——(2009b). 'China: Car Capital of the World?' *BusinessWeek*, available at: http://www.businessweek.com/globalbiz/content/may2009/gb20090518_095449.htm (created 18 May 2009, accessed 16 August 2009).

Schiefferes, S. (2007). 'Rivals Chase GM in Chinese Markets', *BBC News*, available at: <http://news.bbc.co.uk/2/hi/business/6576825.stm> (created 20 April 2007, accessed 1 August 2009).

Schipani, C. and Liu, J. (2002). 'Corporate Governance in China: Then and Now'. *Columbia Business Law Review*, 1/1: 1–69.

Shane, S. and Cable, D. (2002). 'Network Ties, Reputation, and the Financing of New Ventures'. *Management Science*, 48/3: 364–81.

Shaw, E. (1973). *Financial Deepening in Economic Development.* Oxford and New York: Oxford University Press.

Shen, D. (2008). 'What's Happening in China's Textile and Clothing Industries?' *Clothing and Textiles Research Journal*, 26: 203–24.

Shen, Y., Shen, M., Xu, Z., and Bai, Y. (2009). 'Bank Size and Small and Medium-sized Enterprise (SME) Lending: Evidence from China'. *World Development*, 37/4: 800–11.

Shih, V., Zhang, Q. and Liu, M. (2007). 'Comparing the Performance of Chinese Banks: A Principal Component Approach'. *China Economic Review*, 18: 15–34.

Shirai, S. (2002). 'Banks' Lending Behaviour and Firms' Corporate Financing Pattern in the People's Republic of China'. ADB Institute Research Paper No. 161, pp. 1–33.

Shleifer, A. and Vishny, R. W. (1994). 'Politicians and Firms'. *Quarterly Journal of Economics*, 109/4, 995–1025.

Sicular, T. (1988). 'Plan and Market in China's Agricultural Commerce'. *Journal of Political Economy*, 96: 283–307.

Sims, C. (1972). 'Money, Income, and Causality'. *American Economic Review*, 62/4: 540–52.

——(1980). 'Macroeconomics and Reality'. *Econometrica*, 48/1: 1–48.

Sinha, A., Iqbal, G. M., and Inggi, B. L. (2006). 'Asian Textile Industry: Review and Outlook'. *Journal for Asia on Textile and Apparel*, February edition, available at: http://www.adsaleata.com/Publicity/ePub/lang-eng/asid-71/article-10/Article.aspx (accessed on 24 August 2008).

Solinger, D. J. (1991). *From Lathes to Looms: China's Industrial Policy in Comparative Perspective, 1979–1982*. Stanford: Stanford University Press.

——(1999). *Contesting Citizenship in Urban China: Peasant Migrants, the State, and the Logic of the Market*. Berkeley: University of California Press.

Sonobe, T. and Otsuka, K. (2003). 'Productivity Effects of TVE Privatization: The Case Study of Garment and Metal Casting Enterprises in the Greater Yangtze Region'. National Bureau of Economic Research Working Paper WP(9621), pp. 1–35.

Spencer, J. (2007). 'China Pays Steep Price as Textile Exports Boom'. *Wall Street Journal*, 22 August, p. A5.

Spencer, R. (2007). 'The Most Valuable Bank in the World?' *Daily Telegraph*, 11 January, p. 34.

Staiger, D. and Stock, J. H. (1997). 'Instrumental Variable Regression with Weak Instruments'. *Econometrica*, 65/3: 557–86.

Stern, N. (2002). *A Strategy for Development*. Washington DC: World Bank Publications.

Stiglitz, J. (2003). *Globalization and its Discontents*. New York: Penguin.

Stock, J. and Watson, M. (2001). 'Forecasting Output and Inflation: The Role of Asset Prices'. National Bureau of Economic Research (NBER) Working Paper No. 8180. Cambridge, Massachusetts.

Su, D. and Fleisher, B. M. (1998). 'What Explains the High IPO Returns in China?' *Emerging Market Quarterly*, 2/Summer: 5–20.

——(1999). 'An Empirical Investigation of Underpricing in Chinese IPOs.' *Pacific-Basin Finance Journal*, 7/1: 173–202.

Sun, L. and Tobin, D. (2009). 'International Listing as a Means to Mobilize the Benefits of Financial Globalization: Micro-level Evidence from China'. *World Development*, 37/4: 825–38.

Sun, Q., and Tong, W. H. S. (2003). 'China's Share Issue Privatization: The Extent of its Success'. *Journal of Financial Economics*, 70: 183–222.

The Economist (2009). 'The China Car Industry: The Ambition of Geely', available at: <http://www.economist.com/businessfinance/displaystory.cfm?story_id=14140382> (created 30 July 2009, accessed 15 August 2009).

Thun, E. (2004). 'Industrial Policy, Chinese-style: FDI, Regulation, and Dreams of National Champions in the Auto Sector'. *Journal of East Asian Studies*, 4: 453–89.

——(2006). *Changing Lanes in China: Foreign Direct Investment, Local Governments, and Auto Sector Development*. Cambridge: Cambridge University Press.

Tian, L. and Megginson, W. L. (2007). 'Extreme Underpricing: Determinants of Chinese IPO Initial Returns', available at SSRN: http://ssrn.com/abstract=891042.

Törnroos, J. Å. (2003). 'Nokia Mobile Phones & the Chinese Market—Managing Culturally Based Strategic Nets'. VALUENET Research Project Working Paper No. 1, pp. 1–23.

Ulrich, Jing. (2008) 'Dividends from China's State-owned Enterprises', *Financial Times*, 21 January, p. 31.

UNCTAD (United Nations Conference on Trade and Development) (2006). *World Investment Report*. Washington DC: United Nations Publications.

——(2008). *World Investment Report: Transnational Corporations, and the Infrastructure Challenge*. Switzerland: United Nations Publication.

Verbrugge, J., Owens, W., and Megginson, W. (2000). 'State Ownership and the Financial Performance of Privatized Banks: An Empirical Analysis'. World Bank Conference on

Banking Privatization, 15–16 March, available online: http://faculty-staff.ou.edu/M/William.
L.Megginson-1/prvbkpap.pdf, pp. 1–50.

Voss, H., Buckley, P. J., and Cross, A. R. (2008). 'Thirty Years of Chinese Outward Foreign
Direct Investment'. Paper presented at the Chinese Economic Association (UK) Conference,
'Three Decades of Economic Reform (1978–2008)'. Cambridge University, Cambridge,
1–2 April 2008.

Walder, A. (1995). 'Local Governments as Industrial Firms: An Organizational Analysis of
China's Transitional Economy'. *American Journal of Sociology* 101/2: 263–301.

Wang, Y. and Yao, Y. (2001). 'Market Reforms, Technological Capabilities, and the Performance
of Small Enterprises in China'. World Bank Working Paper No. 37187, pp. 1–33.

——(2003). 'Sources of China's Economic Growth, 1952–99: Incorporating Human Capital
Accumulation'. *China Economic Review,* 14/1: 32–52.

Wedeman, A. H. (2003). *From Mao to Market: Rent-seeking, Local Protectionism and
Marketization in China.* Cambridge: Cambridge University Press.

Weitzman, M. and Xu, C. (1994). 'Chinese Township Village Enterprises as Vaguely Defined
Cooperatives.' *Journal of Comparative Economics,* 18/2, 121–45.

Wen, H. (2007). 'A Confucian Capitalist Goes Global'. *CommonWealth Magazine (Taiwan),* 364
(31st January): 10–22.

White, S. and Xie, W. (2006). 'Lenovo's Pursuit of Dynamic Strategic Fit', in A. Tsui, Y. Bian, and
L. Cheng (eds.), *China's Domestic Private Firms: Multidisciplinary Perspectives on Management
and Performance.* Armonk, NY: M.E. Sharpe, 277–96.

——(2004). 'Sequential Learning in a Chinese Spin-off: The Case of Lenovo Group Limited'.
R&D Management, 34: 407–22.

Whiting, S. H. (2001). *Power and Wealth in Rural China: The Political Economy of Institutional
Change.* Cambridge: Cambridge University Press.

Williamson, O. E. (2002). 'The Theory of the Firm as Governance Structure: From Choice to
Contract'. *Journal of Economic Perspectives,* 16/3: 171–95.

Wong, C. and Bird, R. M. (2008). 'China's Fiscal System: A Work in Progress', in L. Brandt and
T. G. Rawski (eds.), *China's Great Economic Transformation.* Cambridge: Cambridge
University Press, 429–66.

Wong, Y. C. R. and Wong, M. L. S. (2001). 'Competition in China's Domestic Banking Industry'.
Cato Journal, 21/1: 19–44.

Wu, M. (2007). 'Piercing China's Corporate Veil: Open Questions about the New Company
Law'. *Yale Law Journal,* 117/2: 329–39.

Wu, X. (2002). 'Embracing the Market: Entry into Self-Employment in Transitional China,
1978–1996'. William Davidson Working Paper No. 512, pp. 1–44.

Wu, Y. (2003). 'China's Refrigerator Magnate'. *McKinsey Quarterly,* 3: 5–8.

Xiao, G. (2004). 'Round-tripping Foreign Direct Investment in the People's Republic of China:
Scale, Causes and Implications'. Asian Development Bank Discussion Paper No. 7, Manila,
the Philippines, pp. 1–48.

Xie, W. and White, S. (2006). 'Windows of Opportunity, Learning Strategies and the Rise of
China's Handset Makers'. *International Journal of Technology Management,* 36/1–3: 230–48.

Xinhua (2005). 'Review: ICBC Cannot Afford Failure in Joint-Stock Reform', 29 April, p. 13.

——(2006a). 'Nation's Largest Commercial Bank Launches IPO', 27 September, p. 1.

——(2006b). 'Market Opinion Divided on ICBC's Bullish Performance', 27 December, p. 14.

——(2006c). 'China to Raise Threshold on Car Exports', available at: <http://english.people.
com.cn/200608/30/eng20060830_298249.html> (created 30 August 2006, accessed 1 August
2009).

Xinhua (2009a). 'Top 3 Chinese Automakers take 48.7% of Domestic Market', available at: <http://www.chinadaily.com.cn/bizchina/2009-01/27/content_7429641.htm> (created 27 January 2009, accessed 1 August 2009).

——(2009b). 'China's 2008 Auto Sales Growth hits 10-year Low', available at: <http://www.chinadaily.com.cn/bizchina/2009-01/12/content_7390508.htm> (created 12 January 2009, accessed 14 August 2009).

Xu, Q., Zhu, L., Zheng, G., and Wang, F. (2007). 'Haier's Tao of Innovation: A Case Study of the Emerging Total Innovation Management Model'. *Journal of Technology Transfer*, 32/1–2: 27–47.

Yan, Y. (1996). *The Flow of Gifts: Reciprocity and Social Networks in a Chinese Village*. Stanford: Stanford University Press.

Yang, M. (1994). *Gifts, Favors, and Banquets: The Art of Social Relationships in China*. Ithaca: Cornell University Press.

Yang, Y. and Zhong, C. (1998). 'China's Textiles and Clothing Exports in a Changing World Economy'. *The Developing Economies*, 36/1: 3–23.

Yao, Y. (1998). 'China's Textile and Clothing Exports: Changing International Comparative Advantage and Its Policy Implications'. Asia Pacific School of Economics and Management Working Paper, No. 3, pp. 1–21.

——(2004). 'China's Integration into the World Economy: Implications for Developing Countries'. *Asian Pacific Economic Literature*, 1/1: 40–57.

——and Yueh, L. (2009). 'Law, Finance and Economic Growth in China: An Introduction'. *World Development*, 37/4: 753–62.

——and Zhong, C. (1998). 'China's Textile and Clothing Exports in a Changing World Economy'. *The Developing Economies*, 36/1: 3–23.

Yeung, A. and DeWoskin, K. (1998). 'From Survival to Success: The Journey of Corporate Transformation at Haier'. William Davidson Institute Working Paper 207/1, pp. 1–41.

Yeung, G. and Mok, V. (2004). 'Does WTO Accession Matter for the Chinese Textile and Clothing Industry?' *Cambridge Journal of Economics*, 28: 937–54.

Young, A. (2000). 'The Razor's Edge: Distortions and Incremental Reform in the People's Republic of China'. *Quarterly Journal of Economics*, 115/4: 1091–35.

Yueh, L. (2004). 'Wage Reforms in China During the 1990s'. *Asian Economic Journal*, 18/2: 149–64.

——(2006). 'China's Competitiveness, Intra-industry and Intra-regional Trade in Asia', in Y. Yao and L. Yueh (eds.), *Globalisation and Economic Growth in China*. London: World Scientific Publishing Co. Pte. Ltd, 141–60.

——(2007). 'Global Intellectual Property Rights and Economic Growth'. *Northwestern Journal of Technology and Intellectual Property*, 5/3: 436–48.

——(2009a). 'China's Entrepreneurs.' *World Development*, 37/4: 778–86.

——(2009b). 'Patent Laws and Innovation in China'. *International Review of Law and Economics,* 29/4: 304–13.

Yusuf, S., Nabeshima, K., and Perkins, D. H. (2006). *Under New Ownership: Privatizing China's State-owned Enterprises*. Stanford: Stanford University Press.

Zhang, J., Zhang, L., Rozelle, S., and Boucher, S. (2006). 'Self-employment with Chinese characteristics: The Forgotten Engine of Rural China's Growth'. *Contemporary Economic Policy*, 24/3: 446–58.

Zhang, Z., To, C., and Cao, N. (2004). 'How Do Industry Clusters Succeed: A Case Study in China's Textiles and Apparel Industries'. *Journal of Textile and Apparel, Technology and Management*, 4/2: 10–25.

Zheng, J., Bigsten, A., and Hu, A. (2009). 'Can China's Growth be Sustained? A Productivity Perspective'. *World Development*, 37/4: 874–88.

Zhou, W. (2009). 'Bank Financing in China's Private Sector: The Payoffs of Political Capital'. *World Development*, 37/4: 787–99.

Zhu, S. (2000). *Securities Regulation in China*. Ardsley, NY: Transnational Publishers; London: Simmonds & Hill Publishing.

——(2005). 'Civil Litigation Arising from False Statements on China's Securities Market.' *North Carolina Journal of International Law and Commercial Regulation*, 31/2: 377–429.

——(2007). *Securities Dispute Resolution in China*. Aldershot, England, and Burlington, VT: Ashgate.

——(2009). 'The Role of Law and Governance in Financial Market: The Case of Emerging Chinese Securities Market'. Paper presented at the WG Hart Legal Workshop 2009: Law Reform and Financial Markets, 23–25 June 2009, Institute of Advanced Legal Studies, London.

Zhu, T. (1998). 'A Theory of Contract and Ownership Choice in Public Enterprises Under Reformed Socialism: The case of China's TVEs'. *China Economic Review*, 9/1: 59–71.

■ Index